TWELVE ORDINARY MEN

TWELVE EXTRAORDINARY WOMEN

JOHN MACARTHUR

THOMAS NELSON
Since 1798

NASHVILLE   DALLAS   MEXICO CITY   RIO DE JANEIRO   BEIJING

Published in Nashville, Tennessee, by Thomas Nelson. Thomas Nelson is a registered trademark of Thomas Nelson, Inc.

Published in association with the literary agency of Wolgemuth & Associates, Inc.
Thomas Nelson, Inc., titles may be purchased in bulk for educational, business, fund-raising, or sales promotional use. For information, please e-mail SpecialMarkets@ThomasNelson.com.

Unless otherwise noted, Scripture quotations are taken from THE NEW KING JAMES VERSION, © 1982 by Thomas Nelson, Inc. Used by permission. All rights reserved.

Scripture quotations marked NASB are from the NEW AMERICAN STANDARD BIBLE®, © The Lockman Foundation 1960, 1962, 1963, 1968, 1971, 1972, 1973, 1975, 1977. Used by permission.

Scripture quotations marked NIV are from the HOLY BIBLE: NEW INTERNATIONAL VERSION®,

© 1973, 1978, 1984 by International Bible Society. Used by permission of Zondervan Publishing House. All rights reserved.

Scripture quotations marked KJV are from the King James Version of the Bible.

ISBN 978-1-4002-8063-6 (SE)
ISBN 978-1-4002-8048-3

Printed in the United States of America
09 10 11 12 QW 6 5 4 3 2 1

For Birgie and Charles
with much love –
Dec. 25, 2010

TWELVE ORDINARY MEN

Merry Christmas !

HOW *the* MASTER
SHAPED HIS DISCIPLES *for* GREATNESS,
and WHAT HE WANTS *to* DO *with* YOU

Don and Cynthia

with much love –
Dec. 25, 2010

Merry Christmas!

Don and Gretta

DEDICATION

To Irv Busenitz, for his loyal friendship and devoted service over three decades. Irv is a true teacher and selfless servant who has faithfully invested his own life in the lives of other men who come to study at The Master's Seminary. Irv is the ideal model of both disciple and disciple-maker, having dedicated himself to fulfilling 2 Timothy 2:2: "The things you have heard from me among many witnesses, commit these to faithful men who will be able to teach others also."

Acknowledgments

THIS BOOK IS IN NO SMALL MEASURE THANKS TO THE faithful support and encouragement of David Moberg, Mark Sweeney, and the rest of the staff of Thomas Nelson. We have enjoyed a close and fruitful partnership over the years, and I am grateful to the Lord for the ministry these dear friends have had in so many of my published works.

I am particularly grateful to Mary Hollingsworth and Kathryn Murray of Thomas Nelson, who worked hard under very short deadlines to keep this book on schedule throughout the editorial and typesetting process. Their kindness, patience, and diligence have been exemplary, even under difficult circumstances.

Thanks also to Garry Knussman, who proofread this material at several different stages and offered many helpful editorial suggestions.

My special thanks goes to Phil Johnson, who has worked alongside me as my main editor for more than twenty years. He applied his skills in the process of translating this material from transcripts of my sermons on Matthew 10 and Luke 6, collating both series into one seamless whole and making sure the text was clear and readable.

CONTENTS

ℭ

INTRODUCTION

MORE THAN TWENTY YEARS AGO, WHILE PREACHING through the Gospel of Matthew, I gave a series of character studies on the twelve apostles. The messages were extremely well received, and we produced a tape album and study guide from that series, titled *The Master's Men*. Over the years we have broadcast the entire series several times on the *Grace to You* radio broadcast. Each time it airs, it generates a greater outpouring of affirmative response from listeners. After twenty years, that album continues to be one of the most popular series we have ever produced.

A few years ago, I started teaching a verse-by-verse exposition of Luke's Gospel in our church. When I reached Luke 6:13–16 (where Luke records Jesus' calling of the Twelve) I preached a new series of messages on the apostles. Once again, the response was overwhelming and enthusiastic. While preaching the series I realized that an entire generation had been born and reached adulthood in the years since we had last studied the lives of the disciples. They identified with these men in the same way their parents had done more than two decades before.

Even people who had practically memorized the tapes from the earlier series said they still found the lives of the disciples as fresh and relevant and practical as ever. The new series quickly became another favorite, and people began urging me to combine all the material on the apostles in a book. I didn't need much prodding for such a project. The book you are holding in your hands is the result.

I have always been fascinated with the lives of the twelve apostles. Who isn't? The personality types of these men are familiar to us. They are just like us, and they are like other people we know. They are approachable. They are real and living characters we can identify with. Their faults and foibles, as well as their triumphs and endearing features, are chronicled in some of the most fascinating accounts of the Bible. These are men we *want* to know.

That's because they were perfectly ordinary men in every way. Not one of them was renowned for scholarship or great erudition. They had no track record as orators or theologians. In fact, they were outsiders as far as the religious establishment of Jesus' day was concerned. They were not outstanding because of any natural talents or intellectual abilities. On the contrary, they were all too prone to mistakes, misstatements, wrong attitudes, lapses of faith, and bitter failure—no one more so than the leader of the group, Peter. Even Jesus remarked that they were slow learners and somewhat spiritually dense (Luke 24:25).

They spanned the political spectrum. One was a former Zealot—a radical, determined to overthrow Roman rule. But another had been a tax collector—virtually a traitor to the Jewish nation and in collusion with Rome. At least four, and possibly seven, were fishermen and close friends from Capernaum, probably having known one another from childhood. The others must have been tradesmen or craftsmen, but we are not told what they did before becoming followers of Christ. Most of them were from Galilee, an agricultural region at the intersection of trade routes. And Galilee remained their home base for most of Jesus' ministry—not (as some might think) Jerusalem in Judea, which was the political and religious capital of Israel.

Yet with all their faults and character flaws—as remarkably ordinary as they were—these men carried on a ministry after Jesus' ascension that left an indelible impact on the world. Their ministry continues to influence us even today. God graciously empowered and used these men to inaugurate the spread of the gospel message and to turn the world upside down (Acts 17:6). Ordinary men—people like you and me—became the instruments by which Christ's message was carried to the ends of the earth. No wonder they are such fascinating characters.

The Twelve were personally selected and called by Christ. He knew them as only their Creator could know them (cf. John 1:47). In other words, He knew all their faults long before He chose them. He even knew Judas would betray Him (John 6:70; 13:21–27), and yet He chose the traitor anyway and gave him all the same privileges and blessings He gave to the others.

Think about the ramifications of this: From our human perspective, the propagation of the gospel and the founding of the church hinged entirely on twelve men whose most outstanding characteristic was their ordinariness. They were chosen by Christ and trained for a time that is best measured in months, not years. He taught them the Scriptures and theology. He discipled them in the ways of godly living (teaching them and showing them how to pray, how to forgive, and how to serve one another with humility). He gave them moral instruction. He spoke to them of things to come. And He employed them as His instruments to heal the sick, cast out demons, and do other miraculous works. Three of them—Peter, James, and John— even got a brief glimpse of Him in His glory on the Mount of Transfiguration (Matthew 17:1–9).

It was a brief but intensive schedule of discipleship. And when it was over, on the night of Jesus' betrayal, "all the disciples forsook Him and fled" (Matthew 26:56). From an earthly point of view, the training program looked like a monumental failure. It seemed the disciples had forgotten or ignored everything Christ had ever taught them about taking up the cross and following Him. In fact, their own sense of failure was so profound that they went back to their old vocations for a time. And even at that, it appeared they would fail (John 21:3–4).

But encouraged by the risen Lord, they returned to their apostolic calling. Empowered by the Holy Spirit at Pentecost, they valiantly undertook the task to which Jesus had called them. The work they subsequently began continues today, two thousand years later. They are living proof that God's strength is made perfect in weakness. In and of themselves they were clearly not sufficient for the task (cf. 2 Corinthians 2:16). But God led them in triumph in Christ, and through them He diffused "the fragrance of His knowledge in every place" (v. 14).

To get an appreciation for the brevity of their earthly time with Christ, consider the fact that Jesus' entire ministry from baptism to resurrection lasted only about three years. And the intensive training time with the disciples was only about half that long. In A. B. Bruce's classic work, *The Training of the Twelve,* he points out that by the time Jesus identified and called the Twelve from the larger group of His followers (Matthew 10:1–4; Luke 6:12–16), half of his earthly ministry was already over:

> The selection by Jesus of the twelve . . . is an important landmark in the Gospel history. It divides the ministry of our Lord into two portions, nearly equal, probably, as to duration, but unequal as to the extent and importance of the work done in each respectively. In the earlier period Jesus labored single-handed; His miraculous deeds were confined for the most part to a limited area, and His teaching was in the main of an elementary character. But by the time when the twelve were chosen, the work of the kingdom had assumed such dimensions as to require organization and division of labor; and the teaching of Jesus was beginning to be of a deeper and more elaborate nature, and His gracious activities were taking on ever-widening range.

It is probable that the selection of a limited number to be His close and constant companions had become a necessity to Christ, in consequence of His very success in gaining disciples. His followers, we imagine, had grown so numerous as to be an incumbrance and an impediment to his movements, especially in the long journeys which mark the later part of His ministry. It was impossible that all who believed could continue henceforth to follow Him, in the literal sense, whithersoever He might go: the greater number could now only be occasional followers. But it was His wish that certain selected men should be with Him at all times and in all places,—His traveling companions in all His wanderings, witnessing all His work, and ministering to His daily needs. And so, in the quaint words of Mark, "Jesus calleth unto Him whom He would, and they came unto Him, and He [ordained] twelve, that they should be with Him." (Mark 3:13–14)[1]

That means these few men, whose backgrounds were in mundane trades and earthly occupations, had little more than eighteen months' training for the monumental task to which they were called. There was no second string, no backup players, no plan B if the Twelve should fail.

The strategy sounds risky in the extreme. In earthly terms, the founding of the church and the spread of the gospel message depended entirely on those twelve ordinary men with their many obvious weaknesses—and one of them so devilish as to betray the Lord of the universe. And the entirety of their training for the task took less than half as long as it typically takes to get a degree from a seminary today.

But Christ knew what He was doing. From His divine perspective, the ultimate success of the strategy actually depended on the Holy Spirit working in those men to accomplish His sovereign will. It was a mission that could not be thwarted. That's why it was a work for which God alone deserves praise and glory. Those men were merely instruments in His hands—just as you and I can be God's instruments today. God delights to use such ordinary means—"the foolish things of the world to put to shame the things which are mighty; and the base things of the world and the things which are despised God has chosen, and the things which are not, to bring to nothing the things that are, that no flesh should glory in His presence" (1 Corinthians 1:27–29). The two-thousand-year triumph of the apostolic endeavor is a testimony to the wisdom and power of the divine strategy.

Sometimes in Scripture the Twelve are called "disciples"—*mathetes* in the Greek text (Matthew 10:1; 11:1; 20:17; Luke 9:1). The word means "learners, students." That is what they were during those months they spent under the direct and personal tutelage of the Lord. He had multitudes of disciples, but these twelve were specifically called and chosen to a unique apostolic office. Therefore they are also designated "apostles"—*apostoloi* in the Greek. The word simply means "messengers, sent ones." They were given a unique ambassadorial office of authority and spokesmanship for Christ. Luke especially uses this term in his gospel and throughout the Book of Acts, and he reserves the term almost exclusively for the Twelve. Matthew speaks of "apostles" only once (Matthew 10:2); elsewhere, he refers to "twelve disciples" (11:1; 20:17) or "the twelve" (26:14, 20, 47). Likewise, Mark uses the term "apostles" only once (Mark 6:30). Other than that, he always refers to the apostles as "the twelve" (3:14; 4:10; 6:7; 9:35; 10:32; 11:11; 14:10, 17, 20, 43). John, too, uses the word *apostolos* just once, in a nontechnical sense (John 13:16—where most English versions render the expression, "he who is sent"). Like Mark, John always refers to the apostolic band as "the twelve" (John 6:67, 70–71; 20:24).

Luke 10 describes an incident where seventy of Jesus' followers were chosen and sent out two by two. They were obviously "sent ones" and some commentators therefore refer to them as "apostles," but Luke does not employ that term to describe them.

The Twelve were called to a specific office. And in the Gospels and Acts, the term *apostoloi* almost always refers to that office and the twelve men who were specifically called and ordained to the office.

Acts 14:14 and the Pauline epistles make it clear that the apostle Paul was likewise called to fill a special apostolic office—that of "apostle to the Gentiles" (Romans 11:13; 1 Timothy 2:7; 2 Timothy 1:11). Paul's apostleship was a unique calling. He obviously had the same authority and privileges as that of the Twelve (2 Corinthians 11:5). But Paul's apostleship is not subject matter for this book, because our focus here is on the twelve men who shared Jesus' public ministry with Him as His closest friends and companions. Paul wasn't converted until after Christ's ascension (Acts 9). He was an apostle "born out of due time" (1 Corinthians 15:8). He spoke with the same authority and manifested the same miraculous ability as the Twelve—and the Twelve embraced him and recognized his authority (cf. 2 Peter 3:15–16)—but he was not one of them.

The number twelve was significant, because Luke describes how, after Jesus' ascension, the apostles chose Matthias to fill the office vacated by Judas (Acts 1:23–26).

The role of an apostle (including the special office to which the apostle Paul was called) involved a position of leadership and exclusive teaching authority in the early church. The New Testament Scriptures were all written by the apostles or their close associates. And before the New Testament was written, the apostles' teaching was the rule in the early church. Beginning with the very first converts at Pentecost, all true believers looked to the apostles' leadership (Acts 2:37). And as the church grew, its faithfulness to the truth was described in these terms: "They continued steadfastly in the apostles' doctrine" (Acts 2:42).

The apostles were given a supernatural power to work signs and wonders (Matthew 10:1; Mark 6:7, 13; Luke 9:1–2; Acts 2:3–4; 5:12). Those signs bore witness to the truth of the gospel, which the apostles had received from Christ, and which they introduced on His behalf to the world (2 Corinthians 12:12; Hebrews 2:3–4).

In other words, their role was a pivotal, foundational role. They *are* in a true sense, the very foundation of the Christian church, "Jesus Christ Himself being the chief cornerstone" (Ephesians 2:20).

INTRODUCTION

These studies in the lives of the apostles have been a particular delight for me—and one of the most fruitful endeavors of my life. My greatest joy is preaching Christ. Eleven of these men shared that passion, devoted their lives to it, and triumphed in it against overwhelming opposition. They are fitting heroes and role models for us, despite their shortcomings. To study their lives is to get to know the men who were closest to Christ during His earthly life. To realize that they were ordinary people just like us is a great blessing. May the Spirit of Christ who taught them transform us the way He transformed them, into precious vessels fit for the Master's use. And may we learn from their example what it means to be disciples indeed.

1

COMMON MEN, UNCOMMON CALLING

❧

*For you see your calling, brethren, that not many wise according to the
flesh, not many mighty, not many noble, are called. But God has chosen
the foolish things of the world to put to shame the wise, and God has
chosen the weak things of the world to put to shame the things which are
mighty; and the base things of the world and the things which are
despised God has chosen, and the things which are not, to bring to nothing the things that are, that no flesh should glory in His presence.*

—1 CORINTHIANS 1:26–29

F ROM THE TIME JESUS BEGAN HIS PUBLIC MINISTRY IN HIS
    hometown of Nazareth, He was enormously controversial. The
    people from His own community literally tried to kill Him
immediately after His first public message in the local synagogue. "All
those in the synagogue, when they heard these things, were filled with
wrath, and rose up and thrust Him out of the city; and they led Him
to the brow of the hill on which their city was built, that they might
throw Him down over the cliff. Then passing through the midst of
them, He went His way" (Luke 4:28–30).

Ironically, Jesus became tremendously popular among the people
of the larger Galilee region. As word of His miracles began to circu-
late throughout the district, massive hordes of people came out to see
Him and hear Him speak. Luke 5:1 records how "the multitude
pressed about Him to hear the word of God." One day, the crowds
were so thick and so aggressive that He got into a boat, pushed it

offshore far enough to get away from the press of people, and taught the multitudes from there. Not by mere happenstance, the boat Jesus chose belonged to Simon. Jesus would rename him Peter, and he would become the dominant person in Jesus' closest inner circle of disciples.

Some might imagine that if Christ had wanted His message to have maximum impact, He could have played off His popularity more effectively. Modern conventional wisdom would suggest that Jesus ought to have done everything possible to exploit His fame, tone down the controversies that arose out of His teaching, and employ whatever strategies He could use to maximize the crowds around Him. But He did not do that. In fact, He did precisely the opposite. Instead of taking the populist route and exploiting His fame, He began to emphasize the very things that made His message so controversial. At about the time the crowds reached their peak, He preached a message so boldly confrontive and so offensive in its content that the multitude melted away, leaving only the most devoted few (John 6:66–67).

Among those who stayed with Christ were the Twelve, whom He had personally selected and appointed to represent Him. They were twelve perfectly ordinary, unexceptional men. But Christ's strategy for advancing His kingdom hinged on those twelve men rather than on the clamoring multitudes. He chose to work through the instrumentality of those few fallible individuals rather than advance His agenda through mob force, military might, personal popularity, or a public-relations campaign. From a human perspective, the future of the church and the long-term success of the gospel depended entirely on the faithfulness of that handful of disciples. There was no plan B if they failed.

The strategy Jesus chose typified the character of the kingdom itself. "The kingdom of God does not come with observation; nor will they say, 'See here!' or 'See there!' For indeed, the kingdom of God is within you" (Luke 17:20–21). The kingdom advances " 'Not by might nor by power, but by My Spirit,' says the LORD of hosts" (Zechariah 4:6). A dozen men under the power of the Holy Spirit are a more potent force than the teeming masses whose initial enthusiasm for Jesus was apparently provoked by little more than sheer curiosity.

Christ personally chose the Twelve and invested most of His energies in them. He chose them before they chose Him (John 15:16). The process of choosing and calling them happened in distinct stages. Careless readers of Scripture sometimes imagine that John 1:35–51, Luke 5:3-11, and the formal calling of the Twelve in Luke 6:12–16 are contradictory accounts of how Christ called His apostles. But there is no contradiction. The passages are simply describing different stages of the apostles' calling.

In John 1:35–51, for example, Andrew, John, Peter, Philip, and Nathaniel encounter Jesus for the first time. This event occurs near the beginning of Jesus' ministry, in the wilderness near the Jordan River, where John the Baptist was ministering. Andrew, John, and the others were there because they were already disciples of John the Baptist. But when they heard their teacher single out Jesus and say, "Behold the Lamb of God!" they followed Jesus.

That was phase one of their calling. It was a calling to *conversion*. It illustrates how every disciple is called first to salvation. We must recognize Jesus as the true Lamb of God and Lord of all, and embrace Him by faith. That stage of the disciples' call did not involve full-time discipleship. The Gospel narratives suggest that although they followed Jesus in the sense that they gladly heard His teaching and submitted to Him as their Teacher, they remained at their full-time jobs, earning a living through regular employment. That is why from this point until Jesus called them to full-time ministry, we often see them fishing and mending their nets.

Phase two of their calling was a call to *ministry*. Luke 5 describes the event in detail. This was the occasion when Jesus pushed out from shore to escape the press of the multitudes and taught from Peter's boat. After He finished teaching, He instructed Peter to launch out to the deep water and put in his nets. Peter did so, even though the timing was wrong (fish were easier to catch at night when the water was cooler and the fish surfaced to feed), the place was wrong (fish normally fed in shallower waters and were easier to catch there), and Peter was exhausted (having fished all night without any success). He told Jesus, "Master, we have toiled all night and caught nothing; nevertheless at Your word I will let down the net" (Luke 5:5). The resulting catch of fish overwhelmed their nets and nearly sank two of their fishing boats! (vv. 6–7).

It was on the heels of that miracle that Jesus said, "Follow Me, and I will make you fishers of men" (Matthew 4:19). Scripture says it was at this point that "they forsook all and followed Him" (Luke 5:11). According to Matthew, Andrew and Peter "immediately left their nets and followed Him" (Matthew 4:20). And James and John "immediately . . . left the boat and their father, and followed Him" (v. 22). From that point on, they were inseparable from the Lord.

Matthew 10:1–4 and Luke 6:12–16 describe a third phase of their calling. This was their calling to *apostleship*. It was at this point that Christ selected and appointed twelve men in particular and made them His apostles. Here is Luke's account of the incident:

> Now it came to pass in those days that He went out to the mountain to pray, and continued all night in prayer to God. And when it was day, He called His disciples to Himself; and from them He chose twelve whom He also named apostles: Simon, whom He also named Peter, and Andrew his brother; James and John; Philip and Bartholomew; Matthew and Thomas; James the son of Alphaeus, and Simon called the Zealot; Judas the son of James, and Judas Iscariot who also became a traitor.

Their apostleship began with a kind of internship. Christ sends them out. Mark 6:7 says they were sent out two by two. At this stage they were not quite ready to go out alone, so Christ teamed them in pairs, so that they would offer one another mutual support.

Throughout this phase of their training, the Lord Himself stuck closely with them. He was like a mother eagle, watching the eaglets as they began to fly. They were always checking back with Him, reporting on how things were going (cf. Luke 9:10; 10:17). And after a couple of seasons of evangelistic labor, they returned to the Lord and remained with Him for an extended time of teaching, ministry, fellowship, and rest (Mark 6:30–34).

There was a fourth phase of their calling, which occurred after Jesus' resurrection. Judas was now missing from the group, having hanged himself after his betrayal of Christ. Jesus appeared to the remaining eleven in His resurrection body and sent them into all the world, commanding them to disciple the nations. This was, in effect, a call to *martyrdom*. Each of them ultimately gave his life for the sake of the gospel. History records that all but one of them were killed for their testimony. Only John is said to have lived to old age, and he was severely persecuted for Christ's sake, then exiled to the tiny island of Patmos.

Despite the obstacles they faced, they triumphed. In the midst of great persecution and even martyrdom, they fulfilled their task. Against all odds, they entered victorious into glory. And the continuing witness of the gospel—spanning two thousand years' time and reaching into virtually every corner of the world—is a testimony to the wisdom of the divine strategy. No wonder we are fascinated by these men.

Let's begin our study of the Twelve by looking carefully at phase three of their calling—their selection and appointment to *apostleship*. Notice the details as Luke gives them to us.

THE TIMING

First, the timing of this event is significant. Luke notes this with his opening phrase in Luke 6:12: "Now it came to pass in those days." The New American Standard Bible renders the phrase this way: "And it was at this time." Luke is not talking about clock time, or the specific days of a specific month. "At this time" and "in those days" refers to a period of time, a season, a distinct phase in Jesus' ministry.

It was an interval in His ministry when the opposition to Him peaked.

"In those days" refers back to the immediately preceding account. This section of Luke's Gospel records the vicious opposition Christ was beginning to receive from the scribes and Pharisees. Luke 5:17 is Luke's first mention of the Pharisees, and verse 21 is his first use of the word "scribes." (The scribes are mentioned alongside the Pharisees as "teachers of the law" in verse 17.)

So we are first introduced to Jesus' chief adversaries in Luke 5:17, and Luke's account of their opposition fills the text through the end of chapter 5 and well into chapter 6. Luke describes the escalating conflict between Jesus and the religious leaders of Judaism. They opposed Him when He healed a paralytic and forgave his sins (5:17–26). They opposed Him for eating and drinking with tax collectors and sinners (5:27–39). They opposed Him when He permitted His disciples to pluck heads of grain and eat them on the Sabbath (6:1-5). And they opposed him for healing a man with a withered hand on the Sabbath (6:6–11). One after another, Luke recounts those incidents and highlights the growing opposition of the religious leaders.

The conflict reaches a high point in Luke 6:11. The scribes and Pharisees "were filled with rage, and discussed with one another what they might do to Jesus." Both Mark and Matthew are even more graphic. They report that the religious leaders wanted to destroy Jesus (Matthew 12:14; Mark 3:6). Mark says the religious leaders even got the Herodians involved in their plot. The Herodians were a political faction that supported the dynasty of the Herods. They were not normally allied with the Pharisees, but the two groups joined together in collusion against Jesus. They were already hatching plans to murder Him.

It is at this precise point that Luke interjects his account of how the Twelve were chosen and appointed to be apostles. "It came to pass in those days"—when the hostility against Christ had escalated to a murderous fever pitch. Hatred for Him among the religious elite had reached its apex. Jesus could already feel the heat of His coming death. The crucifixion was now less than two years away. He already knew that He would suffer death on the cross, that He would rise from the dead, and that after forty days He would ascend to His Father. He therefore also knew that His earthly work would have to be handed off to someone else.

It was now time to select and prepare His official representatives. Jesus—knowing the hatred of the religious leaders, fully aware of the hostility against Him, seeing the inevitability of His execution—therefore chose twelve key men to carry on the proclamation of His gospel for the salvation of Israel and the establishment of the church. Time was of the essence. There weren't many days left (about eighteen months, by most estimates) before His earthly ministry would end. Now was the time to choose His apostles. Their most intensive training would begin immediately and be complete within a matter of months.

The focus of Christ's ministry therefore turned at this point from the multitudes to the few. Clearly, it was the looming reality of His death at the hands of His adversaries that signaled the turning point.

There's another striking reality in this. When Jesus chose the Twelve to be His official representatives—preachers of the gospel who would carry both His message and His authority—He didn't choose a single rabbi. He didn't choose a scribe. He didn't choose a Pharisee. He didn't choose a Sadducee. He didn't choose a priest. Not one of the men He chose came from the religious establishment. The choosing of the twelve apostles was a judgment against institutionalized Judaism. It was a renunciation of those men and their organizations, which had become totally corrupt. That is why the Lord didn't choose one recognized religious leader. He chose instead men who were not theologically trained—fishermen, a tax collector, and other common men.

Jesus had long been at war with those who saw themselves as the religious nobility of Israel. They resented Him. They rejected Him and His message. They hated Him. The Gospel of John puts it this way: "He came to His own, and His own did not receive Him" (John 1:11).

The religious leaders of Judaism constituted the core of those who rejected Him.

Nearly a year and a half before this, in one of the first official acts of Jesus' ministry, He had challenged Israel's religious establishment on their own turf in Jerusalem during the Passover—the one time of year when the city was most populated with pilgrims coming to offer sacrifices. Jesus went to the temple mount, made a whip of small cords, drove the thieving money-changers out of the temple, poured out their money, overturned their tables, and chased their animals away (John 2:13–16). In doing that, He struck a devastating blow at institutionalized Judaism. He unmasked the religious nobility as thieves and hypocrites. He condemned their spiritual bankruptcy. He exposed their apostasy. He publicly rebuked their sin. He indicted them for gross corruption. He denounced their deception. That is how He *began* His ministry. It was an all-out assault on the religion of the Jewish establishment.

Now, many months later, at the height of His Galilean ministry, far removed from Jerusalem, the resentment that must have been inaugurated at that first event had reached a fever pitch. The religious leaders were now bloodthirsty. And they began to devise a scheme to execute Him.

Their rejection of Him was complete. They were hostile to the gospel He preached. They despised the doctrines of grace He stood for, spurned the repentance He demanded, looked with disdain upon the forgiveness He offered, and repudiated the faith He epitomized. In spite of the many miracles that proved His messianic credentials—despite actually seeing Him cast out demons, heal every conceivable sickness, and raise dead people to life—they would not accept the fact that He was God in human flesh. They hated Him. They hated His message. He was a threat to their power. And they desperately wanted to see Him dead.

So when it was time for Jesus to select twelve apostles, He naturally did not choose people from the establishment that was so determined to destroy Him. He turned instead to His own humble followers and selected twelve simple, ordinary, working-class men.

THE TWELVE

If you've ever visited the great cathedrals in Europe, you might assume that the apostles were larger-than-life stained-glass saints with shining halos who represented an exalted degree of spirituality. The fact of the matter is that they were very, very common men.

It's a shame they have so often been put on pedestals as magnificent marble figures or portrayed in paintings like some kind of Roman gods. That dehumanizes them. They were just twelve completely ordinary men—perfectly human in every way. We mustn't lose touch with who they really were.

I recently read a biography of William Tyndale, who pioneered the translation of Scripture into English. He thought it wrong that common people heard the Bible only in Latin and not in their own language. The church leaders of his day, incredibly, did not want the Bible in the language of the people because (like the Pharisees of Jesus' day) they feared losing their ecclesiastical power. But against their opposition, Tyndale translated the New Testament into English and had it published. For his efforts he was rewarded with exile, poverty, and persecution. Finally, in 1536, he was strangled and burned at the stake.

One of the main things that motivated Tyndale to translate Scripture into the common language was a survey of English clergy that revealed that most of them did not even know who the twelve apostles were. Only a few of them could name more than four or five of the apostles. Church leaders and Christians of today might fare just as poorly on the test. The way the institutional church has canonized these men has actually dehumanized them and made them seem remote and otherworldly. It is a strange irony, because when Jesus chose them, He selected them not for any extraordinary abilities or spiritual superiority. He seems to have deliberately chosen men who were notable only for their ordinariness.

What qualified these men to be apostles? Obviously it was not any intrinsic ability or outstanding talent of their own. They were

Galileans. They were not the elite. Galileans were deemed low-class, rural, uneducated people. They were commoners—nobodies. But again, they were not selected because they were any more distinguished or more talented than others in Israel at the time.

Certainly, there are some rather clear moral and spiritual qualifications that have to be met by men who would fill this or any other kind of leadership role in the church. In fact, the standard for spiritual leadership in the church is extremely high. Consider, for example, the qualifications for being an elder or a pastor, listed in 1 Timothy 3:2–7:

> [He] must be blameless, the husband of one wife, temperate, sober-minded, of good behavior, hospitable, able to teach; not given to wine, not violent, not greedy for money, but gentle, not quarrelsome, not covetous; one who rules his own house well, having his children in submission with all reverence (for if a man does not know how to rule his own house, how will he take care of the church of God?); not a novice, lest being puffed up with pride he fall into the same condemnation as the devil. Moreover he must have a good testimony among those who are outside, lest he fall into reproach and the snare of the devil.

Titus 1:6–9 gives a similar list. Hebrews 13:7 also suggests that church leaders must be exemplary moral and spiritual examples, because their faith must be the kind others can follow, and they will be required to give an account to God for how they conduct themselves. These are very, very high standards.

By the way, the standard is no lower for people in the congregation. Leaders are examples for everyone else. There's no acceptable "lower" standard for rank-and-file church members. In fact, in Matthew 5:48, Jesus said to *all* believers, "Be perfect, just as your Father in heaven is perfect."

Frankly, no one meets such a standard. Humanly speaking, no one "qualifies" when the standard is utter perfection. No one is fit to be in God's kingdom, and no one is inherently worthy to be in God's service. All have sinned and fall short of God's glory (Romans 3:23). There is none righteous, no not one (Romans 3:10). Remember, it was the mature apostle Paul who confessed, "I know that in me (that is, in my flesh) nothing good dwells" (Romans 7:18). In 1 Timothy 1:15 he called himself the chief of sinners.

So there are no intrinsically qualified people. God Himself must save sinners, sanctify them, and then transform them from unqualified into instruments He can use.

The Twelve were like the rest of us; they were selected from the unworthy and the unqualified. They were, like Elijah, men "with a nature like ours" (James 5:17). They did not rise to the highest usefulness because they were somehow *different* from us. Their transformation into vessels of honor was solely the work of the Potter.

Many Christians become discouraged and disheartened when their spiritual life and witness suffer because of sin or failure. We tend to think we're worthless nobodies—and left to ourselves, that would be true! But worthless nobodies are just the kind of people God uses, because that is all He has to work with.

Satan may even attempt to convince us that our shortcomings render us useless to God and to His church. But Christ's choice of the apostles testifies to the fact that God can use the unworthy and the unqualified. He can use nobodies. They turned the world upside down, these twelve (Acts 17:6). It was not because they had extraordinary talents, unusual intellectual abilities, powerful political influence, or some special social status. They turned the world upside down because God worked in them to do it.

God chooses the humble, the lowly, the meek, and the weak so that there's never any question about the source of power when their lives change the world. It's not the man; it's the truth of God and the power of God *in* the man. (We need to remind some preachers today of this. It's not their cleverness or their personality. The power is in the Word—the truth that we preach—not in us.) And apart from one Person—one extraordinary human being who was God incarnate, the Lord Jesus Christ—the history of God's work on earth is the story

11

of His using the unworthy and molding them for His use the same careful way a potter fashions clay. The Twelve were no exception to that.

The apostles properly hold an exalted place in redemptive history, of course. They are certainly worthy of being regarded as heroes of the faith. The book of Revelation describes how their names will adorn the twelve gates of the heavenly city, the New Jerusalem. So heaven itself features an eternal tribute to them. But that doesn't diminish the truth that they were as ordinary as you and I. We need to remember them not from their stained-glass images, but from the down-to-earth way the Bible presents them to us. We need to lift them out of their otherworldly obscurity and get to know them as real people. We need to think of them as actual men, and not as some kind of exalted figures from the pantheon of religious ritualism.

Let's not, however, underestimate the importance of their office. Upon their selection, the twelve apostles in effect became the true spiritual leaders of Israel. The religious elite of *apostate* Israel were symbolically set aside when Jesus chose them. The apostles became the first preachers of the new covenant. They were the ones to whom the Christian gospel was first entrusted. They represented the true Israel of God—a genuinely repentant and believing Israel. They also became the foundation stones of the church, with Jesus Himself as the chief cornerstone (Ephesians 2:20). Those truths are heightened, not diminished, by the fact that these men were so ordinary.

Again, that is perfectly consistent with the way the Lord always works. In 1 Corinthians 1:20–21 we read, "Where is the wise? Where is the scribe? Where is the disputer of this age? Has not God made foolish the wisdom of this world? For since, in the wisdom of God, the world through wisdom did not know God, it pleased God through the foolishness of the message preached to save those who believe." That is the very reason there were no philosophers, no brilliant writers, no famous debaters, no eminent teachers, and no men who had ever distinguished themselves as great orators among the twelve men Christ chose. They *became* great spiritual leaders and great preachers under the power of the Holy Spirit, but it was not because of any innate oratorical skill, leadership abilities, or academic qualifications these men had. Their influence is owing to one thing and one thing only: the power of the message they preached.

On a human level, the gospel was thought a foolish message and the apostles were deemed unsophisticated preachers. Their teaching was beneath the elite. They were mere fishermen and working-class nobodies. Peons. Rabble. That was the assessment of their contemporaries. (The same thing has been true of the genuine church of Christ throughout history. It is true in the evangelical world today. Where are the impressive intellects, the great writers, and the great orators esteemed by the world? They're not found, for the most part, in the church.) "For you see your calling, brethren, that not many wise according to the flesh, not many mighty, not many noble, are called" (v. 26).

"But God has chosen the foolish things of the world to put to shame the wise, and God has chosen the weak things of the world to put to shame the things which are mighty; and the base things of the world and the things which are despised God has chosen, and the things which are not, to bring to nothing the things that are, that no flesh should glory in His presence" (vv. 27–29). God's favorite instruments are nobodies, so that no man can boast before God. In other words, God chooses whom He chooses in order that *He* might receive the glory. He chooses weak instruments so that no one will attribute the power to human instruments rather than to God, who wields those instruments. Such a strategy is unacceptable to those whose whole pursuit in life is aimed toward the goal of human glory.

With the notable exception of Judas Iscariot, these men were not like that. They certainly struggled with pride and arrogance like every fallen human being. But the driving passion of their lives became the glory of Christ. And it was that passion, subjected to the influence of the Holy Spirit—not any innate skill or human talent—that explains why they left such an indelible impact on the world.

13

THE TEACHER

Bear in mind, then, that the selection of the Twelve took place at a time when Jesus was faced with the reality of His impending death. He had experienced the rising hostility of the religious leaders. He knew His earthly mission would soon culminate in His death, resurrection, and ascension. And so from this point on, the whole character of His ministry changed. It became his top priority to train the men who would be the chief spokesmen for the gospel after He was gone.

How did He choose them? He first went off to commune with His Father. "He went out to the mountain to pray, and continued all night in prayer to God" (Luke 6:12).

Throughout the first five chapters of his Gospel, Luke has already made clear that prayer was a pattern in the life of Jesus. Luke 5:16 says, "He Himself often withdrew into the wilderness and prayed." It was His habit to slip away in solitude to talk to His Father. He was always under pressure from the massive multitudes when He was in the towns and villages of Galilee. The wilderness and the mountain regions afforded solitude where He could pray.

We don't know *which* mountain this was. If it mattered, Scripture would tell us. There are lots of hills and mountains around the northern Galilee area. This one was probably in close walking distance to Capernaum, which was a sort of home base for Jesus' ministry. He went there and spent the entire night in prayer.

We often see Him praying in anticipation of crucial events in His ministry. (Remember, that is what He was doing on the night of His betrayal—praying in a garden where he found some solitude from the hectic atmosphere in Jerusalem. Judas knew he would find Jesus there because according to Luke 22:39 it was His habit to go there and pray.)

Here is Jesus in His true humanity. He was standing in a very volatile situation. The brewing hostility against Him was already threatening to bring about His death. He had a very brief amount of time remaining to train the men who would carry the gospel to the world after His departure. And the chilling reality of those matters drove Him to the top of a mountain so He could pray to God in total solitude. He had made Himself of no reputation and had taken the form of a bondservant, coming to earth as a man. The time was now approaching when He would further humble Himself unto death—even the death of the cross. And thus He goes to God as a man would go, to seek God's face in prayer and to commune with the Father about the men whom He would choose for this vital office.

Notice that He spent the entire night in prayer. If He went to the mountain before dark, that was probably around seven or eight o'clock in the evening. If He came back down after dawn, that would have been around six in the morning. In other words, He prayed for at least ten hours straight.

To say He spent the whole night requires several words in English. It's only one word in the Greek: *dianuktereuo*. The word is significant. It speaks of enduring at a task through the night. The word could not be used of sleeping all night. It's not an expression you would use if you wanted to say it was dark all night. It has the sense of toiling through the night, staying at a task all night. It suggests that He remained awake through the darkness until morning and that He was persevering all that time in prayer with an immense weight of duty upon Him.

Another interesting note comes through in the Greek language although we don't see it in the English. Our English version says that He "continued all night in prayer to God." Actually, the Greek expression means that He spent the whole night in the prayer *of* God. Whenever He prayed, it was quite literally the prayer of God. He was engaged in inter-Trinitarian communion. The prayer being offered was the very prayer of God. The Members of the Trinity were communing with one another. His prayers were all perfectly consistent with the mind and the will of God—for He Himself is God. And therein do we see the incredible mystery of His humanity and His deity brought together. Jesus in His humanity needed to pray all night, and Jesus in His deity was praying the very prayer of God.

Don't miss the point: The choice Christ would soon make was of such monumental importance that it required ten to twelve hours of prayer in preparation. What was He praying for? Clarity in the matter of whom to choose? I don't think so. As omniscient God incarnate, the divine will was no mystery to Him. He was no doubt praying for the men He would soon appoint, communing with the Father about the absolute wisdom of His choice, and acting in His capacity as Mediator on their behalf.

When the night of prayer was over, He returned to where His disciples were and summoned them. ("And when it was day, He called His disciples to Himself"—Luke 6:13.) It was not only the Twelve whom He summoned. The word *disciple* in this context speaks of His followers in a broad sense. The word itself means "student, learner." There must have been numerous disciples, and from them, He would choose twelve to fill the office of an apostle.

It was common, both in the Greek culture and the Jewish culture of Jesus' day, for a prominent rabbi or philosopher to attract students. Their teaching venue was not necessarily a classroom or an auditorium. Most were peripatetic instructors whose disciples simply followed them through the normal course of everyday life. That is the kind of ministry Jesus maintained with His followers. He was an itinerant teacher. He simply went from place to place, and as He taught, He attracted people who followed His movements and listened to His teaching. We get a picture of this back in verse 1: "Now it happened on the second Sabbath after the first that He went through the grainfields. And His disciples plucked the heads of grain and ate them, rubbing them in their hands." They were walking with Him, following Him from place to place as He taught, gleaning grain for food as they walked.

We don't know how many disciples Jesus had. At one point, he sent seventy out in pairs to evangelize in communities where He was preparing to visit (Luke 10:1). But the total number of His followers was undoubtedly far more than seventy. Scripture indicates that multitudes followed Him. And why not? His teaching was absolutely unlike anything anyone had ever heard in its clarity and obvious, inherent authority; He had the ability to heal diseases, cast out demons, and raise the dead; He was full of grace and truth. It's not amazing that He drew so many disciples. What is amazing is that anyone rejected Him. But reject Him they did, because His message was more than they could bear.

We see something of the dynamics of this in John 6. At the beginning of the chapter, He feeds more than five thousand people who had come out to see Him. (John 6:10 says the men alone numbered five thousand. Counting women and children, the crowd might have easily been double that number or more.) It was an amazing day. Many of those people were already following Him as disciples; many others were no doubt prepared to do so. John writes, "Then those men, when they had seen the sign that Jesus did, said, 'This is truly the Prophet who is to come into the world'" (v. 14). Who was this man who could produce food out of nothing? *They* spent most of their lives farming, harvesting, raising animals, and preparing meals. *Jesus* could just create food! That would change their lives. They must have had visions of leisure and free food, already prepared. This was the kind of Messiah they had hoped for! According to John, "They were about to come and take Him by force to make Him king" (v. 15). He escaped by a series of supernatural events that culminated in His walking on the water.

The next day the people found Him in Capernaum, on the other side of the lake. Crowds of them had come looking for Him, obviously hoping He would give them more food. He chided them for following Him out of wrong motives: "You seek Me, not because you saw the signs, but because you ate of the loaves and were filled" (v. 26). When they continued to ask for more food, He told them, "I am the living bread which came down from heaven. If anyone eats of this bread, he will live forever; and the bread that I shall give is My flesh, which I shall give for the life of the world" (v. 51). The saying was so hard for them to understand that they pressed Him to explain. He continued:

> "Most assuredly, I say to you, unless you eat the flesh of the Son of Man and drink His blood, you have no life in you. Whoever eats My

flesh and drinks My blood has eternal life, and I will raise him up at the last day. For My flesh is food indeed, and My blood is drink indeed. He who eats My flesh and drinks My blood abides in Me, and I in him. As the living Father sent Me, and I live because of the Father, so he who feeds on Me will live because of Me. This is the bread which came down from heaven; not as your fathers ate the manna, and are dead. He who eats this bread will live forever." These things He said in the synagogue as He taught in Capernaum. (vv. 53–59)

This was so offensive that even many of His disciples began to have second thoughts about following Him. John writes, "From that time many of His disciples went back and walked with Him no more" (v. 66).

So disciples were coming and going. People were attracted, then disillusioned. And on that particular occasion described in John 6, Jesus even said to the Twelve, "Do you also want to go away?" (v. 67). Peter spoke for the group when he answered, "Lord, to whom shall we go? You have the words of eternal life. Also we have come to believe and know that You are the Christ, the Son of the living God" (vv. 68–69).

Those who stayed were people whom God had sovereignly drawn to His own Son (v. 44). Jesus had also drawn them to Himself in particular. He told them, "You did not choose Me, but I chose you and appointed you that you should go and bear fruit, and that your fruit should remain" (John 15:16). He sovereignly selected them and (with the exception of Judas Iscariot, whom Christ knew would betray Him) He sovereignly worked in them and through them to guarantee that they would persevere with Him, that they would bear fruit, and that their fruit would remain. Here we see the principle of God's electing grace at work.

The sovereignty of His choice is seen in an extraordinary way by the selection of the Twelve. Out of the larger group of disciples, perhaps hundreds of them, He chose twelve men in particular and appointed them to the apostolic office. It was not a job for which applicants or volunteers were sought. Christ *chose* them sovereignly and appointed them, in the presence of the larger group. This was a remarkable moment for those twelve. Up to this point, Peter, James, John, Andrew, Nathanael, Matthew, and the others were just part of the crowd. They were learners like everyone else in the group. They had been following and listening and observing and absorbing His teaching. But they didn't yet have any official role of leadership. They had not yet been appointed to any role that set them apart from the others. They were faces in the crowd until Christ selected them and made twelve of them apostles.

Why twelve? Why not eight? Why not twenty-four? The number twelve was filled with symbolic importance. There were twelve tribes in Israel. But Israel was apostate. The Judaism of Jesus' time represented a corruption of the faith of the Old Testament. Israel had abandoned divine grace in favor of works-religion. Their religion was legalistic. It was shot through with hypocrisy, self-righteous works, man-made regulations, and meaningless ceremonies. It was heretical. It was based on physical descent from Abraham rather than the *faith* of Abraham. In choosing twelve apostles, Christ was in effect appointing new leadership for the new covenant. And the apostles represented the new leaders of the true Israel of God—consisting of people who believed the gospel and were following the faith of Abraham (cf. Romans 4:16). In other words, the twelve apostles symbolized judgment against the twelve tribes of Old Testament Israel.

Jesus Himself made the connection plainly. In Luke 22:29–30, He told the apostles, "I bestow upon you a kingdom, just as My Father bestowed one upon Me, that you may eat and drink at My table in My kingdom, and sit on thrones judging the twelve tribes of Israel."

The significance of the number twelve would have been immediately obvious to almost every Israelite. Jesus' messianic claims were clear to all who listened to His teaching. He constantly spoke of His coming kingdom. Meanwhile, throughout Israel, expectation was running high that the Messiah would very soon appear and establish

His kingdom. Some had thought John the Baptist would be that Messiah, but John pointed them to Christ (cf. John 1:19–27). They knew very well that Christ had all the messianic credentials (John 10:41-42). He wasn't the kind of political leader they expected, so they were slow to believe (John 10:24–25). But they surely understood the claims He was making, and they were filled with anticipation.

So when He publicly appointed twelve men to be His apostles, the significance of that number was loud and clear. The apostles represented a whole new Israel, under the new covenant. And their appointment—bypassing the religious establishment of official Judaism—signified a message of judgment against national Israel. Clearly, these twelve ordinary men were not destined for an ordinary role. They stood in the place of the heads of twelve tribes. They were living proof that the kingdom Jesus was about to establish was altogether different from the kingdom most Israelites anticipated.

Luke 6:13 says, "He chose twelve whom He also named apostles." The title alone was significant. The Greek verb *apostello* means "to send out." The noun form, *apostolos,* means "one who is sent." The English word *apostle* is a transliteration, rather than a translation, of the Greek word. The apostles were "sent ones." But they were not mere messengers. The Greek word for "messenger" was *angelos,* from which we get our word "angel." An *apostolos* was something more significant than a courier or a herald; *apostolos* conveyed the idea of an ambassador, a delegate, an official representative.

The word has an exact parallel in Aramaic—*shaliah.* (Remember that the common language in Israel in Jesus' time—the language Jesus Himself spoke—was not Hebrew, but Aramaic.) In that first-century Jewish culture, the *shaliah* was an official representative of the Sanhedrin, the ruling council of Israel. A *shaliah* exercised the full rights of the Sanhedrin. He spoke for them, and when he spoke, he spoke with their authority. He was owed the same respect and deference as the council itself. But he never delivered his own message; his task was to deliver the message of the group whom he represented. The office of a *shaliah* was well known. *Shaliah* were sent out to settle legal or religious disputes, and they acted with the full authority of the whole council. Some prominent rabbis also had their *shaliah*, "sent ones" who taught their message and represented them with their full authority. Even the Jewish Mishnah (a collection of oral traditions originally conceived as a commentary on the Law) recognized the role of the *shaliah*. It says, "The one sent by the man is as the man himself." So the nature of the office was well known to the Jewish people.

Thus when Jesus appointed apostles, He was saying something very familiar to people in that culture. These were His delegates. They were His trusted *shaliah*. They spoke with His authority, delivered His message, and exercised His authority.

THE TASK

The familiar role of the *shaliah* in that culture virtually defined the task of the apostles. Obviously, Christ would delegate His authority to these twelve and send them out with His message. They would represent Him as official delegates. Virtually everyone in that culture would have instantly understood the nature of the office. These twelve men, commissioned as Jesus' apostles, would speak and act with the same authority as the One who sent them. "Apostle" was therefore a title of great respect and privilege.

Mark 3:14 records this same event: "Then He appointed twelve, that they might be with Him and that He might send them out to preach." Notice the two-step process. Before they could be sent out to preach, they had to be pulled in. It was absolutely critical that they be with Jesus before they be sent out. In fact, it isn't until Luke 9:1 that Jesus calls the Twelve together and gives them authority over the demons and power to heal diseases. At that point, He literally delegates to them His miracle power. So in Luke 6, He identifies and appoints them and brings them under His direct and personal tutelage ("that they might be with Him"). In Luke 9, several months later, He gives them power to work miracles and cast out demons. Not until then did He "send them out to preach."

Up to this point, Jesus was speaking to huge crowds most of the time. With the calling of the Twelve in Luke 6, His teaching ministry becomes more intimate, focused primarily on them. He would still draw large crowds and teach them, but His focus was on the disciples and their training.

Notice the natural progression in their training program. At first, they simply followed Jesus, gleaning from His sermons to the multitudes and listening to His instructions along with a larger group of disciples. They apparently did not do this full-time, but as opportunity allowed in the course of their regular lives. Next (as recorded in Matthew 4), He called them to leave everything and follow Him exclusively. Now (in the incident recorded in Luke 6 and Matthew 10), He selects twelve men out of that group of full-time disciples, identifies them as apostles, and begins to focus most of His energies on their personal instruction. Later, He will gift them with authority and miracle power. Finally, He will send them out. At first, they go on short-term mission assignments, but they keep coming back. But when He leaves to return to the Father, they will go out for good on their own. There's a clear progression in their training and entry into full-time ministry.

No longer just disciples, they are now apostles—*shaliah*. They occupy an important office. Luke uses the word "apostles" six times in his Gospel and about thirty times in the book of Acts. Their role in the Gospels pertains primarily to taking the kingdom message to Israel. In Acts, they are engaged in the founding of the church.

Although they were common men, theirs was an uncommon calling. In other words, the task they were called to, and not anything about the men per se, is what makes them so important. Consider how unique their role was to be.

Not only would they found the church and play a pivotal leadership role as the early church grew and branched out, but they also became the channels through which most of the New Testament would be given. They received truth from God by divine revelation. Ephesians 3:5 is very explicit. Paul says that the mystery of Christ,

22

which in earlier ages was not made known, "has now been revealed by the Spirit to His holy apostles and prophets." They did not preach a human message. The truth was given to them by direct revelation. They were therefore the source of all true church doctrine. Acts 2:42 describes the activities of the early church in these terms: "They continued steadfastly in the apostles' doctrine and fellowship, in the breaking of bread, and in prayers." Before the New Testament was complete, the apostles' teaching was the *only* source of truth about Christ and church doctrine. And their teaching was received with the same authority as the written Word. In fact, the written New Testament is nothing other than the Spirit-inspired, inscripturated record of the apostles' teaching.

In short, the apostles were given to edify the church. Ephesians 4:11–12 says Christ gave the apostles "for the equipping of the saints for the work of ministry, for the edifying of the body of Christ." They were the original Christian teachers and preachers. Their teaching, as recorded in the New Testament, is the only rule by which sound doctrine can be tested, even today.

They were also examples of virtue. Ephesians 3:5 calls them "holy apostles." They set a standard for godliness and true spirituality. They were the first examples for believers to emulate. They were men of character and integrity, and they set the standard for all who would subsequently become leaders in the church.

They had unique power to perform miracles that confirmed their message. Hebrews 2:3–4 says that the gospel "first began to be spoken by the Lord, and was confirmed to us by those who heard Him, God also bearing witness both with signs and wonders, with various miracles, and gifts of the Holy Spirit." In other words, God confirmed His Word through the apostles by the miracles that they were able to do. The New Testament indicates that *only* the apostles and those who were closely associated with them had the power to do miracles. That is why 2 Corinthians 12:12 speaks of such miracles as "the signs of an apostle."

As a result of all this, the disciples were greatly blessed and held in high esteem by the people of God. Jesus' expectations for them were met through their faithful perseverance. And His promise to them was fulfilled in the growth and expansion of the church. You may recall that in Luke 18:28, Peter said to Jesus, "See, we have left all and followed You." The disciples were apparently concerned about the way things were going and what might happen to them. Peter's words were actually a plea. It is as if he was saying, on behalf of the others, "What's going to happen to us?"

Jesus replied, "Assuredly, I say to you, there is no one who has left house or parents or brothers or wife or children, for the sake of the kingdom of God, who shall not receive many times more in this present time, and in the age to come eternal life." They had not left anything that He would not more than make up to them. And God did bless them in this life (even though, as we shall see when we examine each life, most of them were martyred). God blessed them in this life through the founding and growth of the church. They not only gained influence, respect, and honor among the people of God; but as for their homes and families, they gained multitudes of spiritual children and brethren as the church grew and believers multiplied. And they will be greatly honored in the age to come as well.

THE TRAINING

All of that might have seemed remote and uncertain on the morning Jesus summoned His disciples and appointed the Twelve. They still needed to be taught. All their shortcomings and human failings seemed to overshadow their potential. Time was short. They had already left whatever vocations they were expert in. They had abandoned their nets, forsaken their fields, and left the tax tables behind. They had relinquished everything they knew, in order to be trained for something for which they had no natural aptitude.

But when they forsook their jobs, they by no means became idle. They became full-time students, learners—*disciples*. Now the next eighteen months of their lives would be filled with even more intensive training—the best seminary education ever. They had the example of Christ perpetually before them. They could listen to His teaching, ask Him questions, watch how He dealt with people, and enjoy intimate fellowship with Him in every kind of setting. He gave them ministry opportunities, instructing them and sending them out on special assignments. He graciously encouraged them, lovingly corrected them, and patiently instructed them. That is how the best learning always occurs. It isn't just information passed on; it's one life invested in another.

But it was not an *easy* process. The Twelve could be amazingly thick headed. There was a reason they weren't the academic elite. Jesus Himself often said things like, "Are you also still without understanding? Do you not yet understand?" (Matthew 15:16–17; cf. 16:9). "O foolish ones, and slow of heart to believe" (Luke 24:25). It is significant that Scripture doesn't cover their defects. The point is not to portray them as superholy luminaries or to elevate them above mere mortals. If that were the aim, there would be no reason to record their character flaws. But instead of whitewashing the blemishes, Scripture seems to make a great deal of their human weaknesses. It's a brilliant reminder that "[our] faith should not be in the wisdom of men but in the power of God" (1 Corinthians 2:5).

Why was the learning process so difficult for the apostles? First of all, they lacked spiritual understanding. They were slow to hear and slow to understand. They were at various times thick, dull, stupid, and blind. All those terms or their equivalents are used to describe them in the New Testament. So how did Jesus remedy their lack of spiritual understanding? He just kept teaching. Even after His resurrection, He stayed forty days on earth. Acts 1:3 says that during that time He was "speaking of the things pertaining to the kingdom of God." He was still persistently teaching them until the moment He ascended into heaven.

A second problem that made the learning process difficult for the disciples is that they lacked humility. They were self-absorbed, self-centered, self-promoting, and proud. They spent an enormous amount of time arguing about who would be the greatest among them (Matthew 20:20–28; Mark 9:33–37; Luke 9:46). How did Jesus overcome their lack of humility? By being an example of humility to them. He washed their feet. He modeled servanthood. He humbled Himself, even unto the death of the cross.

Third, not only did they lack understanding and humility, but they also lacked faith. Four times in the Gospel of Matthew alone Jesus says to them, "O you of little faith" (6:30; 8:26; 14:31; 16:8). In Mark 4:40, He asked them, "How is it that you have no faith?" At the end of Mark's Gospel, after they had spent months in intensive training with Jesus—even after He had risen from the dead—Mark writes, "He rebuked their unbelief and hardness of heart" (Mark 16:14). What remedy did Jesus have for their lack of faith? He kept doing miracles and wonderful works. The miracles were not primarily for the benefit of unbelievers; most of His miracles were deliberately done "in the presence of His disciples" so that *their* faith could be strengthened (John 20:30).

Fourth, they lacked commitment. While the crowds were cheering and the miracles were being multiplied, they were thrilled. But as soon as the soldiers came into the garden to arrest Jesus, they all forsook Him and fled (Mark 14:50). Their leader ended up denying Jesus and swearing he didn't even know the man. How did Jesus remedy their proneness to defection? By interceding for them in prayer. John 17 records how Jesus prayed that they would remain ultimately faithful and that the Father would bring them to heaven (vv. 11–26).

Fifth, they lacked power. On their own, they were weak and help-less, especially when confronted with the enemy. There were times when they tried but could not cast out demons. Their faithlessness left them unable to harness the power that was available to them. What did Jesus do to remedy their weakness? On the day of Pentecost He sent the Holy Spirit to indwell and empower them. This was His promise to them: "You shall receive power when the Holy Spirit has come upon you; and you shall be witnesses to Me in Jerusalem, and in all Judea and Samaria, and to the end of the earth" (Acts 1:8). That promise was mightily fulfilled.

We're inclined to look at this group with all their weaknesses and wonder why Jesus did not simply pick a different group of men. Why would He single out men with no understanding, no humility, no faith, no commitment, and no power? Simply this: His strength is made perfect in weakness (2 Corinthians 12:9). Again we see how He chooses the weak things of this world to confound the mighty. No one could ever examine this group of men and conclude that they did what they did because of their own innate abilities. There is no human explanation for the influence of the apostles. The glory goes to God alone.

Acts 4:13 says this about how the people of Jerusalem perceived the apostles: "Now when they saw the boldness of Peter and John, and perceived that they were uneducated and untrained men, they marveled. And they realized that they had been with Jesus." The Greek text says people perceived that they were *"aggramatoi . . . idiotai"*—literally, "illiterate ignoramuses." And that was true from a worldly viewpoint. But it was obvious that they had been with Jesus. The same thing should be said of every true disciple. Luke 6:40 says, "A disciple is not above his teacher, but everyone who is perfectly trained will be like his teacher."

The apostles' relatively brief time of training with Jesus bore eternal fruit. At first, it might have seemed that everything would be for naught. The night Jesus was betrayed, they were scattered like sheep whose shepherd had been smitten (Matthew 26:31). Even after the resurrection, they seemed timid, full of remorse over their failure, and too aware of their own weaknesses to minister with confidence.

But after Jesus ascended to heaven, the Holy Spirit came, infused them with power, and enabled them to do what Christ had trained them to do. The book of Acts records how the church was launched, and the rest is history. Those men, through the legacy of New Testament Scripture and the testimony they left, are still changing the world even today.

2
PETER—THE APOSTLE WITH THE FOOT-SHAPED MOUTH

And the Lord said, "Simon, Simon! Indeed, Satan has asked for you, that he may sift you as wheat. But I have prayed for you, that your faith should not fail; and when you have returned to Me, strengthen your brethren."

—LUKE 22:31–32

WE HAVE FOUR LISTS OF THE TWELVE APOSTLES IN THE New Testament: Matthew 10:2–4, Mark 3:16–19, Luke 6:13–16, and Acts 1:13. Here's how the list appears in Luke's Gospel: "He chose twelve whom He also named apostles: Simon, whom He also named Peter, and Andrew his brother; James and John; Philip and Bartholomew; Matthew and Thomas; James the son of Alphaeus, and Simon called the Zealot; Judas the son of James, and Judas Iscariot who also became a traitor."

In all four biblical lists, the same twelve men are named, and the order in which they are given is strikingly similar. The first name in all four lists is Peter. He thus stands out as the leader and spokesman for the whole company of twelve. The Twelve are then arranged in three groups of four. Group one always has Peter at the head of the list, and that group always includes Andrew, James, and John. Group two always features Philip first and includes Bartholomew, Matthew, and Thomas.

Group three is always led by James the son of Alphaeus, and it includes Simon the Zealot; Judas son of James (called "Thaddeaus" in Mark and "Lebbaeus, whose surname was Thaddeaus" in Matthew); and finally, Judas Iscariot. (Judas Iscariot is omitted from the list in Acts 1 because he was already dead by then. In the three lists where Judas's name is included, it always appears last, along with a remark identifying him as the traitor.)

The three names at the head of each group seem to have been the group leaders. The three groups always appear in the same order: first Peter's group, then the group led by Philip, then the group headed by James.

Matthew 10:2–4	Mark 3:16–19	Luke 6:14–16	Acts 1:13
Peter	Peter	Peter	Peter
Andrew	James	Andrew	James
James	John	James	John
John	Andrew	John	Andrew
Philip	Philip	Philip	Philip
Bartholomew	Bartholomew	Bartholomew	Thomas
Thomas	Matthew	Matthew	Bartholomew
Matthew	Thomas	Thomas	Matthew
James (son of Alphaeus)	James (son of Alphaeus)	James (son of Alphaeus)	James (son of Alphaeus)
Lebbaeus (surn. Thaddeus)	Thaddeus	Simon	Simon
Simon	Simon	Judas (son of James)	Judas (son of James)
Judas Iscariot	Judas Iscariot	Judas Iscariot	

The groups appear to be listed in descending order based on their level of intimacy with Christ. The members of group one were in all likelihood the first disciples Jesus called to Himself (John 1:35–42). Therefore they had been with Him the longest and occupied the most trusted position in His inner circle. They are often seen together in the presence of Christ at key times. Of the four in the first group, three—Peter, James, and John—form an even closer inner circle. Those three are with Jesus at major events in His ministry when the other apostles are either not present or not as close. The three in the inner circle were together, for example, on the Mount of Transfiguration and in the heart of the Garden of Gethsemane (cf. Matthew 17:1; Mark 5:37; 13:3; 14:33).

Group two does not have such a high profile, but they are still significant figures in the Gospel accounts. Group three is more distant, and they are rarely mentioned in the narrative accounts of Jesus' ministry. The only member of group three we know much about is Judas Iscariot—and we know him only because of his treachery at the very end. So although there were twelve apostles, only three seem to have had the most intimate relationship with Christ. The others seemed to enjoy somewhat lesser degrees of personal familiarity with Him.

This suggests that even a relatively small group of twelve is too large for one person to maintain the closest intimacy with each group member. Jesus kept three men very close to Him—Peter, James, and John. Next came Andrew, and then the others, obviously in declining degrees of close friendship. If Christ in His perfect humanity could not pour equal amounts of time and energy into everyone He drew around Him, no leader should expect to be able to do that.

The Twelve were an amazingly varied group. Their personalities and interests swept the spectrum. The four in group one seem to be the only ones tied together by common denominators. They were all four fishermen, they were two sets of brothers, they came from the same community, and they had apparently all been friends for a long time. By contrast, Matthew was a tax collector and a loner. Simon was a Zealot—a political activist—and a different kind of loner. The others all came from unknown occupations.

They all had vastly differing personalities. Peter was eager, aggressive, bold, and outspoken—with a habit of revving his mouth while his brain was in neutral. I have often referred to him as the apostle with the foot-shaped mouth. John, on the other hand, spoke very little. In the first twelve chapters of Acts, he and Peter are constant companions, but no words of John are ever recorded. Bartholomew (also known sometimes as Nathanael), was a true believer, openly confessing his faith in Christ and quick to have faith (cf. John 1:47–50). Significantly, he is in the same group as (and sometimes paired with) Thomas, who was an outspoken skeptic and doubter and wanted to have proof for everything.

Their political backgrounds were different, too. Matthew, the former tax collector (who was sometimes called Levi), was considered one of the most despicable people in Israel before Jesus called him. He had taken a job with the Roman government to extort taxes from his own people—and that tax money went to pay for the Roman occupation army. The lesser-known of the two Simons, on the other hand, is called "the Zealot" in Luke 6:15 and Acts 1:13. Zealots were an outlaw political party who took their hatred of Rome to an extreme and conspired to overthrow Roman rule. Many of them were violent outlaws. Since they did not have an army, they used sabotage and assassination to advance their political agenda. They were, in effect, terrorists. One faction of the Zealots was known as *sicarii* (literally, "dagger-men") because of the small, curved blades they carried. They concealed those weapons beneath their robes and used them to dispatch people they perceived as political enemies—people like tax collectors. Roman soldiers were also favorite targets for their assassinations. The *sicarii* usually staged these acts of execution at public functions in order to heighten fear. That Matthew, a former tax collector, and Simon, a former Zealot, could be part of the same company of twelve apostles is a testimony to the life-changing power and grace of Christ.

It is interesting that the key men in the first and second groups of apostles were originally called at the very outset of Christ's ministry. John 1:35–42 describes how Jesus called John and Andrew. They, in turn, on that very same day, brought Peter, who was Andrew's brother.

James, the remaining member of that group, was John's brother, so it was undoubtedly Andrew and John who brought him to Christ, too. In other words, the first group's association with Jesus went back to the very start of His public ministry.

John 1:43–51 likewise describes the calling of Philip and Nathanael (also known as Bartholomew). They were called "the following day" (v. 43). So that group also had a history that went back to the beginning of Jesus' ministry. These were men who had known Jesus well and followed Him closely for a long time.

The first person in the first group—the man who became the spokesman and the overall leader of the group—was "Simon, whom He also named Peter" (Luke 6:14).

"SIMON . . . ALSO NAMED PETER"

Simon was a very common name. There are at least seven Simons in the Gospel accounts alone. Among the Twelve were two named Simon (Simon Peter and Simon the Zealot). In Matthew 13:55, Jesus' half brothers are listed, and one of them was also named Simon. Judas Iscariot's father was called Simon as well (John 6:71). Matthew 26:6 mentions that Jesus had a meal at the home of a man in Bethany named Simon the leper. Another Simon—a Pharisee—hosted Jesus at a similar meal (Luke 7:36–40). And the man conscripted to carry Jesus' cross partway to Calvary was Simon the Cyrene (Matthew 27:32).

Our Simon's full name at birth was Simon Bar-Jonah (Matthew 16:17), meaning "Simon, son of Jonah" (John 21:15–17). Simon Peter's father's name, then, was John (sometimes rendered Jonas or Jonah). We know nothing more about his parents.

But notice that the Lord gave him another name. Luke introduces him this way: "Simon, whom He also named Peter" (Luke 6:14). Luke's choice of words here is important. Jesus didn't merely give him a new name to replace the old one. He "also" named him Peter. This disciple was known sometimes as Simon, sometimes as Peter, and sometimes as Simon Peter.

"Peter" was a sort of nickname. It means "Rock." (*Petros* is the Greek word for "a piece of rock, a stone.") The Aramaic equivalent was *Cephas* (cf. 1 Corinthians 1:12; 3:22; 9:5; 15:5; Galatians 2:9). John 1:42 describes Jesus' first face-to-face meeting with Simon Peter: "Now when Jesus looked at him, He said, 'You are Simon the son of Jonah. You shall be called Cephas' (which is translated, A Stone)." Those were apparently the first words Jesus ever said to Peter. And from then on, "Rock" was his nickname.

Sometimes, however, the Lord continued to refer to him as Simon anyway. When you see that in Scripture, it is often a signal that Peter has done something that needs rebuke or correction.

The nickname was significant, and the Lord had a specific reason for choosing it. By nature Simon was brash, vacillating, and un-dependable. He tended to make great promises he couldn't follow through with. He was one of those people who appears to lunge wholeheartedly into something but then bails out before finishing. He was usually the first one in; and too often, he was the first one out. When Jesus met him, he fit James's description of a double-minded man, unstable in all his ways (James 1:8). Jesus changed Simon's name, it appears, because He wanted the nickname to be a perpetual reminder to him about who he *should* be. And from that point on, whatever Jesus called him sent him a subtle message. If He called him Simon, He was signaling him that he was acting like his old self. If He called him Rock, He was commending him for acting the way he ought to be acting.

Tommy Lasorda, former manager of the Los Angeles Dodgers, tells the story of a young, skinny pitcher who was new in the Dodgers' minor league system. The youngster was somewhat timid but had an extraordinarily powerful and accurate arm. Lasorda was convinced that the young pitcher had the potential to be one of the greatest ever. But, Lasorda says, the young man needed to be more fierce and competitive. He needed to lose his timidity. So Lasorda gave him a nickname that was exactly the opposite of his personality: "Bulldog." Over the years, that is exactly what Orel Hershiser became—one of the most tenacious competitors who ever took the mound in the major leagues. The nickname became a perpetual reminder of what he *ought* to be, and before long, it shaped his whole attitude.

This young man named Simon, who would become Peter, was impetuous, impulsive, and overeager. He needed to become like a rock, so that is what Jesus named him. From then on, the Lord could gently chide or commend him just by using one name or the other.

After Christ's first encounter with Simon Peter, we find two distinct contexts in which the name Simon is regularly applied to him. One is a *secular* context. When Scripture refers to his house, for example, it's usually "Simon's house" (Mark 1:29; Luke 4:38; Acts 10:17). When it speaks of his mother-in-law, it does so in similar terms: "Simon's wife's mother" (Mark 1:30; Luke 4:38). Luke 5, describing the fishing business, mentions "one of the boats, which was Simon's" (v. 3)—and Luke says James and John were "partners with Simon" (v. 10). All of those expressions refer to Simon by his given name in purely secular contexts. When he is called Simon in such a context, the use of his old name usually has nothing to do with his spirituality or his character. That is just the normal way of signifying what pertained to him as a natural man—his work, his home, or his family life. These are called "Simon's" things.

The second category of references where he is called Simon is seen whenever Peter was displaying the characteristics of his un-regenerate self—when he was sinning in word, attitude, or action. Whenever he begins to act like his old self, Jesus and the Gospel writers revert to calling him Simon. In Luke 5:5, for example, Luke writes, "Simon answered and said to Him, 'Master, we have toiled all night and caught nothing; nevertheless at Your word I will let down the net.' " That is young Simon the fisherman speaking. He is skeptical and reluctant. But as he obeys and his eyes are opened to who Jesus really is, Luke begins to refer to him by his new name. Verse 8 says, "When Simon Peter saw it, he fell down at Jesus' knees, saying, 'Depart from me, for I am a sinful man, O Lord!' "

We see Jesus calling him Simon in reference to the key failures in his career. In Luke 22:31, foretelling Peter's betrayal, Jesus said, "Simon, Simon! Indeed, Satan has asked for you, that he may sift you as wheat." Later, in the Garden of Gethsemane, when Peter should have been watching and praying with Christ, he fell asleep. Mark writes, "[Jesus] came and found them sleeping, and said to Peter, 'Simon, are you sleeping? Could you not watch one hour? Watch and pray, lest you enter into temptation. The spirit indeed is willing, but the flesh is weak'" (Mark 14:37–38). Thus usually when Peter needed rebuke or admonishment, Jesus referred to him as Simon. It must have reached the point where whenever the Lord said "Simon," Peter cringed. He must have been thinking, *Please call me Rock!* And the Lord might have replied, "I'll call you Rock when you act like a rock."

It is obvious from the Gospel narratives that the apostle John knew Peter very, very well. They were lifelong friends, business associates, and neighbors. Interestingly, in the Gospel of John, John refers to his friend fifteen times as "Simon Peter." Apparently John couldn't make up his mind which name to use, because he saw both sides of Peter constantly. So he simply put both names together. In fact, "Simon Peter" is what Peter calls himself in the address of his second epistle: "Simon Peter, a bondservant and apostle of Jesus Christ" (2 Peter 1:1). In effect, he took Jesus' nickname for him and made it his surname (cf. Acts 10:32).

After the resurrection, Jesus instructed His disciples to return to Galilee, where He planned to appear to them (Matthew 28:7). Impatient Simon apparently got tired of waiting, so he announced that he was going back to fishing (John 21:3). As usual, the other disciples dutifully followed their leader. They got into the boat, fished all night, and caught nothing.

But Jesus met them on the shore the following morning, where He had prepared breakfast for them. The main purpose of the breakfast meeting seemed to be the restoration of Peter (who, of course, had sinned egregiously by denying Christ with curses on the night the Lord was betrayed). Three times Jesus addressed him as Simon and

PETER

asked, "Simon, son of Jonah, do you love Me?" (John 21:15–17).
Three times, Peter affirmed his love.

That was the last time Jesus ever had to call him Simon. A few
weeks later, on Pentecost, Peter and the rest of the apostles were filled
with the Holy Spirit. It was Peter, the Rock, who stood up and
preached that day. Peter was exactly like most Christians—both carnal and spiritual.
He succumbed to the habits of the flesh sometimes; he functioned in
the Spirit other times. He was sinful sometimes, but other times he
acted the way a righteous man ought to act. This vacillating man—
sometimes Simon, sometimes Peter—was the leader of the Twelve.

"FOLLOW ME, AND I WILL MAKE YOU FISHERS OF MEN"

Simon Peter was a fisherman by trade. He and his brother Andrew
were heirs to a family fishing business, centered in Capernaum. They
caught fish on the Sea of Galilee. Commercial fishermen on that lake
in Jesus' day caught three types of fish. The "small fish" mentioned in
John 6:9 in connection with the feeding of the five thousand are
sardines. Sardines and a kind of flat bread were the staples of the region.
Another kind of fish, known as *barbels* (because of the fleshy filaments
at the corners of their mouths) are a kind of carp and hence are somewhat bony, but they can grow to be very large—weighing as much as
fifteen pounds. (A barbel was probably the kind of fish Peter caught
with a coin in its mouth in Matthew 17:27, because it is the only fish
in the Sea of Galilee large enough to swallow a coin and also be caught
on a hook.) The third and most common type of commercial fish are
musht—a type of fish that swims and feeds in shoals and has a comb-
like dorsal fin. Musht of edible size range from six inches to a foot and
a half long. Fried musht are still served in restaurants near the Sea of
Galilee and are popularly known today as "St. Peter's Fish."

Simon and Andrew spent their nights netting those fish. The
brothers were originally from a small village called Bethsaida on the

north shore of the lake (John 1:44), but they had moved to a larger town nearby called Capernaum (Mark 1:21, 29).

In Jesus' day, Capernaum was the major town on the north tip of the Sea of Galilee. Jesus made Capernaum His home and the base of His ministry for several months. But He pronounced woe on both Capernaum and Bethsaida in Matthew 11:21–24. And those cities are merely ruins today. The ruins of the synagogue in Capernaum are still visible. Nearby (just a block to the south) archaeologists found the ruins of an ancient church. Early tradition, dating back at least to the third century, claims this church was built over the house of Peter. Indeed, archaeologists have found many signs that Christians in the second century venerated this site. It may very well be the house where Peter lived. It is a short walk from there to the edge of the lake.

Simon Peter had a wife. We know this because in Luke 4:38 Jesus healed his mother-in-law. The apostle Paul said in 1 Corinthians 9:5 that Peter took his wife on his apostolic mission. That may indicate either that they had no children or that their children were already grown by the time he took his wife. However, Scripture doesn't expressly say that they had any children. Peter was married. That's really all we know for certain about his domestic life.

We know Simon Peter was the leader of the apostles—and not only from the fact that his name heads every list of the Twelve. We also have the explicit statement of Matthew 10:2: "Now the names of the twelve apostles are these: first, Simon, who is called Peter." The word translated "first" in that verse is the Greek term *protos*. It doesn't refer to the first in a list; it speaks of the chief, the leader of the group. Peter's leadership is further evident in the way he normally acts as spokesman for the whole group. He is always in the foreground, taking the lead. He seems to have had a naturally dominant personality, and the Lord put it to good use among the Twelve.

It was, after all, the Lord who chose him to be the leader. Peter was formed and equipped by God's sovereign design to be the leader. Moreover, Christ Himself shaped and trained Peter to be the leader. Therefore when we look at Peter, we see how God builds a leader.

Peter's name is mentioned in the Gospels more than any other name except Jesus. No one speaks as often as Peter, and no one is spoken to by the Lord as often as Peter. No disciple is so frequently rebuked by the Lord as Peter; and no disciple ever rebukes the Lord except Peter (Matthew 16:22). No one else confessed Christ more boldly or acknowledged His lordship more explicitly; yet no other disciple ever verbally denied Christ as forcefully or as publicly as Peter did. No one is praised and blessed by Christ the way Peter was; yet Peter was also the only one Christ ever addressed as Satan. The Lord had harsher things to say to Peter than He ever said to any of the others.

All of that contributed to making him the leader Christ wanted him to be. God took a common man with an ambivalent, vacillating, impulsive, unsubmissive personality and shaped him into a rocklike leader—the greatest preacher among the apostles and in every sense the dominant figure in the first twelve chapters of Acts, where the church was born.

We see in Peter's life three key elements that go into the making of a true leader: the right raw material, the right life experiences, and the right character qualities. Let me show you exactly what I mean.

THE RAW MATERIAL THAT MAKES A TRUE LEADER

There is an age-old debate about whether true leaders are born or made. Peter is a strong argument for the belief that leaders are born with certain innate gifts, but must also be properly shaped and made into a true leader.

Peter had the God-given fabric of leadership woven into his personality from the beginning. He was made of the right raw material. Of course, it was the Lord who fashioned him this way in his mother's womb (cf. Psalm 139:13–16).

There are certain rather obvious features in Simon Peter's natural disposition that were critical to his leadership ability. These are not generally characteristics that can be developed merely by training; they were innate features of Peter's temperament.

The first one is *inquisitiveness.* When you're looking for a leader, you want someone who asks lots of questions. People who are not inquisitive simply don't make good leaders. Curiosity is crucial to leadership. People who are content with what they don't know, happy to remain ignorant about what they don't understand, complacent about what they haven't analyzed, and comfortable living with problems they haven't solved—such people cannot lead. Leaders need to have an insatiable curiosity. They need to be people who are hungry to find answers. Knowledge is power. Whoever has the information has the lead. If you want to find a leader, look for someone who is asking the right questions and genuinely looking for answers.

This sort of inquisitiveness normally manifests itself in early childhood. Most of us have encountered children who ask question after question—wearying their parents and other adults with a nonstop barrage of petty puzzlers. (Some of us can even remember being like that as children!) That is part of the fabric of leadership. The best problem-solvers are people who are driven by an unquenchable enthusiasm for knowing and understanding things.

In the Gospel accounts, Peter asks more questions than all the other apostles combined. It was usually Peter who asked the Lord to explain His difficult sayings (Matthew 15:15; Luke 12:41). It was Peter who asked how often he needed to forgive (Matthew 18:21). It was Peter who asked what reward the disciples would get for having left everything to follow Jesus (Matthew 19:27). It was Peter who asked about the withered fig tree (Mark 11:21). It was Peter who asked questions of the risen Christ (John 21:20–22). He always wanted to know more, to understand better. And that sort of inquisitiveness is a foundational element of a true leader.

Another necessary ingredient is *initiative.* If a man is wired for leadership, he will have drive, ambition, and energy. A true leader must be the kind of person who makes things happen. He is a starter. Notice that Peter not only *asked* questions; he was also usually the first one to *answer* any question posed by Christ. He often charged right in where angels fear to tread.

There was that famous occasion when Jesus asked, "Who do men say that I, the Son of Man, am?" (Matthew 16:13). Several opinions were circulating among the people about that. "So they said, 'Some say John the Baptist, some Elijah, and others Jeremiah or one of the prophets'" (v. 14). Jesus then asked the disciples in particular, "But who do *you* say that I am?" (v. 15, emphasis added). It was at that point that Peter boldly spoke out above the rest: "You are the Christ, the Son of the living God" (v. 16). The other disciples were still processing the question, like schoolboys afraid to speak up lest they give the wrong answer. Peter was bold and decisive. That's a vital characteristic of all great leaders. Sometimes he had to take a step back, undo, retract, or be rebuked. But the fact that he was always willing to grab opportunity by the throat marked him as a natural leader.

In the Garden of Gethsemane, when Roman soldiers from Fort Antonia came to arrest Jesus, all three synoptic Gospel writers say there was a "great multitude" armed "with swords and staves" (Matthew 26:47; cf. Mark 14:43; Luke 22:47). A typical Roman cohort consisted of six hundred soldiers, so in all likelihood there were hundreds of battle-ready Roman troops in and around the garden that night. Without hesitating, Peter pulled out his sword and took a swing at the head of Malchus, the servant of the high priest. (The high priest and his personal staff would have been in the front of the mob, because he was the dignitary ordering the arrest.) Peter was undoubtedly trying to cut the man's head off. But Peter was a fisherman, not a swordsman. Malchus ducked, and his ear was severed. So Jesus "touched his ear and healed him" (Luke 22:51). Then He told Peter, "Put your sword in its place, for all who take the sword will perish by the sword" (Matthew 26:52). (Thus He affirmed the equity of capital punishment as a divine law.)

Think about that incident. There was an entire detachment of

Roman soldiers there—perhaps numbering in the hundreds. What did Peter think he was going to do? Behead them all, one by one? Sometimes in Peter's passion for taking the initiative, he overlooked the obvious big-picture realities.

But with all his brashness, Peter had the raw material from which a leader could be made. Better to work with a man like that than to try to motivate someone who is always passive and hesitant. As the familiar saying goes, it is much easier to tone down a fanatic than to resurrect a corpse. Some people have to be dragged tediously in any forward direction. Not Peter. He always wanted to move ahead. He wanted to know what he didn't know. He wanted to understand what he didn't understand. He was the first to ask questions and the first to try to answer questions. He was a man who always took the initiative, seized the moment, and charged ahead. That's the stuff of leadership.

Remember, these characteristics are only the raw material from which a leader is made. Peter needed to be trained and shaped and matured. But to do the task Christ had for him, he needed moxie, chutzpa—courage to stand up in Jerusalem on Pentecost and preach the gospel in the face of the same population who had lately executed their own Messiah. But Peter was just the sort of fellow who could be trained to take that kind of courageous initiative.

There's a third element of the raw material that makes a true leader: *involvement*. True leaders are always in the middle of the action. They do not sit in the background telling everyone else what to do while they live a life of comfort away from the fray. A true leader goes through life with a cloud of dust around him. That is precisely why people follow him. People cannot *follow* someone who remains distant. The true leader must show the way. He goes before his followers into the battle.

Jesus came to the disciples one night out in the middle of the Sea of Galilee, walking on the water in the midst of a violent storm. Who out of all the disciples jumped out of the boat? Peter. *There's the Lord,* he must have thought. *I'm here; I've got to go where the action is.* The other disciples wondered if they were seeing a ghost (Matthew 14:26). But Peter said, "Lord, if it is You, command me to come to You on the water." Jesus answered, "Come" (vv. 27–29)—and before anyone knew it, Peter was out of the boat, walking on the water. The rest of the disciples were still clinging to their seats, trying to make sure they didn't fall overboard in the storm. But Peter was out of the boat without giving it a second thought. That is involvement—*serious* involvement. Only after he left the boat and walked some distance did Peter think about the danger and start to sink.

People often look at that incident and criticize Peter's lack of faith. But let's give him credit for having faith to leave that boat in the first place. Before we disparage Peter for the weakness that almost brought him down, we ought to remember where he was when he began to sink.

Similarly, although Peter denied Christ, keep in mind one significant fact: He and one other disciple (probably his lifelong friend, John) were the only ones who followed Jesus to the high priest's house to see what would become of Jesus (John 18:15). And in the courtyard of the high priest's house, Peter was the only one close enough for Jesus to turn and look him in the eyes when the rooster crowed (Luke 22:61). Long after the other disciples had forsaken Christ and fled in fear for their lives, Peter was virtually alone in a position where such a temptation could snare him, because despite his fear and weakness, he couldn't abandon Christ completely. That's the sign of a true leader. When almost everyone else bailed out, he tried to stay as close to his Lord as he could get. He wasn't the kind of leader who is content to send messages to the troops from afar. He had a passion to be personally involved, so he is always found close to the heart of the action.

That was the raw fabric of which Peter was made: an insatiable inquisitiveness, a willingness to take the initiative, and a passion to be personally involved. Now it was up to the Lord to train and shape him, because frankly, that kind of raw material, if not submitted to the Lord's control, can be downright dangerous.

THE LIFE EXPERIENCES
THAT SHAPE A TRUE LEADER

How did the Lord take a man cut from such rough fabric and refine him into a leader? For one thing, he made sure Peter had the kind of life experiences that formed him into the kind of leader Christ wanted him to be. It is in this sense that true leaders are made, not just born.

Experience can be a hard teacher. In Peter's case the ups and downs of his experience were dramatic and often painful. His life was filled with tortuous zigs and zags. The Lord dragged him through three years of tests and difficulties that gave him a lifetime of the kind of experiences every true leader must endure.

Why did Jesus do this? Did He take some glee in tormenting Peter? Not at all; the experiences—even the difficult ones—were all necessary to shape Peter into the man he needed to become.

Recently I read the results of a study involving all the young people in America who have been involved in the epidemic of school shooting rampages. It turns out that the common denominator among the shooters is that virtually all of them are young people who were prescribed Ritalin or other antidepressant drugs to control behavior problems. Instead of being disciplined for wrong attitudes and bad behavior, they were drugged into a stupor. Instead of training them to behave and teaching them self-control, child psychologists prescribed mind-numbing drugs that only temporarily curbed their rebellious behavior. The defiant, rebellious attitudes that were the root of the problem were never confronted or dealt with. Those kids had been artificially sheltered from the consequences of their rebellion in their younger childhood. They missed the life experiences that might have shaped their character differently.

The apostle Peter learned a lot through hard experience. He learned, for example, that crushing defeat and deep humiliation often follow hard on the heels of our greatest victories. Just after Christ commended him for his great confession in Matthew 16:16 ("You are the Christ, the Son of the living God"), Peter suffered the harshest rebuke ever recorded of a disciple in the New Testament. One moment Christ called Peter blessed, promising him the keys of the kingdom (vv. 17–19). In the next paragraph, Christ addressed Peter as Satan and said, "Get behind me!" (v. 23)—meaning, "Don't stand in My way!"

That incident occurred shortly after Peter's triumphant confession. Jesus announced to the disciples that He was going to Jerusalem, where He would be turned over to the chief priests and scribes and be killed. Upon hearing that, "Peter took Him aside and began to rebuke Him, saying, 'Far be it from You, Lord; this shall not happen to You!'" (Matthew 16:22). Peter's sentiment is perfectly understandable. But he was thinking only from a human standpoint. He did not know the plan of God. Without realizing it, he was trying to dissuade Christ from the very thing He came to earth to do. As usual, he was speaking when he ought to have been listening. Jesus' words to Peter were as stern as anything He ever spoke to any individual: "He turned and said to Peter, 'Get behind Me, Satan! You are an offense to Me, for you are not mindful of the things of God, but the things of men'" (v. 23).

Peter had just learned that God would reveal truth to him and guide his speech as he submitted his mind to the truth. He wasn't dependent upon a human message. The message he was to proclaim was given to him by God (v. 17). He would also be given the keys to the kingdom—meaning that his life and message would be the unlocking of the kingdom of God for the salvation of many (v. 19).

But now, through the painful experience of being rebuked by the Lord, Peter also learned that he was vulnerable to Satan. Satan could fill his mouth just as surely as the Lord could fill it. If Peter minded the things of men rather than the things of God, or if he did not do the will of God, he could be an instrument of the enemy.

Later, Peter fell victim to Satan again on the night of Jesus' arrest. This time he learned the hard way that he was humanly weak and could not trust his own resolve. All his boasting promises and earnest resolutions did not keep him from falling. After declaring in front of everyone that he would *never* deny Christ, he denied Him anyway, and he punctuated his denials with passionate curses. Satan was sifting him as wheat. Thus Peter learned how much chaff and how little substance there was in him and how watchful and careful he must be to rely only on the Lord's strength.

At the same time, he learned that in spite of his own sinful tendencies and spiritual weaknesses, the Lord wanted to use him and would sustain him and preserve him no matter what.

All those things Peter learned by experience. Sometimes the experiences were bitter, distressing, humiliating, and painful. Other times they were encouraging, uplifting, and perfectly glorious—such as when Peter saw Christ's divine brilliance on the Mount of Transfiguration. Either way, Peter made the most of his experiences, gleaning from them lessons that helped make him the great leader he became.

THE CHARACTER QUALITIES
THAT DEFINE A TRUE LEADER

A third element in the making of a leader—besides the right raw material and the right life experiences—is the right character. Character, of course, is absolutely critical in leadership. America's current moral decline is directly linked to the fact that we have elected, appointed, and hired too many leaders who have no character. In recent years, some have tried to argue that character doesn't really matter in leadership; what a man does in his private life supposedly should not be a factor in whether he is deemed fit for a public leadership role. That perspective is diametrically opposed to what the Bible teaches. Character does matter in leadership. It matters a lot.

In fact, character is what makes leadership possible. People simply cannot respect or trust those who lack character. And if they do not respect a man, they will not follow him. Time and truth go hand in hand. Leaders without character eventually disappoint their followers and lose their confidence. The only reason such people are often popular is that they make other people who have no character feel better about themselves. But they aren't *real* leaders.

Lasting leadership is grounded in character. Character produces respect. Respect produces trust. And trust motivates followers.

Even in the purely human realm, most people do recognize that true leadership is properly associated with character qualities like integrity, trustworthiness, respectability, unselfishness, humility, self-discipline, self-control, and courage. Such virtues reflect the image of God in man. Although the divine image is severely tarnished in fallen humanity, it has not been entirely erased. That's why even pagans recognize those qualities as desirable virtues, important requirements for true leadership.

Christ Himself is the epitome of what a true leader ought to be like. He is perfect in all the attributes that make up the character of a leader. He is the embodiment of all the truest, purest, highest, and noblest qualities of leadership.

Obviously, in *spiritual* leadership, the great goal and objective is to bring people to Christlikeness. That is why the leader himself must manifest Christlike character. That is why the standard for leadership in the church is set so high. The apostle Paul summarized the spirit of the true leader when he wrote, "Imitate me, just as I also imitate Christ" (1 Corinthians 11:1).

Peter might just as well have written the same thing. His character was molded and shaped after the example he had witnessed in Christ. He had the raw material for becoming a leader, and that was important. His life experiences helped hone and sharpen his natural leadership abilities, and that was also vital. But the real key to everything—the essential foundation upon which true leadership always rises or falls—is character. It was the character qualities Peter developed through his intimate association with Christ that ultimately made him the great leader he became.

J. R. Miller wrote, "The only thing that walks back from the tomb with the mourners and refuses to be buried is the character of a man.

What a man is survives him. It can never be buried."[1] That is a true sentiment, but there is something more important than what people think of us after we are dead. What is far more important is the impact we have while we are here.

What are some of the character qualities of a spiritual leader that were developed in the life of Peter? One is *submission*. At first glance that may seem an unusual quality to cultivate in a leader. After all, the leader is the person in charge, and he expects other people to submit to him, right? But a true leader doesn't just demand submission; he is an example of submission by the way he submits to the Lord and to those in authority over him. Everything the true spiritual leader does ought to be marked by submission to every legitimate authority—especially submission to God and to His Word.

Leaders tend to be confident and aggressive. They naturally dominate. Peter had that tendency in him. He was quick to speak and quick to act. As we have seen, he was a man of initiative. That means he was always inclined to try to take control of every situation. In order to balance that side of him, the Lord taught him submission.

He did it in some rather remarkable ways. One classic example of this is found in Matthew 17. This account comes at a time when Jesus was returning with the Twelve to Capernaum, their home base, after a period of itinerant ministry. A tax collector was in town making the rounds to collect the annual two-drachma (half-shekel) tax from each person twenty years old or older. This was not a tax paid to Rome, but a tax paid for the upkeep of the temple. It was prescribed in Exodus 30:11–16 (cf. 2 Chronicles 24:9). The tax was equal to two days' wages, so it was no small amount.

Matthew writes, "Those who received the temple tax came to Peter and said, 'Does your Teacher not pay the temple tax?' " (Matthew 17:24). Peter assured him that Jesus did pay His taxes.

But this particular tax apparently posed a bit of a problem in Peter's mind. Was Jesus morally obliged, as the incarnate Son of God, to pay for the upkeep of the temple like any mere man? The sons of earthly kings don't pay taxes in their fathers' kingdoms; why should

Jesus? Jesus knew what Peter was thinking, so "when he had come into the house, Jesus anticipated him, saying, 'What do you think, Simon? From whom do the kings of the earth take customs or taxes, from their sons or from strangers?'" (v. 25).

Peter answered, "From strangers." Kings don't tax their own children.

Jesus drew the logical conclusion for Peter: "Then the sons are free" (v. 26). In other words, Jesus had absolute heavenly authority, if He desired, to opt out of the temple tax.

But if He did that, it would send the wrong message as far as *earthly* authority is concerned. Better to submit, pay the tax, and avoid a situation most people would not understand. So although Jesus was not technically *obligated* to pay the temple tax, he said, "Nevertheless, lest we offend them, go to the sea, cast in a hook, and take the fish that comes up first. And when you have opened its mouth, you will find a piece of money; take that and give it to them for Me and you" (v. 27).

The coin in the mouth of the fish was a stater—a single coin worth a shekel, or four drachma. It was exactly enough to pay the temple tax for two. In other words, Jesus arranged for Peter's tax to be paid in full, too.

It's intriguing that the miracle Jesus worked demonstrated His absolute *sovereignty,* and yet at the same time, He was being an example of human *submission.* Christ supernaturally directed a fish that had swallowed a coin to take the bait on Peter's hook. If Jesus was Lord over nature to such a degree, He certainly had authority to opt out of the temple tax. And yet he taught Peter by example how to submit willingly.

Submission is an indispensible character quality for leaders to cultivate. If they would teach people to submit, they must be examples of submission themselves. And sometimes a leader must submit even when there might seem to be very good arguments *against* submitting.

Peter learned the lesson well. Years later, in 1 Peter 2:13–18, he would write,

> Therefore submit yourselves to every ordinance of man for the Lord's
> sake, whether to the king as supreme, or to governors, as to those who
> are sent by him for the punishment of evildoers and for the praise of
> those who do good. For this is the will of God, that by doing good you
> may put to silence the ignorance of foolish men; as free, yet not using
> liberty as a cloak for vice, but as bondservants of God. Honor all
> people. Love the brotherhood. Fear God. Honor the king. Servants, be
> submissive to your masters with all fear, not only to the good and
> gentle, but also to the harsh.

This was the same lesson Peter learned from Christ: You are free in
one sense, but don't use your freedom as a covering for evil. Rather,
regard yourself as the Lord's bondslave. You are a citizen of heaven and
merely a sojourner on earth, but submit to every ordinance of man *for
the Lord's sake.* You are first and foremost a subject of Christ's kingdom
and a mere stranger and pilgrim on this earth. Nonetheless, to avoid
offense, honor the earthly king. Honor all people. This is the will of
God, and by submitting, you will put to silence the ignorance of
ungodly men.

Remember, the man who wrote that epistle was the same man
who when he was young and brash slashed off the ear of the high
priest's servant. He is the same man who once struggled over the idea
of Jesus' paying taxes. But he *learned* to submit—not an easy lesson for
a natural leader. Peter especially was inclined to be dominant, forceful,
aggressive, and resistant to the idea of submission. But Jesus taught
him to submit willingly, even when he thought he had a good argument for refusing to submit.

A second character quality Peter learned was *restraint.* Most people
with natural leadership abilities do not naturally excel when it comes
to exercising restraint. Self-control, discipline, moderation, and
reserve don't necessarily come naturally to someone who lives life at
the head of the pack. That is why so many leaders have problems with
anger and out-of-control passions. Perhaps you have noticed recently
that anger-management seminars have become the latest fad for

CEOs and people in high positions of leadership in American business. It is clear that anger is a common and serious problem among people who rise to such a high level of leadership.

Peter had similar tendencies. Hotheadedness goes naturally with the sort of active, decisive, initiative-taking personality that made him a leader in the first place. Such a man easily grows impatient with people who lack vision or underperform. He can be quickly irritated by those who throw up obstacles to success. Therefore he must learn restraint in order to be a good leader.

The Lord more or less put a bit in Peter's mouth and taught him restraint. That is one of the main reasons Peter bore the brunt of so many rebukes when he spoke too soon or acted too hastily. The Lord was *constantly* teaching him restraint.

That scene in the garden where Peter tried to decapitate Malchus is a classic example of his natural lack of restraint. Even surrounded by hundreds of Roman soldiers, all armed to the teeth, Peter unthinkingly pulled out his sword and was ready to wade into the crowd, swinging. It was fortunate for him that Malchus lost nothing more than an ear and that Jesus immediately healed the damage. As we have already seen, Jesus rebuked Peter sternly.

That rebuke must have been especially difficult for Peter, coming as it did in front of a horde of enemies. But he learned much from what he witnessed that night. Later in life, he would write, "Christ also suffered for us, leaving us an example, that you should follow His steps: 'Who committed no sin, nor was deceit found in His mouth'; who, when He was reviled, did not revile in return; when He suffered, He did not threaten, but committed Himself to Him who judges righteously" (1 Peter 2:21–23).

How different that is from the young man who tried to grab a sword and whack his way through his opposers! Peter had learned the lesson of restraint.

He also had to learn *humility*. Leaders are often tempted by the sin of pride. In fact, the besetting sin of leadership may be the tendency to think more of oneself than one ought to think. When people are following your lead, constantly praising you, looking up to you, and admiring you, it is too easy to be overcome with pride.

We can observe in Peter a tremendous amount of self-confidence. It is obvious by the way he jumps in with answers to all the questions. It is obvious in most of his actions, such as when he stepped out of the boat and began to walk on water. It became obvious in the worst and most disastrous way on that fateful occasion when Jesus foretold that His disciples would forsake Him.

Jesus said, "All of you will be made to stumble because of Me this night, for it is written:'I will strike the Shepherd, and the sheep of the flock will be scattered'" (Matthew 26:31).

But Peter was cocksure: "Even if all are made to stumble because of You, I will *never* be made to stumble" (v. 33, emphasis added). Then he added, "Lord, I am ready to go with You, both to prison and to death" (Luke 22:33).

Of course, as usual, Peter was wrong and Jesus was right. Peter *did* deny Christ not once, but multiple times, just as Jesus had warned. Peter's shame and disgrace at having dishonored Christ so flagrantly were only magnified by the fact he had boasted so stubbornly about being impervious to such sins!

But the Lord used all of this to make Peter humble. And when Peter wrote his first epistle, he said, "be clothed with humility, for 'God resists the proud, but gives grace to the humble.' Therefore humble yourselves under the mighty hand of God, that He may exalt you in due time" (1 Peter 5:5–6). He specifically told church leaders, "[Don't act like] lords over those entrusted to you, but [be] examples to the flock" (v. 3). Humility became one of the virtues that characterized Peter's life, his message, and his leadership style.

Peter also learned *love.* All the disciples struggled with learning that true spiritual leadership means loving service to one another. The real leader is someone who serves, not someone who demands to be waited upon.

This is a hard lesson for many natural leaders to learn. They tend to see people as a means to their end. Leaders are usually task-oriented rather than people-oriented. And so they often use people, or plow over people, in order to achieve their goals. Peter and the rest of the disciples needed to learn that leadership is rooted and grounded in loving service to others. The true leader loves and serves those whom he leads.

Jesus said, "If anyone desires to be first, he shall be last of all and servant of all" (Mark 9:35). The Lord Himself constantly modeled that kind of loving servant-leadership for the disciples. But nowhere is it more plainly on display than in the Upper Room on the night of His betrayal.

Jesus and the disciples had come to celebrate the Passover in a rented room in Jerusalem. The Passover seder was an extended, ceremonious meal lasting as long as four or five hours. Celebrants in that culture usually reclined at a low table rather than sitting upright in chairs. That meant one person's head would be next to another person's feet. Of course, all the roads were either muddy or dusty, so feet were constantly dirty. Therefore the common custom was that when you went into a house for a meal, there was usually a servant whose job it was to wash guests' feet. This was practically the lowliest and least desirable of all jobs. But for any host to neglect to arrange for his guests' feet to be washed was a significant affront (cf. Luke 7:44).

Apparently on this busy Passover night, in that rented room, no provision had been made for any servant to wash the guests' feet. The disciples were evidently prepared to overlook the breach of etiquette rather than volunteering to do such a menial task themselves. So they gathered around the table as if they were prepared to start the meal without any foot-washing. Therefore, Scripture says, Jesus Himself "rose from supper and laid aside His garments, took a towel and girded Himself. After that, He poured water into a basin and began to wash the disciples' feet, and to wipe them with the towel with which He was girded" (John 13:4–5).[2]

Jesus Himself—the One they rightly called Lord—took on the role of the lowest slave and washed the dirty feet of His disciples. According to Luke, at about the same time this occurred, the disciples were in the midst of an argument about which one of them was the greatest (Luke 22:24). They were interested in being elevated, not humiliated. So Jesus did what none of them would do. He gave them a lesson about the humility of genuine love.

Most of them probably sat there in stunned silence. But when the Lord came to Simon Peter, "Peter said to Him, 'Lord, are You washing my feet?'" (John 13:6). The sense of the statement is, *What do You think You're doing?* Here is the brash and bold Simon, speaking without carefully thinking things through. He even went on to say, "You shall never wash my feet!" (v. 8).

Peter was the master of the absolute statement: "I will *never* deny You" (cf. Matthew 26:33). "You shall *never* wash my feet!" There are no shades of gray in Peter's life; everything is in absolute black and white.

Jesus answered him, "If I do not wash you, you have no part with Me" (John 13:8). Jesus, of course, was speaking of the necessity of *spiritual* cleansing. Obviously, it wasn't the literal foot-washing that made the disciples fit for fellowship with Christ; Jesus was speaking about cleansing from sin. That was the spiritual reality this humble act of foot-washing was meant to symbolize. (Proof that He was speaking of *spiritual* cleansing is found in verse 10, when He said, "You are clean, but not all of you." He had just washed their feet, so they were all clean in the external, physical sense. But the apostle John says in verse 11, "He knew who would betray Him; therefore He said, 'You are not all clean'"—signifying that Judas was not clean in the spiritual sense of which He spoke.)

Peter's answer is typical of his usual unbridled wholeheartedness: "Lord, not my feet only, but also my hands and my head!" (v. 9). Again, there was never any middle ground with Peter. It was always all or nothing. So Jesus assured him that he was already "completely clean." (The Lord was still speaking in spiritual terms about forgiveness and cleansing from sin.) Peter now needed nothing more than a foot-washing.

In other words, Peter, as a believer, was already fully justified. The forgiveness and cleansing he needed was not the kind of summary pardon one would seek from the Judge of the universe—as if Peter were seeking to have his eternal destiny settled. He had already received that kind of cleansing and forgiveness. But now Peter was coming to God as any child would approach a parent, seeking fatherly grace and forgiveness for his wrongdoings. That was the kind of cleansing Peter needed. It is the same kind of forgiveness Jesus taught all believers to pray for daily (Luke 11:4). Here, Jesus likens such daily forgiveness to a foot-washing.

Those truths were all wrapped up in the symbolism when Jesus washed the disciples' feet. But the central lesson was about the way love ought to be shown. Jesus' example was a consummate act of loving, lowly service.

Later that evening, after Judas had left, Jesus told the other eleven, "A new commandment I give to you, that you love one another; as I have loved you, that you also love one another. By this all will know that you are My disciples, if you have love for one another" (vv. 34–35). How had He loved them? He washed their feet. While they were arguing about who was the greatest, He showed them what loving, humble service for one another looks like.

It's hard for most leaders to stoop and wash the feet of those whom they perceive as subordinates. But that was the example of leadership Jesus gave, and He urged His disciples to follow it. In fact, He told them that showing love to one another in such a way was the mark of a true disciple.

Did Peter learn to love? He certainly did. Love became one of the hallmarks of his teaching. In 1 Peter 4:8 he wrote, "Above all things have fervent love for one another, for 'love will cover a multitude of sins.'" The Greek word translated "fervent" in that verse is *ektenes*, literally meaning "stretched to the limit." Peter was urging us to love to the maximum of our capacity. The love he spoke of is not about a feeling. It's not about how we respond to people who are naturally lovable. It's about a love that covers and compensates for others' failures and weaknesses: "Love will cover a multitude of sins." This is the sort of love that washes a brother's dirty feet. Peter himself had learned that lesson from Christ's example.

Another important character quality Peter needed to learn was *compassion*. When the Lord warned Peter that he would deny Him, He said, "Satan has asked for you, that he may sift you as wheat" (Luke 22:31). Wheat was typically separated from the chaff by being shaken and tossed up into the air in a stiff wind. The chaff was blown away and the wheat would fall into a pile, thus purified.

We might have expected Jesus to reassure Peter by saying, "I'm not going to allow Satan to sift you." But He didn't. He essentially let Peter know that He had given Satan the permission he sought. He would allow the devil to put Peter to the test (as God did in the case of Job). He said, in essence, "I'm going to let him do it. I'm going to let Satan shake the very foundations of your life. Then I'm going to let him toss you to the wind—until there's nothing left but the reality of your faith." Jesus did reassure Peter that the apostle's faith would survive the ordeal. "I have prayed for you," Jesus told him, "that your faith should not fail; and when you have returned to Me, strengthen your brethren" (v. 32).

It was then that Peter arrogantly insisted that he would never stumble. Yet despite his protestations, before the night was over, he *did* deny Jesus, and his whole world was severely shaken. His ego was deflated. His self-confidence was annihilated. His pride suffered greatly. But his faith never failed.

What was this all about? Jesus was equipping Peter to strengthen the brethren. People with natural leadership abilities often tend to be short on compassion, lousy comforters, and impatient with others. They don't stop very long to care for the wounded as they pursue their goals. Peter needed to learn compassion through his own ordeal, so that when it was over, he could strengthen others in theirs.

For the rest of his life, Peter would need to show compassion to people who were struggling. After being sifted by Satan, Peter was well equipped to empathize with others' weaknesses. He could hardly help having great compassion for those who succumbed to temptation or fell into sin. He had been there. And by that experience he learned to be compassionate, tender-hearted, gracious, kind, and comforting to others who were lacerated by sin and personal failure.

In 1 Peter 5:8–10, he wrote, "Be sober, be vigilant; because your adversary the devil walks about like a roaring lion, seeking whom he may devour. Resist him, steadfast in the faith, knowing that the same sufferings are experienced by your brotherhood in the world. But may the God of all grace, who called us to His eternal glory by Christ Jesus, after you have suffered a while, perfect, establish, strengthen, and settle you."

Peter understood human weakness, and he understood it well. He had been to the bottom. His own weaknesses had been thrown in his face. But he had been perfected, established, strengthened, and settled by the Lord. As usual, he was writing out of his own experience. These were not theoretical precepts he taught.

Finally, he had to learn *courage*. Not the impetuous, headlong, false kind of "courage" that caused him to swing his sword so wildly at Malchus, but a mature, settled, intrepid willingness to suffer for Christ's sake.

The kingdom of darkness is set against the kingdom of light. Lies are set against the truth. Satan is set against God. And demons are set against the holy purposes of Christ. Therefore Peter would face difficulty wherever he went. Christ told him, "Most assuredly, I say to you, when you were younger, you girded yourself and walked where you wished; but when you are old, you will stretch out your hands, and another will gird you and carry you where you do not wish" (John 21:18).

What did that mean? The apostle John gives a clear answer: "This He spoke, signifying by what death [Peter] would glorify God" (v. 19).

The price of preaching would be death for Peter. Persecution. Oppression. Trouble. Torture. Ultimately, martyrdom. Peter would need rock-solid courage to persevere.

You can practically see the birth of real courage in Peter's heart at Pentecost, when he was filled and empowered by the Holy Spirit. Prior to that, he had shown flashes of a fickle kind of courage. That is why he impetuously drew his sword in front of a multitude of armed soldiers one minute but denied Jesus when challenged by a servant girl a few hours later. His courage, like everything in his life, was marred by instability.

After Pentecost, however, we see a different Peter. Acts 4 describes how Peter and John were brought before the Sanhedrin, the Jewish ruling counsel. They were solemnly instructed "not to speak at all nor teach in the name of Jesus" (v. 18).

Peter and John boldly replied, "Whether it is right in the sight of God to listen to you more than to God, you judge. For we cannot but speak the things which we have seen and heard" (vv. 19–20). Soon they were brought back before the Sanhedrin for continuing to preach. Again they told them the same thing: "We ought to obey God rather than men" (Acts 5:29). Peter, filled with the Holy Spirit and driven by the knowledge that Christ had risen from the dead, had acquired an unshakable, rock-solid courage.

In Peter's first epistle we get a hint of why he was filled with such courage. Writing to Christians dispersed all over the Roman Empire because of persecution, he tells them:

Blessed be the God and Father of our Lord Jesus Christ, who according to His abundant mercy has begotten us again to a living hope through the resurrection of Jesus Christ from the dead, to an inheritance incorruptible and undefiled and that does not fade away, reserved in heaven for you, who are kept by the power of God through faith for salvation ready to be revealed in the last time. In this you greatly rejoice, though now for a little while, if need be, you have been grieved by various trials, that the genuineness of your faith, being much more precious than gold that perishes, though it is tested by fire, may be found to praise, honor, and glory at the revelation of Jesus Christ. (1 Peter 1:3–7)

He was secure in Christ, and he knew it. He had seen the risen Christ, so he knew Christ had conquered death. He knew that whatever earthly trials came his way, they were merely temporary. The trials, though often painful and always distasteful, were nothing compared to the hope of eternal glory (cf. Romans 8:18). The genuineness of true faith, he knew, was infinitely more precious than any perishing earthly riches, because his faith would redound to the praise and glory of Christ at His appearing. That hope is what gave Peter such courage.

As Peter learned all these lessons and his character was transformed—as he became the man Christ wanted him to be—he gradually changed from Simon into Rock. He learned submission, restraint, humility, love, compassion, and courage from the Lord's example. And because of the Holy Spirit's work in his heart, he did become a great leader.

He preached at Pentecost and three thousand people were saved (Acts 2:14–41). He and John healed a lame man (Acts 3:1–10). He was so powerful that people were healed in his shadow (Acts 5:15–16). He raised Dorcas from the dead (Acts 9:36–42). He introduced the gospel to the Gentiles (Acts 10). And he wrote two epistles, 1 and 2 Peter, in which he featured the very same lessons he had learned from the Lord about true character.

What a man Peter was! Was he perfect? No. In Galatians 2 the apostle Paul relates an incident in which Peter compromised. He acted like a hypocrite. We see a brief flash of the old Simon. Peter was eating with Gentiles, fellowshiping with them as true brethren in Christ—until some false teachers showed up. These heretics insisted that unless the Gentiles were circumcised and following Old Testament ceremonial law, they could not be saved and should not be treated as brethren. Peter, apparently intimidated by the false teachers, stopped eating with the Gentile brethren (Galatians 2:12). Verse 13 says that when Peter did it, everybody else did it, too, because Peter was their leader. So the apostle Paul writes, "I withstood him to his face, because he was to be blamed" (v. 11). Paul rebuked Peter in the presence of everyone (v. 14).

To Peter's credit, he responded to Paul's correction. And when the error of the Judaizers was finally confronted at a full council of church leaders and apostles in Jerusalem, it was Peter who spoke up first in defense of the gospel of divine grace. He introduced the argument that won the day (Acts 15:7–14). He was in effect defending the apostle Paul's ministry. The whole episode shows how Simon Peter remained teachable, humble, and sensitive to the Holy Spirit's conviction and correction.

How did Peter's life end? We know that Jesus told Peter he would die as a martyr (John 21:18–19). But Scripture doesn't record the death of Peter. All the records of early church history indicate that Peter was crucified. Eusebius cites the testimony of Clement, who says that before Peter was crucified he was forced to watch the crucifixion of his own wife. As he watched her being led to her death, Clement says, Peter called to her by name, saying, "Remember the Lord." When it was Peter's turn to die, he pleaded to be crucified upside down because he wasn't worthy to die as his Lord had died. And thus he was nailed to a cross head-downward.[3]

Peter's life could be summed up in the final words of his second epistle: "Grow in grace and in the knowledge of our Lord and Savior, Jesus Christ" (2 Peter 3:18). That is exactly what Simon Peter did, and that is why he became Rock—the great leader of the early church.

3

ANDREW—THE APOSTLE OF SMALL THINGS

❧

One of the two who heard John speak, and followed Him, was Andrew,
Simon Peter's brother. He first found his own brother Simon, and said to
him, "We have found the Messiah" (which is translated, the Christ).
And he brought him to Jesus.

—JOHN 1:40–42

PETER'S BROTHER, ANDREW, IS THE LEAST-KNOWN OF THE FOUR disciples in the lead group. Although he was a member of that dominant foursome, Andrew ordinarily is left very much in the background. He was not included in several of the important events where we see Peter, James, and John together with Christ (Matthew 17:1; Mark 5:37; 14:33). At other key times, however, he was featured as part of the inner circle (cf. Mark 1:29; 13:3). There is no question that he had a particularly close relationship with Christ, because he was so often the means by which other people were personally introduced to the Master.

Andrew was the first of all the disciples to be called (John 1:35–40). As we shall shortly see, he was responsible for introducing his more dominant brother, Peter, to Christ (vv. 41–42). His eagerness to follow Christ, combined with his zeal for introducing others to Him, fairly typifies Andrew's character.

Peter and Andrew were originally from the village of Bethsaida

(John 1:44). Archaeologists have not yet determined the exact location of Bethsaida, but from its description in the New Testament, it is clear that it lay in the northern Galilee region. At some point, the brothers relocated to the larger city of Capernaum, close by their hometown. In fact, Peter and Andrew shared a house in Capernaum (Mark 1:29) and operated a fishing business together from there. Capernaum afforded an especially advantageous location, situated as it was on the north shore of the Sea of Galilee (where fishing was good)—and located at the junction of key trade routes.

Peter and Andrew had probably been lifelong companions with the other set of fishermen—brothers from Capernaum—James and John, sons of Zebedee. The four of them apparently shared common spiritual interests even before they met Christ. They evidently took a sabbatical from the fishing business, visited the wilderness where John the Baptist was preaching, and became disciples of John. That is where they were when they first met Christ. And when they returned to fishing (before Jesus called them to be full-time disciples), they remained together as partners. So it was quite natural that this little group formed a cohesive unit within the Twelve. In many ways these four seemed inseparable.

All four of them obviously *wanted* to be leaders. As a group, they exercised a sort of collective leadership over the other disciples. We have already seen that Peter was without question the dominant one of the group and the usual spokesman for all twelve—sometimes whether they liked it or not. But it is clear that the four disciples in the inner circle all aspired to be leaders. That is why they sometimes had those shameful arguments over who was the greatest.

Their eagerness to lead, which caused so many clashes when they were together as a group, ultimately became immensely valuable when these men went their separate ways as apostles in the early church. Jesus was training them for leadership, and in the end, they all filled important leadership roles in the early church. That is why Scripture likens them to the very foundation of the church: "Jesus Christ Himself being the chief cornerstone" (Ephesians 2:20).

Of the four in the inner circle, however, Andrew was the least conspicuous. Scripture doesn't tell us a lot about him. You can practically count on your fingers the number of times he is mentioned specifically in the Gospels. (In fact, apart from the places where all twelve disciples are listed, Andrew's name appears in the New Testament only nine times, and most of those references simply mention him in passing.)

Andrew lived his life in the shadow of his better-known brother. Many of the verses that name him add that he was Peter's brother, as if that were the fact that made him significant.

In such situations, where one brother overshadows another to such a degree, it is common to find resentment, strong sibling rivalry, or even estrangement. But in Andrew's case, there is no evidence that he begrudged Peter's dominance. Again, it was Andrew who brought Peter to Christ in the first place. He did this immediately and without hesitation. Of course, Andrew would have been fully aware of Peter's tendency to domineer. He must have known full well that as soon as Peter entered the company of disciples, he would take charge and Andrew would be relegated to a secondary status. Yet Andrew brought his older brother anyway. That fact alone says much about his character.

Almost everything Scripture tells us about Andrew shows that he had the right heart for effective ministry in the background. He did not seek to be the center of attention. He did not seem to resent those who labored in the limelight. He was evidently pleased to do what he could with the gifts and calling God had bestowed on him, and he allowed the others to do likewise.

Of all the disciples in the inner circle, Andrew appears the least contentious and the most thoughtful. As we know already, Peter tended to be impetuous, to rush ahead foolishly, and to say the wrong thing at the wrong time. He was often brash, clumsy, hasty, and impulsive. James and John were nicknamed "Sons of Thunder" because of their reckless tendencies. They were also evidently the ones who provoked many of the arguments about who was the greatest. But there's never a hint of that with Andrew. Whenever he speaks—which is rare in Scripture—he always says the right thing, not the wrong thing. Whenever he acts apart from the other disciples, he does what is right. Scripture never attaches any dishonor to Andrew's actions when it mentions him by name.

There were certainly times when, following Peter's lead, or acting in concert with all the disciples, Andrew made the same mistakes they made. But whenever his name is expressly mentioned—whenever he rises above the others and acts or speaks as an individual—Scripture commends him for what he does. He was an effective leader even though he never took the spotlight.

Andrew and Peter, though brothers, had totally different leadership styles. But just as Peter was perfectly suited for his calling, Andrew was perfectly suited for his. In fact, Andrew may be a *better* model for most church leaders than Peter, because most who enter the ministry will labor in relative obscurity, like Andrew, as opposed to being renowned and prominent, like Peter.

Andrew's name means "manly," and it seems a fitting description. Of course, the kind of net-fishing he and the others did required no small degree of physical strength and machismo. But Andrew also had other characteristics of manliness. He was bold, decisive, and deliberate. Nothing about him is feeble or wimpish. He was driven by a hearty passion for the truth, and he was willing to subject himself to the most extreme kinds of hardship and austerity in pursuit of that objective.

Remember that when Jesus met him for the first time, Andrew was already a devout man who had joined the ranks of John the Baptist's disciples. The Baptist was well known for his rugged appearance and his spartan lifestyle. He "was clothed in camel's hair, with a leather belt around his waist; and his food was locusts and wild honey" (Matthew 3:4). He lived and ministered in the wilderness, cut off from all the comforts and conveniences of city life. To follow John the Baptist as a disciple, one could hardly be soft.

John's Gospel describes Andrew's first meeting with Jesus. It took place in the wilderness, where John the Baptist was preaching repentance and baptizing converts. The apostle John records the incident as an eyewitness, because he and Andrew were there together as disciples of John the Baptist. (The apostle John doesn't identify himself by name. He keeps himself anonymous in his Gospel right up to the very end. But the way he relates the details of this encounter, right down to giving us the time of day, suggests that he had firsthand knowledge of this incident. He was obviously the other disciple mentioned in the account.)

Andrew's personal encounter with Jesus took place a few months after Jesus' baptism (1 John 29–34). Andrew and John were standing next to the Baptist when Jesus walked by and John the Baptist said, "Behold the Lamb of God!" (vv. 35–36). They immediately left John's side and began to follow Jesus (v. 37). Don't imagine that they were being fickle or untrue to their mentor. Quite the opposite. John the Baptist had already expressly denied that he was the Messiah: "When the Jews sent priests and Levites from Jerusalem to ask him, 'Who are you?' He confessed, and did not deny, but confessed, 'I am not the Christ' " (vv. 19–20). When people pressed John for an explanation of who he was, he said, "I am 'The voice of one crying in the wilderness: "Make straight the way of the LORD," ' as the prophet Isaiah said" (v. 23).

So John had already said in the most plain and forthright terms that he was only the forerunner of the Messiah. He had come to prepare the way and to point people in the right direction. In fact, the very heart of John the Baptist's message was preparation for the Messiah, who was coming speedily. Andrew and John would therefore have been caught up in the thrill of messianic expectation, waiting only for the right Person to be identified. That is why as soon as they heard John the Baptist identify Christ as the Lamb of God, the two disciples instantly, eagerly left John to follow Christ. They did the right thing. The Baptist himself surely would have approved of their choice.

The biblical account continues: "Then Jesus turned, and seeing them following, said to them, 'What do you seek?' They said to Him, 'Rabbi' (which is to say, when translated, Teacher), 'where are You staying?' He said to them, 'Come and see.' They came and saw where He was staying, and remained with Him that day" (vv. 38–39).

It was about four o' clock in the afternoon ("the tenth hour," according to verse 39) when they met Christ. They followed Him to the place where He was staying and spent the remainder of that day with Him. Since this was near John the Baptist in the wilderness, it was probably a rented house or possibly just a room in a rustic inn. But these two disciples were privileged to spend the afternoon and evening in private fellowship with Jesus, and they left convinced that they had found the true Messiah. They met, became acquainted, and began to be taught by Jesus that very day. Thus Andrew and John became Jesus' first disciples.

Notice the first thing Andrew did: "He first found his own brother Simon, and said to him, 'We have found the Messiah' (which is translated, the Christ). And he brought him to Jesus" (vv. 41–42). The news was too good to keep to himself, so Andrew went and found the one person in the world whom he most loved—whom he most wanted to know Jesus—and he led him to Christ.

As we saw in the previous chapter, Peter and Andrew went back to Capernaum and continued their fishing career after that initial meeting with Christ. It was at a later time—perhaps several months later—that Jesus came to Galilee to minister. He had begun His ministry in and around Jerusalem, where He cleansed the temple and stirred the hostility of the religious leaders. But then He returned to Galilee to preach and heal, and He eventually came to Capernaum. There He encountered the four brothers again, while they were fishing.

Matthew 4 records that encounter:

And Jesus, walking by the Sea of Galilee, saw two brothers, Simon called Peter, and Andrew his brother, casting a net into the sea; for they were fishermen. Then He said to them, "Follow Me, and I will make you fishers of men." They immediately left their nets and followed Him. Going on from there, He saw two other brothers, James the son of Zebedee, and John his brother, in the boat with Zebedee their

66

father, mending their nets. He called them, and immediately they left the boat and their father, and followed Him. (vv. 18–22)

This was where they left fishing for a more permanent, full-time discipleship.

A parallel account of this event is recorded in Luke 5:1–11. But in Luke's account, Andrew's name is not mentioned. We know he was there and was included, because Matthew's record makes that clear. But Andrew was so much in the background that Luke doesn't even mention his name. Again, he was the kind of person who seldom came to the forefront. He remained somewhat hidden. He was certainly part of the group, and he must have followed Christ as eagerly and as quickly as the others, but he played a quiet, unsung role in obscurity.

He had lived his whole life in the shadow of Peter, and he apparently accepted that role. This was the very thing that made him so useful. His willingness to be a supporting actor often gave him insights into things the other disciples had trouble grasping. Thus whenever he does come to the forefront, the thing that shines is his uncanny ability to see immense value in small and modest things.

HE SAW THE VALUE OF INDIVIDUAL PEOPLE

When it came to dealing with people, for example, Andrew fully appreciated the value of a single soul. He was known for bringing individuals, not crowds, to Jesus. Almost every time we see him in the Gospel accounts, he is bringing someone to Jesus.

Remember that his first act after discovering Christ was to go and get Peter. That incident set the tone for Andrew's style of ministry. At the feeding of the five thousand, for example, it was Andrew who brought the boy with the loaves and fishes to Christ. All the other disciples were at a loss to know how to obtain food for the multitude. It was Andrew who took the young boy to Jesus and said, "There is a lad here who has five barley loaves and two small fish" (John 6:9).

John 12:20–22 tells of some Greeks who sought out Philip and asked to see Jesus. These were probably Gentiles who knew of Jesus' reputation and wanted to meet Him. John 12:21 says these men "came to Philip, who was from Bethsaida of Galilee, and asked him, saying, 'Sir, we wish to see Jesus.' Philip came and told Andrew, and in turn Andrew and Philip told Jesus."

It is significant that these men approached Philip, but Philip took the men to Andrew and let Andrew introduce them to the Master. Why didn't Philip just take them to Jesus himself? Perhaps he was naturally timid, or maybe he wasn't confident enough in his own relationship with Christ. Maybe Philip just became flustered and confused about the proper protocol. Or it's possible that Philip wasn't sure Jesus would want to see *them*. In any case, Philip knew Andrew could introduce individuals to Christ.

Andrew was not confused when someone wanted to see Jesus. He simply brought them to Him. He understood that Jesus would want to meet anyone who wanted to meet Him (cf. John 6:37).

Andrew was obviously poised and comfortable introducing people to Christ, because he did it so often. He apparently knew Jesus well and had no insecurities about bringing others to Him. In John 1 he brought Peter to Christ, which made him the first home missionary. Now he brings some Greeks to Christ, making him the first foreign missionary.

One thing I have observed in all my years of ministry is that the most effective and important aspects of evangelism usually take place on an individual, personal level. Most people do not come to Christ as an immediate response to a sermon they hear in a crowded setting. They come to Christ because of the influence of an individual.

The church I pastor seeks to foster an evangelistic environment. And people are coming to Christ on a regular basis. Almost every Sunday in our evening services we baptize several new believers. Each one gives a testimony before being baptized. And in the overwhelming majority of instances, they tell us they came to Christ primarily because of the testimony of a coworker, a neighbor, a relative, or a friend. Occasionally we hear people say they were converted in direct response to a message they heard in church or a sermon that was broadcast on the radio. But even in those cases, it is usually owing to the influence of an individual who encouraged the person to listen or brought him to church in the first place. There's no question that the most effective means for bringing people to Christ is one at a time, on an individual basis.

Both Andrew and his brother Peter had evangelistic hearts, but their methods were dramatically different. Peter preached at Pentecost, and three thousand people were added to the church. Nothing in Scripture indicates that Andrew ever preached to a crowd or stirred masses of people. But remember that it was he who brought Peter to Christ. In the sovereign providence of God, Andrew's act of faithfulness in bringing his own brother to Christ was the individual act that led to the conversion of the man who would preach that great sermon at Pentecost. All the fruit of Peter's ministry is ultimately also the fruit of Andrew's faithful, individual witness.

God often works that way. Few have ever heard of Edward Kimball. His name is a footnote in the annals of church history. But he was the Sunday school teacher who led D. L. Moody to Christ. He went one afternoon to the Boston shoe store where the nineteen-year-old Moody was working, cornered him in the stockroom, and introduced him to Christ.

Kimball was the antithesis of the bold evangelist. He was a timid, soft-spoken man. He went to that shoe shop frightened, trembling, and unsure of whether he had enough courage to confront this young man with the gospel. At the time, Moody was crude and obviously illiterate, but the thought of speaking to him about Christ had Kimball trembling in his boots. Kimball recalled the incident years later. Moody had begun to attend his Sunday school class. It was obvious that Moody was totally untaught and ignorant about the Bible. Kimball said,

> I decided to speak to Moody about Christ and about his soul. I started down town to Holton's shoe store. When I was nearly there I

began to wonder whether I ought to go just then during business hours. And I thought maybe my mission might embarrass the boy, that when I went away the other clerks might ask who I was, and when they learned might taunt Moody and ask if I was trying to make a good boy out of him. While I was pondering over it all I passed the store without noticing it. Then, when I found I had gone by the door I determined to make a dash for it and have it over at once.[1]

Kimball found Moody working in the stockroom, wrapping and shelving shoes. Kimball said he spoke with "limping words." He later said, "I never could remember just what I *did* say: something about Christ and His love; that was all." He admitted it was "a weak appeal."[2] But Moody then and there gave his heart to Christ.

Of course, D. L. Moody was used mightily by the Lord as an evangelist both in America and in England. His ministry made a massive impact on both sides of the Atlantic, spanning most of the second half of the nineteenth century. Tens of thousands testified that they came to Christ because of his ministry. Among Moody's converts were people like C. T. Studd, the great pioneer missionary, and Wilbur Chapman, who himself became a well-known evangelist. Moody subsequently founded Moody Bible Institute, where thousands of missionaries, evangelists, and other Christian workers have been trained during the past century and sent out into all the world. All of that began when one man was faithful to introduce another individual to Christ.

That's the way Andrew usually seemed to minister: one-on-one. Most pastors would love to have their churches populated by people with Andrew's mentality. Too many Christians think that because they can't speak in front of groups or because they don't have leadership gifts, they aren't responsible to evangelize. There are few who, like Andrew, understand the value of befriending just one person and bringing him or her to Christ.

HE SAW THE VALUE OF
INSIGNIFICANT GIFTS

Some people see the big picture more clearly just because they appreciate the value of small things. Andrew fits that category. This comes through clearly in John's account of the feeding of the five thousand. Jesus had gone to a mountain to try to be alone with His disciples. As often happened when He took a break from public ministry, the clamoring multitudes tracked Him down. It was just before Passover, the most important holiday on the Jewish calendar. That means it was precisely one year before Christ would be crucified.

Suddenly a huge throng of people approached. Somehow they had discovered where Jesus was. It was nearing time to eat, and bread would be the object lesson in the message Jesus would preach to the multitude. So He made it clear that He wanted to feed the multitude. He asked Philip where they might buy bread. John adds an editorial comment to stress the fact that Christ was sovereignly in control of these circumstances: "This He said to test him, for He Himself knew what He would do" (John 6:6).

Philip did a quick accounting and determined that they had only two hundred denarii in their treasury. A denarius was a day's pay for a common laborer, so two hundred denarii would be approximately eight months' wages. It was a significant sum, but the crowd was so large that even two hundred denarii was inadequate to buy enough food for them. Philip's vision was overwhelmed by the size of the need. He and the other disciples were at a loss to know what to do. Matthew, recounting this same incident, reports that the disciples said, "This is a deserted place, and the hour is already late. Send the multitudes away, that they may go into the villages and buy themselves food" (Matthew 14:15).

But Jesus answered, "They do not need to go away. You give them something to eat" (v. 16). The disciples must have been stymied by this. Jesus' demand seemed unreasonable.

At that point, Andrew spoke up. "There is a lad here who has five barley loaves and two small fish" (John 6:9). Of course, even Andrew knew that five barley loaves and two small fish would not be enough to feed five thousand people, but (in his typical fashion) he brought the boy to Jesus anyway. Jesus had commanded the disciples to feed the people, and Andrew knew He would not issue such a command without making it possible for them to obey. So Andrew did the best he could. He identified the one food source available, and he made sure Jesus knew about it. Something in him seemed to understand that no gift is insignificant in the hands of Jesus.

John continues the narrative:

> Then Jesus said, "Make the people sit down." Now there was much grass in the place. So the men sat down, in number about five thousand. And Jesus took the loaves, and when He had given thanks He distributed them to the disciples, and the disciples to those sitting down; and likewise of the fish, as much as they wanted. So when they were filled, He said to His disciples, "Gather up the fragments that remain, so that nothing is lost." Therefore they gathered them up, and filled twelve baskets with the fragments of the five barley loaves which were left over by those who had eaten. (vv. 10–13)

What an amazing lesson! That so little could be used to accomplish so much was a testimony to the power of Christ. No gift is really insignificant in His hands.

Our Lord Himself taught the disciples that same lesson in Luke 21:1–4: "He looked up and saw the rich putting their gifts into the treasury, and He saw also a certain poor widow putting in two mites. So He said, 'Truly I say to you that this poor widow has put in more than all; for all these out of their abundance have put in offerings for God, but she out of her poverty put in all the livelihood that she had.'"

In other words, the poor person who gives everything he or she has is giving a greater gift than rich people who gave much more out of their abundance. God's ability to use a gift is in no way hindered or enhanced by the size of that gift. And it is the sacrificial faithfulness of the giver, not the size of the gift, that is the true measure of the gift's significance.

That's a difficult concept for the human mind to comprehend. But somehow, Andrew seemed instinctively to know that he was not wasting Jesus' time by bringing such a paltry gift. It is not the greatness of the gift that counts, but rather the greatness of the God to whom it is given. Andrew set the stage for the miracle.

Of course, Jesus didn't even need to have that boy's lunch in order to serve the crowd. He could have created food from nothing just as easily. But the way He fed the five thousand illustrates the way God always works. He takes the sacrificial and often insignificant gifts of people who give faithfully, and He multiplies them to accomplish monumental things.

HE SAW THE VALUE OF INCONSPICUOUS SERVICE

Some people won't play in the band unless they can hit the big drum. James and John had that tendency. So did Peter. But not Andrew. He is never named as a participant in the big debates. He was more concerned about bringing people to Jesus than about who got the credit or who was in charge. He had little craving for honor. We never hear him say anything unless it related to bringing someone to Jesus.

Andrew is the very picture of all those who labor quietly in humble places, "not with eyeservice, as men-pleasers, but as bond-servants of Christ, doing the will of God from the heart" (Ephesians 6:6). He was not an impressive pillar like Peter, James, and John. He was a humbler stone. He was one of those rare people who is willing to take second place and to be in the place of support. He did not mind being hidden as long as the work was being done.

This is a lesson many Christians today would do well to learn. Scripture cautions against seeking roles of prominence, and it warns those who would be teachers that they face a higher standard of judgment: "My brethren, let not many of you become teachers, knowing that we shall receive a stricter judgment" (James 3:11).

Jesus taught the disciples, "If any man desire to be first, the same shall be last of all, and servant of all" (Mark 9:35). It takes a special kind of person to be a leader with a servant's heart. Andrew was like that.

As far as we know, Andrew never preached to multitudes or founded any churches. He never wrote an epistle. He isn't mentioned in the book of Acts or any of the epistles. Andrew is more a silhouette than a portrait on the pages of Scripture.

In fact, the Bible does not record what happened to Andrew after Pentecost. Whatever role he played in early church history, he remained behind the scenes. Tradition says he took the gospel north. Eusebius, the ancient church historian, says Andrew went as far as Scythia. (That's why Andrew is the patron saint of Russia. He is also the patron saint of Scotland.) He was ultimately crucified in Achaia, which is in southern Greece, near Athens. One account says he led the wife of a provincial Roman governor to Christ, and that infuriated her husband. He demanded that his wife recant her devotion to Jesus Christ and she refused. So the governor had Andrew crucified.

By the governor's orders, those who crucified him lashed him to his cross instead of nailing him, in order to prolong his sufferings. (Tradition says it was a saltire, or an X-shaped cross.) By most accounts, he hung on the cross for two days, exhorting passersby to turn to Christ for salvation. After a lifetime of ministry in the shadow of his more famous brother and in the service of His Lord, he met a similar fate as theirs, remaining faithful and still endeavoring to bring people to Christ, right to the end.

Was he slighted? No. He was privileged. He was the first to hear that Jesus was the Lamb of God. He was the first to follow Christ. He was part of the inner circle, given intimate access to Christ. His name will be inscribed, along with the names of the other apostles, on the foundations of the eternal city—the New Jerusalem. Best of all, he had a whole lifetime of privilege, doing what he loved best: introducing individuals to the Lord.

Thank God for people like Andrew. They're the quiet individuals, laboring faithfully but inconspicuously, giving insignificant, sacrificial gifts, who accomplish the most for the Lord. They don't receive much recognition, but they don't seek it. They only want to hear the Lord say, "Well done."

And Andrew's legacy is the example he left to show us that in effective ministry it's often the little things that count—the individual people, the insignificant gifts, and the inconspicuous service. God delights to use such things, because He has "chosen the foolish things of the world to put to shame the wise, and God has chosen the weak things of the world to put to shame the things which are mighty; and the base things of the world and the things which are despised God has chosen, and the things which are not, to bring to nothing the things that are, that no flesh should glory in His presence" (1 Corinthians 1:27–29).

4
JAMES—THE APOSTLE OF PASSION

Herod the king stretched out his hand to harass some from the church.
Then he killed James the brother of John with the sword.

—ACTS 12:1–2

O F THE THREE DISCIPLES IN JESUS' CLOSEST INNER CIRCLE, James is the least familiar to us. The biblical account is practically devoid of any explicit details about his life and character. He never appears as a stand-alone character in the Gospel accounts, but he is always paired with his younger and better-known brother, John. The only time he is mentioned by himself is in the book of Acts, where his martyrdom is recorded.

This relative silence about James is ironic, because from a human perspective, he might have seemed the logical one to dominate the group. Between James and John, James was the eldest. (That is doubtless why his name always appears first when those two names appear together.) And between the two sets of brothers, the family of James and John seems to have been much more prominent than the family of Peter and Andrew. This is hinted at by the fact that James and John are often referred to simply as "the sons of Zebedee" (Matthew 20:20;

26:37; 27:56; Mark 10:35; Luke 5:10; John 21:2)—signifying that Zebedee was a man of some importance.

Zebedee's prestige might have stemmed from his financial success, his family lineage, or both. He was apparently quite well-to-do. His fishing business was large enough to employ multiple hired servants (Mark 1:20). Moreover, Zebedee's entire family had enough status that the apostle John "was known to the high priest," and that is how John was able to get Peter admitted to the high priest's courtyard on the night of Jesus' arrest (John 18:15–16). There is some evidence from the early church record that Zebedee was a Levite and closely related to the high priest's family. Whatever the reason for Zebedee's prominence, it is clear from Scripture that he was a man of importance, and his family's reputation reached from Galilee all the way to the high priest's household in Jerusalem.

James, as the elder brother from such a prominent family, might have felt that by all rights he ought to have been the chief apostle. Indeed, that may be one of the main reasons there were so many disputes about "which of them should be considered the greatest" (Luke 22:24). But James never did actually take first place among the apostles except in one regard: He was the first to be martyred.

James is a much more significant figure than we might consider, based on the little we know about him. In two of the lists of apostles his name comes immediately after Peter's (Mark 3:16–19; Acts 1:13). So there is good reason to assume he was a strong leader—and probably second in influence after Peter.

Of course, James also figures prominently in the close inner circle of three. He, Peter, and John were the only ones Jesus permitted to go with Him when He raised Jairus's daughter from the dead (Mark 5:37). The same group of three witnessed Jesus' glory on the Mount of Transfiguration (Matthew 17:1). James was among four disciples who questioned Jesus privately on the Mount of Olives (Mark 13:3). And he was included again with John and Peter when the Lord urged those three to pray with Him privately in Gethsemane (Mark 14:33). So as a member of the small inner circle, he was privileged to witness

Jesus' *power* in the raising of the dead, he saw His *glory* when Jesus was transfigured, he saw Christ's *sovereignty* in the way the Lord unfolded the future to them on the Mount of Olives, and he saw the Savior's *agony* in the garden. All of these events must have strengthened his faith immensely and equipped him for the suffering and martyrdom he himself would eventually face.

If there's a key word that applies to the life of the apostle James, that word is *passion*. From the little we know about him, it is obvious that he was a man of intense fervor and intensity. In fact, Jesus gave James and John a nickname: *Boanerges*—"Sons of Thunder." That defines James's personality in very vivid terms. He was zealous, thunderous, passionate, and fervent. He reminds us of Jehu in the Old Testament, who was known for driving his chariot at breakneck speed (2 Kings 9:20), and who said, "Come with me, and see my zeal for the LORD"—then annihilated the house of Ahab and swept away Baal-worship from the land. But Jehu's passion was a passion out of control, and his "zeal for the Lord" turned out to be tainted with selfish, worldly ambition and the most bloodthirsty kinds of cruelty. Scripture says, "Jehu took no heed to walk in the law of the LORD God of Israel with all his heart; for he did not depart from the sins of Jeroboam, who had made Israel sin" (2 Kings 10:31). The apostle James's zeal was mixed with similar ambitious and bloodthirsty tendencies (though in much milder doses), and he may have even been headed down a similar road to ruin when Jesus met him. But by God's grace, he was transformed into a man of God and became one of the leading apostles.

Mark, who records that Jesus called James and John "Sons of Thunder," includes that fact in his list of the Twelve, mentioning it in the same way he notes that Simon was named Peter (Mark 3:17). We don't know how often Jesus employed His nickname for James and John; Mark's mention of it is the only time it appears in all of Scripture. Unlike Peter's name, which was obviously intended to help encourage and shape Peter's character toward a rocklike steadfastness, "Boanerges" seems to have been bestowed on the sons of Zebedee to chide them when they allowed their naturally feverish temperaments to get out of hand. Perhaps the Lord even used it for humorous effect while employing it as a gentle admonishment.

What little we know about James underscores the fact that he had a fiery, vehement disposition. While Andrew was quietly bringing individuals to Jesus, James was wishing he could call down fire from heaven and destroy whole villages of people. Even the fact that James was the first to be martyred—and that his martyrdom was accomplished by no less a figure than Herod—suggests that James was not a passive or subtle man, but rather he had a style that stirred things up, so that he made deadly enemies very rapidly.

There is a legitimate place in spiritual leadership for people who have thunderous personalities. Elijah was that kind of character. (Indeed, Elijah was the role model James thought he was following when he pleaded for fire from heaven.) Nehemiah was similarly passionate (cf. Nehemiah 13:25). John the Baptist had a fiery temperament, too. James apparently was cut from similar fabric. He was outspoken, intense, and impatient with evildoers.

There is nothing inherently wrong with such zeal. Remember that Jesus Himself made a whip and cleansed the temple. And when he did, "His disciples remembered that it was written, 'Zeal for Your house has eaten Me up'" (John 2:17; cf. Psalm 69:9). James of all people knew what it was to be eaten up with zeal for the Lord. Much of what James saw Jesus do probably helped stoke his zeal—such as when the Lord rebuked the Jewish leaders, when He cursed the cities of Chorazin and Bethsaida, and when He confronted and destroyed demonic powers. Zeal is a virtue when it is truly zeal for righteousness' sake.

But sometimes zeal is less than righteous. Zeal apart from knowledge can be damning (cf. Romans 10:2). Zeal without wisdom is dangerous. Zeal mixed with insensitivity is often cruel. Whenever zeal disintegrates into uncontrolled passion, it can be deadly. And James sometimes had a tendency to let such misguided zeal get the better of him. Two incidents in particular illustrate this. One is the episode where James wanted to call down fire. The other is the time James and

John enlisted their mother's help to lobby for the highest seats in the kingdom. Let's look at these individually.

FIRE FROM HEAVEN

We get our best glimpse of why James and John were known as the Sons of Thunder in Luke 9:51–56. Jesus was preparing to pass through Samaria. He was headed to Jerusalem for the final Passover, which He knew would culminate in His death, burial, and resurrection. Luke writes, "Now it came to pass, when the time had come for Him to be received up, that He steadfastly set His face to go to Jerusalem, and sent messengers before His face. And as they went, they entered a village of the Samaritans, to prepare for Him. But they did not receive Him, because His face was set for the journey to Jerusalem" (vv. 51–53).

It was significant that Jesus chose to travel through Samaria. Even though the shortest route from Galilee to Jerusalem went right through Samaria, most Jews traveling between those two places deliberately took a route that required them to travel many miles out of the way through the barren desert of Perea—requiring them to cross the Jordan twice—just so that they could avoid Samaria.

The Samaritans were the mixed-race offspring of Israelites from the Northern Kingdom. When Israel was conquered by the Assyrians, the most prominent and influential people in their tribes were taken into captivity, and the land was resettled with pagans and foreigners who were loyal to the Assyrian king (2 Kings 17:24–34). Poor Israelites who remained in the land intermarried with those pagans.

From the very beginning, the interloping pagans did not prosper in the land because they did not fear the Lord. So the king of Assyria sent back one of the priests whom he had taken captive, in order to teach people how to fear the Lord (2 Kings 17:28). The result was a religion that blended elements of truth and paganism. "They feared the LORD, yet served their own gods; according to the rituals of the nations from among whom they were carried away" (v. 33). In other words, they still *claimed* to worship Jehovah as God (and ostensibly they accepted the Pentateuch as Scripture), but they founded their own priesthood, built their own temple, and devised a sacrificial system of their own making. In short, they made a new religion based in large part on pagan traditions. The Samaritans' religion is a classic example of what happens when the authority of Scripture is subjugated to human tradition.

The original site of the Samaritans' temple was on Mount Gerizim, in Samaria. That temple was built during the time of Alexander the Great, but it had been destroyed about one hundred twenty-five years before the birth of Christ. Gerizim was still deemed holy by the Samaritans, however, and they were convinced the mountain was the only place where God could properly be worshiped. That is why the Samaritan woman in John 4:20 said to Jesus, "Our fathers worshiped on this mountain, and you Jews say that in Jerusalem is the place where one ought to worship." Obviously, this was one of the chief points under dispute between the Jews and the Samaritans. (To this day a small group of the Samaritans' descendants still worship on Mount Gerizim.)

Many of the original Israelites' descendants who later returned to Samaria from captivity were also the product of intermarriage with pagans, so the culture of Samaria suited them perfectly. Of course, the Jews regarded the Samaritans as a mongrel race and their religion as a mongrel religion. That is why, during the time of Christ, such pains were taken to avoid all travel through Samaria. The entire region was deemed unclean.

But in this instance, Jesus' face was set for Jerusalem, and as He had done before (John 4:4), He chose the more direct route through Samaria. Along the way, He and His followers would need places to eat and spend the night. Since the party traveling with Jesus was fairly large, He sent messengers ahead to arrange accommodations.

Because it was obvious that Jesus was headed for Jerusalem to celebrate the Passover, and the Samaritans were of the opinion that all such feasts and ceremonies ought to be observed on Mount Gerizim, Jesus' messengers were refused all accommodations. The Samaritans not only hated the Jews, but they also hated the worship that took place in Jerusalem. They therefore had no interest in Christ's agenda at all. He represented everything Jewish that they despised. So they summarily rejected the request. The problem was not that there was no room for them in the inn; the problem was that the Samaritans were being deliberately inhospitable. If Jesus intended to pass through their city on His way to Jerusalem to worship, they were going to make it as hard as possible for Him. They hated the Jews and their worship as much as the Jews hated them and their worship. As far as the Samaritans were concerned, turnabout was fair play.

Of course, Jesus had never shown anything but goodwill toward the Samaritans. He had healed a Samaritan's leprosy and commended that man for his gratefulness (Luke 17:16). He had accepted water from a Samaritan woman and given her the water of life (John 4:7–29). He had stayed in that woman's village for two days, evangelizing her neighbors (John 4:39–43). He had made a Samaritan the hero of one of His best-known parables (Luke 10:30–37). Later He would command His disciples to preach the gospel in Samaria (Acts 1:8). He had always been full of kindness and goodwill toward the Samaritans.

But now they were treating Him with deliberate contempt.

James and John, the Sons of Thunder, were instantly filled with passionate outrage. They already had in mind a remedy for this situation. They said, "Lord, do You want us to command fire to come down from heaven and consume them, just as Elijah did?" (Luke 9:54).

The reference to Elijah was full of significance. The incident to which James and John were referring had taken place in this very region. They were familiar with the Old Testament account, and they knew its historical relevance to Samaria. We see here how deeply the Jews felt their resentment toward Samaria.

It was a matter of historical fact that the name of Samaria had been associated with idolatry and apostasy long before the Assyrian conquest. *Samaria* was originally the name of one of the most important cities in the Northern Kingdom. During Ahab's reign, in the days of Elijah, Samaria was turned into a center for Baal-worship (1 Kings

16:32). This was also where Ahab had built his famous ivory palace (1 Kings 22:39; cf. Amos 3:12–15).

Ahab's palace became the permanent residence for subsequent kings of the Northern Kingdom. In fact, it was the very place where King Ahaziah fell through the lattice in his upper chamber and was seriously injured (2 Kings 1:2).

A *lattice* is a screen or a grate made of crisscrossed wooden strips. This could have been a decorative window covering. More likely it was a flimsy substitute for a parapet around the perimeter of the roof. Apparently, Ahaziah carelessly backed into some latticework or stupidly leaned on it, and when it gave way, he fell to the ground from the upper level of the palace.

Ahaziah was the son and successor of Ahab. His mother, Jezebel, was still living during his reign and still exercising her evil influence through her son's throne. When Ahaziah's accident occurred, the injuries were apparently life-threatening, and he wanted to know his fate. So he dispatched messengers, telling them, "Go, inquire of Baal-Zebub, the god of Ekron, whether I shall recover from this injury" (v. 2).

Inquiring of soothsayers was strictly forbidden by Moses' law, of course (Deuteronomy 18:10–12). Seeking prophecies from fortune-tellers who were associated with Baal-Zebub was even worse. Baal–Zebub was a Philistine deity. His name meant "lord of the flies." The land of the Philistines was thick with flies, and the Philistines believed the lord of the flies lived in their land, so they made this fly-god one of their main deities. They had some famous oracles who claimed to be able to tell the future. They usually gave flattering prophecies with predictions so ambiguous they could hardly miss, but those oracles nonetheless had gained fame throughout Israel. They were the "Psychic Friends Network" of Elijah's time.

But Baal-Zebub was as vile a deity as anyone ever invented. He supposedly ruled the flies—those abhorrent insects that swarm around every kind of decay and filth and spread disease and spawn maggots. It was a fitting image for this kind of god. Who would ever think of worshiping a deity whose realm was everything foul and unclean? Such a god was so revolting to the Jews that they altered the name *Baal-Zebub* slightly to make it "Beelzebul," which means "god of dung." This vile being epitomized everything impure and unholy—everything that opposes the true God. (That is why, by the time of Jesus, the name *Beelzebub* had become a way to refer to Satan—Luke 11:15.) This was the god from whom Ahaziah sought knowledge of the future.

So the Lord sent Elijah to intercept the messengers. Scripture says, "The angel of the LORD said to Elijah the Tishbite, 'Arise, go up to meet the messengers of the king of Samaria, and say to them, "Is it because there is no God in Israel that you are going to inquire of Baal-Zebub, the god of Ekron?" ' " (2 Kings 1:3). The angel also gave Elijah a solemn message for the injured king: "Now therefore, thus says the LORD: 'You shall not come down from the bed to which you have gone up, but you shall surely die' " (v. 4).

Elijah did as he was told and sent the prophecy back to Ahaziah via the king's messengers. The messengers did not even know who Elijah was. When they reported back to the king, they simply told him the prophecy had been given them by "a man [who] came up to meet us" (v. 6).

Ahaziah asked, "What kind of man was it who came up to meet you and told you these words?" (v. 7).

They answered, "A hairy man wearing a leather belt around his waist" (v. 8).

Ahaziah instantly knew who it was: "It is Elijah the Tishbite" (v. 8).

Elijah had been Ahab and Jezebel's nemesis for years, so he was well known to Ahaziah. Naturally, Ahaziah hated him and probably decided then and there to kill him. So he sent "a captain of fifty with his fifty men" to confront Elijah (v. 9). The fact that Ahaziah sent so many soldiers is proof his intentions were not peaceful. Their orders were probably to arrest him and bring him back to Ahaziah so that the king could actually witness Elijah's execution and gloat over it.

"So [the captain of the fifty] went up to him; and there he was, sitting on the top of a hill" (v. 9). Elijah was totally unfazed by the size of the regiment that came to get him. He wasn't hiding or running from them; he was sitting placidly atop the hill, where they would be sure to find him.

The captain spoke: "Man of God, the king has said, 'Come down!'" (v. 9).

Elijah's reply was to the point: "'If I am a man of God, then let fire come down from heaven and consume you and your fifty men.' And fire came down from heaven and consumed him and his fifty" (v. 10). The Hebrew expression suggests that the entire company was utterly consumed, reduced to ashes in an instant. This apparently occurred in the presence of witnesses, who reported the matter back to the king.

But Ahaziah was a foolishly stubborn man. "Then he sent to him another captain of fifty with his fifty men. And he answered and said to him: 'Man of God, thus has the king said, "Come down quickly!"' So Elijah answered and said to them, 'If I am a man of God, let fire come down from heaven and consume you and your fifty men.' And the fire of God came down from heaven and consumed him and his fifty" (vv. 11–12).

Incredibly, Ahaziah was not through. He sent *another* company of fifty men. But the captain of this third group was wise. He approached Elijah humbly and pleaded for the lives of his men. So this time the angel of the Lord instructed Elijah to go with the soldiers and confront Ahaziah personally. Elijah went with them and delivered the message of doom to Ahaziah personally.

And Ahaziah died "according to the word of the LORD which Elijah had spoken" (vv. 13–17).

All of that had taken place in the very region through which Jesus proposed to travel to Jerusalem. The story of Elijah's fiery triumph was well known to the disciples. It was one of the classic Old Testament episodes they would have been reminded of merely by traveling through that district.

So when James and John suggested fire from heaven as a fitting response to the Samaritans' inhospitality, they probably thought they were standing on solid precedent. After all, Elijah was not condemned for his actions. On the contrary, at that time and under those circumstances, it was the appropriate response from Elijah.

But it was not a proper response for James and John. In the first place, their motives were wrong. A tone of arrogance is evident in the way they asked the question: "Lord, do You want *us* to command fire to come down from heaven and consume them, just as Elijah did?" Of course, they did not have the power to call down fire from heaven. Christ was the only one in their company who had such power. If that were an appropriate response, He could well have done it Himself. James and John were brazenly suggesting that He should give *them* power to call down fire. Christ Himself had been challenged many times by His adversaries to produce such cosmic miracles, and He had always declined (cf. Matthew 12:39). James and John were in effect asking Jesus to enable them to do what they knew He would not do.

Furthermore, Jesus' mission was very different from Elijah's. Christ had come to save, not to destroy. Therefore He responded to the Boanerges Brothers with a firm reproof: "But He turned and rebuked them, and said, 'You do not know what manner of spirit you are of. For the Son of Man did not come to destroy men's lives but to save them'" (Luke 9:55–56).

After all this time with Jesus, how could they have missed the spirit of so much He had taught? "The Son of Man has come to seek and to save that which was lost" (Luke 19:10). He was on a mission of rescue, not judgment. Although He had every right to demand absolute worship, "The Son of Man did not come to be served, but to serve, and to give His life a ransom for many" (Matthew 20:28). "For God did not send His Son into the world to condemn the world, but that the world through Him might be saved" (John 3:17). Jesus Himself had said, "I have come as a light into the world, that whoever believes in Me should not abide in darkness. And if anyone hears My words and does not believe, I do not judge him; for I did not come to judge the world but to save the world" (John 12:46–47).

Of course, a time is coming when Christ *will* judge the world.

Scripture says He will be "revealed from heaven with His mighty angels, in flaming fire taking vengeance on those who do not know God, and on those who do not obey the gospel of our Lord Jesus Christ. These shall be punished with everlasting destruction from the presence of the Lord and from the glory of His power" (2 Thessalonians 1:7–9). But this was not the time or the place for that.

As Solomon wrote, "To everything there is a season, a time for every purpose under heaven. . . . A time to kill, and a time to heal; a time to break down, and a time to build up . . . a time to cast away stones, and a time to gather stones . . . a time to keep silence, and a time to speak; a time to love, and a time to hate; a time of war, and a time of peace" (Ecclesiastes 3:1–8). James and John momentarily forgot that "now is the day of salvation" (2 Corinthians 6:2).

Perhaps, however, there is a touch of nobility in their indignation against the Samaritans. Their zeal to defend Christ's honor is surely a great virtue. It is far better to get fired up with righteous wrath than to sit passively and endure insults against Christ. So their resentment over seeing Christ deliberately slighted is admirable in some measure, even though their reaction was tainted with arrogance and their proposed remedy to the problem was completely out of line.

Note also that Jesus was not by any means condemning what Elijah had done in his day. Nor was our Lord advocating a purely pacifist approach to every conflict. What Elijah did he did for the sake of God's glory and with God's express approval. That fire from heaven was a public display of *God's* wrath (not Elijah's), and it was a deservedly severe judgment against an unthinkably evil regime that had sat on Israel's throne for generations. Such extreme wickedness called for extreme measures of judgment.

Of course, such instant destruction would be fitting every time anyone sinned, if that were how God chose to deal with us. But, thankfully, it ordinarily is not. "His tender mercies are over all His works" (Psalm 145:9). He is "merciful and gracious, longsuffering, and abounding in goodness and truth" (Exodus 34:6). He has "no pleasure in the death of the wicked, but that the wicked turn from his way and live" (Ezekiel 33:11).

Jesus' example taught James that loving-kindness and mercy are virtues to be cultivated as much as (and sometimes more than) righteous indignation and fiery zeal. Notice what happened. Instead of calling down fire from heaven, "They went to another village" (Luke 9:56). They simply found accommodations elsewhere. It was a little inconvenient, perhaps, but far better and far more appropriate in those circumstances than James and John's proposed remedy for the Samaritans' inhospitality.

A few years after this, as the early church began to grow and the gospel message spread beyond Judea, Philip the deacon "went down to the city of Samaria and preached Christ to them" (Acts 8:5). A marvelous thing happened. "The multitudes with one accord heeded the things spoken by Philip, hearing and seeing the miracles which he did. For unclean spirits, crying with a loud voice, came out of many who were possessed; and many who were paralyzed and lame were healed. And there was great joy in that city" (vv. 6–8).

Undoubtedly, many who were saved under Philip's preaching were some of the same people whom Jesus spared when James had wanted to incinerate them. And we can be certain that even James himself rejoiced greatly in the salvation of so many who once had dishonored Christ so flagrantly.

THRONES IN THE KINGDOM

We get another insight into James's character in Matthew 20:20–24. Here we discover that James was not only fervent, passionate, zealous, and insensitive; he was also ambitious and overconfident. And in this case, he and his brother John engaged in a furtive attempt to gain status over the other apostles:

> Then the mother of Zebedee's sons came to Him with her sons, kneeling down and asking something from Him. And He said to her,

"What do you wish?" She said to Him, "Grant that these two sons of mine may sit, one on Your right hand and the other on the left, in Your kingdom." But Jesus answered and said, "You do not know what you ask. Are you able to drink the cup that I am about to drink, and be baptized with the baptism that I am baptized with?" They said to Him, "We are able." So He said to them, "You will indeed drink My cup, and be baptized with the baptism that I am baptized with; but to sit on My right hand and on My left is not Mine to give, but it is for those for whom it is prepared by My Father." And when the ten heard it, they were greatly displeased with the two brothers.

Mark also records this incident, but he doesn't mention that James and John enlisted their mother's intercession. Although Matthew records that she is the one who made this request of Jesus, a comparison with Mark's account makes it clear that she was put up to it by her sons.

By comparing Matthew 27:56 with Mark 16:1, we further discover that the mother of James and John was named Salome. She was one of "many women who followed Jesus from Galilee, ministering to Him" (Matthew 27:55)—meaning that they supplied financial support and probably helped prepare meals (cf. Luke 8:1–3). Because of the family's affluence, Salome would have been able to join her sons for extended periods of time, traveling with the company that followed Jesus everywhere and helping meet logistical, practical, and financial needs.

The idea for Salome's bold request was undoubtedly hatched in the minds of James and John because of Jesus' promise in Matthew 19:28: "Assuredly I say to you, that in the regeneration, when the Son of Man sits on the throne of His glory, you who have followed Me will also sit on twelve thrones, judging the twelve tribes of Israel." Jesus immediately followed up that promise with a reminder that "Many who are first will be last, and the last first" (v. 30). But it was the promise of thrones that caught the attention of James and John. So they decided to have their mother request that they be given the most prominent thrones.

They were already in the intimate circle of three. They had been disciples as long as anyone. They probably thought of numerous reasons why they deserved this honor, so why not simply ask for it?

For her part, Salome was clearly a willing participant. Obviously she had encouraged her sons' ambitions, which may help explain where some of their attitudes came from.

Jesus' reply subtly reminded them that suffering is the prelude to glory: "Are you able to drink the cup that I drink, and be baptized with the baptism that I am baptized with?" Although He had explained to them numerous times that He was about to be crucified, they clearly did not understand what kind of baptism He meant. They had no real concept of what was stirring in the cup He was asking them to drink.

So, of course, in their foolish, ambitious self-confidence, they assured Him, "We are able." They were clamoring for honor and position, so they were *still* eager to hear Him promise them those highest thrones.

But He did not make that promise. Instead, He assured them that they would indeed drink His cup and be baptized with the same baptism he was about to undergo. (At that moment they could not have appreciated what they had just volunteered for.) But the chief thrones, Jesus said, were not necessarily part of the bargain. "To sit on My right hand and on My left is not Mine to give, but it is for those for whom it is prepared by My Father" (Matthew 20:23).

Their ambition ultimately created conflicts among the apostles, because the other ten heard about it and were displeased. The question of who deserved the most prominent thrones became the big debate among them, and they carried it right to the table at the Last Supper (Luke 22:24).

James wanted a crown of glory; Jesus gave him a cup of suffering. He wanted power; Jesus gave him servanthood. He wanted a place of prominence; Jesus gave him a martyr's grave. He wanted to rule; Jesus gave him a sword—not to wield, but to be the instrument of his own execution. Fourteen years after this, James would become the first of the Twelve to be killed for his faith.

A CUP OF SUFFERING

The end of James's story from an earthly perspective is recorded in Acts 12:1–3: "Now about that time Herod the king stretched out his hand to harass some from the church. Then he killed James the brother of John with the sword. And because he saw that it pleased the Jews, he proceeded further to seize Peter also."

Remember, this is the one place in Scripture where James appears alone, apart from even his brother. Few details of James's martyrdom are given. Scripture records that Herod was the one who had him killed and that the instrument of execution was a sword (meaning, of course, that he was beheaded). This was not Herod Antipas, the one who killed John the Baptist and put Jesus on trial; this was his nephew and successor, Herod Agrippa I. We don't know why this Herod would be so hostile to the church. Of course, it was well known that his uncle had participated in the conspiracy to kill Christ, so the preaching of the cross would surely have been an embarrassment to the Herodian Dynasty per se (cf. Acts 4:27). In addition to that, it is clear that Herod wanted to use the tensions between the church and the Jewish religious leaders to his political advantage. He began with a campaign of harassment against Christians and soon moved to murder. When he saw how this pleased the Jewish leaders, he decided to target Peter as well.

Peter miraculously escaped, and Herod himself died under God's judgment shortly afterward. Scripture says that after Peter's escape, Herod had the prison guards killed and went to Caesarea (Acts 12:19). While there, he accepted the kind of worship that is appropriate only for God. "The people kept shouting, 'The voice of a god and not of a man!' Then immediately an angel of the Lord struck him, because he did not give glory to God. And he was eaten by worms and died" (vv. 22–23). And thus the immediate threat against the church posed by Herod's campaign of harassment and murder was ended.

But it is significant that James was the first of the apostles to be killed. (James is the only apostle whose death is actually recorded in

Scripture.) Clearly, James was still a man of passion. His passion, now under the Holy Spirit's control, had been so instrumental in the spread of the truth that it had aroused the wrath of Herod. Obviously, James was right where he had always hoped to be and where Christ had trained him to be—on the front line as the gospel advanced and the church grew.

That Son of Thunder had been mentored by Christ, empowered by the Holy Spirit, and shaped by those means into a man whose zeal and ambition were useful instruments in the hands of God for spreading of the kingdom. Still courageous, zealous, and committed to the truth, he had apparently learned to use those qualities for the Lord's service, rather than for his own self-aggrandizement. And now his strength was so great that when Herod decided it was time to stop the church, James was the first man who had to die. He thus drank the cup Christ gave him to drink. His life was short, but his influence continues to this day.

History records that James's testimony bore fruit right up until the moment of his execution. Eusebius, the early church historian, passes on an account of James's death that came from Clement of Alexandria: "[Clement] says that the one who led James to the judgment-seat, when he saw him bearing his testimony, was moved, and confessed that he was himself also a Christian. They were both therefore, he says, led away together; and on the way he begged James to forgive him. And [James], after considering a little, said, 'Peace be with thee,' and kissed him. And thus they were both beheaded at the same time."[1] Thus in the end, James had learned to be more like Andrew, bringing people to Christ instead of itching to execute judgment.

James is the prototype of the passionate, zealous, front runner who is dynamic, strong, and ambitious. Ultimately, his passions were tempered by sensitivity and grace. Somewhere along the line he had learned to control his anger, bridle his tongue, redirect his zeal, eliminate his thirst for revenge, and completely lose his selfish ambition. And the Lord used him to do a wonderful work in the early church.

Such lessons are sometimes hard for a man of James's passions to learn. But if I have to choose between a man of burning, flaming, passionate, enthusiasm with a potential for failure on the one hand, and a cold compromiser on the other hand, I'll take the man with passion every time. Such zeal must always be harnessed and tempered with love. But if it is surrendered to the control of the Holy Spirit and blended with patience and longsuffering, such zeal is a marvelous instrument in the hands of God. The life of James offers clear proof of that.

5

JOHN—THE APOSTLE OF LOVE

Now there was leaning on Jesus' bosom one of His disciples, whom Jesus loved.

—JOHN 13:23

THE APOSTLE JOHN IS FAMILIAR TO US BECAUSE HE WROTE so much of the New Testament. He was the human author of a Gospel and three epistles that bear his name, as well as the book of Revelation. Aside from Luke and the apostle Paul, John wrote more of the New Testament than any other human author. Scripture is therefore full of insights into his personality and character. In fact, most of what we know about John we extract from his own writings. We see through his Gospel how he views Christ. We observe in his epistles how he dealt with the church. And in the book of Revelation we even see the future through the visions God gave him.

Both Scripture and history record that John played a major role in the early church. Of course, he was a member of the Lord's most intimate inner circle, but he was by no means the dominant member of that group. He was the younger brother of James, and although he was a frequent companion to Peter in the first twelve chapters of Acts,

Peter remained in the foreground and John remained in the background.

But John also had his turn at leadership. Ultimately, because he outlived all the others, he filled a unique and patriarchal role in the early church that lasted nearly to the end of the first century and reached deep into Asia Minor. His personal influence was therefore indelibly stamped on the primitive church, well into the post-apostolic era.

Almost everything we observed about the personality and character of James is also true of John, the younger half of the Boanerges Brothers' duo. The two men had similar temperaments, and as we noted in the previous chapter, they were inseparable in the Gospel accounts. John was right there with James, eager to call down fire from heaven against the Samaritans. He was also in the thick of the debates about who was the greatest. His zeal and ambition mirrored that of his elder brother.

Therefore it is all the more remarkable that John has often been nicknamed "the apostle of love." Indeed, he wrote more than any other New Testament author about the importance of love—laying particular stress on the Christian's love for Christ, Christ's love for His church, and the love for one another that is supposed to be the hallmark of true believers. The theme of love flows through his writings.

But love was a quality he *learned* from Christ, not something that came naturally to him. In his younger years, he was as much a Son of Thunder as James. If you imagine that John was the way he was often portrayed in medieval art—a meek, mild, pale-skinned, effeminate person, lying around on Jesus' shoulder looking up at Him with a dove-eyed stare—forget that caricature. He was rugged and hard-edged, just like the rest of the fishermen-disciples. And again, he was every bit as intolerant, ambitious, zealous, and explosive as his elder brother. In fact, the one and only time the synoptic Gospel writers recorded John speaking for himself, he displayed his trademark aggressive, self-assertive, impertinent intolerance.

If you study Matthew, Mark, and Luke you'll notice that John is nearly always named along with someone else—with Jesus, with

Peter, or with James. Only one time does John appear and speak alone. And that was when he confessed to the Lord that he had rebuked a man for casting out demons in Jesus' name, because the man was not part of the disciples' group (Mark 9:38). We'll examine that episode shortly.

So it is clear from the Gospel accounts that John was capable of behaving in the most sectarian, narrow-minded, unbending, reckless, and impetuous fashion. He was volatile. He was brash. He was aggressive. He was passionate, zealous, and personally ambitious—just like his brother James. They were cut from the same bolt of cloth.

But John aged well. Under the control of the Holy Spirit, all his liabilities were exchanged for assets. Compare the young disciple with the aged patriarch, and you'll see that as he matured, his areas of greatest weakness all developed into his greatest strengths. He's an amazing example of what should happen to us as we grow in Christ—allowing the Lord's strength to be made perfect in our weakness.

When we think of the apostle John today, we usually think of a tender-hearted, elderly apostle. As the elder statesman of the church near the end of the first century, he was universally beloved and respected for his devotion to Christ and his great love for the saints worldwide. That is precisely why he earned the epithet, "apostle of love."

As we shall see, however, love did not nullify the apostle John's passion for truth. Rather, it gave him the balance he needed. He retained to the end of his life a deep and abiding love for God's truth, and he remained bold in proclaiming it to the very end.

John's zeal for the truth shaped the way he wrote. Of all the writers of the New Testament, he is the most black and white in his thinking. He thinks and writes in absolutes. He deals with certainties. Everything is cut-and-dried with him. There aren't many gray areas in his teaching, because he tends to state things in unqualified, antithetical language.

For example, in his Gospel, he sets light against darkness, life against death, the kingdom of God against the kingdom of the devil, the children of God against the children of Satan, the judgment of the righteous against the judgment of the wicked, the resurrection of life against the resurrection of damnation, receiving Christ against rejecting Christ, fruit against fruitlessness, obedience against disobedience, and love against hatred. He loves dealing with truth in absolutes and opposites. He understands the necessity of drawing a clear line.

The same approach carries through in his epistles. He tells us we are either walking in the light or dwelling in darkness. If we are born of God, we do not sin—indeed, we *cannot* sin (1 John 3:9). We are either "of God" or "of the world" (1 John 4:4–5). If we love, we are born of God; and if we don't love, we are not born of God (vv. 7–8). John writes, "Whoever abides in Him does not sin. Whoever sins has neither seen Him nor known Him" (1 John 3:6). He says all these things without qualification and without any softening of the hard lines.

In his second epistle, he calls for complete, total separation from all that is false: "Whoever transgresses and does not abide in the doctrine of Christ does not have God. He who abides in the doctrine of Christ has both the Father and the Son. If anyone comes to you and does not bring this doctrine, do not receive him into your house nor greet him; for he who greets him shares in his evil deeds" (vv. 9–11). He ends his third epistle with these words in verse 11: "He who does good is of God, but he who does evil has not seen God."

John is just that black and white.

Of course, even as John is writing such things, he knows and understands very well that believers *do* sin (cf. 1 John 2:1; 1:8, 10), but he doesn't belabor or even develop the point. He is concerned primarily with the overall pattern of a person's life. He wants to underscore the fact that righteousness, not sin, is the dominant principle in a true believer's life. Those who read John carelessly or superficially might almost think he is saying there are no exceptions.

Paul is the apostle of the exceptions. Paul took time to explain the struggle all believers experience with sin in their lives (Romans 7). While Paul also states that those who are born of God do not continue in habitual sin as a pattern of life (Romans 6:6–7), he nonetheless acknowledges that we must still wage war against the remnants of sin in our members, resist the tendencies of our flesh, put off the old man, put on the new, and so on. From reading John, one might think that righteousness comes so easily and naturally to the Christian that every failure would be enough to shatter our assurance completely. That is why when I read heavy doses of John, I sometimes have to turn to Paul's epistles just to find some breathing space.

Of course, both Paul's and John's epistles are inspired Scripture, and both emphases are necessary. The exceptions dealt with by Paul don't nullify the truths stated so definitively by John. And the relentlessly unequivocal statements of John don't rule out the careful qualifications given by Paul. Both are necessary aspects of God's revealed truth.

But the way John wrote was a reflection of his personality. Truth was his passion, and he seemed to bend over backwards not to make it fuzzy. He spoke in black-and-white, absolute, certain terms, and he did not waste ink coloring in all the gray areas. He gave rules of thumb without listing all the exceptions. Jesus Himself often spoke in absolutes just like that, and John no doubt learned his teaching style from the Lord. Although John always wrote with a warm, personal, pastoral tone, what he wrote does not always make for soothing reading. It does, however, always reflect his deep convictions and his absolute devotion to the truth.

It is probably fair to say that one of the dangerous tendencies for a man with John's personality is that he would have a natural inclination to push things to extremes. And indeed, it does seem that John in his younger years was a bit of an extremist. He seemed to lack a sense of spiritual equilibrium. His zeal, his sectarianism, his intolerance, and his selfish ambition were all sins of *imbalance*. They were all potential virtues, pushed to sinful extremes. That is why the greatest strengths of his character sometimes ironically *caused* his most prominent failures. Peter and James had a similar tendency to turn their greatest strengths into weaknesses. Their *best* characteristics frequently became pitfalls for them.

We all fall prey to this principle from time to time. It is one of the effects of human depravity. Even our best characteristics, corrupted by sin, become an occasion of stumbling. It is wonderful to have a high regard for the truth, but zeal for the truth must be balanced by a love for people, or it can give way to judgmentalism, harshness, and a lack of compassion. It is fine to be hardworking and ambitious, but if ambition is not balanced with humility, it becomes sinful pride—self-promotion at the expense of others. Confidence is a wonderful virtue, too, but when confidence becomes a sinful *self*-confidence, we become smug and spiritually careless.

Clearly, there is nothing inherently wrong with zeal for the truth, a desire to succeed, or a sense of confidence. Those are all legitimate virtues. But even a virtue out of balance can become an impediment to spiritual health—just as truth out of balance can lead to serious error. A person out of balance is unsteady. Imbalance in one's personal character is a form of intemperance—a lack of self-control—and that is a sin in and of itself. So it is a very dangerous thing to push any point of truth or any character quality to an undue extreme.

That is what we see in the life of the younger disciple John. At various times he behaved like an extremist, a bigot, and a harsh, reckless man who was selfishly committed to his own narrow perception of truth. In his early years he was the most *unlikely* candidate to be remembered as the apostle of love.

But three years with Jesus began to transform a self-centered fanatic into a mature man of balance. Three years with Jesus moved this Son of Thunder toward becoming an apostle of love. At the very points where he was most imbalanced, Christ gave him equilibrium, and in the process John was transformed from a bigoted hothead into a loving, godly elder statesman for the early church.

HE LEARNED THE BALANCE OF LOVE AND TRUTH

John seems to have been committed to truth very early in life. From the beginning we see him as a spiritually aware man who sought to know and follow the truth. When we first encounter John (John

1:35–37), both he and Andrew are disciples of John the Baptist. But like Andrew, John without hesitation began following Jesus as soon as John the Baptist singled Him out as the true Messiah. It was not that they were fickle or disloyal to the Baptist. But John the Baptist himself said of Jesus, "He must increase, but I must decrease" (John 3:30). John the disciple was interested in the truth; he hadn't followed the Baptist in order to join a personality cult. Therefore he left John to follow Jesus as soon as John clearly identified Him as the Lamb of God.

John's love of truth is evident in all his writings. He uses the Greek word for *truth* twenty-five times in his Gospel and twenty more times in his epistles. He wrote, "I have no greater joy than to hear that my children walk in truth" (3 John 4). His strongest epithet for someone who claimed to be a believer while walking in darkness was to describe the person as "a liar, and the truth is not in him" (1 John 2:4; cf. 1:6, 8). No one in all of Scripture, except the Lord Himself, had more to say extolling the very concept of truth.

But sometimes in his younger years, John's zeal for truth was lacking in love and compassion for people. He needed to learn the balance. The incident in Mark 9 where John forbade a man to cast out demons in Jesus' name is a good illustration of this.

Again, this is the one place in the synoptic Gospels where John acts and speaks alone, so it is an important insight into his character. Here we see a rare glimpse of John without James and without Peter, speaking for himself. This is pure John. This same incident is also recorded in Luke 9, just before Luke's account of the episode at the Samaritan village, when James and John wanted to call down fire. The similarity of the two occasions is striking. In both cases, John is displaying an appalling intolerance, elitism, and a lack of genuine love for people. In the incident with the Samaritans, James and John showed a lack of love for unbelievers. Here John is guilty of a similar kind of unloving spirit toward a fellow believer. He forbade the man to minister in Jesus' name "because he does not follow us" (Mark 9:38)—because he was not officially a member of the group.

This incident occurred shortly after Jesus' transfiguration. That glorious mountaintop experience, which was witnessed only by the inner circle of three (Peter, James, and John), actually sets the context for what happens later in the chapter. As always, it is vital that we understand the context.

In Mark 9:1, Jesus tells the disciples, "Assuredly, I say to you that there are some standing here who will not taste death till they see the kingdom of God present with power." Of course, that sounded to the disciples like a promise that the millennial kingdom would come in their lifetimes. Yet even today, more than nineteen hundred years after the death of the last disciple, we're still waiting for the establishment of the millennial kingdom on earth. So what was this promise about?

What happened immediately afterward clearly answers that question. Jesus was promising them a preview of coming attractions. Three of them would have the privilege of witnessing a brilliant foretaste of glory divine. They would see a glimpse of the glory and power of the coming kingdom. It happened less than a week after Jesus' promised that some of them would see the kingdom, present with power: "Now after six days Jesus took Peter, James, and John, and led them up on a high mountain apart by themselves; and He was transfigured before them" (v. 2).

Christ took His three most trusted, intimate friends and disciples to a mountain, where He pulled back the veil of His human flesh so that the shekinah glory—the very essence of the nature of the eternal God—was shining out in blazing brilliance. "His clothes became shining, exceedingly white, like snow, such as no launderer on earth can whiten them" (v. 3). Matthew says the sight was so shocking that the disciples fell on their faces (Matthew 17:6). No one on earth had experienced anything remotely like this since Moses caught a glimpse of God's back after being shielded in the cleft of a rock from the full display of His glory (Exodus 33:20–23). It was a transcendental experience, the likes of which the disciples had never even imagined.

To top that off, "Elijah appeared to them with Moses, and they were talking with Jesus" (Mark 9:4). According to verse 6, the disciples were so frightened, they didn't know what to say.

Peter, in typical fashion, spoke anyway: "Rabbi, it is good for us to be here; and let us make three tabernacles: one for You, one for Moses, and one for Elijah" (v. 5). Peter probably thought this appearance of Elijah and Moses signified the inauguration of the kingdom, and he was eager to make it permanent. He also seems to have been erroneously thinking of the three of them as a kind of triumvirate of equals, rather than realizing Christ was the one to whom Moses and Elijah had pointed, making Him superior to them. And so at that very moment ("While he was still speaking"—Matthew 17:5), "A cloud came and overshadowed them; and a voice came out of the cloud, saying, 'This is My beloved Son. Hear Him!' " (Mark 9:7). Those were virtually the same words that had come from heaven at Jesus' baptism (Mark 1:11).

This was an amazing experience for Peter, James, and John to behold. They were being given a unique privilege, unparalleled in the annals of redemptive history. But Mark 9:9 says, "As they came down from the mountain, [Jesus] commanded them that they should tell no one the things they had seen, till the Son of Man had risen from the dead."

Can you imagine how difficult that would have been? They had just witnessed the most incredible thing anyone had ever seen, but they weren't allowed to tell anyone else about it. It was a formidable restraint to put upon them.

After all, the disciples—and these three in particular—were constantly arguing about who was the greatest among them. The subject seemed never very far from their thoughts (and they are about to give evidence of that just a few verses further into Mark's narrative). So it must have been exceedingly difficult for them not to use this experience as ammunition for their own case. They might have come down the mountain and said to the rest of the disciples, "Guys, guess where we have been? We were up there on the mountain and guess who showed up? Elijah and Moses!" They had been given a glimpse of the kingdom. They had seen things that never could be seen or known by anyone. They had a vivid preview of the glory to come. How difficult it must have been to keep this experience to themselves!

It does seem to have fueled the debate about who was the greatest.

Later in the chapter, Mark says they came to Capernaum. "And when He was in the house He asked them, 'What was it you disputed among yourselves on the road?'" (Mark 9:33). Jesus did not ask because He needed the *information;* He was looking for a *confession.* He knew exactly what they were talking about.

But they were embarrassed. So "they kept silent, for on the road they had disputed among themselves who would be the greatest" (v. 34). It's not hard to understand how the argument began. Peter, James, and John, brimming with confidence after their mountaintop experience, surely felt that now they had the inside track. They had seen things so wonderful that they were not permitted even to speak of them. And each one now was probably looking for some sign that he was the greatest of the three—possibly arguing among themselves about things like which one was standing closer to Jesus when He was trans-figured, reminding Peter that he was rebuked by a voice from heaven, and so on.

But when Jesus asked them what they were arguing about, they instantly grew silent. They realized they were wrong to debate these things. Their own consciences obviously were smiting them. That is why they couldn't bear to admit what all the fuss was about.

Of course, Jesus knew. And He seized the opportunity to teach them once again. "He sat down, called the twelve, and said to them, 'If anyone desires to be first, he shall be last of all and servant of all.' Then He took a little child and set him in the midst of them. And when He had taken him in His arms, He said to them, 'Whoever receives one of these little children in My name receives Me; and whoever receives Me, receives not Me but Him who sent Me'" (vv. 35–37).

They had it backward. If they wanted to be first in the kingdom, they needed to be servants. If they wanted to be truly great, they needed to be more childlike. Instead of arguing and fighting with each other, instead of putting each other down, instead of rejecting each other and exalting themselves, they needed to take the role of a servant.

It was a lesson about love. "Love does not parade itself, is not puffed up; does not behave rudely, does not seek its own" (1 Corinthians 13:4–5). Love is manifested in service to one another, not by lording it over each other.

This apparently cut John to the heart. It was a serious rebuke, and John obviously got the message. This is where we find the only time John speaks in the synoptic Gospels: "Now John answered Him, saying, 'Teacher, we saw someone who does not follow us casting out demons in Your name, and we forbade him because he does not follow us'" (v. 38). This was sectarianism—rebuking a man for ministering in Jesus' name just because he didn't belong to the group. This shows the intolerance of John, a Son of Thunder. This was the narrowness, the ambition, the desire to have the status all for himself and not share it with anybody else—all of which too often characterized John in his younger years.

Here we see clearly that John was not a passive personality. He was aggressive. He was competitive. He condemned a man who was ministering in the name of Jesus, just because the man wasn't part of the group. John had actually stepped in and tried to shut down this man's ministry for no other reason than that.

I am inclined to think John confessed this to Jesus because he was convicted. I believe he was feeling the sting of Jesus' rebuke, and he spoke these words as a penitent. Something in John was beginning to change, and he was beginning to see his own lack of love as undesirable. The fact that John made this confession was indicative of the transformation that was taking place in him. His conscience was bothering him. He was being tenderized. He had always been zealous and passionate for the truth, but now the Lord was teaching him to love. This is a major turning point in his life and thinking. He was beginning to understand the necessary equilibrium between love and truth.

The kingdom needs men who have courage, ambition, drive, passion, boldness, and a zeal for the truth. John certainly had all of those things. But to reach his full potential, he needed to balance those things with love. I think this episode was a critical rebuke that started to move him toward becoming the apostle of love he ultimately became.

John was always committed to truth, and there's certainly nothing wrong with that, but it is not enough. Zeal for the truth must be balanced by love for people. Truth without love has no decency; it's just *brutality*. On the other hand, love without truth has no character; it's just *hypocrisy*.

Many people are just as imbalanced as John was, only in the other direction. They place too much emphasis on the love side of the fulcrum. Some are merely ignorant; others are deceived; still others simply do not care about what is true. In each case, truth is missing, and all they are left with is error, clothed in a shallow, tolerant sentimentality. It is a poor substitute for genuine love. They talk a lot about love and tolerance, but they utterly lack any concern for the truth. Therefore even the "love" they speak of is a tainted love. Real love "does not rejoice in iniquity, but rejoices in the truth" (1 Corinthians 13:6).

On the other hand, there are many who have all their theological ducks in a row and know their doctrine but are unloving and self-exalting. They are left with truth as cold facts, stifling and unattractive. Their lack of love cripples the power of the truth they profess to revere.

The truly godly person must cultivate both virtues in equal proportions. If you could wish for anything in your sanctification, wish for that. If you pursue anything in the spiritual realm, pursue a perfect balance of truth and love. Know the truth, and uphold it in love.

In Ephesians 4, the apostle Paul describes this balance of truth and love as the very pinnacle of spiritual maturity. He writes of "the measure of the stature of the fullness of Christ" (v. 13). He is speaking about full maturity, perfect Christlikeness. This is how he epitomizes the goal for which we ought to strive: "[That] speaking the truth in love, [we] may grow up in all things into Him who is the head; Christ" (v. 15). This is what it means to share Christ's likeness. He is the perfect expression of truth and the perfect expression of love. He is our model.

Manifesting both truth and love is possible only for the mature believer who has grown into the measure of the stature that belongs to the fullness of Christ. That is how true spiritual maturity is defined. The authentically Christlike person knows the truth and speaks it in love. He knows the truth as Christ has revealed it, and he loves as Christ loves.

As a mature apostle, John learned the lesson well. His brief second epistle offers vivid proof of how well he balanced the twin virtues of truth and love. Throughout that epistle, John repeatedly couples the concepts of love and truth. He writes, "To the elect lady and her children, whom I love in truth" (v. 1). He says, "I rejoiced greatly that I have found some of your children walking in truth" (v. 4), and then he spends the first half of the epistle urging them to walk in love as well. He reminds them of the New Commandment, which of course is not really new, but simply restates the commandment we have heard from the beginning: "that we love one another" (v. 5).

So the first half of this short epistle is all about love. He urges this woman and her children not only to continue walking in truth, but also to remember that the sum and substance of God's law is *love*. There is therefore no greater truth than love. The two are inseparable. After all, the First and Great Commandment is this: "You shall love the LORD your God with all your heart, with all your soul, and with all your mind" (Matthew 22:37). And the second is like unto it: "You shall love your neighbor as yourself" (v. 39). In other words, love is what real truth is ultimately all about.

But John balances that emphasis on love in the second half of the epistle by urging this woman not to compromise her love by receiving and blessing false teachers who undermine the truth. Genuine love is not some saccharine sentiment that disregards the truth and tolerates everything:

> For many deceivers have gone out into the world who do not confess Jesus Christ as coming in the flesh. This is a deceiver and an antichrist. Look to yourselves, that we do not lose those things we worked for, but that we may receive a full reward. Whoever transgresses and does not abide in the doctrine of Christ does not have God. He who abides in the

doctrine of Christ has both the Father and the Son. If anyone comes to you and does not bring this doctrine, do not receive him into your house nor greet him; for he who greets him shares in his evil deeds. (vv. 7–11)

John is no longer calling down fire from heaven against the enemies of truth, but he cautions this lady not to go to the other extreme, either. She is not to open her home or even bestow a verbal blessing on people who make a living twisting and opposing the truth.

Of course, the apostle is not urging this woman to be unkind or abusive to anyone. We are commanded to do good to those who persecute us, be kind to those who hate us, bless those who oppose us, and pray for those who despitefully use us (Luke 6:27–28). But our blessing on our enemies must stop short of encouraging or assisting a false teacher who is corrupting the gospel.

Love and truth must be maintained in perfect balance. Truth is never to be abandoned in the name of love. But love is not to be deposed in the name of truth. That is what John learned from Christ, and it gave him the balance he so desperately needed.

HE LEARNED THE BALANCE
OF AMBITION AND HUMILITY

In his youth, John had some ambitious plans for himself. It's not inherently wrong to aspire to have influence or to desire success. But it is wrong to have selfish motives, as John apparently did. And it is especially wrong to be ambitious without also being humble.

Here is another important balance that must be struck, or else a virtue turns into a vice. Ambition without humility becomes egotism, or even megalomania.

In Mark 10, one chapter after the incident where John rebuked a man who was ministering in Jesus' name, we find Mark's description of how James and John approached Jesus with their request to be seated on His right and left in the kingdom. Ironically, Jesus had just reiterated the importance of humility. In Mark 10:31, He told them, "Many who are first will be last, and the last first." (Remember, this was virtually the same statement that provoked John's earlier confession in Mark 9. There, Jesus had set a child in their midst as an object lesson about humility and told them, "If anyone desires to be first, he shall be last of all and servant of all"—Mark 9:35.) Jesus was simply reiterating the same lesson He had taught them over and over about humility.

Nonetheless, just a few verses later (10:35–37), Mark records that James and John came to Jesus with their infamous request for the chief thrones. In our study of the apostle James, we looked at Matthew's account of this incident, and we learned that James and John actually enlisted their mother to intercede for them. Here we discover that they were seeking this favor secretly, because the other disciples learned of it afterward (v. 41).

Coming as it did on the heels of so many admonitions from Jesus about humility, the brothers' request shows amazing audacity. It reveals how utterly devoid of true humility they were.

Again, there is nothing wrong with ambition. In fact, there was nothing intrinsically wrong with James and John's desire to sit next to Jesus in the kingdom. Who would not desire that? The other disciples certainly desired it, and that is why they were displeased with James and John. Jesus did not rebuke them for that desire per se.

Their error was in desiring *to obtain* the position more than they desired *to be worthy* of such a position. Their ambition was untempered by humility. And Jesus had repeatedly made clear that the highest positions in the kingdom are reserved for the most humble saints on earth. Notice His response in verses 42–45:

> Jesus called them to Himself and said to them, "You know that those who are considered rulers over the Gentiles lord it over them, and their great ones exercise authority over them. Yet it shall not be so among you; but whoever desires to become great among you shall be your servant. And whoever of you desires to be first shall be slave of all. For even the Son of Man did not come to be served, but to serve, and to give His life a ransom for many."

Those who want to be great must first learn to be humble. Christ Himself was the perfection of true humility. Furthermore, His kingdom is advanced by humble service, not by politics, status, power, or dominion. This was Jesus' whole point when He set the child in the midst of the disciples and talked to them about the childlikeness of the true believer. Elsewhere, He had also told them, "Everyone who exalts himself will be humbled, and he who humbles himself will be exalted" (Luke 18:14). Even before that, He had said,

> When you are invited by anyone to a wedding feast, do not sit down in the best place, lest one more honorable than you be invited by him; and he who invited you and him come and say to you, "Give place to this man," and then you begin with shame to take the lowest place. But when you are invited, go and sit down in the lowest place, so that when he who invited you comes he may say to you, "Friend, go up higher." Then you will have glory in the presence of those who sit at the table with you. For whoever exalts himself will be humbled, and he who humbles himself will be exalted. (Luke 14:8–11)

Again and again, Christ had emphasized this truth: if you want to be great in the kingdom, you must become the servant of all.

It is astonishing how little this truth penetrated the disciples' consciousness, even after three years with Jesus. But on the final night of His earthly ministry, not one of them had the humility to pick up the towel and washbasin and perform the task of a servant (John 13:1–17). So Jesus did it Himself.

John *did* eventually learn the balance between ambition and humility. In fact, humility is one of the great virtues that comes through in his writings.

Throughout John's Gospel, for instance, he never once mentions his own name. (The only "John" who is mentioned by name in the Gospel of John is John the Baptist.) The apostle John refuses to speak of himself in reference to himself. Instead, he speaks of himself in reference to Jesus. He never paints himself in the foreground as a hero, but uses every reference to himself to honor Christ. Rather than write his name, which might focus attention on him, he refers to himself as "the disciple whom Jesus loved" (John 13:23; 20:2; 21:7, 20), giving glory to Jesus for having loved such a man. In fact, he seems utterly in awe of the marvel that Christ loved him. Of course, according to John 13:1–2, Jesus loved *all* His apostles to perfection. But it seems there was a unique way in which John gripped this reality, and he was humbled by it.

In fact, it is John's Gospel alone that records in detail Jesus' act of washing the disciples' feet. It is clear that Jesus' own humility on the night of His betrayal made a lasting impression on John.

John's humility also comes through in the gentle way he appeals to his readers in every one of his epistles. He calls them "little children," "beloved"—and he includes himself as a brother and fellow child of God (cf. 1 John 3:2). There's a tenderness and compassion in those expressions that shows his humility. His last contribution to the canon was the book of Revelation, where he describes himself as "your brother and companion in the tribulation and kingdom and patience of Jesus Christ" (Revelation 1:9). Even though he was the last remaining apostle and the patriarch of the church, we never find him lording it over anyone.

Somewhere along the line, John's ambition found balance in humility. John himself was mellowed—although he remained courageous, confident, bold, and passionate.

HE LEARNED THE BALANCE
OF SUFFERING AND GLORY

As noted, in his early years, the apostle John had a thirst for glory and an aversion to suffering. His thirst for glory is seen in his desire for the chief throne. His aversion to suffering is seen in the fact that he and the other apostles forsook Jesus and fled on the night of His arrest (Mark 14:50).

Both desires are perfectly understandable. After all, John had seen Jesus' glory firsthand on the Mount of Transfiguration, and he treasured

Jesus' promise that he would share that glory (Matthew 19:28–29). How could he *not* desire such a blessing? On the other hand, no one but a madman enjoys suffering.

There was nothing inherently sinful about John's desire to participate in the glory of Jesus' eternal kingdom. Christ had promised him a throne and an inheritance in glory. Moreover, it is my conviction that when we see Christ's glory fully unveiled we will finally understand why the glory of Christ is the greatest reward of all in heaven. One glimpse of Jesus in the fullness of His glory will be worth all the pain and sorrow and suffering we have endured here on earth (cf. Psalm 17:15; 1 John 3:2). Participation in Christ's glory is therefore a fitting desire for every child of God.

But if we desire to participate in heavenly glory, we must also be willing to partake of earthly sufferings. This was the apostle Paul's desire: "That I may know Him and the power of His resurrection, and the fellowship of His sufferings, being conformed to His death" (Philippians 3:10). Paul wasn't saying he had a masochistic lust for pain; he was simply recognizing that glory and suffering are inseparable. Those who desire the reward of glory must be willing to endure the suffering.

Suffering is the price of glory. We are "heirs of God and joint heirs with Christ, if indeed we suffer with Him, that we may also be glorified together" (Romans 8:17). Jesus taught this principle again and again. "If anyone desires to come after Me, let him deny himself, and take up his cross, and follow Me. For whoever desires to save his life will lose it, but whoever loses his life for My sake will find it" (Matthew 16:24–25). "Unless a grain of wheat falls into the ground and dies, it remains alone; but if it dies, it produces much grain. He who loves his life will lose it, and he who hates his life in this world will keep it for eternal life" (John 12:24–25).

Suffering is the prelude to glory. Our suffering as believers is the assurance of the glory that is yet to come (1 Peter 1:6–7). And "the sufferings of this present time are not worthy to be compared with the glory which shall be revealed in us" (Romans 8:18). Meanwhile, those who thirst for glory must balance that desire with a willingness to suffer.

All the disciples needed to learn this. Remember, they *all* wanted the chief seats in glory. But Jesus said there is a price for those seats. Not only are those seats reserved for the humble, but those who sit in those seats will first be prepared for the place of honor by enduring the humility of suffering. That is why Jesus told James and John that before they would receive any throne at all, they would be required to "drink the cup that I drink, and be baptized with the baptism that I am baptized with" (Mark 10:38).

How eagerly and how naively James and John assured the Lord that they would be able to drink of the cup He would drink and be baptized with a baptism of suffering! "They said to Him, 'We are able'" (v. 39). At that moment they had no real clue what they were volunteering for. They were like Peter, boasting that they would follow Jesus to the death—but when faced with the opportunity, they all forsook Him and fled.

Thankfully, Christ does not regard such failures as final. All eleven of the disciples fled on the night of Jesus' betrayal and arrest. But every one of them was recovered, and every one of them ultimately learned to suffer willingly for Christ's sake.

In fact, all of them except John suffered and ultimately died for the faith. They were martyred one by one in the prime of life. John was the only disciple who lived to old age. But he suffered, too, in ways the others did not. He was still enduring earthly anguish and persecution long after the others were already in glory.

On the night of Jesus' arrest, John probably began to understand the bitterness of the cup he would have to drink. We know from his account of Jesus' trial that he and Peter followed Jesus to the house of the high priest (John 18:15). There he watched as Jesus was bound and beaten. As far as we know, John was the only disciple who was an actual eyewitness to Jesus' crucifixion. He was standing close enough to the cross for Jesus to see him (John 19:26). He probably watched as the Roman soldiers drove in the nails. He was there when a soldier finally pierced his Lord's side with a spear. And perhaps as he watched he remembered that he had agreed to partake of this same baptism. If so, he surely realized then and there how awful the cup was he had so easily volunteered to drink!

When John's brother James became the church's first martyr, John bore the loss in a more personal way than the others. As each of the other disciples was martyred one by one, John suffered the grief and pain of additional loss. These were his friends and companions. Soon he alone was left. In some ways, that may have been the most painful suffering of all.

Virtually all reliable sources in early church history attest to the fact that John became the pastor of the church the apostle Paul had founded at Ephesus. From there, during a great persecution of the church under the Roman Emperor Domitian (brother and successor of Titus, who destroyed Jerusalem), John was banished to a prison community on Patmos, one of the small Dodecanese Islands in the Aegean Sea off the west coast of modern Turkey. He lived in a cave there. It was while there that he received and recorded the apocalyptic visions described in the book of Revelation (cf. Revelation 1:9). I have been to the cave in which he is thought to have lived and in which he is believed to have written the Apocalypse. It was a harsh environment for an aged man. He was cut off from those whom he loved, treated with cruelty and reproach, and made to sleep on a stone slab with a rock for a pillow as the years passed slowly.

But John learned to bear suffering willingly. There is no complaint about his sufferings anywhere in his epistles or the book of Revelation. It is certain that he wrote Revelation under the most extreme kind of hardship and deprivation. But he makes scant mention of his difficulties, referring to himself as "both your brother and companion in the tribulation and kingdom and patience of Jesus Christ" (Revelation 1:9). Notice that in the same breath he mentioned "tribulation," he speaks of the patience that enabled him to bear his sufferings willingly. He was looking forward calmly to the day when he would partake in the promised glory of the kingdom. That is the right balance and a healthy perspective. He had learned to look beyond his earthly sufferings in anticipation of the heavenly glory. John got the message. He learned the lessons. He grasped the character of Christ in a powerful way. And he became a choice human model of what righteous, Christlike character ought to be.

Powerful proof of this is seen in a vignette from the cross. Remember, John is the only one of the apostles whom the biblical record places as an eyewitness to the crucifixion. John himself describes the scene as Jesus looked down from the cross and saw His mother, Mary, along with her sister, another Mary (wife of Clopas), Mary Magdalene, and John (John 19:25). John writes, "When Jesus therefore saw His mother, and the disciple whom He loved standing by, He said to His mother, 'Woman, behold your son!' Then He said to the disciple, 'Behold your mother!' And from that hour that disciple took her to his own home" (vv. 26–27).

Obviously, John had learned the lessons he needed to learn. He had learned to be a humble, loving servant—or else Jesus would not have given him the care of His own mother. He told Peter, "Feed My sheep" (John 21:17). He told John, "Care for My mother." Several witnesses in early church history record that John never left Jerusalem and never left the care of Mary until she died.

John reminds me of many seminary graduates whom I have known, including myself as a younger man. I recall when I came out of seminary. I was loaded to the gills with truth but somewhat short on patience. It was a strong temptation to come blasting into the church, dump the truth on everyone, and expect an immediate response. I needed to learn patience, tolerance, mercy, grace, forgiveness, tenderness, compassion—all the characteristics of love. It is wonderful to be bold and thunderous, but love is the necessary balance. John is a superb model for such young men.

It may seem amazing that Jesus loved a man who wanted to burn up the Samaritans. He loved a man who was obsessed with status and position. He loved a man who forsook Him and fled rather than suffer for His sake. But in loving John, Jesus transformed him into a different man—a man who modeled the same kind of love Jesus had shown him.

We noted earlier that John used the word *truth* some forty-five times in his Gospel and epistles. But it is interesting that he also used the word *love* more than eighty times. Clearly, he learned the balance Christ taught Him. He learned to love others as the Lord had loved him. Love became the anchor and centerpiece of the truth he was most concerned with.

In fact, John's theology is best described as a theology of love. He taught that God is a God of love, that God loved His own Son, that God loved the world, that God is loved by Christ, that Christ loved His disciples, that Christ's disciples loved Him, that all men should love Christ, that we should love one another, and that love fulfills the law. Love was a critical part of every element of John's teaching. It was the dominant theme of his theology.

And yet his love never slid into indulgent sentimentality. To the very end of his life John was still a thunderous defender of the truth. He lost none of his intolerance for lies. In his epistles, written near the end of his life, he was still thundering out against errant Christologies, against anti-Christian deceptions, against sin, and against immorality. He was in that sense a Son of Thunder to the end. I think the Lord knew that the most powerful advocate of love needed to be a man who never compromised the truth.

Another favorite word of John's was *witness*. He used it nearly seventy times. He refers to the witness of John the Baptist, the witness of Scripture, the witness of the Father, the witness of Christ, the witness of the miracles, the witness of the Holy Spirit, and the witness of the apostles. In each case, these were witnesses to the *truth*. So his love for the truth remained undiminished.

In fact, I am convinced John leaned on Jesus' shoulder (John 13:23), not only because he enjoyed the pure love his Lord gave him, but also because he wanted to hear every word of truth that came out of the mouth of Christ.

John died, by most accounts, around A.D. 98, during the reign of

Emperor Trajan. Jerome says in his commentary on Galatians that the aged apostle John was so frail in his final days at Ephesus that he had to be carried into the church. One phrase was constantly on his lips: "My little children, love one another." Asked why he always said this, he replied, "It is the Lord's command, and if this alone be done, it is enough."

Thus the fishermen of Galilee—Peter, Andrew, James, and John—became fishers of men on a tremendous scale, gathering souls into the church. In a sense, they are still casting their nets into the sea of the world by their testimony in the Gospels and their epistles. They are still bringing multitudes of people to Christ. Although they were common men, theirs was an uncommon calling.

6
PHILIP—THE BEAN COUNTER

Philip answered Him, "Two hundred denarii worth of bread is not sufficient for them, that every one of them may have a little."

—JOHN 6:7

I N THE FOUR BIBLICAL LISTS OF THE TWELVE APOSTLES, THE fifth name on every list is Philip. As we noted in chapter 2, this apparently signifies that Philip was the leader of the second group of four. As far as the biblical record is concerned, Philip plays something of a minor role compared to the four men in group one, but he nonetheless is mentioned on several occasions, so he emerges from the larger group of twelve as a distinct character in his own right.

Philip is a Greek name, meaning "lover of horses." He must also have had a Jewish name, because all twelve apostles were Jewish. But his Jewish name is never given. Greek civilization had spread through the Mediterranean after the conquests of Alexander the Great in the fourth century B.C., and many people in the Middle East had adopted the Greek language, Greek culture, and Greek customs. They were known as "Hellenists" (cf. Acts 6:1). Perhaps Philip came from a family of Hellenistic Jews. Custom would have dictated that he have a Hebrew name as well, but for whatever reasons, he seems to have used his Greek name exclusively. So we know him only as Philip.

Don't confuse him with Philip the deacon, the man we meet in Acts 6 who became an evangelist and led the Ethiopian eunuch to Christ. Philip the apostle was a completely different individual.

The apostle Philip "was from Bethsaida, the city of Andrew and Peter" (John 1:44). Since they were all God-fearing Jews, Philip probably grew up attending the same synagogue as Peter and Andrew. Because of the relationship that existed between them and the sons of Zebedee, Philip was possibly acquainted with all four. There is good biblical evidence that Philip, Nathanael, and Thomas were all fishermen from Galilee, because in John 21, after the resurrection, when the apostles returned to Galilee and Peter said, "I am going fishing" (John 21:3), the others who were there all answered, "We are going with you also." According to John 21:2, that group included "Simon Peter, Thomas called the Twin, Nathanael of Cana in Galilee, the sons of Zebedee, and two others of His disciples." The unnamed "two others" were most likely Philip and Andrew, because elsewhere they are always seen in the company of the men who are named in that passage.

If all seven of these men were professional fishermen, they were most likely all friends and close coworkers a long time before they followed Christ. This shows what a close-knit group the apostles were, with at least half of the group—including all the core members—having come from one small region, most likely engaged in the same occupation, and probably having known and befriended each other long before they became disciples.

In a sense that is somewhat surprising. We might have expected Jesus to take a different approach in choosing the Twelve. After all, He was appointing them to the formidable task of being apostles, proxies for Him after He departed the earth, men with full power of attorney to speak and act on His behalf. You might think He would scour the whole earth to find the most gifted and qualified men. But instead, He singled out a small group of fishermen, a diverse yet common group of men with unexceptional talents and average abilities who already knew each other. And He said, "They will do."

All He really required of them was availability. He would draw them to Himself, train them, gift them, and empower them to serve Him. Because they would preach *Jesus'* message and do miracles by *His* power, these rugged fishermen were better suited to the task than a group of glittering prodigies trying to operate on their own talent might have been. After all, even these men behaved like prima donnas at times. So perhaps one of the reasons Christ selected and called this particular group is that for the most part they already got along well with one another. In any case, after already choosing Peter, Andrew, and John, Jesus located and called Philip, a native of the same little village from which Peter and Andrew originally hailed.

What do we know about Philip? Matthew, Mark, and Luke give no details at all about him. All the vignettes of Philip appear in the Gospel of John. And from John's Gospel, we discover that Philip was a completely different kind of person from either Peter, Andrew, James, or John. In John's narrative, Philip is often paired with Nathanael (also known as Bartholomew), so we can assume the two of them were close comrades. But Philip is singularly different from even his closest companion. He is unique among all the disciples.

Piecing together all that the apostle John records about him, it seems Philip was a classic "process person." He was a facts-and-figures guy—a by-the-book, practical-minded, non-forward-thinking type of individual. He was the kind who tends to be a corporate killjoy, pessimistic, narrowly focused, sometimes missing the big picture, often obsessed with identifying reasons things can't be done rather than finding ways to do them. He was predisposed to be a pragmatist and a cynic—and sometimes a defeatist—rather than a visionary.

HIS CALL

We first meet Philip in John 1, the day after Jesus had first called Andrew, John, and Peter. You will remember that Jesus had called those first three in the wilderness, where they were sitting at the feet of John the Baptist. John pointed them to the Messiah, and they left John to follow Jesus.

John writes, "The following day Jesus wanted to go to Galilee, and He found Philip and said to him, 'Follow Me'" (John 1:43). Apparently, Philip was also in the wilderness with John the Baptist, and before returning to Galilee, Jesus sought him out and invited him to join the other disciples.

Peter, Andrew, and John (and likely James as well) had more or less found Jesus. To be precise, they had been directed to Him by John the Baptist. So this is the first time we read that Jesus Himself actually sought and found one of them.

That is not to say He didn't sovereignly seek and call the rest. In fact, we know that He had chosen them all before the foundation of the world. In John 15:16, Jesus told them, "You did not choose Me, but I chose you and appointed you." But in the descriptions of how they first encountered Christ, this language is unique to the call of Philip. He is the first one whom Jesus physically sought out, and the first one to whom Jesus actually said, "Follow Me."

It is interesting, incidentally, to note that at the *end* of His earthly ministry, Jesus had to say, "Follow Me" to Peter (John 21:19, 22). Peter apparently still needed that encouragement after his failure on the night of Jesus' betrayal. But Philip was the first to hear and obey those words. From the outset, Jesus actively sought Philip. He found him. He invited him to follow. And He found in Philip an eager and willing disciple.

It is obvious that Philip already had a seeking heart. Of course, a seeking heart is always evidence that God is sovereignly drawing the person, for as Jesus said, "No one can come to Me unless the Father who sent Me draws him" (John 6:44); and again, "No one can come to Me unless it has been granted to him by My Father" (v. 65).

Philip's seeking heart is evident in how he responded to Jesus. "Philip found Nathanael and said to him, 'We have found Him of whom Moses in the law, and also the prophets, wrote; Jesus of Nazareth, the son of Joseph'" (John 1:45). Obviously, Philip and

PHILIP

Nathanael, like the first four disciples, had been studying the Law and the Prophets and were seeking the Messiah. That is why they had all gone to the wilderness to hear John the Baptist in the first place. So when Jesus came to Philip and said, "Follow Me," his ears, his eyes, and his heart were already open, and he was prepared to follow.

Notice something interesting about the expression Philip used with Nathanael: *"We* have found *Him."* As far as Philip was concerned, he had found the Messiah rather than being found by Him. Here we see the classic tension between sovereign election and human choice. Philip's call is a perfect illustration of how both exist in perfect harmony. The Lord found Philip, but Philip felt he found the Lord. Both things were true from the human perspective. But from a biblical perspective, we know that God's choice is the determinative one. "You did not choose Me, but I chose you and appointed you" (John 15:16).

Still, from a human perspective—from *Philip's* point of view—this was the end of his search. By God's grace, he had been a faithful and true seeker. He was devoted to the Word of God, and he believed the Old Testament promise of a Messiah. Now he had found Him—or rather had been found by Him.

Philip not only had a seeking heart, but he also had the heart of a personal evangelist. His first response upon meeting Jesus was to find his friend Nathanael and tell him about the Messiah.

I am convinced, by the way, that friendships provide the most fertile soil for evangelism. When the reality of Christ is introduced into a relationship of love and trust that has already been established, the effect is powerful. And it seems that invariably, when someone becomes a true follower of Christ, that person's first impulse is to want to find a friend and introduce that friend to Christ. That dynamic is seen in Philip's spontaneous instinct to go find Nathanael and tell him about the Messiah.

The language Philip used betrayed his amazement at discovering who the Messiah was. The One of whom Moses wrote, and the One foretold by the prophets, was none other than "Jesus of Nazareth, the son of Joseph," a lowly carpenter's son.

Nathanael, as we shall see in the chapter that follows, was at first nonplused. "Nathanael said to him, 'Can anything good come out of Nazareth?'" (John 1:46). Bethsaida was slightly north of Nazareth, but both were in Galilee, not far from each other. Nathanael himself came from Cana (John 21:2), a village just north of Nazareth. Nazareth by all measures would have been a more significant place than Cana, so there may have been some local rivalry reflected in Nathanael's skepticism.

But Philip was undaunted: "Come and see" (1:46). The ease with which Philip believed is remarkable. In human terms, no one had brought Philip to Jesus. He was like Simeon, "waiting for the Consolation of Israel, and the Holy Spirit was upon him" (Luke 2:25). He knew the Old Testament promises. He was ready. He was expectant. His heart was prepared. And he received Jesus gladly, unhesitatingly, as Messiah. No reluctance. No disbelief. It mattered not to him what kind of one-horse town the Messiah had grown up in. He knew instantly that he had come to the end of his search.

That is frankly out of character for Philip, and it reveals to what a great degree the Lord had prepared his heart. His *natural* tendency might have been to hold back, doubt, ask questions, and wait and see. As we are about to discover, he was not usually a very decisive person. But thankfully, in this case, He was already being drawn to Christ by the Father. And as Jesus said, "All that the Father gives Me *will* come to Me" (John 6:37, emphasis added).

THE FEEDING OF THE FIVE THOUSAND

Our next glimpse of Philip occurs in John 6, at the feeding of the five thousand. We referred to this episode in chapter 1. We took a closer look at it in chapter 3 when we studied the character of Andrew. We return now for another look at the feeding of the five thousand, this time through Philip's eyes. And here we discover what Philip as a natural man was like. We already know he was a student of the Old Testament. We know he interpreted it literally and believed in the Messiah. So when the Messiah came to him and said, "Follow Me," he embraced Jesus immediately and followed Him without hesitation. That was Philip's spiritual side. His heart was right. He was a man of faith. But often he was a man of *weak* faith.

Here his personality begins to show through. John describes how a great multitude had sought out Jesus and found Him on a mountainside with His disciples. As we saw in chapter 1, to say this was a crowd of five thousand doesn't do justice to the size of the multitude. John 6:10 says there were five thousand *men* in the crowd. There must have been several more thousand women and children. (Ten or twenty thousand would not be impossible). In any case, it was a huge throng, and according to Matthew 14:15, evening was approaching. The people needed to eat.

John 6:5 says, "Then Jesus lifted up His eyes, and seeing a great multitude coming toward Him, He said to Philip, 'Where shall we buy bread, that these may eat?'"

Why did He single Philip out and ask him? John says, "This He said to test him, for He Himself knew what He would do" (v. 6).

Philip was apparently the apostolic administrator—the bean counter. It is likely that he was charged with arranging meals and logistics. We know that Judas was in charge of keeping the money (John 13:29), so it makes sense that someone was also charged with coordinating the acquisition and distribution of meals and supplies. It was a task that certainly suited Philip's personality. Whether officially or unofficially, he seems to have been the one who was always concerned with organization and protocol. He was the type of person who in every meeting says, "I don't think we can do that"—the master of the impossible. And apparently, as far as he was concerned, almost everything fit into that category.

So Jesus was testing him. He wasn't testing him to find out what he was thinking; Jesus already knew that (cf. John 2:25). He wasn't asking for a plan; John says Jesus also already knew what He Himself was going to do. He was testing Philip so that Philip would reveal to himself what he was like. That is why Jesus turned to Philip, the classic administrative personality, and asked, "How do you propose to feed all these people?"

Of course, Jesus knew exactly what Philip was thinking. I believe Philip had already begun counting heads. When the crowd started moving in, he was already doing estimates. It was late in the day; this was a huge crowd; they were going to be hungry. And eating in those days was no easy thing. There were no fast-food franchises on that mountainside. So by the time Jesus asked the question, Philip already had his calculations prepared: "Philip answered Him, 'Two hundred denarii worth of bread is not sufficient for them, that every one of them may have a little' " (John 6:7). He had apparently been thinking through the difficulties of the food supply from the moment he first saw the crowd. Instead of thinking, *What a glorious occasion! Jesus is going to teach this crowd. What a tremendous opportunity for the Lord!*—all pessimistic Philip could see was the impossibility of the situation.

Philip had been there when the Lord created wine out of water (John 2:2). He had already seen numerous times when Jesus had healed people, including several creative and regenerative miracles. But when he saw that great crowd, he began to feel overwhelmed by the impossible. He lapsed into materialistic thinking. And when Jesus tested his faith, he responded with open unbelief. *It can't be done.*

From a purely human perspective, he was absolutely right. A denarius was one day's wages for a common laborer (cf. Matthew 20:2). In other words, between all the disciples—at least twelve of them and probably many more—they had no more than eight months' worth of a single day-laborer's wages to meet their own needs. That is not a large sum, considering all that had to be done to care for the disciples' own food and lodging. With such a small amount, they couldn't afford even a meager snack for so many people. Philip was probably thinking, *One denarius would buy twelve wheat biscuits. Barley's cheaper. So with one denarius we could buy twenty barley biscuits. If we get the small biscuits and break them in half . . . Nah, it simply can't be done.* He had already figured out that four thousand barley cakes would never be enough to go around. His thoughts were pessimistic, analytical, and pragmatic—completely materialistic and earthbound.

126

One of the supreme essentials of leadership is a sense of vision—and this is especially true for anyone whose Master is Christ. But Philip was obsessed with mundane matters and therefore overwhelmed by the impossibility of the immediate problem. He knew too much arithmetic to be adventurous. The reality of the raw facts clouded his faith. He was so obsessed with this temporal predicament that he was oblivious to the transcendental possibilities that lay in Jesus' power. He was so enthralled with common-sense calculations that he didn't see the opportunity the situation presented. He *should* have said, "Lord, if You want to feed them, feed them. I'm just going to stand back and watch how You do it. I know You can do it, Lord. You made wine at Cana and fed Your children manna in the wilderness. Do it. We will tell everyone to get in line, and You just make the food." That would have been the right response. But Philip was convinced it simply couldn't be done. The limitless supernatural power of Christ had completely escaped his thinking.

On the other hand, Andrew seemed to have a glimmer of the possible. He found one little boy with two pickled fish and five barley crackers and brought him to Christ. Even Andrew's faith was challenged by the colossal size of the logistical problem. He said to Jesus, "There is a lad here who has five barley loaves and two small fish, but what are they among so many?" (v. 9). Either Andrew had some faint ray of hope that Jesus would do *something* (because he brought the boy to Jesus anyway), or he was influenced by Philip's pessimism, and by this act supported the claim that the situation was impossible.

Either way, Philip lost the opportunity to see the reward of faith; and the action of Andrew (which probably indicated some meager degree of faith) was honored. As Jesus taught them elsewhere, "If you have faith as a mustard seed, you will say to this mountain, 'Move from here to there,' and it will move; and nothing will be impossible for you" (Matthew 17:20).

Philip needed to learn that lesson. *Everything* seemed impossible to him. He needed to set aside his materialistic, pragmatic, common-sense concerns and learn to lay hold of the supernatural potential of faith.

THE VISIT OF THE GREEKS

John 12 gives us another insight into Philip's character. Again, we see his overanalytical temperament. He was concerned too much about methods and protocol. He lacked boldness and vision. It made him too timid and too apprehensive. And when he has another opportunity to step out in faith, he misses it again.

John 12:20–21 says, "Now there were certain Greeks among those who came up to worship at the feast. Then they came to Philip, who was from Bethsaida of Galilee, and asked him, saying, 'Sir, we wish to see Jesus.'" These were either God-fearing Gentiles or full-fledged proselytes to Judaism who were coming to Jerusalem to worship God at the Passover. This was the final Passover of the Old Testament economy, during which Jesus Himself would be slain as the true Lamb of God. He was on His way to Jerusalem to die for the sins of the world.

These Greeks were very interested in Jesus. They sought out Philip in particular. Perhaps because of his Greek name, they thought he was the best contact. Or maybe they had learned that he was more or less the administrator of the group, the one who made all the arrangements on behalf of the disciples. Again we see that whether Philip held that position officially or by default, he seems to have been the one in charge of operations. So these men approached him to arrange a meeting with Jesus.

Philip, being the typical administrative type, probably carried around in his head a full manual of protocols and procedures. (In fact, if he was like many administrators I have known, he might have had an actual written policy manual, which he fastidiously devised and insisted on following to the letter. He strikes me as that kind of by-the-book type of person.) Somehow these Greeks knew he was the policy person, so they asked him to arrange a meeting with Jesus.

It was not a difficult or complex request. And yet Philip seems to have been unsure what to do with them. If he checked the manual on Gentiles and Jesus, he might have noticed that Jesus said on one occasion when He sent the disciples out, "Do not go into the way of the Gentiles, and do not enter a city of the Samaritans. But go rather to the lost sheep of the house of Israel" (Matthew 10:5–6). On another occasion, Jesus said, "I was not sent except to the lost sheep of the house of Israel" (Matthew 15:24).

Was that principle meant to prohibit Gentiles from ever being introduced to Jesus? Of course not. Jesus was simply identifying the normal priority of His ministry: "to the Jew first and also to the Greek" (Romans 2:10). It was a general principle, not an ironclad law. Greeks and other Gentiles were expressly included among those to whom He ministered. Jesus Himself had originally revealed that He was the Messiah to a Samaritan woman. Although the focus of His ministry was to Israel first and foremost, He was, after all, the Savior of the world, not just Israel. "He came to His own, and His own did not receive Him. But as many as received Him, to them He gave the right to become children of God, to those who believe in His name" (John 1:11–12).

But people like Philip don't appreciate general rules of thumb; they want every rule to be rigid and inviolable. There was no protocol in the manual for introducing Greeks to Jesus. And Philip wasn't prepared to do something so unconventional.

Nonetheless, Philip had a good heart. So he took the Greeks to Andrew. Andrew would bring anyone to Jesus. So "Philip came and told Andrew, and in turn Andrew and Philip told Jesus" (John 12:22). Obviously, Philip was not a decisive man. There was no precedent for introducing Gentiles to Jesus, so he enlisted Andrew's help before doing anything. This way no one could fault Philip for not going by the book. After all, Andrew was *always* bringing people to Jesus. Andrew would get the blame if anyone objected.

We may safely assume that Jesus received the Greeks gladly. He Himself said, "the one who comes to Me I will by no means cast out" (John 6:37). John 12 doesn't record anything about Jesus' meeting with the Greeks except the discourse Jesus gave on that occasion:

Jesus answered them, saying, "The hour has come that the Son of Man should be glorified. Most assuredly, I say to you, unless a grain of wheat falls into the ground and dies, it remains alone; but if it dies, it produces much grain. He who loves his life will lose it, and he who hates his life in this world will keep it for eternal life. If anyone serves Me, let him follow Me; and where I am, there My servant will be also. If anyone serves Me, him My Father will honor." (12:23–26)

In short, He preached the gospel to them and invited them to become His disciples.

Was it the right thing to bring those Greeks to Jesus? Absolutely. Jesus Himself welcomes all comers to drink freely of the water of life (Revelation 22:17). It would have been wrong to turn those men away. Philip seemed to know that in his heart, even if his head was obsessed with protocol and procedure.

THE UPPER ROOM

Our final glimpse of Philip comes just a short time later, in the Upper Room with the disciples on the occasion of the Last Supper. It is significant to note that this was the last night of Jesus' earthly ministry—the eve of His crucifixion. The formal training of the Twelve had officially come to an end. And yet their faith was still pathetically weak. This was the same evening when they sat around the table arguing about who was the greatest, rather than taking up the towel and basin and washing Jesus' feet. Many of the most important lessons He had taught them appear to have gone unheeded. As Jesus said, they were "foolish . . . and slow of heart to believe" (Luke 24:25).

This was true of Philip in particular. Of all the foolish, impetuous, heartbreakingly ignorant statements that occasionally escaped the lips of the disciples, none was more disappointing than Philip's remark in the Upper Room.

That night Jesus' heart was heavy. He knew what lay ahead for Him on the following day. He knew His time with the disciples was at an end, and although they still seemed rather ill-prepared from a purely human perspective, He was going to send the Holy Spirit to empower them as His witnesses. His earthly work with them was nearly finished. He was sending them out as sheep in the midst of wolves (cf. Matthew 10:16). So He was eager to comfort them and encourage them about the Holy Spirit, who would come to empower them.

He urged them not to be troubled in their hearts and promised them He was going to prepare a place for them (John 14:1–2). He further promised to return to receive them to Himself so that they could be where He was going (v. 3). Then He added this: "And where I go you know, and the way you know" (v. 4). Obviously, the *where* was heaven, and the *way* there was the way He had outlined in the gospel.

But they were slow to catch his meaning, and Thomas probably spoke for them all when he said, "Lord, we do not know where You are going, and how can we know the way?" (v. 5).

Jesus said to him, "I am the way, the truth, and the life. No one comes to the Father except through Me" (John 14:6). By now His meaning certainly ought to have been clear. He was going to the Father in heaven, and the only way there for them was through faith in Christ. Of course, that is one of the key biblical texts about the exclusivity of Christ. He was expressly teaching that no one can go to heaven who does not trust Him and embrace Him alone as Savior. He is the way—the *only* way—to the Father.

Then Jesus added an explicit claim about His own deity: "If you had known Me, you would have known My Father also; and from now on you know Him and have seen Him" (John 14:7). He was stating in the clearest possible language that He is God. Christ and His Father are of the same essence. To know Christ is to know the Father, because the different Persons of the Trinity are one in their very essence. Jesus *is* God. To see Him is to see God. They had both seen Him and known Him, so in effect, they already knew the Father as well.

It was at this point that Philip spoke up: "Philip said to Him, 'Lord, show us the Father, and it is sufficient for us' " (v. 8).

"Show us the Father"? How could Philip say such a thing, immediately on the heels of what Jesus had just told them? This is profoundly sad. You would think that by the time Philip got to this point, so long a time after he had begun to follow Jesus, he would know better. All that time, he had heard Jesus teach. He had witnessed untold numbers of miracles. He had seen people healed of the worst kinds of diseases and deformities. He had been there when Jesus cast out demons. He had spent time in intimate fellowship with Christ, day in and day out, twenty-four hours a day, seven days a week, for many months. If he had truly known Christ, he would have known the Father also (v. 7). How could he now say, "Show us the Father"? Where had he been?

"Jesus said to him, 'Have I been with you so long, and yet you have not known Me, Philip? He who has seen Me has seen the Father; so how can you say, "Show us the Father"?' " (v. 9). What did Philip think had been going on for the past two or three years? How could Philip of all people, who had responded with such enthusiastic faith at the beginning, be making a request like this at the end? Where was his faith?

Jesus asked him, "Do you not believe that I am in the Father, and the Father in Me? The words that I speak to you I do not speak on My own authority; but the Father who dwells in Me does the works. Believe Me that I am in the Father and the Father in Me, or else believe Me for the sake of the works themselves" (vv. 10–11). Jesus was saying in essence, "I am to the Father what you are to Me. I am the Father's apostle. I am His *shaliah*. I act with His full power of attorney.

"More than that, I am one with the Father. I am in the Father and the Father is in Me. We share the same divine essence."

Notice the appeal: "Do you not believe? . . . *Believe"!* Philip had already embraced Jesus as Messiah. Christ was urging him to take his faith to its logical conclusion: Philip was already in the presence of the living and eternal God Himself. He did not need to see any greater miracles. He did not need any more dramatic proof. "Show us the Father"? What was he saying? What did he think Jesus had been doing?

For three years Philip had gazed into the very face of God, and it still was not clear to him. His earthbound thinking, his materialism, his skepticism, his obsession with mundane details, his preoccupation with business details, and his small-mindedness had shut him off from a full apprehension of whose presence he had enjoyed.

Philip, like the other disciples, was a man of limited ability. He was a man of weak faith. He was a man of imperfect understanding. He was skeptical, analytical, pessimistic, reluctant, and unsure. He wanted to go by the book all the time. Facts and figures filled his thoughts. So he was unable to grasp the big picture of Christ's divine power, Person, and grace. He was slow to understand, slow to trust, and slow to see beyond the immediate circumstances. He still wanted more proof.

If we were interviewing Philip for the role to which Jesus called him, we might say, "He's out. You can't make him one of the twelve most important people in the history of the world."

But Jesus said, "He's exactly what I'm looking for. My strength is made perfect in weakness. I'll make him into a preacher. He'll be one of the founders of the church. I will make him a ruler in the kingdom and give him an eternal reward in heaven. And I will write his name on one of the twelve gates of the New Jerusalem." Thankfully, the Lord uses people like Philip—lots of them.

Tradition tells us that Philip was greatly used in the spread of the early church and was among the first of the apostles to suffer martyrdom. By most accounts he was put to death by stoning at Heliopolis, in Phrygia (Asia Minor), eight years after the martyrdom of James. Before his death, multitudes came to Christ under his preaching.

Philip obviously overcame the human tendencies that so often hampered his faith, and he stands with the other apostles as proof that "God has chosen the foolish things of the world to put to shame the wise, and God has chosen the weak things of the world to put to shame the things which are mighty; and the base things of the world and the things which are despised God has chosen, and the things which are not, to bring to nothing the things that are, that no flesh should glory in His presence" (1 Corinthians 1:27–29).

7

NATHANAEL—THE GUILELESS ONE

Nathanael answered and said to Him, "Rabbi, You are the Son of God! You are the King of Israel!"

—JOHN 1:49

PHILIP'S CLOSEST COMPANION, NATHANAEL, IS LISTED AS Bartholomew in all four lists of the Twelve. In the Gospel of John he is always called Nathanael. *Bartholomew* is a Hebrew surname meaning "son of Tolmai." *Nathanael* means "God has given." So he is Nathanael, son of Tolmai, or Nathanael Bar-Tolmai.

The synoptic Gospels and the book of Acts contain no details about Nathanael's background, character, or personality. In fact, they each mention him only once—when they list all twelve disciples. John's Gospel features Nathanael in just two passages: in John 1, where his call is recorded, and in John 21:2, where he is named as one of those who returned to Galilee and went fishing with Peter after Jesus' resurrection and before the ascension.

According to John 21:2, Nathanael came from the small town of Cana in Galilee, the place where Jesus did His first miracle, changing water into wine (John 2:11). Cana was very close to Jesus' own hometown, Nazareth.

As we saw in the previous chapter, Nathanael was brought to Jesus by Philip immediately after Philip was sought and called by Christ. Philip and Nathanael were apparently close friends, because in each of the synoptic Gospels' lists of the twelve apostles, the names of Philip and Bartholomew are linked. In the earliest church histories and many of the early legends about the apostles, their names are often linked as well. Apparently, they were friends throughout the years of their journey with Christ. Not unlike Peter and Andrew (who were so often named together as brothers) and James and John (who likewise were brothers), we find these two always side by side, not as brothers, but as close companions.

Virtually everything we know about Nathanael Bar-Tolmai comes from John's account of his call to discipleship. Remember, that event took place in the wilderness, shortly after Jesus' baptism, when John the Baptist pointed to Christ as the Lamb of God who takes away the sin of the world (John 1:29). Andrew, John, and Peter (and possibly James as well) were the first to be called (vv. 35–42). The next day, having purposed to go to Galilee, Jesus sought out Philip and called him, too (v. 43).

According to verse 45, "Philip found Nathanael." They were obviously friends. Whether this was a business relationship, a family relationship, or just a social relationship, Scripture does not say. But Philip obviously was close to Nathanael, and he knew Nathanael would be interested in the news that the long-awaited Messiah had finally been identified. In fact, he couldn't wait to share the news with him. So he immediately pursued him and brought him to Jesus.

Apparently Nathanael was found by Philip in or near the same place where Philip was found by the Lord Himself. The brief description of how Nathanael came to Jesus is full of insight into his character. From it, we learn quite a lot about what kind of person Nathanael was.

HIS LOVE OF SCRIPTURE

One striking fact about Nathanael is obvious from how Philip announced to him that he had found the Messiah: "Philip found Nathanael and said to him, 'We have found Him of whom Moses in the law, and also the prophets, wrote'" (John 1:45). Obviously, the truth of Scripture was something that mattered to Nathanael. Philip knew Nathanael, so he knew Nathanael would be intrigued by the news that Jesus was the One prophesied by Moses and the prophets in Scripture. Therefore, when Philip told Nathanael about the Messiah whom he had found, he did so from the standpoint of Old Testament prophecy. The fact that Philip introduced Jesus this way suggests that Nathanael *knew* the Old Testament prophecies.

This probably indicates that Nathanael and Philip were students of the Old Testament together. In all likelihood, they had come to the wilderness to hear John the Baptist together. They had a shared interest in the fulfillment of Old Testament prophecy. Philip obviously knew the news of Jesus would excite Nathanael.

Notice that he didn't say to him, "I found a man who has a wonderful plan for your life." He didn't say, "I found a man who will fix your marriage and your personal problems and give your life meaning." He didn't appeal to Nathanael on the basis of how Jesus might make *Nathanael's* life better. Philip spoke of Jesus as the fulfillment of Old Testament prophecies, because he knew that would pique Nathanael's interest. Nathanael, as an eager student of the Old Testament, was already a seeker after divine truth.

Incidentally, it appears that all the apostles, with the exception of Judas Iscariot, were to some degree already true seekers after divine truth before they met Jesus. They were already being drawn by the Spirit of God. Their hearts were open to the truth and hungry to know it. They were sincere in their love for God and their desire to know the truth and receive the Messiah. In that sense they were very different from the religious establishment, which was dominated by hypocrisy and false piety. The disciples were the real thing.

Most likely, Philip and Nathaniel had pored long hours over the Scripture together, searching the Law and the Prophets to discern the truth about the coming of the Messiah. And the fact that they were so well trained in Scripture no doubt explains why they were so quick to respond to Jesus. In Nathanael's case, this would become especially evident. He was able to recognize Jesus clearly and instantly because he had a clear understanding of what the Scripture said about Him. Nathanael knew what the promises said, so he recognized the fulfillment when he saw it. He knew Him of whom Moses and the prophets had written, and he recognized Jesus as that One after the briefest of conversations with Him. Nathanael sized Him up quickly and received Him on the spot. The reason that was possible was because Nathanael had been such a diligent student of Scripture.

Philip told him, "[It is] Jesus of Nazareth, the son of Joseph." "Jesus" was a common name—*Y'shua* in its Aramaic form. It is the same name rendered "Joshua" in the Old Testament. It meant, significantly, "Yahweh is salvation" ("for He will save His people from their sins"—Matthew 1:21). Philip was using the expression "son of Joseph" as a kind of surname—"Jesus Bar-Joseph," just as his friend was "Nathanael Bar-Tolmai." That is how people were commonly identified. (It was the Hebrew equivalent of modern surnames like Josephson or Johnson. People throughout history have been identified this way—with surnames derived from their fathers.)

There must have been a certain amount of surprise in the voice of Philip. It was as if he were saying, "You'll never believe this, but Jesus, son of Joseph, the carpenter's son from Nazareth is the Messiah!"

HIS PREJUDICE

Verse 46 then gives us a further insight into Nathanael's character. Although he was as a student of Scripture and a searcher for the true knowledge of God; although he had strong spiritual interests and had been faithful, diligent, and honest in his devotion to the Word of God;

he was human. He had certain prejudices. Here is his response: "Can anything good come out of Nazareth?"

He *might* have said, "As I read the Old Testament, Micah the prophet says Messiah comes out of Bethlehem [Micah 5:2], not Nazareth." He could have said, "But Philip, Messiah is identified with Jerusalem, because He's going to reign in Jerusalem." But the depth of his prejudice comes through in the words he chose: "Can anything good come out of Nazareth?"

That was not a rational or biblical objection; it was based on sheer emotion and bigotry. It reveals what contempt Nathanael had for the whole town of Nazareth. Frankly, Cana wasn't such a prestigious town, either. To this day it is utterly unexceptional. Unless you are looking for the shrine built on the supposed location where Jesus turned water to wine, you probably won't want to go there. Cana was off the beaten track, while Nazareth was at least at a crossroads. To travel from the Mediterranean to Galilee, people traveled through Nazareth. One of the main routes going north and south between Jerusalem and Lebanon passed through Nazareth. No one ever "passed through" Cana; Cana was a side trip from everything. So the lack of anything attractive in Nazareth doesn't fully explain Nathanael's prejudice. His remark probably reflects some kind of civic rivalry between Nazareth and Cana.

Nazareth was a rough town. Its culture was largely unrefined and uneducated. (It is still much the same today.) It isn't a particularly picturesque place. Although it has a nice setting on the slopes of the hills in Galilee, it is not a very memorable town, and it was even less so in Jesus' time. The Judaeans looked down on all Galileans, but even the Galileans looked down on the Nazarenes. Nathanael, though he came from an even more lowly village, was simply echoing the Galileans' general contempt for Nazareth. This was the same kind of regional pride that might cause someone from, say, Cleveland, to speak with disdain about Buffalo.

Here again we see that God takes pleasure in using the common, weak, and lowly things of this world to confound the wise and powerful (cf. 1 Corinthians 1:27). He even calls people from the most despised locations. He can also take a flawed person who is blinded by prejudice, and He can change that person into someone used to transform the world. In the end the only explanation is the power of God, so all the glory goes to Him.

It was inconceivable to Nathanael that the Messiah would come out of a tacky place like Nazareth. It was an uncultured place, full of evil, corrupt, and populated with sinful people. Nathanael simply did not anticipate that anything good could come from there. And he was oblivious to the rather obvious fact that he himself had come from an equally contemptible community.

Prejudice is ugly. Generalizations based on feelings of superiority, not on fact, can be spiritually debilitating. Prejudice cuts a lot of people off from the truth. As a matter of fact, much of the nation of Israel rejected their Messiah because of prejudice. They did not believe their Messiah should come out of Nazareth, either. It was inconceivable to them that the Messiah and all His apostles would come from Galilee. They mocked the apostles as uneducated Galileans. The Pharisees taunted Nicodemus by saying, "Are you also from Galilee? Search and look, for no prophet has arisen out of Galilee" (John 7:52). They did not like the fact that Jesus spoke against the religious establishment from Jerusalem. And from the religious leaders down to the people sitting in the synagogues, it was to some degree their prejudice that caused them to reject Him. This happened even in Jesus' own hometown. They derided Jesus as Joseph's son (Luke 4:22). He was without honor even in His own country, because he was nothing but a carpenter's son (v. 24). And the entire synagogue in Nazareth—His own synagogue, where He had grown up—were so filled with prejudice against Him that after He preached a single message to them, they tried to take Him to a cliff on the edge of town and throw Him off to kill Him (vv. 28–29).

Prejudice skewed their view of the Messiah. The people of Israel were prejudiced against Him as a Galilean and a Nazarene. They were prejudiced against Him as an uneducated person outside the religious establishment. They were particularly prejudiced against His message. And their prejudice against Him shut them off from the gospel. They refused to hear Him because they were cultural and religious bigots.

John Bunyan understood the danger of prejudice. In his famous allegory *The Holy War*, he pictures the forces of Immanuel coming to bring the gospel to the town of Mansoul. They directed their assault on Mansoul at the Ear-gate, because faith comes by hearing. But Diabolus, the enemy of Immanuel and His forces, wanted to hold Mansoul captive to hell. So Diabolus decided to meet the attack by stationing a special guard at Ear-gate. The guard he chose was "one old Mr. Prejudice, an angry and ill-conditioned fellow." According to Bunyan, they made Mr. Prejudice "captain of the ward at that gate, and put under his power sixty men, called deaf men; men advantageous for that service, forasmuch as they mattered no words of the captains, nor of the soldiers." That is a very vivid description of precisely how many people are rendered impervious to the truth of the gospel. Their own prejudice renders them deaf to the truth.

Men's ears are closed to the gospel by many kinds of prejudice—racial prejudice, social prejudice, religious prejudice, and intellectual prejudice. Prejudice effectively caused the majority of the Jewish nation to remain deaf to the Messiah. Satan had stationed at the Ear-gate of Israel Mr. Prejudice and his band of deaf men. That is why when Jesus "came to His own, . . . His own did not receive Him" (John 1:11).

John Bunyan used the imagery of deafness. The apostle Paul used the metaphor of blindness: "If our gospel is veiled, it is veiled to those who are perishing, whose minds the god of this age has blinded, who do not believe, lest the light of the gospel of the glory of Christ, who is the image of God, should shine on them" (2 Corinthians 4:3–4). Rendered deaf and blind by prejudice against the truth, they missed the message. It's still that way today.

Nathanael lived in a society that was prejudicial by temperament. In reality, all sinful people are. We make prejudicial statements. We draw prejudiced conclusions about individuals, classes of people, and whole societies. Nathanael, like the rest of us, had that sinful tendency. And his prejudice caused him at first to be skeptical when Philip told him the Messiah was a Nazarene.

Fortunately, his prejudice wasn't strong enough to keep him from Christ. "Philip said to him, 'Come and see' " (v. 46). That is the right way to deal with prejudice: Confront it with the facts. Prejudice is feeling-based. It is subjective. It does not necessarily reflect the reality of the matter. So the remedy for prejudice is an honest look at objective reality—"come and see."

And Nathanael went. Fortunately, his prejudiced mind was not as powerful as his seeking heart.

HIS SINCERITY OF HEART

The most important aspect of Nathanael's character is expressed from the lips of Jesus. Jesus knew Nathanael already. He "had no need that anyone should testify of man, for He knew what was in man" (John 2:25). So His first words upon seeing Nathanael were a powerful commendation of Nathanael's character. Jesus saw Nathanael coming toward Him and said of him, "Behold, an Israelite indeed, in whom is no deceit!" (John 1:47).

Can you imagine a more wonderful thing than to have words of approval like that come out of the mouth of Jesus? It would be one thing to hear that at the end of your life, along with, "Well done, good and faithful servant; you have been faithful over a few things, I will make you ruler over many things. Enter into the joy of your lord" (cf. Matthew 25:21, 23). We often hear eulogies at funerals that extol the virtues of the deceased. But how would you like Jesus to say that about you from the very start?

This speaks volumes about Nathanael's character. He was pure-hearted from the beginning. Certainly, he was human. He had sinful faults. His mind was tainted by a degree of prejudice. But His heart was not poisoned by deceit. He was no hypocrite. His love for God, and His desire to see the Messiah, were genuine. His heart was sincere and without guile.

Jesus refers to him as "an Israelite indeed." The word in the Greek text is *alethos,* meaning "truly, genuinely." He was an authentic Israelite. This is not a reference to his physical descent from Abraham. Jesus was not talking about genetics. He was linking Nathanael's status as a true Israelite to the fact that he was without deceit. His guilelessness is what defined him as a true Israelite. For the most part, the Israelites of Jesus' day were not real, because they were hypocrites. They were phonies. They lived life with a veneer of spirituality, but it was not real, and therefore they were not genuine spiritual children of Abraham. Nathanael, however, was real.

In Romans 9:6–7, the apostle Paul says, "For they are not all Israel who are of Israel, nor are they all children because they are the seed of Abraham." In Romans 2:28–29, he writes, "He is not a Jew who is one outwardly, nor is circumcision that which is outward in the flesh; but he is a Jew who is one inwardly; and circumcision is that of the heart, in the Spirit, not in the letter; whose praise is not from men but from God."

Here was an authentic Jew, one of the true spiritual offspring of Abraham. Here was one who worshiped the true and living God without deceit and without hypocrisy. Nathanael was the authentic item. Jesus would later say, in John 8:31, "If you abide in My word, you are My disciples indeed." The Greek word is the same–*alethos.*

Nathanael was a true disciple from the start. There was no hypocrisy in him. This is very unusual, and it was particularly rare in first-century Israel. Remember, Jesus indicted the entire religious establishment of His day as hypocrites. Matthew 23:13–33 records an amazing diatribe against the scribes and Pharisees in which Jesus calls them hypocrites from every possible angle. The synagogues were full of hypocrites, too. From the highest leaders to the people on the street, hypocrisy was a plague on that culture. But here was a true, nonhypocritical Jew. Here was a man whose heart was circumcised, cleansed of defilement. His faith was authentic. His devotion to God was real. He was without guile, not like the scribes and Pharisees. He was a truly righteous man—flawed by sin as we all are—but justified before God through a true and living faith.

HIS EAGER FAITH

Because his heart was sincere and his faith was real, Nathanael overcame his prejudice. His response to Jesus and the narrative that follows reveal his true character. At first, he was simply amazed that Jesus seemed to know anything about him. "Nathanael said to Him, 'How do You know me?'" (John 1:48).

We have to assume that Nathanael was still questioning whether this Man could truly be the Messiah. It was not that he questioned Philip's judgment; Philip was his friend, so he surely knew enough about Philip to know that Philip—the indecisive process-person—wouldn't have made any hasty judgment. It was certainly not that he questioned Scripture or that he was prone to skepticism. It was just that this man from Nazareth did not seem to fit the picture of the Messiah in Nathanael's mind. Jesus was the son of a carpenter, a no-name, non-descript man from a town that had no connection to any prophecy. (Nazareth did not even exist in the Old Testament.) And now Jesus had spoken to him as if he knew all about him and could even see inside his heart. Nathanael was just trying to come to grips with it all.

"How do You know me?" He might have meant, "Are You just flattering me? Are You trying to make me one of Your followers by paying me compliments? How could You possibly know what is in my heart?"

"Jesus answered and said to him, 'Before Philip called you, when you were under the fig tree, I saw you.'" (v. 48). This put a whole different spin on things. This was not flattery; it was omniscience! Jesus wasn't physically present to see Nathanael under the fig tree; Nathanael knew that. Suddenly he realized he was standing in the presence of Someone who could see into his very heart with an omniscient eye.

What was the significance of the fig tree? It was most likely the place where Nathanael went to study and meditate on Scripture. Houses in that culture were mostly small, one-room affairs. Most of the cooking was done inside, so a fire was kept burning even in the summer. The house could get full of smoke and stuffy. Trees were planted around houses to keep them cool and shaded. One of the best trees to plant near a house was a fig tree, because it bore wonderful fruit and gave good shade. Fig trees grow to a height of only about fifteen feet. They have a fairly short, gnarled trunk, and their branches are low and spread as far as twenty-five or thirty feet. A fig tree near a house provided a large, shady, protected place outdoors. If you wanted to escape the noise and stifling atmosphere of the house, you could go outside and rest under its shade. It was a kind of private outdoor place, perfect for meditation, reflection, and solitude. No doubt that is where Nathanael went to study Scripture and pray.

In effect, Jesus was saying, "I know the state of your heart because I saw you under the fig tree. I knew what you were doing. That was your private chamber. That is where you would go to study and pray. That's where you would go to meditate. And I saw you in that secret place. I knew what you were doing." It was not only that Jesus saw his *location,* but that He saw his *heart* as well. He knew the sincerity of Nathanael's character because He saw right into him when he was under the fig tree.

That was enough for Nathanael. He "answered and said to Him, 'Rabbi, You are the Son of God! You are the King of Israel!' " (v. 49).

John's whole Gospel was written to prove that Jesus is the Son of God (John 20:31). John's first words are a powerful declaration of Jesus' deity ("In the beginning was the Word, and the Word was with God, and the Word was God.") Every point in his Gospel is designed to prove that Jesus is the Son of God—sharing the same essence as God—by highlighting His miracles, His sinless character, the divine wisdom of His teaching, and His attributes, which are the very attributes of God. John is writing to show the many ways in which Jesus manifested Himself as God. And here in the first chapter he gives the testimony of Nathanael that this Jesus is the omniscient Son of God. He is of the very same essence as God.

Remember, this is the very same truth Nathanael's friend Philip still hadn't quite grasped two years later, because he said to Jesus in the Upper Room, "Show us the Father" (John 14:8–9). What Philip didn't get until the end, his friend Nathanael understood at the very start.

Nathanael knew the Old Testament. He was familiar with what the prophets had said. He knew whom to look for. And now, regardless of the fact that Jesus came from Nazareth, His omniscience, His spiritual insight, His ability to read the heart of Nathanael was enough to convince Nathanael that He was indeed the true Messiah.

Nathanael's familiarity with the Old Testament messianic prophecies is clearly seen in his reply to Jesus ("You are the Son of God! You are the King of Israel!"). Psalm 2 clearly indicated that the Messiah would be the Son of God. Many Old Testament prophecies spoke of Him as "King of Israel," including Zephaniah 3:15 ("The LORD has taken away your judgments, He has cast out your enemy. The King of Israel, the LORD, is in your midst; You shall see disaster no more") and Zechariah 9:9 ("Rejoice greatly, O daughter of Zion! Shout, O daughter of Jerusalem! Behold, your King is coming to you; He is just and having salvation, lowly and riding on a donkey, a colt, the foal of a donkey"). Micah 5:2, the same verse that predicted His birth in Bethlehem, referred to him as "The One to be Ruler in Israel, whose goings forth are from of old, from everlasting"—identifying Him not only as King but also as the Eternal One. So when Nathanael saw proof of Jesus' omniscience, he instantly recognized Him as the promised Messiah, the Son of God and King of Israel.

Nathanael was like Simeon, who lifted up the infant Jesus and said, "Lord, now You are letting Your servant depart in peace, according to Your word; for my eyes have seen Your salvation which You have prepared before the face of all peoples, a light to bring revelation to the Gentiles, and the glory of Your people Israel" (Luke 2:29–32). He recognized Jesus instantly as the One he had been waiting for. Nathanael, a careful student of Scripture, was a true Jew who waited for the Messiah and knew that when He came He would be Son of God and King. He was never one of the half-committed. He came to full understanding and total commitment on day one.

"Jesus answered and said to him, 'Because I said to you, "I saw you under the fig tree," do you believe? You will see greater things than these.' And He said to him, 'Most assuredly, I say to you, hereafter you shall see heaven open, and the angels of God ascending and descending upon the Son of Man'" (John 1:50-51). He affirmed Nathanael's faith and promised that he would see even greater things than a simple show of Jesus' omniscience. If one simple statement about the fig tree was enough to convince Nathanael that this was the Son of God and the King of Israel, he had not seen anything yet. From here on out, everything he would see would enrich and enlarge his faith.

Most of the disciples struggled just to come to the place where Nathanael stood after his first meeting with Christ. But for Nathanael, the ministry of Christ only affirmed what he already knew to be true. How wonderful to see someone so trustworthy and trusting from the very beginning, so that for him the whole three years with Jesus was just an unfolding panorama of supernatural reality!

In the Old Testament, Jacob had a dream in which "a ladder was set up on the earth, and its top reached to heaven; and there the angels of God were ascending and descending on it" (Genesis 28:12). Jesus' words to Nathanael were a reference to that Old Testament account. *He* was the ladder. And Nathanael would see the angels of God ascending and descending upon Him. In other words, Jesus *is* the ladder that connects heaven and earth.

That's all we know about Nathanael from Scripture. Early church records suggest that he ministered in Persia and India and took the gospel as far as Armenia. There is no reliable record of how he died. One tradition says he was tied up in a sack and cast into the sea. Another tradition says he was crucified. By all accounts, he was martyred like all the apostles except John.

What we *do* know is that Nathanael was faithful to the end because he was faithful from the start. Everything he experienced with Christ and whatever he experienced after the birth of the New Testament church ultimately only made his faith stronger. And Nathanael, like the other apostles, stands as proof that God can take the most common people, from the most insignificant places, and use them to His glory.

8

MATTHEW—THE TAX COLLECTOR; AND THOMAS—THE TWIN

As Jesus passed on from there, He saw a man named Matthew sitting at the tax office. And He said to him, "Follow Me." So he arose and followed Him.

—MATTHEW 9:9

Then Thomas, who is called the Twin, said to his fellow disciples, "Let us also go, that we may die with Him."

—JOHN 11:16

A S WE HAVE SEEN ALL ALONG, ONE OF THE FACTS THAT stands out in the lives of all twelve apostles is how ordinary and unrefined they were when Jesus met them. All twelve, with the exception of Judas Iscariot, were from Galilee. That whole region was predominantly rural, consisting of small towns and villages. Its people were not elite. They were not known for their education. They were the commonest of the common. They were fishermen and farmers.

Such were the disciples as well. Christ deliberately passed over those who were aristocratic and influential and chose men mostly from the dregs of society.

That is how it has always been in God's economy. He exalts the humble and lays low those who are proud. "Out of the mouth of babes and nursing infants [He has] ordained strength" (Psalm 8:2). "For He brings down those who dwell on high, the lofty city; He lays it low, He lays it low to the ground, He brings it down to the dust. The foot shall tread it down; the feet of the poor and the steps of the needy" (Isaiah 26:5–6). God told Israel, "I will leave in your midst a meek and humble people, and they shall trust in the name of the LORD" (Zephaniah 3:12). "Thus says the Lord GOD: 'Remove the turban, and take off the crown; nothing shall remain the same. Exalt the humble, and humble the exalted'" (Ezekiel 21:26).

It should be no surprise, then, that Christ disdained religious elitism. The religious leaders of Jesus' day (like the vast majority of religious celebrities even today) were blind leaders of the blind. Most members of the Jewish establishment in Jesus' day were so spiritually blind that when the Messiah came and did miracles before their eyes, they still did not see Him as the Messiah. They saw Him rather as an interloper and an intruder. They regarded Him as an enemy. And from the very outset, from the first time He preached in public, they sought a way to have Him murdered (Luke 4:28–29).

In the end, it was the chief priests and ruling council of Israel who led the crowd in a cry for Jesus' blood. The religious establishment hated Him. So it is no wonder that when the time came for Jesus to choose and appoint apostles, He looked away from the religious elite and chose instead simple men of faith who were, by every earthly standard, commonplace.

It wasn't that the self-righteous religious leaders did not believe in Jesus' miracles. Nowhere on the pages of the Gospel record did anyone ever deny the *reality* of Jesus' miracles. Who could deny them? There were too many, and they had been done too publicly to be dismissed by even the most skeptical gainsayers. Of course, some desperately tried to attribute Jesus' miracles to the power of Satan (Matthew 12:24). No one, however, ever denied that the miracles were *real*. Anyone could see that He had the power to cast out demons and do miracles at will. No one could honestly question whether He truly had power over the supernatural world.

But what irritated the religious leaders was not the miracles. They could have lived with the fact that He could walk on water or that He could make food to feed thousands of people. What they could *not* tolerate was being called sinners. They would not acknowledge themselves as poor, prisoners, blind, and oppressed (Luke 4:18). They were too smugly self-righteous. So when Jesus came (as John the Baptist had come before Him) preaching repentance and saying they were sinners, wretched, poor, blind, lost people under the bondage of their own iniquity, needing forgiveness and cleansing—they could not and would not tolerate that. Therefore it was ultimately because of His *message* that they hated Him, vilified Him, and finally executed Him.

That is precisely why when it came time for Him to appoint apostles, He chose lowly, ordinary men. These were men who were not reluctant to acknowledge their own sinfulness.

MATTHEW, THE PUBLICAN

In all likelihood, none of the Twelve was more notorious as a sinner than Matthew. He is called by his Jewish name, "Levi the son of Alphaeus," in Mark 2:14. Luke refers to him as "Levi" in Luke 5:27–29, and as "Matthew" when he lists the Twelve in Luke 6:15 and Acts 1:13.

Matthew, of course, is the author of the Gospel that bears his name. For that reason, we might expect to have a lot of detail about this man and his character. But the fact of the matter is that we know very little about Matthew. The only thing we know for sure is he was a humble, self-effacing man who kept himself almost completely in the background throughout his lengthy account of Jesus' life and ministry. In his entire Gospel he mentions his own name only two times. (Once is where he records his call, and the other is when he lists all twelve apostles.)

Matthew was a tax collector—a publican—when Jesus called him. That is the *last* credential we might expect to see from a man who would become an apostle of Christ, a top leader in the church, and a preacher of the gospel. After all, tax collectors were the most despised people in Israel. They were hated and vilified by all of Jewish society. They were deemed lower than Herodians (Jews loyal to the Idumean dynasty of Herods) and more worthy of scorn than the occupying Roman soldiers. Publicans were men who had bought tax franchises from the Roman emperor and then extorted money from the people of Israel to feed the Roman coffers and to pad their own pockets. They often strong-armed money out of people with the use of thugs. Most were despicable, vile, unprincipled scoundrels.

Matthew 9:9 records the call of this man. It comes out of nowhere, completely catching the reader by surprise: "As Jesus passed on from [Capernaum], He saw a man named Matthew sitting at the tax office. And He said to him, 'Follow Me.' So he arose and followed Him." That is the only glimpse of Matthew we have from his own Gospel.

Matthew goes on in the next few verses to say, "Now it happened, as Jesus sat at the table in the house, that behold, many tax collectors and sinners came and sat down with Him and His disciples" (v. 10). Luke reveals that this was actually an enormous banquet that Matthew himself held at his own house in Jesus' honor. It seems he invited a large number of his fellow tax collectors and various other kinds of scoundrels and social outcasts to meet Jesus. As we saw in the case of Philip and Andrew, Matthew's first impulse after following Jesus was to bring his closest friends and introduce them to the Savior. He was so thrilled to have found the Messiah that he wanted to introduce Jesus to everyone he knew. So he held a large banquet in Jesus' honor and invited them all.

Luke records what happened on that occasion: "Then Levi gave Him a great feast in his own house. And there were a great number of tax collectors and others who sat down with them. And their scribes and the Pharisees complained against His disciples, saying, 'Why do You eat and drink with tax collectors and sinners?' Jesus answered and said to them, 'Those who are well have no need of a physician, but those who are sick. I have not come to call the righteous, but sinners, to repentance'" (Luke 5:29–32).

Why did Matthew invite tax gatherers and other lowlifes? Because they were the only kind of people he knew. They were the only ones who would associate with a man like Matthew. He didn't know any of the social elite well enough to invite them to his house. He was a tax collector, and tax collectors were on the same level socially as harlots (Matthew 21:32). For a *Jewish* man like Matthew to be a tax collector was even worse. His occupation made him a traitor to the nation, a social pariah, the rankest of the rank. He would also have been a religious outcast, forbidden to enter any synagogue.

Therefore Matthew's only friends were the riffraff of society—petty criminals, hoodlums, prostitutes, and their ilk. They were the ones he invited to his house to meet Jesus. Jesus and the apostles, according to Matthew's own account, gladly came and ate with such people.

Of course, the people of the religious establishment were outraged and scandalized. They wasted no time voicing their criticism to the disciples. But Jesus replied by saying sick people are the very ones who need a physician. He had not come to call the self-righteous, but sinners, to repentance. In other words, there was nothing He could do for the religious elite as long as they insisted on keeping up their pious, hypocritical veneer. But people like Matthew who were prepared to confess their sin could be forgiven and redeemed.

It is interesting to note that three tax collectors are specifically mentioned in the Gospels, and each one of them found forgiveness. There was Zaccheus, in Luke 19:2–10; the publican mentioned in the parable of Luke 18:10–14; and Matthew. Furthermore, Luke 15:1 says that "all the tax collectors and the sinners drew near to Him to hear Him." Luke 7:29 says after Jesus commended John the Baptist's ministry, that "when all the people heard Him, even the tax collectors justified God, having been baptized with the baptism of John." Jesus admonished the religious leaders with these words: "Assuredly, I say to you that tax collectors and harlots enter the kingdom of God before you. For John came to you in the way of righteousness, and you did not believe him; but tax collectors and harlots believed him; and when you saw it, you did not afterward relent and believe him" (Matthew 21:31–32).

The parable of the publican and the sinner in Luke 18:10–14 might well have been based on an actual incident. Jesus said,

Two men went up to the temple to pray, one a Pharisee and the other a tax collector. The Pharisee stood and prayed thus with himself, "God, I thank You that I am not like other men; extortioners, unjust, adulterers, or even as this tax collector. I fast twice a week; I give tithes of all that I possess." And the tax collector, standing afar off, would not so much as raise his eyes to heaven, but beat his breast, saying, "God, be merciful to me a sinner!" I tell you, this man went down to his house justified rather than the other; for everyone who exalts himself will be humbled, and he who humbles himself will be exalted.

Notice that the tax collector stood "afar off." He had to. He would not have been permitted past the court of the Gentiles in the temple. In fact, tax collectors had to keep their distance from any group, because they were so hated. The Jewish Talmud taught that it was righteous to lie and deceive a tax collector, because that was what a professional extortioner deserved.

Obviously, tax collectors had a certain amount that was legitimate to collect for the government (cf. Matthew 22:21; Romans 13:7). But there was an unspoken agreement with the Roman emperor that they could assess whatever other fees and additional taxes they could collect, and they were allowed to keep a percentage for themselves.

There were two kinds of tax collectors, the *Gabbai* and the *Mokhes*. The Gabbai were general tax collectors. They collected property tax, income tax, and the poll tax. These taxes were set by official assessments, so there was not as much graft at this level. The Mokhes, however, collected a duty on imports and exports, goods for domestic trade, and virtually anything that was moved by road. They set tolls on roads and bridges, they taxed beasts of burden and axles on transport wagons, and they charged a tariff on parcels, letters, and whatever else they could find to tax. Their assessments were often arbitrary and capricious.

There were two kinds of Mokhes—the Great Mokhes and the Little Mokhes. A Great Mokhes stayed behind the scenes and hired others to collect taxes for him. (Zaccheus was apparently a Great

Mokhes—a "chief tax collector"—Luke 19:2). Matthew was evidently a Little Mokhes, because he manned a tax office where he dealt with people face to face (Matthew 9:9). He was the one the people saw and resented most. He was the worst of the worst. No self-respecting Jew in his right mind would ever choose to be a tax collector. He had effectively cut himself off not only from his own people, but also from his God. After all, since he was banned from the synagogue and forbidden to sacrifice and worship in the temple, he was in essence worse off religiously than a Gentile.

Therefore it must have been a stunning reality to Matthew when Jesus chose him. It came out of the blue. By Matthew's own account, Jesus saw him sitting in the tax office and simply said, "Follow Me" (Matthew 9:9).

Matthew instantly and without hesitation "arose and followed Him." He abandoned the tax office. He left his toll booth and walked away from his cursed profession forever.

The decision was irreversible as soon as he made it. There was no shortage of money-grubbing piranha who coveted a tax franchise like Matthew's, and as soon as he stepped away, you can be sure that someone else stepped in and took over. Once Matthew walked away, he could never go back. Nor did he ever regret his decision.

What was it in a man like Matthew that caused him to drop everything at once like that? We might assume that he was a materialist. And at one time he must have been, or he never would have gotten into a position like that in the first place. So why would he walk away from everything and follow Jesus, not knowing what the future held?

The best answer we can deduce is that whatever Matthew's tortured soul may have experienced because of the profession he had chosen to be in, down deep inside he was a Jew who knew and loved the Old Testament. He was spiritually hungry. At some point in his life, most likely *after* he had chosen his despicable career, he was smitten with a gnawing spiritual hunger and became a true seeker. Of course, God was seeking and drawing *him,* and the draw was irresistible.

We know that Matthew knew the Old Testament very well,

because his Gospel quotes the Old Testament ninety-nine times. That is more times than Mark, Luke, and John combined. Matthew obviously had extensive familiarity with the Old Testament. In fact, he quotes out of the Law, out of the Psalms, and out of the Prophets—every section of the Old Testament. So he had a good working knowledge of all the Scriptures that were available to him. He must have pursued his study of the Old Testament on his own, because he couldn't hear the Word of God explained in any synagogue. Apparently, in a quest to fill the spiritual void in his life, he had turned to the Scriptures.

He believed in the true God. And because he knew the record of God's revelation, he understood the promises of the Messiah. He must have also known about Jesus, because sitting on the crossroads in a tax booth, he would have heard information all the time about this miracle worker who was banishing disease from Palestine, casting demons out of people, and doing miracles. So when Jesus showed up and called him to follow Him, he had enough faith to drop everything and follow. His faith is clearly indicated not only in the immediacy of his response, but also in the fact that after following Jesus, he held this evangelistic banquet in his home.

This is virtually all we know of Matthew: He knew the Old Testament, he believed in God, he looked for the Messiah, he dropped everything immediately when he met Jesus, and in the joy of his newfound relationship, he embraced the outcasts of his world and introduced them to Jesus. He became a man of quiet humility who loved the outcasts and gave no place to religious hypocrisy—a man of great faith and complete surrender to the lordship of Christ. He stands as a vivid reminder that the Lord often chooses the most despicable people of this world, redeems them, gives them new hearts, and uses them in remarkable ways.

Forgiveness is the thread that runs through Matthew 9 after the account of Matthew's conversion. Of course, even as a tax collector, Matthew knew his sin, his greed, his betrayal of his own people. He knew he was guilty of graft, extortion, oppression, and abuse. But when Jesus said to him, "Follow Me," Matthew knew there was inherent in that command a promise of the forgiveness of his sin. His heart had long hungered for such forgiveness. And that is why he arose without hesitation and devoted the rest of his life to following Christ.

We know that Matthew wrote his Gospel with a Jewish audience in mind. Tradition says he ministered to the Jews both in Israel and abroad for many years before being martyred for his faith. There is no reliable record of how he was put to death, but the earliest traditions indicate he was burned at the stake. Thus this man who walked away from a lucrative career without ever giving it a second thought remained willing to give his all for Christ to the very end.

THOMAS, THE PESSIMIST

The final apostle in the second group of four is also a familiar name: Thomas. He is usually nicknamed "Doubting Thomas," but that may not be the most fitting label for him. He was a better man than the popular lore would indicate.

It probably is fair, however, to say that Thomas was a somewhat negative person. He was a worrywart. He was a brooder. He tended to be anxious and angst-ridden. He was like Eeyore in Winnie the Pooh. He anticipated the worst all the time. Pessimism, rather than doubt, seems to have been his besetting sin.

Thomas, according to John 11:16 (KJV), was also called "Didymus," which means "the twin." Apparently he had a twin brother or a twin sister, but his twin is never identified in Scriptures.

Like Nathanael, Thomas is mentioned only once each in the three synoptic Gospels. In each case, he is simply named with the other eleven apostles in a list. No details about him are given by Matthew, Mark, or Luke. We learn everything we know about his character from John's Gospel.

It becomes obvious from John's record that Thomas had a tendency to look only into the darkest corners of life. He seemed always to anticipate the worst of everything. Yet despite his pessimism, some

157

wonderfully redeeming elements of his character come through in John's account of him.

John's first mention of Thomas is found in John 11:16. It is a single verse, but it speaks volumes about Thomas's real character.

In this context, John is describing the prelude to the raising of Lazarus. Jesus had left Jerusalem because His life was in jeopardy there, and "He went away again beyond the Jordan to the place where John was baptizing at first, and there He stayed" (John 10:40). Great crowds of people came out to hear Jesus preach. John says, "And many believed in Him there" (v. 42). This may have been the most fruitful time of ministry the disciples had witnessed in all the time since they had begun to follow Christ. People were responsive. Souls were being converted. And Jesus was able to minister freely without the opposition of the religious rulers of Jerusalem.

But something happened to interrupt their time in the wilderness. John writes, "Now a certain man was sick, Lazarus of Bethany, the town of Mary and her sister Martha. It was that Mary who anointed the Lord with fragrant oil and wiped His feet with her hair, whose brother Lazarus was sick" (John 11:1–2). Bethany was on the outskirts of Jerusalem. And Jesus had formed a close and loving relationship with this little family who lived there. He loved them with a special affection. He had stayed with them, and they had provided for His needs.

Now His dear friend Lazarus was sick, and Mary and Martha sent word to Jesus saying, "Lord, behold, he whom You love is sick" (v. 3). They knew if Jesus came to see Lazarus, He would be able to heal him.

This presented a quandary. If Jesus went that close to Jerusalem, he was walking into the very teeth of the worst kind of hostility. John 10:39 says the Jewish leaders were seeking to seize Him. They were already determined to kill Him. He had eluded their grasp once already, but if He returned to Bethany, they were certain to find out, and they would try again to seize Him.

The disciples must have breathed a sigh of relief when Jesus answered, "This sickness is not unto death, but for the glory of God, that the Son of God may be glorified through it" (John 11:4). What He *meant*, of course, was that Lazarus's death would not be the *ultimate* result of his sickness. The Son of God would glorify Himself by raising Lazarus from the dead. Jesus knew, of course, that Lazarus would die. In fact, He knew the very hour of his death.

John writes, "Now Jesus loved Martha and her sister and Lazarus. So, when He heard that he was sick, He stayed two more days in the place where He was" (vv. 5–6). At first glance, that seems a strange juxtaposition of statements: Jesus loved Lazarus and his family, so He stayed put while Lazarus was dying. He deliberately tarried to give Lazarus time to die. But this *was* an act of love, because ultimately, the blessing they received when Lazarus was raised from the dead was a greater blessing than if he had merely been healed of his sickness. It glorified Jesus in a greater way. It strengthened their faith in Him immeasurably more. Therefore Jesus waited a couple of extra days so that Lazarus was already dead four days by the time He arrived (v. 39).

Of course, Jesus, with His supernatural knowledge, knew exactly when Lazarus died. That is *why* He waited. "Then after this He said to the disciples, 'Let us go to Judea again' " (v. 7).

The disciples thought this was crazy. They said, "Rabbi, lately the Jews sought to stone You, and are You going there again?" (v. 8). They frankly did not want to go back to Jerusalem. The ministry in the wilderness was phenomenal. In Jerusalem they all risked being stoned. Now was not a good time for a visit to Bethany, which was virtually within sight of the temple, where Jesus' bitterest enemies had their headquarters.

Jesus' answer is interesting. He gives them an illustration. "Are there not twelve hours in the day? If anyone walks in the day, he does not stumble, because he sees the light of this world. But if one walks in the night, he stumbles, because the light is not in him" (vv. 9–10). In other words, there was no need for Him to skulk around like a common criminal. He was determined to do His work in the bright light of day, because that's what you do in order *not* to stumble. Those who were walking in darkness are the ones in danger of stumbling—

particularly the religious leaders who were secretly looking for a way to kill Him.

He said that to the disciples to calm them down. They obviously did not want to go back and die. But Jesus reassured them they had nothing to fear. And of course, He knew His time to die was in God's timing, not His enemies'. Our Lord made His purpose clear when He said, "Our friend Lazarus sleeps, but I go that I may wake him up" (v. 11).

The disciples missed His meaning. They said, "Lord, if he sleeps he will get well" (v. 12). If he's only asleep, why not let him rest? After all, Jesus had already said his sickness was not unto death. The disciples couldn't see the urgency of the situation. It sounded to them like Lazarus was already on the road to recovery.

"However, Jesus spoke of his death, but they thought that He was speaking about taking rest in sleep. Then Jesus said to them plainly, 'Lazarus is dead. And I am glad for your sakes that I was not there, that you may believe. Nevertheless let us go to him' " (vv. 13–15).

Now they understood. Jesus *had* to go back. He was determined to do so. There would be no talking Him out of it. To them, it must have seemed like the worst possible disaster. They were floundering in fear. They were convinced that if Jesus returned to Bethany, He would be killed. But He had made up His mind.

It was at this point that Thomas spoke up. Here is where we meet him for the first time in all the Gospel records. "Then Thomas, who is called the Twin, said to his fellow disciples, 'Let us also go, that we may die with Him' " (v. 16).

Now that is pessimistic, and that's typical for Thomas. But it is a heroic pessimism. He could see nothing but disaster ahead. He was convinced Jesus was heading straight for a stoning. But if that is what the Lord was determined to do, Thomas was grimly determined to go and die with Him. You have to admire his courage.

It is not easy to be a pessimist. It is a miserable way to live. An optimist might have said, "Let's go; everything will work out. The Lord knows what He is doing. He says we won't stumble. We will be fine." But the pessimist says, "He's going to die, and we're going to die with

Him." Thomas at least had the courage to be loyal, even in the face of his pessimism. It is much easier for an optimist to be loyal. He always expects the best. It is hard for a pessimist to be loyal, because he is convinced the worst is going to happen. This is heroic pessimism. This is real courage.

Thomas was devoted to Christ. He may have been the equal to John in this regard. When we think about someone who loved Jesus and was intimate with Him, we usually think of John, because he was always near Jesus. But it is clear from this account that Thomas did not want to live without Jesus. If Jesus was going to die, Thomas was prepared to die with Him. In essence he says, "Guys, suck it up; let's go and die. Better to die and be with Christ than to be left behind."

Thomas was an example of strength to the rest of the apostles. It appears they collectively followed his lead at this point and said, "OK, let's go and die"—because they *did* go with Him to Bethany.

Thomas obviously had a deep devotion to Christ that could not be dampened even by his own pessimism. He had no illusion that following Jesus would be easy. All he could see were the jaws of death opening to swallow him. But he followed Jesus with an undaunted courage. He was resolved to die if necessary with his Lord rather than forsake Him. He would rather die than be left behind and separated from Christ.

Thomas's profound love for the Lord shows up again in John 14. You'll recall from our study of Philip that Jesus was telling them of His imminent departure. "I go to prepare a place for you" (John 14:2). "And where I go you know, and the way you know" (v. 4).

In verse 5 Thomas speaks: "Thomas said to Him, 'Lord, we do not know where You are going, and how can we know the way?' " Again we see his pessimism. In essence, he was saying, "You're leaving. We'll never get where you are going. We don't even know *how* to get there. How are we supposed to get there? It was a better plan for us to die with You, because then there's no separation. If we died together, we would all be together. But if You just go, how are we ever going to find You? We don't even know how to get there."

161

Here is a man with deep love. He is a man whose relationship with Christ was so strong that he never wanted to be severed from Him. His heart was broken as he heard Jesus speak of leaving them. He was shattered. The thought of losing Christ paralyzed him. He had become so attached to Jesus in those years that he would have been glad to die with Christ, but he could not think of living without Him. You have to admire his devotion to Christ.

This was overwhelming for Thomas. And his worst fears came to pass. Jesus died and he didn't.

We pick up the next picture of Thomas in John 20. After Jesus' death, all the disciples were in deep sorrow. But they all got together to comfort one another. Except for Thomas. John 20:24 says, "Thomas, called the Twin, one of the twelve, was not with them."

It is too bad he wasn't there, because Jesus came and appeared to them. They had locked themselves in a room somewhere (most likely the Upper Room in Jerusalem). John writes, "The doors were shut where the disciples were assembled, for fear of the Jews" (v. 19). Suddenly, although the doors and windows were sealed shut, "Jesus came and stood in the midst, and said to them, 'Peace be with you.' When He had said this, He showed them His hands and His side. Then the disciples were glad when they saw the Lord" (vv. 19–20).

Thomas missed the whole thing. Why wasn't he there? It is possible that he was so negative, so pessimistic, such a melancholy person, that he was absolutely destroyed, and he was probably off somewhere wallowing in his own misery. He could see only the worst of everything. Now his worst fear had been realized. Jesus was gone, and Thomas was sure he would never see Him again. He may have still been thinking he would never find the way to get where Jesus was. He was no doubt regretting the fact that he did not die with Jesus, as he had been so determined to do in the first place.

Thomas may well have felt alone, betrayed, rejected, forsaken. It was over. The One he loved so deeply was gone, and it tore his heart out. He was not in a mood to socialize. He was brokenhearted, shattered, devastated, crushed. He just wanted to be alone. He simply

162

couldn't take the banter. He wasn't in a mood to be in a crowd, even with his friends.

"The other disciples therefore said to him, 'We have seen the Lord'" (v. 25). They were exuberant. They were ecstatic. They were eager to share the good news with Thomas.

But someone in the kind of mood Thomas was in was not going to be cheered up so easily. He was still being a hopeless pessimist. All he could see was the bad side of things, and this was just too good to be true. "So he said to them, 'Unless I see in His hands the print of the nails, and put my finger into the print of the nails, and put my hand into His side, I will not believe'" (v. 25).

It is because of that statement that he has been nicknamed "Doubting Thomas." But don't be too hard on Thomas. Remember, the other disciples did not believe in the resurrection until they saw Jesus, either. Mark 16:10–11 says after Mary Magdalene saw Him, "She went and told those who had been with Him, as they mourned and wept. And when they heard that He was alive and had been seen by her, they did not believe." The two disciples on the road to Emmaus walked with Him a long distance before they even realized who He was. And then "they went and told it to the rest, but they did not believe them either" (v. 13). When Jesus showed up in the room where the disciples are gathered, "He showed them His hands and side" (John 20:20). *Then* they believed. So they were *all* slow to believe. What set Thomas apart from the other ten was not that his doubt was greater, but that his sorrow was greater.

John 20:26 says that eight days passed after Jesus appeared to the disciples again. Finally Thomas's ragged grief had eased a bit, apparently. Because when the apostles were returned to the room where Jesus appeared to them, this time Thomas was with them. Once again, "Jesus came, the doors being shut, and stood in the midst, and said, 'Peace to you!'" (v. 26).

No one needed to tell Jesus what Thomas had said, of course. He looked right at Thomas and said, "Reach your finger here, and look at My hands; and reach your hand here, and put it into My side. Do not be unbelieving, but believing" (v. 27). The Lord was amazingly gentle with him. Thomas had erred because he was more or less wired to be a pessimist. But it was the error of a profound love. It was provoked by grief, brokenheartedness, uncertainty, and the pain of loneliness. No one could feel the way Thomas felt unless he loved Jesus the way Thomas loved Him. So Jesus was tender with him. He understands our weaknesses (Hebrews 4:15). So He understands our doubt. He sympathizes with our uncertainty. He is patient with our pessimism. And while recognizing these as weaknesses, we must also acknowledge Thomas's heroic devotion to Christ, which made him understand that it would be better to die than to be separated from his Lord. The proof of his love was the profoundness of his despair.

Then Thomas made what was probably the greatest statement ever to come from the lips of the apostles: "My Lord and my God!" (v. 28). Let those who question the deity of Christ meet Thomas.

Suddenly, Thomas's melancholy, comfortless, negative, moody tendencies were forever banished by the appearance of Jesus Christ. And in that moment he was transformed into a great evangelist. A short time later, at Pentecost, along with the other apostles, he was filled with the Holy Spirit and empowered for ministry. He, like his comrades, took the gospel to the ends of the earth.

There is a considerable amount of ancient testimony that suggests Thomas carried the gospel as far as India. There is to this day a small hill near the airport in Chennai (Madras), India, where Thomas is said to have been buried. There are churches in south India whose roots are traceable to the beginning of the church age, and tradition says they were founded under the ministry of Thomas. The strongest traditions say he was martyred for his faith by being run through with a spear—a fitting form of martyrdom for one whose faith came of age when he saw the spear mark in his Master's side and for one who longed to be reunited with his Lord.

TWO TRANSFORMED

It's interesting that God used a publican like Matthew and a pessimist like Thomas. Matthew was once the vilest of sinners—a wretched, despicable outcast. Thomas was a tender-hearted, moody, melancholy individual. But both of them were transformed by Christ in the same way He transformed the others. Are you beginning to get the idea of what kind of people God uses? He can use *anyone*. Personality, status, and family background are all immaterial. The one thing all these men except Judas had in common was a willingness to acknowledge their own sinfulness and look to Christ for grace. He met them with grace, mercy, and forgiveness and transformed their lives into lives that would glorify Him. He does that for all who truly trust Him.

9

JAMES—THE LESS; SIMON—THE ZEALOT; AND JUDAS (NOT ISCARIOT)—THE APOSTLE WITH THREE NAMES

James the son of Alphaeus, and Simon called the Zealot; Judas the son of James . . .

—LUKE 6:15–16

T HE FINAL GROUP OF FOUR APOSTLES IS THE LEAST KNOWN to us, except for Judas Iscariot, who made himself notorious by selling Christ to be crucified. This group seems to have been less intimate with Christ than the other eight disciples. They are virtually silent in the Gospel narratives. Little is known about any of them, except the fact that they were appointed to be apostles. We'll deal with three of them in this chapter, and save Judas Iscariot, the traitor, for the final chapter.

It must be borne in mind that the apostles were men who gave up everything to follow Christ. Peter spoke for them all when he said, "See, we have left all and followed You" (Luke 18:28). They had left houses, jobs, lands, family, and friends to follow Christ. Their sacrifice was heroic. With the exception of Judas Iscariot, they all became valiant and intrepid witnesses.

We don't actually see much of their heroism in the Gospel records, because the Gospel writers—two of them apostles (Matthew and John) and the other two (Mark and Luke) close friends of apostles—honestly portrayed their weaknesses as well as their strengths. The apostles are not presented to us as mythic figures, but as real people. They are not depicted as prominent celebrities, but as ordinary men. That is why, as far as the Gospel accounts are concerned, the apostles give color and life to the descriptions of Jesus' life, but they are rarely in the foreground. They are never major role players.

When they do come to the foreground, it is often to manifest doubt, disbelief, or confusion. Sometimes we see them thinking more highly of themselves than they ought to think. Sometimes they speak when they ought to remain silent and seem clueless about things they ought to have understood. Sometimes they exhibit more confidence in their own abilities and their own strengths than they should. So their shortcomings and weaknesses show up more often than their strengths. In that sense, the raw honesty of the Gospel accounts is amazing.

Meanwhile, there are very few manifestations of any great acts by the apostles. We are told that they were empowered to heal, raise the dead, and cast out demons, but even that is narrated in such a way as to highlight the apostles' imperfections (cf. Mark 9:14-29). The one place in all the Gospels where a specific apostle does something truly extraordinary is when Peter began to walk on water—but he immediately found himself sinking.

The Gospel records simply do not portray these men as heroes. Their heroism played out after Jesus went back to heaven, sent the Holy Spirit, and empowered them. Suddenly we begin to see them acting differently. They are strong and courageous. They perform great miracles. They preach with a newfound boldness. But even then, the biblical record is sparse. Primarily, all we see are Peter, John, and later the apostle Paul (who was added to their number as "one born out of due time"—1 Corinthians 15:8). The rest of them went on into obscurity.

The legacy of their true greatness is the church, a living, breathing organism which they helped found and of which they became the very foundation stones ("Jesus Christ Himself being the chief cornerstone"—Ephesians 2:20). The church, now some two thousand years old, exists today because these men launched the expansion of the gospel of Jesus Christ to the ends of the earth. And their heroism will be rewarded and commemorated throughout eternity in the New Jerusalem, where their names will be permanently etched into the foundation of that city.

The Gospels are the record of how Jesus trained them. Scripture deliberately records more about Jesus and His teaching than it does about the lives of these men. It all serves to remind us that the Lord loves to use weak and common people. If the faults and character flaws of the apostles seem like a mirror of your own weaknesses, take heart. These are the kinds of people the Lord delights to use.

The one thing that set these men apart from others in the Gospel accounts was the durability of their faith. Nowhere does this come through more clearly than in John 6, shortly after the feeding of the five thousand, when crowds of people began to flock around Jesus, hoping for more free food. At that very point, Jesus began to preach a message that many found shocking and offensive. He described Himself as the true manna from heaven (v. 32). *That* was shocking enough, because by describing Himself as having come down from heaven (v. 41), He was claiming to be God. The Jewish leaders and the people understood this correctly as a claim of deity (v. 42). Jesus responded by saying again that He was the true bread of life (v. 48). He then added that He would give His flesh for the life of the world, and said, "Whoever eats My flesh and drinks My blood has eternal life, and I will raise him up at the last day. For My flesh is food indeed, and My blood is drink indeed. He who eats My flesh and drinks My blood abides in Me, and I in him" (vv. 54–56). Obviously, He was not talking about literal cannibalism; He was using vivid imagery to speak of the absolute commitment He required of His followers.

John writes, "Therefore many of His disciples, when they heard this, said, 'This is a hard saying; who can understand it?' " (v. 60). The word "disciples" in that verse refers to the larger group of followers who followed Jesus, not the Twelve in particular. John goes on to say, "From that time many of His disciples went back and walked with Him no more" (John 6:66). On that very day, many of the dozens of disciples who had sat under Jesus' teaching and witnessed His miracles stopped following Him. His sayings were too hard and His demands too rigorous for them. But not the Twelve. They remained resolutely with Jesus.

And as the crowd dissipated in shock, Jesus looked around at the Twelve and said, "Do you also want to go away?" (v. 67). Now was the time to leave, if they were inclined to do so.

Peter spoke for the group when he answered, "Lord, to whom shall we go? You have the words of eternal life" (v. 68). They were staying with Him no matter what. Except for Judas Iscariot, they were men of true faith.

Jesus knew all along that some of His disciples were not true believers, and He knew that Judas would betray Him. He told them, "'But there are some of you who do not believe.' For Jesus knew from the beginning who they were who did not believe, and who would betray Him" (v. 64). In verse 70, He answers Peter, "Did I not choose you, the twelve, and one of you is a devil?" He knew their hearts. Except for Judas, they had made the break with their past permanently. They had given up everything to follow Jesus.

That is the single most heroic fact about them revealed in the Gospels. And Judas's failure to make that commitment, while pretending that he had, was what made him so despicable.

As we examine this last group of apostles, we discover that although Scripture says very little about them, they nonetheless have their own distinctions.

JAMES, SON OF ALPHAEUS

The ninth name in Luke's list of the apostles (Luke 6:14–16) is "James the son of Alphaeus" (v. 15). The *only* thing Scripture tells us about this man is his name. If he ever wrote anything, it is lost to history. If he ever asked Jesus any questions or did anything to stand out from the group, Scripture does not record it. He never attained any degree of fame or notoriety. He was not the kind of person who stands out. He was utterly obscure. He even had a common name.

There are several men with the name *James* in the New Testament. We have already met James the son of Zebedee. There was another James, who was the son of Mary and Joseph and therefore a half brother of Christ (Galatians 1:19). The James who was Jesus' half brother apparently became a leader in the Jerusalem church. He was the spokesman who delivered the ruling at the Jerusalem Council in Acts 15:13–21. He is also thought to be the same James who penned the New Testament epistle that bears his name. He is not the same James named as one of the apostles in the third band of four.

Practically all we know about the James with whom we are concerned is that he was the son of Alphaeus (Matthew 10:3; Mark 3:18; Luke 6:15; Acts 1:13). In Mark 15:40, we learn that James's mother was named Mary. That verse, together with Matthew 27:56 and Mark 15:47 mention another of this woman's sons, Joses. Joses must have been well-known as a follower of the Lord (though not an apostle), because his name is mentioned repeatedly. Their mother, Mary, was obviously a devoted follower of Christ as well. She was an eyewitness to the crucifixion. She is also one of the women who came to prepare Jesus' body for burial (Mark 16:1).

Aside from those scant details that can be gleaned about his family, this James is utterly obscure. His lack of prominence is even reflected in his nickname. In Mark 15:40 he is referred to as "James the Less."

The Greek word for "Less" is *mikros*. It literally means "little." Its primary meaning is "small in stature," so it could refer to his physical features. Perhaps he was a short or small-framed man.

The word can also speak of someone who is young in age. He might have been younger than James the son of Zebedee, so that this title would distinguish him as the younger of the two. In fact, even if this is not what his nickname mainly referred to, it is probably true that he was younger than the other James; otherwise he would more likely have been known as "James the Elder."

But the name most likely refers to his influence. As we have already seen, James the son of Zebedee was a man of prominence. His family was known to the high priest (John 18:15–16). He was part of the Lord's most intimate inner circle. He was the better-known of the two Jameses. Therefore, James the son of Alphaeus was known as "James the Less." *Mikros.* "Little James."

It may well be that all these things were true of James, so that he was a small, young, quiet person who stayed mostly in the background. That would all be consistent with the low profile he had among the Twelve. We might say his distinguishing mark was his obscurity.

That in itself is a significant fact. Apparently he sought no recognition. He displayed no great leadership. He asked no critical questions. He demonstrated no unusual insight. Only his name remains, while his life and his labors are immersed in obscurity.

But he was one of the Twelve. The Lord selected him for a reason, trained and empowered him like the others, and sent him out as a witness. He reminds me of those unnamed people mentioned in Hebrews 11:33–38:

> . . . who through faith subdued kingdoms, worked righteousness, obtained promises, stopped the mouths of lions, quenched the violence of fire, escaped the edge of the sword, out of weakness were made strong, became valiant in battle, turned to flight the armies of the aliens. Women received their dead raised to life again. And others were tortured, not accepting deliverance, that they might obtain a better resurrection. Still others had trial of mockings and scourgings, yes, and of chains and imprisonment. They were stoned, they were sawn in two, were tempted, were slain with the sword. They wandered about in sheepskins and goatskins, being destitute, afflicted, tormented; of whom the world was not worthy. They wandered in deserts and mountains, in dens and caves of the earth.

Eternity will reveal the names and the testimonies of these, like James the Less, whom this world barely remembers and knows nothing about.

Early church history is also mostly silent about this man named James. Some of the earliest legends about him confuse him with James the brother of the Lord. There is some evidence that James the Less took the gospel to Syria and Persia. Accounts of his death differ. Some say he was stoned; others say he was beaten to death; still others say he was crucified like his Lord.

In any case, we can be certain that he became a powerful preacher like the others. He surely performed "the signs of an apostle . . . in signs and wonders and mighty deeds" (2 Corinthians 12:12). And His name will be inscribed on one of the gates of the heavenly city.

Here's an interesting thought about James, son of Alphaeus: You may recall that according to Mark 2:14, Levi (Matthew) was the son of a man named Alphaeus as well. It could be that this James was the brother of Matthew. After all, Peter and Andrew were brothers and James and John were brothers. Why not these two? There is no effort on the part of Scripture to distinguish between the two Alphaeuses. On the other hand, Matthew and James are nowhere identified as brothers. We simply don't know whether they were or not.

Another interesting question about James's lineage comes to light when we compare Mark 15:40 with John 19:25. Both verses mention two other Marys who were standing by the cross of Jesus with Mary the Lord's mother. Mark 15:40 mentions "Mary Magdalene, and Mary the mother of James the less and of Joses." John 19:25 names "[Jesus'] mother's sister, Mary the wife of Clopas, and Mary Magdalene." It is possible, perhaps even likely, that Jesus' mother's sister ("Mary the wife of Clopas") and "Mary the mother of James the less" are the same person. ("Clopas" may have been another name for Alphaeus, or James's mother might have remarried after his father died). That would have made James the Less Jesus' cousin.

Was James the cousin of our Lord? Was he the brother of Matthew? We don't know. Scripture doesn't expressly tell us. The disciples' importance did not stem from their pedigree. Had that been important, Scripture would have recorded it for us. What made these men important was the Lord whom they served and the message they proclaimed. If we lack details about the men themselves, that is OK. Heaven will reveal the full truth of who they were and what they were like. In the meantime, it is enough to know that they were chosen by the Lord, empowered by the Spirit, and used by God to carry the gospel to the world of their day.

All the men themselves more or less disappear from the biblical narrative within a few years after Pentecost. In no case does Scripture give us a full biography. That is because Scripture always keeps the focus on the power of Christ and the power of the Word, not the men who were merely instruments of that power. These men were filled with the Spirit and they preached the Word. That is all we really need to know. The vessel is not the issue; the Master is.

No one epitomizes that truth better than James the Less, son of Alphaeus. He may have been able to claim that he was Matthew's brother or Jesus' cousin, but he went quietly unnoticed through the entire Gospel narrative. This world remembers next to nothing about him. But in eternity, he will receive a full reward (Mark 10:29–31).

SIMON THE ZEALOT

The next name given in Luke 6:15 is "Simon called the Zealot." In Matthew 10:4 and Mark 3:18, he is called "Simon the Cananite." That is not a reference to the land of Canaan or the village of Cana. It comes from the Hebrew root *qanna,* which means "to be zealous."

Simon was apparently at one time a member of the political party known as the Zealots. The fact that he bore the title all his life may also suggest that he had a fiery, zealous temperament. But that term in Jesus' day signified a well-known and widely feared outlaw political sect, and Simon had apparently been a member of that sect.

The historian Josephus described four basic parties among the

Jews of that time. The *Pharisees* were fastidious about the Law; they were the religious fundamentalists of their time. The *Sadducees* were religious liberals; they denied the supernatural. They were also rich, aristocratic, and powerful. They were in charge of the temple. The *Essenes* are not mentioned in Scripture at all, but both Josephus and Philo describe them as ascetics and celibates who lived in the desert and devoted their lives to the study of the Law. The fourth group, the *Zealots,* were more politically minded than any group besides the Herodians. The Zealots hated the Romans, and their goal was to overthrow the Roman occupation. They advanced their agenda primarily through terrorism and surreptitious acts of violence.

The Zealots were extremists in every sense. Like the Pharisees, they interpreted the law literally. Unlike the Pharisees (who were willing to compromise for political reasons), the Zealots were militant, violent outlaws. They believed only God Himself had the right to rule over the Jews. And therefore they believed they were doing God's work by assassinating Roman soldiers, political leaders, and anyone else who opposed them.

The Zealots were hoping for a Messiah who would lead them in overthrowing the Romans and restore the kingdom to Israel with its Solomonic glory. They were red-hot patriots, ready to die in an instant for what they believed in. Josephus wrote of them:

> Of the fourth sect of Jewish philosophy, Judas the Galilean was the author. These men agree in all other things with the Pharisaic notions; but they have an inviolable attachment to liberty, and say that God is to be their only Ruler and Lord. They also do not value dying any kinds of death, nor indeed do they heed the deaths of their relations and friends, nor can any such fear make them call any man lord. And since this immovable resolution of theirs is well known to a great many, I shall speak no further about that matter; nor am I afraid that any thing I have said of them should be disbelieved, but rather fear, that what I have said is beneath the resolution they show when they undergo pain. And it was in Gessius Florus's time that the nation

began to grow mad with this distemper, who was our procurator, and who occasioned the Jews to go wild with it by the abuse of his authority, and to make them revolt from the Romans.[1]

The revolt Josephus describes "in Gessius Florus's time" occurred in A.D. 6, when a group of Zealots waged a violent rebellion against a Roman census tax. The Zealots' leader and founder, also mentioned by Josephus, was Judas the Galilean, who is named in Acts 5:37.

The Zealots were convinced that paying tribute to a pagan king was an act of treason against God. That view found widespread acceptance among people who were already overburdened by Roman taxation. Judas the Galilean seized the opportunity, organized forces, and went on a rampage of murder, plunder, and destruction. From their headquarters in the Galilee region, Judas and his followers carried out guerilla-style warfare and terrorist acts against the Romans. Soon, however, the Romans crushed the rebellion, killed Judas of Galilee, and crucified his sons.

The Zealot party merely went underground. Their acts of terror became more selective and more secretive. As noted in chapter 2, they formed a party of secret assassins called *sicarii*—"dagger-men"—because of the deadly, curved daggers they carried in the folds of their robes. They would sneak up behind Roman soldiers and politicians and stab them in the back, between the ribs, expertly piercing the heart.

They liked to burn Roman targets in Judea, then retreat to the remote areas of Galilee to hide. As Josephus described them in the quotation cited above, their willingness to suffer any kind of death or endure any amount of pain—including the torture of their own kindred—was well known. The Romans might torture them and kill them, but they could not quench their passion.

Many historians believe that when the Romans sacked Jerusalem under Titus Vespasian in A.D. 70, that terrible holocaust was largely precipitated by the Zealots. During the siege of Rome, after the Roman army had already surrounded the city and cut off supplies, the

Zealots actually began killing fellow Jews who wanted to negotiate with Rome to end the siege. They allowed no one to surrender who wanted to save his or her own life. When Titus saw how hopeless the situation was, he destroyed the city, massacring thousands of its inhabitants, and carried off the treasures of the temple. So the Zealots' blind hatred of Rome and everything Roman ultimately provoked the destruction of their own city. The spirit of their movement was an insane, and ultimately self-destructive, fanaticism.

Josephus suggests that the name *Zealots* was a misnomer, "as if they were zealous in good undertakings, and were not rather zealous in the worst actions, and extravagant in them beyond the example of others."[2]

Simon was one of them. It is interesting that when Matthew and Mark list the Twelve, they list Simon just before Judas Iscariot. When Jesus sent the disciples out two by two in Mark 6:7, it is likely that Simon and Judas Iscariot were a team. They probably both originally followed Christ for similar political reasons. But somewhere along the line, Simon became a genuine believer and was transformed. Judas Iscariot never really believed.

When Jesus did not overthrow Rome, but instead talked of dying, some might have expected Simon to be the betrayer—a man of such deep passion, zeal, and political conviction that he would align himself with terrorists. But that was before He met Jesus.

Of course, as one of the Twelve, Simon also had to associate with Matthew, who was at the opposite end of the political spectrum, collecting taxes for the Roman government. At one point in his life, Simon would probably have gladly killed Matthew. In the end, they became spiritual brethren, working side by side for the same cause— the spread of the gospel—and worshiping the same Lord.

It is amazing that Jesus would select a man like Simon to be an apostle. But he was a man of fierce loyalties, amazing passion, courage, and zeal. Simon had believed the truth and embraced Christ as his Lord. The fiery enthusiasm he once had for Israel was now expressed in his devotion to Christ.

Several early sources say that after the destruction of Jerusalem,

Simon took the gospel north and preached in the British Isles. Like so many of the others, Simon simply disappears from the biblical record. There is no reliable record of what happened to him, but all accounts say he was killed for preaching the gospel. This man who was once willing to kill and be killed for a political agenda within the confines of Judea found a more fruitful cause for which to give his life—in the proclamation of salvation for sinners out of every nation, tongue, and tribe.

JUDAS, SON OF JAMES

The last name on the list of faithful disciples is "Judas, the son of James." The name *Judas* in and of itself is a fine name. It means "Jehovah leads." But because of the treachery of Judas Iscariot, the name *Judas* will forever bear a negative connotation. When the apostle John mentions him, he calls him "Judas (not Iscariot)" (John 14:22).

Judas the son of James actually had three names. (Jerome referred to him as "Trinomious"—the man with three names.) In Matthew 10:3, he is called "Lebbaeus, whose surname was Thaddaeus." *Judas* was probably the name given him at birth. *Lebbaeus* and *Thaddaeus* were essentially nicknames. *Thaddaeus* means "breast child"—evoking the idea of a nursing baby. It almost has a derisive sound, like "mamma's boy." Perhaps he was the youngest in his family, and therefore the baby among several siblings—specially cherished by his mother. His other name, *Lebbaeus,* is similar. It is from a Hebrew root that refers to the heart—literally, "heart child."

Both names suggest he had a tender, childlike heart. It is interesting to think of such a gentle soul hanging around in the same group of four apostles as Simon the Zealot. But the Lord can use both kinds. Zealots make great preachers. But so do tender-hearted, compassionate, gentle, sweet-spirited souls like Lebbaeus Thaddaeus. Together, they contribute to a very complex and intriguing group of twelve apostles. There's at least one of every imaginable personality.

Like the other three faithful members of the third apostolic group,

Lebbaeus Thaddaeus is more or less shrouded in obscurity. But that obscurity should not cloud our respect for them. They all became mighty preachers.

The New Testament records one incident involving this Judas Lebbaeus Thaddaeus. To see it, we return to the apostle John's description of Jesus' Upper-Room Discourse. In John 14:21, Jesus says, "He who has My commandments and keeps them, it is he who loves Me. And he who loves Me will be loved by My Father, and I will love him and manifest Myself to him."

Then John adds, "Judas (not Iscariot) said to Him, 'Lord, how is it that You will manifest Yourself to us, and not to the world?'" (v. 22). Here we see the tender-hearted humility of this man. He doesn't say anything brash or bold or overconfident. He doesn't rebuke the Lord like Peter once did. His question is full of gentleness and meekness and devoid of any sort of pride. He couldn't believe that Jesus would manifest Himself to this rag-tag group of eleven, and not to the whole world.

After all, Jesus was the Savior of the world. He was the rightful heir of the earth—King of kings and Lord of lords. They had always assumed that He came to set up His kingdom and subdue all things to Himself. The good news of forgiveness and salvation was certainly good news for all the world. And the disciples knew it well, but the rest of the world was still, by and large, clueless. So Lebbaeus Thaddaeus wanted to know, "Why are you going to disclose Yourself to us and not to the whole world?"

This was a pious, believing disciple. This was a man who loved his Lord and who felt the power of salvation in his own life. He was full of hope for the world, and in his own tender-hearted, childlike way he wanted to know why Jesus wasn't going to make Himself known to everyone. He was obviously still hoping to see the kingdom come to earth. We certainly can't fault him for that; that is how Jesus taught His disciples to pray (Luke 11:2).

Jesus gave him a marvelous answer, and the answer was as tender as the question. "Jesus answered and said to him, 'If anyone loves Me, he will keep My word; and My Father will love him, and We will come to him and make Our home with him'" (John 14:23). Christ would manifest Himself to anyone who loves Him.

Judas Lebbaeus Thaddaeus was still thinking in the political and material realm. "How come You haven't taken over the world yet? Why don't You just manifest Yourself to the world?"

Jesus' answer meant, "I'm not going to take over the world externally; I'm going to take over hearts, one at a time. If anyone loves Me, he will keep My Word. And if he keeps My Word, My Father and I will come to him and together we'll set up the kingdom in his heart."

Most of the early tradition regarding Lebbaeus Thaddaeus suggests that a few years after Pentecost, he took the gospel north, to Edessa, a royal city in Mesopotamia, in the region of Turkey today. There are numerous ancient accounts of how he healed the king of Edessa, a man named Abgar. In the fourth century, Eusebius the historian said the archives at Edessa (now destroyed) contained full records of Thaddaeus's visit and the healing of Abgar.[3]

The traditional apostolic symbol of Judas Lebbaeus Thaddaeus is a club, because tradition says he was clubbed to death for his faith.

Thus this tender-hearted soul followed his Lord faithfully to the end. His testimony was as powerful and as far-reaching as that of the better-known and more outspoken disciples. He, like them, is proof of how God uses perfectly ordinary people in remarkable ways.

10
J U D A S — T H E   T R A I T O R

Then Judas, who was betraying Him, answered and said, "Rabbi, is it I?"

—M ATTHEW 26:25

T HE MOST NOTORIOUS AND UNIVERSALLY SCORNED OF ALL
the disciples is Judas Iscariot, the betrayer. His name appears last
in every biblical list of apostles, except for the list in Acts 1,
where it doesn't appear at all. Every time Judas is mentioned in
Scripture, we also find a notation about his being a traitor. He is the
most colossal failure in all of human history. He committed the most
horrible, heinous act of any individual, ever. He betrayed the perfect,
sinless, holy Son of God for a handful of money. His dark story is a
poignant example of the depths to which the human heart is capable
of sinking. He spent three years with Jesus Christ, but for all that time
his heart was only growing hard and hateful.

The other eleven apostles are all great encouragements to us because
they exemplify how common people with typical failings can be used
by God in *un*common, remarkable ways. Judas, on the other hand,
stands as a warning about the evil potential of spiritual carelessness,

squandered opportunity, sinful lusts, and hardness of the heart. Here was a man who drew as close to the Savior as it is humanly possible to be. He enjoyed every privilege Christ affords. He was intimately familiar with everything Jesus taught. Yet he remained in unbelief and went into a hopeless eternity.

Judas was as common as the rest, without earthly credentials and without any characteristics that made him stand out from the group. He began exactly like the others had begun. But he never laid hold of the truth by faith, so he was never transformed like the rest. While they were increasing in faith as sons of God, he was becoming more and more a child of hell.

The New Testament tells us plenty about Judas—enough to accomplish two things: First, the life of Judas reminds us that it is possible to be near Christ and associate with Him closely (but superficially) and yet become utterly hardened in sin. Second, Judas reminds us that no matter how sinful a person may be, no matter what treachery he or she may attempt against God, the purpose of God cannot be thwarted. Even the worst act of treachery works toward the fulfillment of the divine plan. God's sovereign plan cannot be overthrown even by the most cunning schemes of those who hate Him.

HIS NAME

Judas's name is a form of *Judah*. The name means "Jehovah leads," which indicates that when he was born his parents must have had great hopes for him to be led by God. The irony of the name is that no individual was ever more clearly led by Satan than Judas was.

His surname, *Iscariot,* signifies the region he came from. It is derived from the Hebrew term *ish* ("man") and the name of a town, Kerioth—"man of Kerioth." Judas probably came from Kerioth-hezron (cf. Joshua 15:25), a humble town in the south of Judea. He was apparently the only one of the apostles who did not come from Galilee. As we know, many of the others were brothers, friends, and working companions even before meeting Christ. Judas was a solitary figure who entered their midst from afar. Although there is no evidence that he was ever excluded or looked down upon by the rest of the group, he may have thought of himself as an outsider, which would have helped him justify his own treachery.

The Galilean disciples' unfamiliarity with Judas would have aided and abetted him in his deception. The others knew little about his family, his background, or his life before he became a disciple. So it was easy for him to play the hypocrite. He was able to work his way into a place of trust, which we know he did, because he ultimately became the treasurer of the group and used that position to pilfer funds (John 12:6).

Judas's father was named Simon (John 6:71). This Simon is otherwise unknown to us. It was a common name, obviously, because two of the disciples (Peter and the Zealot) were also named Simon. Beyond that, we know nothing of Judas's family or social background.

Judas was ordinary in every way, just like the others. It is significant that when Jesus predicted one of them would betray Him, no one pointed the finger of suspicion at Judas (Matthew 26:22–23). He was so expert in his hypocrisy that no one seemed to distrust him. But Jesus knew his heart from the beginning (John 6:64).

HIS CALL

The call of Judas is not recorded in Scripture. It is obvious, however, that he followed Jesus willingly. He lived in a time of heightened messianic hope, and like most in Israel, he was eager for the Messiah to come. When he heard about Jesus, he must have become convinced that this must be the true Messiah. Like the other eleven, he left whatever other enterprise he may have been engaged in and began to follow Jesus full-time. Judas even stayed with Jesus when less-devoted disciples began to leave the group (John 6:66–71). He had given his life to following Jesus. But he never gave Jesus his heart.

Judas was probably a young, zealous, patriotic Jew who did not want the Romans to rule and who hoped Christ would overthrow the foreign oppressors and restore the kingdom to Israel. He obviously could see that Jesus had powers like no other man. There was plenty of reason for a man like Judas to be attracted to that.

It is equally obvious, however, that Judas was not attracted to Christ on a spiritual level. He followed Jesus out of a desire for selfish gain, worldly ambition, avarice, and greed. He sensed Jesus' power, and he wanted power like that for himself. He was not interested in the kingdom for salvation's sake or for Christ's sake. He was interested only in what he could get out of it. Wealth, power, and prestige were what fueled his ambitions.

It is clear, on the one hand, that he *chose* to follow. He continued following even when following became difficult. He persisted in following even though it required him to be a more clever hypocrite in order to cover up the reality of what he really was.

On the other hand, Jesus also chose him. The tension between divine sovereignty and human choice is manifest in Judas's calling, just as it is manifest in the calling of the other apostles. They had all chosen Jesus, but He chose them first (John 15:16). Judas had likewise chosen to follow Jesus. And yet he had also been chosen *by* Jesus, but not for redemption. His role of betrayal was ordained before the foundation of the world and even prophesied in the Old Testament.

Psalm 41:9, a messianic prophecy, says, "Even my own familiar friend in whom I trusted, who ate my bread, has lifted up his heel against me." Jesus cited that verse in John 13:18 and said its fulfillment would come in His own betrayal. Psalm 55:12–14 says, "For it is not an enemy who reproaches me; then I could bear it. Nor is it one who hates me who has exalted himself against me; then I could hide from him. But it was you, a man my equal, my companion and my acquaintance. We took sweet counsel together, and walked to the house of God in the throng." That passage also foretold the treachery of Judas. Zechariah 11:12–13 says, "They weighed out for my wages thirty pieces of silver. And the LORD said to me, 'Throw it to the potter'; that princely price they set on me. So I took the thirty pieces of silver and threw them into the house of the LORD for the potter." Matthew

27:9–10 identifies that as another prophecy about Judas. So Judas's role was foreordained.

Scripture even says that when Jesus chose Judas, He *knew* Judas would be the one to fulfill the prophecies of betrayal. He knowingly chose him to fulfill the plan.

And yet Judas was in no sense coerced into doing what he did. No invisible hand forced him to betray Christ. He acted freely and without external compulsion. He was responsible for his own actions. Jesus said he would bear the guilt of his deed throughout eternity. His own greed, his own ambition, and his own wicked desires were the only forces that constrained him to betray Christ.

How do we reconcile the fact that Judas's treachery was prophesied and predetermined with the fact that he acted of his own volition? There is no need to reconcile those two facts. They are not in contradiction. God's plan and Judas's evil deed concurred perfectly. Judas did what he did because his heart was evil. God, who works all things according to the counsel of His own will (Ephesians 1:11), had foreordained that Jesus would be betrayed and that He would die for the sins of the world. Jesus Himself affirmed both truths in Luke 22:22: "Truly the Son of Man goes as it has been determined, but woe to that man by whom He is betrayed!"

Spurgeon said this about the tension between divine sovereignty and human choice:

> If . . . I find taught in one part of the Bible that everything is fore-ordained, that is true; and if I find, in another Scripture, that man is responsible for all his actions, that is true; and it is only my folly that leads me to imagine that these two truths can ever contradict each other. I do not believe they can ever be welded into one upon any earthly anvil, but they certainly shall be one in eternity. They are two lines that are so nearly parallel, that the human mind which pursues them farthest will never discover that they converge, but they do converge, and they will meet somewhere in eternity, close to the throne of God, whence all truth doth spring.[1]

God ordained the events by which Christ would die, and yet Judas carried out his evil deed by his own choice, unfettered and uncoerced by any external force. Both things are true. The perfect will of God and the wicked purposes of Judas concurred to bring about Christ's death. Judas did it for evil, but God meant it for good (cf. Genesis 50:20). There is no contradiction.

From a human perspective, Judas had the same potential as the others. The difference is that he was never really drawn to the Person of Christ. He saw Him only as a means to an end. Judas's secret goal was personal prosperity—gain for himself. He never embraced Jesus' teaching by faith. He never had an ounce of true love for Christ. His heart had never been changed, and therefore the light of truth only hardened him.

Judas had every opportunity to turn from his sin—as much opportunity as was ever afforded anyone. He heard numerous appeals from Christ urging him *not* to do the deed he was planning to do. He heard every lesson Jesus taught during His ministry. Many of those lessons applied directly to him: the parable of the unjust steward (Luke 16:1–13); the message of the wedding garment (Matthew 22:11–14); and Jesus' preaching against the love of money (Matthew 6:19–34), against greed (Luke 13:13–21), and against pride (Matthew 23:1–12). Jesus had even candidly told the Twelve, "One of you is a devil" (John 6:70). He cautioned them about the woe that would come to the person who betrayed him (Matthew 26:24). Judas listened to all of that unmoved. He never applied the lessons. He just kept up his deceit.

HIS DISILLUSIONMENT

Meanwhile, Judas was becoming progressively more disillusioned with Christ. No doubt at the start, *all* the apostles thought of the Jewish Messiah as an oriental monarch who would defeat the enemies of Judea, rid Israel of pagan occupation, and reestablish the Davidic kingdom in unprecedented glory. They knew Jesus was a miracle worker. He obviously had power over the kingdom of darkness. He also had authority to command the physical world. No one ever taught the way He taught, spoke the way He spoke, or lived the way He lived. As far as the disciples were concerned, He was the obvious fulfillment of the Old Testament messianic promises.

But Jesus did not always fulfill their personal expectations and ambitions. To be perfectly honest, their expectations were not all spiritually motivated. We see evidence of this from time to time, such as when James and John asked for the chief seats in the kingdom. Most of them had hoped to see an earthly, materialistic, political, military, and economic kingdom. Although they had left all to follow Jesus, they did so with an expectation that they would be rewarded (Matthew 19:27). The Lord assured them they *would* be rewarded, but their full and final reward would be in the age to come (Luke 18:29–30). If they were counting on immediate, material rewards, they were going to be disappointed.

The rest of the apostles had begun to catch on slowly that the true Messiah was not what they at first expected. They embraced the superior understanding of the biblical promises Jesus unfolded to them. Their love for Christ overcame their worldly ambitions. They received His teaching about the spiritual dimension of the kingdom, and they gladly became partakers.

Judas, meanwhile, simply became disillusioned. For the most part, he hid his disappointment under his blanket of hypocrisy, probably because he was looking for a way to get some money out of the years he had invested with Jesus. The worldliness in his heart was never conquered. He never embraced the spiritual kingdom of Christ. He remained an outsider, albeit secretly.

The few glimpses of Judas that are shown to us from time to time in the Gospels suggest that he had long been growing progressively more disillusioned and embittered but kept it hidden from everyone. As early as John 6, during Jesus' Galilean ministry, Jesus referred to Judas as "a devil." Jesus knew what no one else knew: Judas was becoming disgruntled already. He was still unbelieving, unrepentant, and unregenerate; and he was growing more and more hardhearted all the time.

By the time Jesus and the apostles went to Jerusalem for the Passover in the last year of Jesus' earthly ministry, Judas's spiritual disenfranchisement was complete. At some point in those final few days, his disillusionment turned to hate, and hate mixed with greed finally turned to treachery. Judas probably convinced himself that Jesus had stolen his life—robbed him of three years of money-making potential. That sort of thinking ate away at him until finally he became the monster who betrayed Christ.

HIS AVARICE

Shortly after the raising of Lazarus, and just before Jesus' Triumphal Entry into Jerusalem, Jesus and the disciples returned to Bethany, on the outskirts of the city. This was the place where Lazarus had been raised and where he lived with his sisters, Mary and Martha. Jesus was invited to a meal at the home of one "Simon the Leper" (Matthew 26:6). His dear friend Lazarus was present with Mary and Martha, who were helping serve the meal. John 12:2–3 records what happened: "There they made Him a supper; and Martha served, but Lazarus was one of those who sat at the table with Him. Then Mary took a pound of very costly oil of spikenard, anointed the feet of Jesus, and wiped His feet with her hair. And the house was filled with the fragrance of the oil."

This act was shocking in its extravagance. Not only was it an overt act of worship, but it also had the appearance of wastefulness. Obviously perfume—especially such an expensive fragrance—is designed to be used in small amounts. Once poured out, it cannot be reused. To pour out a pound of expensive oil and use it to anoint someone's feet gave the appearance of gross excess.

"Then one of His disciples, Judas Iscariot, Simon's son, who would betray Him, said, 'Why was this fragrant oil not sold for three hundred denarii and given to the poor?'" (vv. 4–5). Three hundred denarii was a lot of money for perfume by any measure. Remember, a denarius was basically a working man's daily wage (Matthew 20:2). Three hundred denarii is a full year's wages (allowing for Sabbaths and holidays off). I have purchased costly perfume for my wife, but I would never think of spending a year's wages on one dose of perfume! This was an amazingly lavish act on the part of a family who must have had some means.

Judas's response was a clever ploy. He feigned concern for the poor. Apparently, his protest seemed reasonable to the other apostles, too, because Matthew 26:8 says they all echoed Judas's indignation. What an expert Judas had become in his hypocrisy! The apostle John, reflecting on this incident years later, wrote, "This he said, not that he cared for the poor, but because he was a thief, and had the money box; and he used to take what was put in it" (John 12:6). Of course, neither John nor any of the other apostles saw through Judas's deceit at the time, but in retrospect, and writing his book under the Holy Spirit's inspiration, John told us plainly what Judas's motive was: sheer greed.

Jesus responded to Judas in verses 7-8: "Let her alone; she has kept this for the day of My burial. For the poor you have with you always, but Me you do not have always." Given the circumstances, and since Jesus knew perfectly well what was in Judas's heart, this seems a rather mild rebuke. He could have blasted Judas with a fierce condemnation and exposed his real motives, but He did not.

Nonetheless, the gentle reprimand seems to have made Judas resent Jesus even more. He did not repent. He did not even examine his own heart. In fact, this incident seems to have been the turning point in his thinking. Three hundred denarii would have been a lot to add to the treasury, offering a prime opportunity for Judas to skim money for his own pocket. Because of Jesus' willingness to receive such lavish worship, Judas missed a prime opportunity to embezzle funds.

It appears to have been the last straw as far as Judas was concerned, because immediately after telling the story of Jesus' anointing, Matthew says, "Then one of the twelve, called Judas Iscariot, went to the chief priests and said, 'What are you willing to give me if I deliver

Him to you?' And they counted out to him thirty pieces of silver. So from that time he sought opportunity to betray Him" (Matthew 26:14–16). He crept away, left Bethany, walked about a mile and a half to Jerusalem, met with the chief priests, and sold Jesus to His enemies for a pocketful of coins. Thirty pieces of silver. That is all he could get. According to Exodus 21:32, it was the price of a slave. It was not much money. But it was all he could negotiate.

The contrast is staggering: Our Lord is anointed with over-whelming love by Mary and betrayed with overwhelming hate by Judas at the same time.

Notice that this is the first time Judas had ever exposed himself in any way. Up to that point, He had blended in perfectly with the rest of the group. This is the first time on record that he spoke out as an individual, and it is the first time he merited any kind of direct rebuke from Christ. Apparently, that is all that was needed to provoke his betrayal. He had kept his bitterness and disillusionment bottled up as long as he could. Now it spilled forth in secret treachery.

HIS HYPOCRISY

John 13:1 begins the apostle John's lengthy account of what happened in the Upper Room on the night of Jesus' arrest. Having already taken money to betray Christ, Judas came back, blended into the group, and pretended nothing unusual had happened. John says it was the devil who put it in the heart of Judas to betray Jesus (v. 2). That is no surprise. Again, Judas did what he did willingly, without any coercion. Satan could not *force* him to betray Jesus. But Satan through some means suggested the plot, tempted Judas to do this thing, and planted the very seed of treachery in his heart. Judas's heart was so hostile to the truth and so filled with evil that Judas became a willing instrument of Satan himself.

It was at this very point that Jesus gave the apostles a lesson in humility by washing their feet. He washed the feet of all twelve, which means He even washed the feet of Judas. Judas sat there and let

Jesus wash his feet and remained utterly unmoved. The world's worst sinner was also the world's best hypocrite.

Peter, on the other hand, was deeply moved by Jesus' act of humility. At first he was ashamed and refused to let Jesus wash his feet. But when Jesus said, "If I do not wash you, you have no part with Me," (v. 8), Peter replied, "Lord, not my feet only, but also my hands and my head!" (v. 9).

Jesus replied, "He who is bathed needs only to wash his feet, but is completely clean; and you are clean, *but not all of you*" (v. 10, emphasis added). A buzz must have gone around the room when He said that. There were only twelve of them, and Jesus was saying that someone in the group was not clean. John adds, "For He knew who would betray Him; therefore He said, 'You are not all clean' " (v. 11).

In verses 18–19, Jesus spoke even more directly: "I do not speak concerning all of you. I know whom I have chosen; but that the Scripture may be fulfilled, 'He who eats bread with Me has lifted up his heel against Me.' Now I tell you before it comes, that when it does come to pass, you may believe that I am He." Of course, He was saying Judas's act was the fulfillment of Psalm 41:9.

All of that seems to have gone over the heads of most of the apostles. So in verse 21, Jesus makes an even more explicit prediction about the impending act of betrayal: "When Jesus had said these things, He was troubled in spirit, and testified and said, 'Most assuredly, I say to you, one of you will betray Me.' " All the disciples except Judas were perplexed and deeply troubled by this. They apparently began to examine their own hearts, because Matthew 26:22 says, "They were exceedingly sorrowful, and each of them began to say to Him, 'Lord, is it I?' " Even Judas, ever careful to keep up the appearance of being like everyone else, asked, "Rabbi, is it I?" (v. 25). But in his case there had been no sincere self-examination. He asked the question only because he was worried about how the others perceived him; he already knew that he was the one of whom Jesus spoke.

The apostle John concludes his account of this incident:

Now there was leaning on Jesus' bosom one of His disciples, whom Jesus loved. Simon Peter therefore motioned to him to ask who it was of whom He spoke. Then, leaning back on Jesus' breast, he said to Him, "Lord, who is it?" Jesus answered, "It is he to whom I shall give a piece of bread when I have dipped it." And having dipped the bread, He gave it to Judas Iscariot, the son of Simon. Now after the piece of bread, Satan entered him. Then Jesus said to him, "What you do, do quickly." But no one at the table knew for what reason He said this to him. For some thought, because Judas had the money box, that Jesus had said to him, "Buy those things we need for the feast," or that he should give something to the poor. Having received the piece of bread, he then went out immediately. And it was night. (John 12:23–30)

The day of salvation closed for Judas. Divine mercy gave way to divine judgement. Judas was in essence handed over to Satan. Sin had triumphed in his heart. Satan moved in.

Notice, however, that even though Jesus had just spoken of the betrayer and had given Judas the morsel to identify him, it *still* did not compute in the minds of the apostles. No one seemed to anticipate that Judas would be the traitor. So expert was he in his hypocrisy that he fooled everyone but Jesus, right up to the very end.

Jesus sent him away. That is easy to understand. Jesus is pure, sinless, spotless, and holy. Here was this wretched, evil presence into whom Satan had literally entered. Jesus was not about to have the first communion service with the devil and Judas present in the room. *Get out.*

Only after Judas had left did our Lord institute the Lord's Supper. To this day, when we come to the Lord's Table, we are instructed to examine ourselves lest we come hypocritically to the table and bring judgment upon ourselves (1 Corinthians 11:27–32).

The apostle John says that throughout this entire episode, until Judas left the company of apostles, Jesus was deeply "troubled in spirit" (John 13:21). Of course He was troubled! This wicked, wretched, Satan-possessed presence was polluting the fellowship of the apostles. Judas's ingratitude, His rejection of Jesus' kindness, the hate Judas secretly harbored for Jesus, the repulsiveness of the presence of Satan, the heinousness of sin, the horrors of knowing that the gaping jaws of hell were awaiting one of His closest companions—all of that troubled and agitated Jesus. No wonder he sent Judas away.

HIS BETRAYAL

Judas apparently went straight from the Upper Room to the Sanhedrin. He reported to them that the final breach had been made, and he now knew where they could apprehend Jesus under cover of darkness. Judas had been secretly seeking a convenient opportunity to betray Jesus ever since making his bargain with the Sanhedrin (Mark 14:11). Now the time had come.

Remember, Judas did not act in a moment of insanity. This was not a sudden impulse. It was not an act borne only out of passion. This dark deed was deliberately planned and premeditated. He had been planning this for days, if not weeks or even months. He had already taken the money for it (Matthew 26:15). He had just been waiting for an opportune hour. Along the way, he had continued his campaign of embezzlement, kept up the hypocritical facade, and carried on with the rest of the apostles as if he were truly one of them. But now Jesus had spoken openly to the other disciples about Judas's plot to betray Him. Judas had nearly been unmasked in front of the others. It was time for him to act.

What had he been waiting for anyway? According to Luke 22:6, Judas had been seeking an opportunity "to betray [Jesus] to them *in the absence of the multitude*" (emphasis added). He was a coward. He knew the popularity of Jesus. He was afraid of the crowd. Like every hypocrite, he was obsessed with concerns about what people thought of him, so he was hoping to betray Jesus as quietly as possible. He was looking for the doorway to hell that was most convenient. And when he found it, he plunged right in.

So at the very moment when Jesus was instituting the Lord's

Supper in the Upper Room, Judas was making arrangements for His capture. He knew Jesus regularly went to Gethsemane to pray with His disciples. Luke 22:39 says it was Jesus' custom to go there. John 18:2 says Judas "knew the place; for Jesus often met there with His disciples." So Judas knew exactly where to bring the authorities to capture Jesus.

The next time we see Judas is in John 18, when his conspiracy of betrayal reaches its culmination. The evening was at its end. Jesus had gone from the Upper Room to His customary place of prayer in the little olive grove known as Gethsemane. There He poured out his heart to the Father in such agony that His sweat became as great drops of blood. He had left eight of the disciples some distance away and gone deep into the garden with Peter, James, and John (Mark 14:32–33).

"Then Judas, having received a detachment of troops, and officers from the chief priests and Pharisees, came there with lanterns, torches, and weapons" (John 18:3). The "detachment of troops" was most likely a Roman cohort from the Antonio Fortress, adjacent to the temple. A full cohort numbered about six hundred men. No exact figure is given, but all the Gospel writers say it was a great multitude (Matthew 26:47; Mark 14:43; Luke 22:47)—probably hundreds of soldiers. They obviously expected the worst. They came armed to the teeth.

"Jesus therefore, knowing all things that would come upon Him, went forward and said to them, 'Whom are you seeking?' " (John 18:4). He did not wait for Judas to single him out; He did not try to hide; He "went forward," presenting Himself to them, and said, "I am He" (v. 5).

Judas had a prearranged signal to identify Jesus: "Whomever I kiss, He is the One; seize Him" (Matthew 26:48). What a diabolical way to point out Jesus! But his wretchedness was so profound and his hypocrisy so malicious that he seemingly had no conscience. Furthermore, since Jesus stepped forward and identified Himself, the signal would have been unnecessary, but Judas—cynic and scoundrel that he had become—kissed Him anyway (Mark 14:45).

"Jesus said to him, 'Judas, are you betraying the Son of Man with a kiss?' " (Luke 22:48). Kissing is a mark of homage, love, affection, tenderness, respect, and intimacy. Judas's feigned feelings for Christ only made his deed that much darker. It was a devious hypocrisy, trying to keep up the veneer of respect even to the bitter end.

Jesus, ever gracious, even addressed him as "Friend" (Matthew 26:50). Jesus had never been anything but friendly to Judas, but Judas was no true friend of Jesus (cf. John 15:14). He was a betrayer and a deceiver. His kisses were the kisses of the worst kind of treachery.

Judas profaned the Passover that night. He profaned the Lamb of God. He profaned the Son of God. He profaned the place of prayer. He betrayed his Lord with a kiss.

HIS DEATH

Judas sold Jesus for a pittance. But as soon as the deal was complete, Judas's conscience immediately came alive. He found himself in a hell of his own making, hammered by his own mind for what he had done. The money, which had been so important to him before, now did not matter. Matthew 27:3–4 says, "Then Judas, His betrayer, seeing that He had been condemned, was remorseful and brought back the thirty pieces of silver to the chief priests and elders, saying, 'I have sinned by betraying innocent blood.'"

His remorse was not the same as repentance, as subsequent events clearly show. He was sorry, not because he had sinned against Christ, but because his sin did not satisfy him the way he had hoped.

The chief priests and elders were unsympathetic. "They said, 'What is that to us? You see to it!'" (v. 4). They had what they wanted. Judas could do what he liked with the money. Nothing would undo his treachery now.

Matthew says, "Then he threw down the pieces of silver in the temple and departed, and went and hanged himself" (v. 5). Judas was already in a hell of his own making. His conscience would not be silenced, and that is the very essence of hell. Sin brings guilt, and Judas's sin brought him unbearable misery. Again, his remorse was not genuine repentance. If that were the case, he would not have killed himself. He was merely sorry because he did not like what he felt.

Sadly, he did not seek the forgiveness of God. He did not cry out for mercy. He did not seek deliverance from Satan. Instead, he tried to silence his conscience by killing himself. This was the grief of a madman who had lost control.

Matthew concludes his account of Judas: "But the chief priests took the silver pieces and said, 'It is not lawful to put them into the treasury, because they are the price of blood.' And they consulted together and bought with them the potter's field, to bury strangers in. Therefore that field has been called the Field of Blood to this day" (Matthew 27:6–8).

Acts 1:18–19 adds a final note to the tragedy of Judas, with more detail about his death and the acquisition of the Field of Blood: "This man purchased a field with the wages of iniquity; and falling head-long, he burst open in the middle and all his entrails gushed out. And it became known to all those dwelling in Jerusalem; so that field is called in their own language, Akel Dama, that is, Field of Blood."

Some have imagined a contradiction between Matthew and Acts, but all apparent discrepancies are easily reconciled. Matthew indicates that the priests purchased the field with Judas's blood money. Thus it is true that Judas acquired the field "with the wages of iniquity." It was purchased *for* him by the chief priests, but the purchase was made with his money. The field became his possession. His heirs—if he had any—would inherit the field. So it is correct to say that "purchased a field with the wages of iniquity," even though the field was purchased *for* him, by proxy.

Why this particular field? Because it was the very place where Judas hanged himself. Apparently he chose a tree on an overhang above some jagged rocks. (There is a place that precisely fits that description in the field in Jerusalem where tradition says Judas hanged himself.) Either the rope or the tree branch broke, and Judas fell head-long onto the rocks. The biblical description is graphic and ugly: "He burst open in the middle and all his entrails gushed out" (Acts 18:1).

Judas was such a tragic figure that he couldn't even kill himself the way he wanted to. Nonetheless, he died.

This is virtually the last word in Scripture about Judas: "His entrails gushed out." His life and his death were grotesque tragedies. He was a child of hell and a son of perdition, and he went to his own place where he belonged. Jesus said these chilling words: "It would have been good for that man if he had never been born" (Mark 14:21).

THE MORAL OF HIS LIFE

We can draw some important lessons from the life of Judas. *First,* Judas is a tragic example of lost opportunity. He heard Jesus teach day in and day out for some two years. He could have asked Jesus any question he liked. He could have sought and received from the Lord any help he needed. He could have exchanged the oppressive burden of his sin for an easy yoke. Christ had given an open invitation for anyone to do so (Matthew 11:28–30). Yet in the end Judas was damned because of his own failure to heed what he heard.

Second, Judas is the epitome of wasted privilege. He was given the highest place of privilege among all the Lord's followers, but he squandered that privilege—cashed it in for a fistful of coins he decided he did not really want after all. What a stupid bargain!

Third, Judas is the classic illustration of how the love of money is a root of all kinds of evil (1 Timothy 6:10).

Fourth, Judas exemplifies the ugliness and danger of spiritual betrayal. Would that Judas were the only hypocrite who ever betrayed the Lord, but that is not so. There are Judases in every age—people who seem to be true disciples and close followers of Christ but who turn against Him for sinister and selfish reasons. Judas's life is a reminder to each of us about our need for self-examination (cf. 2 Corinthians 13:5).

Fifth, Judas is proof of the patient, forebearing goodness and loving-kindness of Christ. "The LORD is good to all, and His tender mercies are over all His works" (Psalm 145:9). He even shows His loving-kindness to a reprobate like Judas. Remember, Jesus was still calling him "Friend," even in the midst of Judas's betrayal. Jesus never showed Judas anything but kindness and charity, even though the Lord knew all along what Judas was planning to do. In no sense was Judas driven to do what he did by Christ.

Sixth, Judas demonstrates how the sovereign will of God cannot be thwarted by any means. His betrayal of Christ seemed at first glance like Satan's greatest triumph ever. But in reality, it signalled utter defeat for the devil and all his works (Hebrews 2:14; 1 John 3:8).

Seventh, Judas is a vivid demonstration of the deceitfulness and fruitlessness of hypocrisy. He is the branch spoken of in John 15:6 that does not abide in the True Vine. That branch bears no fruit, is cut off, and is thrown into the fire to be destroyed. Judas was so expert at his hypocrisy that none of the other eleven ever suspected him. But he could never fool Jesus. Nor can any hypocrite. And Christ is the righteous Judge who will render to every person his due (John 5:26–27). Hypocrites like Judas will have no one but themselves to blame for the destruction of their souls.

When Judas bartered away the life of Christ, he was in effect selling his own soul to the devil. The tragedy of his life was a tragedy of his own making. He ignored the light he had been exposed to for all those years, and thus he relegated himself to eternal darkness.

After Jesus' resurrection, Judas's office was filled by Matthias (Acts 1:16–26). The apostle Peter said, "For it is written in the Book of Psalms: 'Let his dwelling place be desolate, and let no one live in it'; and, 'Let another take his office'" (v. 20). Matthias was selected because he had been with Jesus and the other apostles "from the baptism of John to that day when He was taken up from us" (v. 22).

Nothing is known of Matthias other than that. His name appears only twice in Scripture, both times in Acts 1, the account of how he was chosen. Thus in the end, another perfectly ordinary man was chosen to fill the place of that extraordinary villain. And so along with the other eleven, Matthias became a powerful witness of Jesus' resurrection (v. 22)—one more ordinary man whom the Lord elevated to an extraordinary calling.

NOTES

INTRODUCTION

1. Alexander Balman Bruce, *The Training of the Twelve* (New York: Doubleday, 1928), 29–30.

CHAPTER 2

1. John C. Maxwell, *The 21 Irrefutable Laws of Leadership* (Nashville: Thomas Nelson, 1998), 71.
2. The King James and New King James Versions seem to suggest that this event occurred after the meal—"supper being ended . . ." Other versions say it occurred "during supper . . ." (NASB) or while "the evening meal was being served" (NIV). The Greek word translated "ended" in the KJV is *ginomai,* a verb with a broad range of meanings, including "to be assembled, to be brought to pass, to be finished." The context makes it clear that it was the preparation of the meal, and not the eating of it, that was "finished" when Jesus arose to wash feet. Obviously, it was after this that Jesus dipped the sop and handed it to Judas (v. 26). So the foot-washing obviously occurred (as protocol demanded) before the meal, not afterward.
3. Eusebius, *Ecclesiastical History,* 3:1, 30.

NOTES

CHAPTER 3

1. John C. Pollock, *Moody: A Biographical Portrait of the Pacesetter in Modern Evangelism* (New York: Macmillan, 1963), 13.
2. Richard Ellsworth Day, *Bush Aglow: The Life Story of Dwight Lyman Moody* (Philadelphia: Judson, 1936), 65.

CHAPTER 4

1. Eusebius, *Ecclesiastical Church History* 2.9.2–3.

CHAPTER 9

1. Josephus, *Antiquities* 18.6.
2. Josephus, *Wars of the Jews* 4.3.9.
3. Eusebius, *Ecclesiastical History* 1.13.5.

CHAPTER 10

1. Charles H. Spurgeon, "A Defense of Calvinism" in Susannah Spurgeon and Joseph Harrald, eds., *The Autobiography of Charles H. Spurgeon,* 4 vols. (Philadelphia: American Baptist Publication Society, 1895), 1:177.

Twelve Extraordinary Women

HOW GOD SHAPED WOMEN *of the* BIBLE,
and WHAT HE WANTS *to* DO *with* YOU

DEDICATION

To all the little girls in my life, my granddaughters, who are on the way to becoming, by God's grace, extraordinary women:

Kathryn

Olivia

Kylee

Jessica

Susannah

Gracie

Brooke

Elizabeth

Audrey

ACKNOWLEDGMENTS

I am grateful for and indebted to Phil Johnson, who has again, as so often before, applied his remarkable editorial skills to my material. For this book, he has done far more than that, by adding his own rich insights to those chapters where my meager material was inadequate.

And very special thanks goes to my extraordinary Patricia, who has faithfully supported this ordinary man through forty-two years of marriage.

CONTENTS

PREFACE

I never anticipated that my book on the apostles *(Twelve Ordinary Men)* would be as well received by readers as it was. People seemed to appreciate and enjoy the character-study format, even though it is a slight departure from my normal expository style. The book's method and arrangement seemed particularly well suited to small-group studies, and that might have helped fuel a still wider interest. Perhaps even more significant was the intensely practical and personal relevance of such character studies. It helps, I think, to see the apostles as they were: *ordinary* men. That was, after all, the whole point of the book. These were men anyone can relate to. Most of us can easily see aspects of our own character in their personalities, their shortcomings, their struggles, their frequent blunders, and their longing to be everything Christ wanted them to be. It gives us great hope to see how wonderfully God used people such as these.

After *Twelve Ordinary Men* had been on the bestseller lists for more than a year, my friends at Thomas Nelson suggested a sequel. Why not deal in a similar format with the lives of twelve of the principal women of Scripture? Everyone who heard the idea was immediately enthusiastic about it. Thus the volume you hold in your hands was born.

Of course, there were no decisions to be made about whom to feature in the first book. *Jesus* chose His twelve disciples; all I had to do was research their lives and write about them. This new book would be a different matter. Faced with a plethora of extraordinary women in the Bible, I made a long list of possibilities. The task of narrowing the roll to twelve was by no means easy. I weighed their relative importance in biblical history and chose twelve women who were critical to the story of redemption.

I hope you'll agree that my final short-list includes a good variety of personality types and an interesting assortment of truly extraordinary women. My hope is that, as with the first book, readers will see aspects of themselves in these studies and be encouraged by the reminder that our personal struggles and temptations are the very same kinds of trials that all believers in all ages have confronted. Thus we are reminded that even in the midst of our trouble, God remains eternally faithful (1 Cor. 10:13). The God of Abraham, Isaac, and Jacob is the God of Sarah, Rebekah, and Rachel too. He is also the God of every believer in *our* generation—men and women alike. We, like all of them, have our shortcomings. But we are His people and the sheep of His pasture (Ps. 100:3). And His faithfulness *still* reaches to the clouds (Ps. 36:5).

Some have already asked me the significance of the delicate shift in titles. If the disciples were "ordinary," how is it that these twelve women are *extra*ordinary?

The answer, of course, is that while the disciples were ordinary in one sense, they were also *extraordinary* in another sense. As far as their innate talents and their human backgrounds are concerned, they were genuinely ordinary, and deliberately so. "God has chosen the foolish things of the world to put to shame the wise, and God has chosen the weak things of the world to put to shame the things which are mighty; and the base things of the world and the things which are despised God has chosen, and the things which are not, to bring to nothing the things that are, that no flesh should glory in His presence" (1 Cor. 1:27–29 NKJV). It was only Christ's work in the disciples' lives that gave them such remarkable power and influence, so that what they became was something quite uncommon—and what they accomplished (Acts 17:6) was something truly extraordinary.

The same thing is true with the women featured in this book. Most of them were unremarkable in and of themselves. They were ordinary, common, and in some cases shockingly low-caste women—in exactly the same way the disciples were common men. Take the Samaritan woman of John 4, for instance. We don't even know her name. Likewise, Anna was an obscure, elderly widow who appears in only one brief vignette in the opening of Luke (2:36–38). Rahab was a common harlot. Even Mary, the mother of Christ, was a young girl of no particular distinction, living in an obscure town in a barren and despised district of Galilee. In each instance, what made them extraordinary was a memorable, life-changing encounter with the God of the universe.

The only real exception is Eve, who *began* life as someone quite extraordinary in every way. She was created by God to be the pure and pristine ideal of womanhood. But she soon spoiled it by sinning. Still, she, too, became a living depiction of the truth that God can recover and redeem those who fall—and make them truly extraordinary trophies of His grace in spite of their failures. In fact, I'm convinced that by God's redeeming grace, the person Eve will be through all eternity is far *more* glorious than she was in her original earthly innocence.

In other words, all these women ultimately became extraordinary not because of any natural qualities of their own, but because the one true God whom they worshiped is great, mighty, glorious, and awesome, and *He* refined them like silver. He redeemed them through the work of an extraordinary Savior—His own divine Son—and conformed them to His image (Rom. 8:29). In other words, the gracious work of God in their lives made each one of these women truly extraordinary.

They therefore stand as reminders of both our fallenness and our potential. Speaking together as one, they all point us to Christ. In every case, He was the One to whom they looked for salvation. We'll see, for example, how Eve, Sarah, Rahab, and Ruth were all in the line of descent that would produce the Promised One who would crush the serpent's head. Hannah likewise longed for a Savior and rejoiced in the promise of salvation. In fact, Hannah's words of praise about the Savior (1 Sam. 2:1–10) are echoed in Mary's Magnificat. That, of course, was Mary's outpouring of praise when she first learned that she would finally be the one—blessed by God above all other women—to give birth to the Savior. Anna, who had hoped for the Savior all her life, was blessed in her old age to be one of the very first to recognize Him in His infancy (Luke 2:36–38). All the other women featured in this book became some of His earliest disciples. Every one of them therefore testifies to us about Christ.

My prayer for you is that as you read this book you will share their faith, imitate their faithfulness, and learn to love the Savior whose work in their lives made them truly extraordinary. Your life can be extraordinary, too, by His wonderful grace.

INTRODUCTION

One of the unique features of the Bible is the way it exalts women. Far from ever demeaning or belittling women, Scripture often seems to go out of the way to pay homage to them, to ennoble their roles in society and family, to acknowledge the importance of their influence, and to exalt the virtues of women who were particularly godly examples.

From the very first chapter of the Bible, we are taught that women, like men, bear the stamp of God's own image (Gen. 1:27; 5:1–2). Women play prominent roles in many key biblical narratives. Wives are seen as venerated partners and cherished companions to their husbands, not merely slaves or pieces of household furniture (Gen. 2:20–24; Prov. 19:14; Eccl. 9:9). At Sinai, God commanded children to honor *both* father and mother (Ex. 20:12). That was a revolutionary concept in an era when most pagan cultures were dominated by men who ruled their households with an iron fist while women were usually regarded as lesser creatures—mere servants to men.

Of course, the Bible recognizes divinely ordained role distinctions between men and women—many of which are perfectly evident from the circumstances of creation alone. For example, women have a unique and vital role in childbearing and nurturing little ones. Women themselves also have a particular need for support and protection, because physically, they are "weaker vessels" (1 Peter 3:7 NKJV). Scripture establishes the proper order in the family and in the church accordingly, assigning the duties of headship and protection in the home to husbands (Eph. 5:23) and appointing men in the church to the teaching and leadership roles (1 Tim. 2:11–15).

Yet women are by no means marginalized or relegated to any second-class status (Gal. 3:28). On the contrary, Scripture seems to set women apart for special honor (1 Peter 3:7). Husbands are commanded to love their wives sacrificially, as Christ loves the church—even, if necessary, at the cost of their own lives (Eph. 5:25–31). The Bible acknowledges and celebrates the priceless value of a virtuous woman (Prov. 12:4; 31:10; 1 Cor. 11:7). In other words, from cover to cover, the Bible portrays women as *extraordinary.*

The biblical accounts of the patriarchs always give due distinction to their wives. Sarah, Rebekah, and Rachel all loom large in the Genesis account of God's dealings with their husbands. Miriam, sister of Moses and Aaron, was both a prophetess and a songwriter—and in Micah 6:4, God Himself honors her alongside her brothers as one of the nation's leaders during the Exodus. Deborah, also a prophetess, was a judge in Israel prior to the monarchy (Judg. 4:4). Scriptural accounts of family life often put wives in the position of wise counselors to their husbands (Judg. 13:23; 2 Kings 4:8–10). When Solomon became king, he publicly paid homage to his mother, standing when she entered his presence, then bowing to her before he sat on his throne (1 Kings 2:19). Sarah and Rahab are expressly named among the heroes of faith in Hebrews 11. Moses' mother (Jochebed) is included as well by implication (v. 23). In Proverbs, wisdom is personified as a woman. The New Testament church is likewise represented as a woman, the bride of Christ.

In the social and religious life of Israel and the New Testament church, women were never relegated to the background. They partook with men in all the feasts and public worship of Israel (Deut. 16:14; Neh. 8:2–3). Women were not required to be veiled or silent in the public square, as they are in some Middle Eastern cultures even today (Gen. 12:14; 24:16; 1 Sam. 1:12). Mothers (not merely fathers) shared teaching responsibilities and authority over their children (Prov. 1:8; 6:20). Women could even be landowners in Israel (Num. 27:8; Prov. 31:16). In fact, wives were expected to administer many of the affairs of their own households (Prov. 14:1; 1 Tim. 5:9–10, 14).

All of that stands in sharp contrast to the way other ancient cultures routinely degraded and debased women. Women in pagan societies during biblical times were often treated with little more dignity than animals. Some of the best-known Greek philosophers—considered the brightest minds of their era—taught that women are inferior creatures by nature. Even in the Roman Empire (perhaps the very pinnacle of pre-Christian civilization) women were usually regarded as mere chattel—personal possessions of their husbands or fathers, with hardly any better standing than household slaves. That, once again, was vastly different from the Hebrew (and biblical) concepts of marriage as a joint inheritance, and parenthood as a partnership where *both* father and mother are to be revered and obeyed by the children (Lev. 19:3).

Pagan *religion* tended to fuel and encourage the devaluation of women even more. Of course, Greek and Roman mythology had its goddesses (such as Diana and Aphrodite). But don't imagine for a moment that goddess-worship in any way raised the status of women in society. The opposite was true. Most temples devoted to goddesses were served by sacred prostitutes—priestesses who sold themselves for money, supposing they were performing a religious sacrament. Both the mythology and the practice of pagan religion has usually been overtly demeaning to women. Male pagan deities were capricious and sometimes wantonly misogynistic. Religious ceremonies were often blatantly obscene— including such things as erotic fertility rites, drunken temple orgies, perverted homosexual practices, and, in the very worst cases, even human sacrifices.

Christianity, born in a world where Roman and Hebrew cultures intersected, elevated the status of women to an unprecedented height. Jesus' disciples included several women (Luke 8:1–3), a practice almost unheard of among the rabbis of His day. Not only that, He *encouraged* their discipleship by portraying it as something more needful than domestic service (Luke 10:38–42). In fact, Christ's first recorded explicit disclosure of His own identity as the true Messiah was made to a Samaritan woman (John 4:25–26). He always treated women with the utmost dignity—even women who might otherwise be regarded as outcasts (Matt. 9:20–22; Luke 7:37–50; John 4:7–27). He blessed their children (Luke 18:15–16), raised their dead (Luke 7:12–15), forgave their sins (Luke 7:44–48), and restored their virtue and honor (John 8:4–11). Thus he exalted the position of womanhood itself.

It is no surprise, therefore, that women became prominent in the ministry of the early church (Acts 12:12–15; 1 Cor. 11:11–15). On the day of Pentecost, when the New Testament church was born, women were there with the chief disciples, praying (Acts 1:12–14). Some were renowned for their good deeds (Acts 9:36); others for their hospitality (Acts 12:12; 16:14–15); still others for their understanding of sound doctrine and their spiritual giftedness (Acts 18:26; 21:8–9). John's second epistle was addressed to a prominent woman in one of the churches under his oversight. Even the apostle Paul, sometimes falsely caricatured by critics of Scripture as a male chauvinist, regularly ministered alongside women (Phil. 4:3). He recognized and applauded their faithfulness and their giftedness (Rom. 16:1–6; 2 Tim. 1:5).

INTRODUCTION

Naturally, as Christianity began to influence Western society, the status of women was dramatically improved. One of the early church fathers, Tertullian, wrote a work titled *On the Apparel of Women* sometime near the end of the second century. He said pagan women who wore elaborate hair ornaments, immodest clothing, and body decorations had actually been forced by society and fashion to abandon the superior splendor of true femininity. He noted, by way of contrast, that as the church had grown and the gospel had borne fruit, one of the visible results was the rise of a trend toward modesty in women's dress and a corresponding elevation of the status of women. He acknowledged that pagan men commonly complained, "Ever since she became a Christian, she walks in poorer garb!"[1] Christian women even became known as "modesty's priestesses."[2] But, Tertullian said, as believers who lived under the lordship of Christ, women were spiritually wealthier, more pure, and thus more glorious than the most extravagant women in pagan society. Clothed "with the silk of uprightness, the fine linen of holiness, the purple of modesty,"[3] they elevated feminine virtue to an unprecedented height.

Even the pagans recognized that. Chrysostom, perhaps the most eloquent preacher of the fourth century, recorded that one of his teachers, a pagan philosopher named Libanius, once said: "Heavens! what women you Christians have!"[4] What prompted Libanius's outburst was hearing how Chrysostom's mother had remained chaste for more than two decades since becoming a widow at age twenty. As the influence of Christianity was felt more and more, women were less and less vilified or mistreated as objects for the amusement of men. Instead, women began to be honored for their virtue and faith.

In fact, Christian women converted out of pagan society were automatically freed from a host of demeaning practices. Emancipated from the public debauchery of temples and theaters (where women were systematically dishonored and devalued), they rose to prominence in home and church, where they were honored and admired for feminine virtues like hospitality, ministry to the sick, the care and nurture of their own families, and the loving labor of their hands (Acts 9:39).

After the Roman emperor Constantine was converted in 312 AD, Christianity was granted legal status in Rome and soon became the dominant religion throughout the Empire. One of the measurable early results of this change was a whole new legal status for women. Rome passed laws recognizing the property rights of women. Legislation governing marriage was revised, so that marriage was legally seen as a partnership, rather than a virtual state of servitude for the wife. In the pre-Christian era, Roman men had power to divorce their wives for virtually any cause, or even for no cause at all. New laws made divorce more difficult, while giving women legal rights against husbands who were guilty of infidelity. Philandering husbands, once an accepted part of Roman society, could no longer sin against their wives with impunity.

This has always been the trend. Wherever the gospel has spread, the social, legal, and spiritual status of women has, as a rule, been elevated. When the gospel has been eclipsed (whether by repression, false religion, secularism, humanistic philosophy, or spiritual decay within the church), the status of women has declined accordingly.

Even when secular movements have arisen claiming to be concerned with women's rights, their efforts have generally been detrimental to the status of women. The feminist movement of our generation, for example, is a case in point. Feminism has devalued and defamed *femininity*. Natural gender distinctions are usually downplayed, dismissed, despised, or denied. As a result, women are now being sent into combat situations, subjected to grueling physical labor once reserved for men, exposed to all kinds of indignities in the workplace, and otherwise encouraged to act and talk like men. Meanwhile, modern feminists heap scorn on women who want family and household to be their first priorities—disparaging the role of motherhood, the one calling that is most uniquely and exclusively feminine. The whole message of feminist egalitarianism is that there is really nothing extraordinary about women.

That is certainly not the message of Scripture. As we have seen, Scripture honors women *as women,* and it encourages them to seek honor in a uniquely feminine way (Prov. 31:10–30).

Scripture never discounts the female intellect, downplays the talents and abilities of women, or discourages the right use of women's spiritual gifts. But whenever the Bible expressly talks about the marks of an excellent woman, the stress is always on feminine *virtue.* The most significant women in Scripture were influential not because of their careers, but because of their *character.* The message these women collectively give is not about "gender equality"; it's about true feminine excellence. And this is always exemplified in moral and spiritual qualities rather than by social standing, wealth, or physical appearance.

According to the apostle Peter, for instance, true feminine beauty is not about external adornment, "arranging the hair, wearing gold, or putting on fine apparel"; *real* beauty is seen instead in "the hidden person of the heart . . . the incorruptible beauty of a gentle and quiet spirit, which is very precious in the sight of God" (1 Peter 3:3–4 NKJV). Paul, likewise, said godliness and good works are the real essence of feminine beauty; not artificial embellishments applied to the outside (1 Tim. 2:9–10). That truth is exemplified to one degree or another by every woman featured in this book.

The *faithfulness* of these women is their true, lasting legacy. I hope as you meet them in Scripture and get to know more about their lives and characters, they will challenge you, motivate you, encourage you, and inspire you with love for the God whom they trusted and served. May your heart be set ablaze with the very same faith, may your life be characterized by a similar faithfulness, and may your soul be overwhelmed with love for the extraordinary God they worshiped.

1

Eve: Mother of All Living

Adam called his wife's name Eve, because she was the mother of all living.

—Genesis 3:20 NKJV

Eve must have been a creature of unsurpassed beauty. She was the crown and the pinnacle of God's amazing creative work. The first female of Adam's race was the last living thing to be called into existence—actually fashioned directly by the Creator's own hand in a way that showed particular care and attention to detail. Remember, Eve wasn't made out of dust like Adam, but carefully designed from living flesh and bone. Adam was refined dirt; Eve was a glorious refinement of humanity itself. She was a special gift to Adam. She was the necessary partner who finally made his existence complete—and whose own existence finally signaled the completion of all creation.

Eve, the *only* being ever directly created by God from the living tissue of another creature, was indeed a singular marvel. God had composed a vast universe of wonders out of nothing. Then He made Adam from a handful of dust. But nothing in the whole expanse of the universe was more wonderful than this woman made from a handful of Adam. If the man represented the supreme species (a race of creatures made in the image of God), Eve was the living embodiment of humanity's glory (1 Cor. 11:7). God had truly saved the best for last. Nothing else would have sufficed quite so perfectly to be the finishing touch and the very zenith of all creation.

In her original state, undefiled by any evil, unblemished by any disease or defect, unspoiled by any imperfection at all, Eve was the flawless archetype of feminine excellence. She was magnificent in every way. Since no other woman has ever come unfallen into a curse-free world, no other woman could possibly surpass Eve's grace, charm, virtue, ingenuity, intelligence, wit, and pure innocence. Physically, too, she must have personified all the best traits of both strength and beauty. There is no doubt that she was a living picture of sheer radiance.

Scripture, however, gives us no physical description of Eve. Her beauty—splendid as it *must* have been—is never mentioned or even alluded to. The focus of the biblical account is on Eve's duty to her Creator and her role alongside her husband. That is a significant fact, reminding us that the chief distinguishing traits of true feminine excellence are nothing superficial. Women who are obsessed with image, cosmetics, body shapes, and other external matters have a distorted view of femininity. Indeed, Western culture as a whole (including a large segment of the visible church) seems hopelessly confused about these very issues. We need to go back to Scripture to see what God's ideal for a woman really is. And the biblical account of Eve is an excellent reminder of what a woman's true priorities ought to be.

As "the mother of all living," Eve is obviously a major character in the story of humanity's fall and redemption. Yet in all of Scripture, her *name* is used only four times—twice in the Old Testament (Gen. 3:20; 4:1), and twice in the New Testament (2 Cor. 11:3; 1 Tim. 2:13). Not only is no physical description of her given; we don't even know such details as how many children she had, how long she lived, or where and how she died (Gen. 5:3–5). The way Scripture tells her story, almost in abbreviated fashion, helps us focus more clearly on the aspects of her life that have the most significance.

Although Scripture is silent about many things we might like to know about Eve, we are given detailed accounts of her creation, her temptation and fall, the curse that was placed on her, and the subsequent hope that she clung to. Naturally, that's where we'll focus our study of this truly extraordinary woman.

HER CREATION

The biblical account of Eve's remarkable creation is given in Genesis 2:20–25:

> *So Adam gave names to all cattle, to the birds of the air, and to every beast of the field. But for Adam there was not found a helper comparable to him. And the LORD God caused a deep sleep to fall on Adam, and he slept; and He took one of his ribs, and closed up the flesh in its place. Then the rib which the LORD God had taken from man He made into a woman, and He brought her to the man. And Adam said: "This is now bone of my bones and flesh of my flesh; she shall be called Woman, because she was taken out of Man." Therefore a man shall leave his father and mother and be joined to his wife, and they shall become one flesh. And they were both naked, the man and his wife, and were not ashamed.* (NKJV)

In other words, God performed a surgical procedure on Adam. Scripture describes the operation with a surprising measure of detail. Adam was anesthetized—not by any artificial means, but God simply caused him to fall into a deep sleep. In such a slumber (especially in a world that was still a perfect paradise), Adam would feel no pain, of course. But, more significantly, the pure, passive restfulness of Adam's sleep makes an ideal illustration of how God's grace is *always* received. Grace is never set in motion by any effort or activity or volunteerism on our part, but it always flows freely from the sovereign will of God. Notice there's nothing to indicate that Adam *asked* God for a wife. Adam certainly wasn't given any conditions to fulfill as a prerequisite to receiving God's kindness. God Himself instigated this whole event and single-handedly brought it to pass—as an expression of sheer grace and benevolence to Adam. Adam was instrumental only in that he contributed a rib, but even that was done while he was asleep. The work was wholly and completely God's.

Adam's side was opened, a rib was carefully removed, and the incision was closed again. With such an infinitely skilled surgeon, and in the paradise of Eden prior to the curse, there was no danger of infection, none of the discomfort of postoperative pain, and (in all likelihood) not even a scar. God took a redundant bone that Adam would never miss and made for him the one thing he lacked: a soul mate. Adam lost a rib, but he gained a loving companion, created especially for him by the Giver of every good and perfect gift (James 1:17).

The Hebrew expression describing how God "made [the rib] into a woman" denotes careful construction and design. Literally, it means God *built* a woman. He carefully assembled a whole new creature with just the right set of attributes to make her the ideal mate for Adam.

Specially created by God for Adam from his own flesh and bone, Eve suited Adam perfectly in every way. She is a wonderful illustration of the goodness of God's grace and the perfect wisdom of His will. Again, God made her while Adam was asleep, without any tips or suggestions from him. Yet she perfectly met every need Adam had, satisfied every longing he may ever have felt, and delighted every faculty of his senses. She answered his need for companionship; she was a source of joy and gladness to him; and she made possible the procreation of the human race. She complemented Adam perfectly, and she enhanced everything about his existence. Eden was now truly a paradise.

When Adam awoke and found Eve, he must have been overjoyed!

The moment he saw her, he loved her. His first words upon meeting her express a profound sense of wonder, genuine delight, and abiding satisfaction: "This is now bone of my bones and flesh of my flesh." Clearly, he already felt a deep, personal attachment to Eve. She was a priceless treasure to be cherished, a worthy partner to encourage him, and a pleasing spouse who would love him in return. Instantly, he adored her and embraced her as his own.

The unique method of Eve's creation is deliberately emphasized, I think, in order to remind us of several crucial truths about womanhood in general.

First, it speaks of Eve's fundamental equality with Adam. The woman was "taken out of man." They shared the same essential nature. She was not a different kind of creature; she was of exactly the same essence as Adam. She was in no way an inferior character made merely to serve him, but she was his spiritual counterpart, his intellectual coequal, and in every sense his perfect mate and companion.

Second, the way Eve was created reminds us of the essential unity that is the ideal in every marriage relationship. Jesus referred to Eve's creation in Matthew 19:4–6 to prove that God's plan for marriage was established at the very beginning of human history and was based on the principles of monogamy, solidarity, and inviolability. "Have you not read that He who made them at the beginning 'made them male and female,' and said, 'For this reason a man shall leave his father and mother and be joined to his wife, and the two shall become one flesh'? So then, they are no longer two but one flesh. Therefore what God has joined together, let not man separate" (NKJV). So the one-flesh principle is perfectly illustrated in the method of Eve's creation. As a matter of fact, this is where that principle finds its true origin.

Third, the circumstances of Eve's creation illustrate how deep and meaningful the marriage of husband and wife is designed to be. It is not *merely* a physical union, but a union of heart and soul as well. Eve was

Adam's complement in every sense, designed by God to be the ideal soul-companion for him. And the intimacy of her relationship with her husband derives from her being literally taken from his side. In his classic commentary on the Bible, Puritan author Matthew Henry wrote these familiar words, which have been adapted and quoted in many marriage ceremonies: "The woman was *made of a rib out of the side of Adam;* not made out of his head to rule over him, nor out of his feet to be trampled upon by him, but out of his side to be equal with him, under his arm to be protected, and near his heart to be beloved."

The symbolism Matthew Henry saw in Adam's rib accords well with what Scripture teaches about the proper relationship between husbands and wives. It reminds us, again, of how Scripture exalts women.

Fourth, Eve's creation contains some important biblical lessons about the divinely-designed role of women. Although Eve was spiritually and intellectually Adam's peer; although they were both of one essence and therefore equals in their standing before God and in their rank above the other creatures; there was nonetheless a clear distinction in their earthly roles. And this was by God's own deliberate creative design. In the words of the apostle Paul, "Man is not from woman, but woman from man. Nor was man created for the woman, but woman for the man" (1 Cor. 11:8–9 NKJV). Adam was created first; then Eve was made to fill a void in his existence. Adam was the head; Eve was his helper. Adam was designed to be a father, provider, protector, and leader. Eve was designed to be a mother, comforter, nurturer, and helper.

That God has ordained these different functions for men and women is clearly evident from nature alone (1 Cor. 11:14). Men and women do not possess equal physical strength. They are bodily and hormonally different (in a number of rather obvious ways). A mountain of empirical and clinical evidence strongly suggests that men and women are also dissimilar in several other important ways—including socially, emotionally, and psychologically.

To acknowledge that there are such fundamental differences between the genders, and that men and women were designed for different roles, may not correspond with modern feminist sensibilities, but this is, after all, what God's own Word says. God created men and women differently with a purpose, and His plan for them reflects their differences. Scripture is clear in teaching that wives should be subject to the authority of their husbands in marriage (Eph. 5:22–24; Col. 3:18; 1 Peter 3:1–6) and that women are to be under the authority and instruction of men in the church (1 Cor. 11:3–7; 14:34–35).

First Timothy 2:11–15 is a key passage on this issue, because that is where the apostle Paul defends the principle of male headship in the church. The *first* reason Paul gives for this arrangement stems from creation, not from the fall: "Adam was formed first, then Eve" (1 Tim. 2:13 NKJV). So the principle of male headship was designed into creation. It was not (as some have suggested) a consequence of Adam's sin and therefore something to be regarded as a fruit of evil. And when Scripture assigns men the role of headship in the church and in marriage, it reflects *God's blueprint as Creator.* I'm convinced that if people today would simply embrace God's purpose and seek to fulfill the roles God has designed for our respective genders, both men and women would be happier, the church would be healthier, and marriages would be stronger.

Adam was the representative head and archetype for the whole human race. But remember, although Eve was given a subordinate role, she remained Adam's spiritual and intellectual equal. She was his "helper," neither his supervisor nor his slave. By calling her Adam's "helper," Scripture stresses the mutuality and the complementary nature of the partnership. Eve was in no way inferior to her husband, but she was nonetheless given a role that was subordinate to his leadership.

Subordinate, yet equal? Yes. The relationships within the Trinity illustrate perfectly how headship and submission can function within a relationship of absolute equals. Christ is in no sense inferior to the Father. "In Him dwells all the fullness of the Godhead bodily" (Col. 2:9 NKJV). He has eternally existed "in the form of God . . . [and] equal with God" (Phil. 2:6 NKJV). "I and My Father are one," He testified (John 10:30 NKJV). The apostle John made it as clear as possible: From eternity past, Jesus was with God and was Himself God (John 1:1–2). Three divine Persons (Father, Son, and Holy Spirit) constitute the one true God of Scripture. All three are fully God and are fully equal. *Yet the Son is subordinate to the Father.* Jesus said, "I do not seek My own will but the will of the Father who sent Me" (John 5:30 NKJV). "I always do those things that please Him" (John 8:29 NKJV).

The apostle Paul drew a clear parallel between Jesus' willing submission to his Father and a wife's willing submission to her husband: "I want you to know that the head of every man is Christ, the head of woman is man, and the head of Christ is God" (1 Cor. 11:3 NKJV). So if you wonder how two persons who are truly equal can have a relationship where one is head and the other submits, you need look no further than the doctrine of the Trinity. God Himself is the pattern for such a relationship.

Eve's creation establishes a similar paradigm for the human race. Here is the sum of it: Men and women, though equal in essence, were designed for different roles. Women are in no sense intellectually or spiritually inferior to men, but they were quite clearly created for a distinctive purpose. In the economy of church and family, the Bible says women should be subordinate to the authority of men. Yet Scripture also recognizes that in a completely different sense, women are exalted *above* men—because they are the living and breathing manifestation of the glory of a race made in God's image (1 Cor. 11:7).

That was precisely Eve's position after creation and before the fall. She was under her husband's headship, yet she was in many ways an even more glorious creature than he, treasured and extolled by him. They were partners and companions, fellow-laborers in the garden. God dealt with Adam as head of the human race, and Eve was accountable to her husband. Far from consigning Eve to menial servitude or a state of domestic enslavement, this arrangement utterly liberated her.

This was true paradise, and Adam and Eve constituted a perfect microcosm of the human race as God designed it to be.

But then it was all ruined by sin. Tragically, Eve was the unwitting portal through which the tempter gained access to assault Adam.

HER TEMPTATION

Genesis 2 ends with a succinct description of the innocence of Eden's paradise: "They were both naked, the man and his wife, and were not ashamed" (v. 25 NKJV).

Genesis 3 then introduces the tempter, a serpent. This is clearly Satan, who has somehow manifested himself in the form of a reptile, though Scripture doesn't formally identify this creature as Satan until the final book of Revelation (Rev. 12:9; 20:2).

Satan was an angel who fell into sin. Isaiah 14:12–15 and Ezekiel 28:12–19 make reference to the demise of a magnificent angelic creature who is described as the highest and most glorious of all created beings. This can only be Satan. We're not told in Scripture precisely when Satan's fall occurred or what circumstances led to it. But it must have been sometime during the events described in Genesis 2, because at the end of Genesis 1, all creation—including everything in the visible universe as well as the spirit world—was complete, pristine, and unblemished. "God saw *everything* that He had made, and *indeed it was very good*"(Gen. 1:31 NKJV, emphasis added). But then in Genesis 3:1, we meet the serpent.

The chronology of the account seems to suggest that a very short time elapsed between the end of creation and the fall of Satan. A similarly short time appears to have elapsed between Satan's fall and Eve's temptation. It might have been only a few days—or perhaps even only a matter of hours. But it could not have been very long. Adam and Eve had not yet even conceived any children.

In fact, that is undoubtedly one of the main reasons the tempter wasted no time deceiving Eve and provoking her husband to sin. He wanted to strike at the head of the human race before the race had any opportunity to multiply. If he could beguile Eve and thereby cause Adam to fall at this moment, he could sabotage all of humanity in one deadly act of treason against God.

Here is the biblical account in full from Genesis 3:1–7:

> *Now the serpent was more cunning than any beast of the field which the LORD God had made. And he said to the woman, "Has God indeed said, 'You shall not eat of every tree of the garden'?"*
>
> *And the woman said to the serpent, "We may eat the fruit of the trees of the garden; but of the fruit of the tree which is in the midst of the garden, God has said, 'You shall not eat it, nor shall you touch it, lest you die.'"*
>
> *Then the serpent said to the woman, "You will not surely die. For God knows that in the day you eat of it your eyes will be opened, and you will be like God, knowing good and evil."*
>
> *So when the woman saw that the tree was good for food, that it was pleasant to the eyes, and a tree desirable to make one wise, she took of its fruit and ate. She also gave to her husband with her, and he ate. Then the eyes of both of them were opened, and they knew that they were naked; and they sewed fig leaves together and made themselves coverings.* (NKJV)

Satan came to Eve in disguise. That epitomizes the subtle way he intended to deceive her. He appears to have singled her out for this cunning deception when she was not in the company of Adam. As the weaker vessel, away from her husband, but close to the forbidden tree, she was in the most vulnerable position possible.

Notice that what the serpent told her was not only plausible; it was even partially true. Eating the fruit would indeed open her eyes to understand good and evil. In her innocence, Eve was susceptible to the devil's half-truths and lies.

The serpent's opening words in verse 1 set the tenor for all his dealings with humanity: "Has God indeed said . . . ?" Skepticism is implicit in the inquiry. This is his classic *modus operandi*. He questions the Word of God, suggesting uncertainty about the meaning of God's statements, raising doubt about the truthfulness of what God has said, insinuating suspicion about the motives behind God's secret purposes, or voicing apprehension about the wisdom of God's plan.

He twists the meaning of God's Word: "Has God indeed said, 'You shall not eat of every tree of the garden'?" God's commandment had actually come to Adam as a positive statement: "Of every tree of the garden *you may freely eat*; but of the tree of the knowledge of good and evil you shall not eat" (Gen. 2:16–17 NKJV, emphasis added). The serpent casts the command in negative language ("You shall *not* eat of every tree"), making God's expression of lavish generosity sound like stinginess. He was deliberately misrepresenting the character and the command of God.

It is likely that Eve had heard about God's only restriction not directly from God, but from her husband. Genesis 2:16–17 records that God gave the prohibition just prior to her creation, at a time when Adam must have been the lone recipient. This concurs perfectly with the biblical truth of Adam's position as the representative and head of the whole human race. God held him directly accountable. Eve's instruction and her protection were his responsibility as head of his family. Consequently, the farther she went from his side, the more she was exposed.

In the innocent bliss of Eden, of course, Eve was unaware that any danger like this existed. Even if (as it appears) the serpent discovered her looking at the tree, she was not thereby sinning. God had not forbidden the couple to *look* at the tree. Contrary to Eve's statement in Genesis 3:3,

God had not even forbidden them to *touch* the tree. She was exaggerating the rigors of God's one restriction.

Notice that she also understated the severity of God's warning, softening God's decisive tone of absolute certainty ("in the day that you eat of it you shall surely die" [Gen. 2:17 NKJV]) to the language of a mere potentiality ("lest you die" [Gen. 3:3 NKJV]).

At this point, however, it seems she was more flustered and confounded than anything else. There's no reason to assume she was purposely misrepresenting the facts. Perhaps for her protection, to put a fence around the danger, *Adam* had advised Eve not to "touch" the forbidden fruit. In any case, Eve was doing nothing wrong by simply looking at it. She would naturally have been curious. Satan seized the opportunity to beguile her, and thereby tempt Adam.

The second time the serpent speaks to Eve he does not merely misquote God's Word in order to put a sinister spin on it. This time he flatly contradicts what God had told Adam. God's word to Adam was, "In the day that you eat of it you shall surely die" (Gen. 2:17 NKJV). Satan's reply to Eve was the exact opposite: "You will not surely die" (3:4 NKJV).

Then Satan went on to confound Eve with his version of what would happen if she ate: "God knows that in the day you eat of it your eyes will be opened, and you will be like God, knowing good and evil" (v. 5 NKJV). This was another partial truth. If Eve ate, her eyes *would* be open to the knowledge of good and evil. In other words, she would forfeit her innocence.

But buried in the middle of those words is the lie of all lies. It is the same falsehood that still feeds the carnal pride of our fallen race and corrupts every human heart. This evil fiction has given birth to every false religion in human history. It is the same error that gave birth to the wickedness of Satan himself. This one lie therefore underlies a whole universe of evil: "You will be like God" (v. 5 NKJV).

Eating the fruit would *not* make Eve anything like God. It would (and did) make her like the devil—fallen, corrupt, and condemned.

But Eve was deceived. She "saw that the tree was good for food, that it was pleasant to the eyes, and a tree desirable to make one wise" (v. 6 NKJV). Notice the natural desires that contributed to Eve's confusion: her bodily appetites (it was good for food); her aesthetic sensibilities (it was pleasant to the eyes); and her intellectual curiosity (it was desirable for wisdom). Those are all good, legitimate, healthy urges—unless the object of desire is sinful, and then natural passion becomes evil lust. That can never result in any good. Thus we are told by the apostle John, "All that is in the world; the lust of the flesh, the lust of the eyes, and the pride of life; is not of the Father but is of the world" (1 John 2:16 NKJV).

Eve ate and then gave to her husband to eat. Scripture doesn't say whether Adam found Eve near the forbidden fruit or she went and found him. Either way, by Adam's act, according to Romans 5:12, "sin entered the world, and death through sin, and thus death spread to all men" (NKJV). That is known as the doctrine of original sin. It's one of the most important, truly foundational doctrines in Christian theology, and therefore certainly worth the effort to understand in the context of Eve's story.

People sometimes ask why it was *Adam's* failure that was so decisive for humanity and why Scripture treats Adam's disobedience as the means by which sin entered the world. After all, Eve actually ate the forbidden fruit first. She was the one who succumbed to the original temptation, allowed herself to be drawn away by an appeal to lust, and disobeyed God's command. Why is Adam's transgression deemed the original sin?

Remember, first of all, that 1 Timothy 2:14 says, "Adam was not deceived, but the woman being deceived, fell into transgression" (NKJV). Adam's sin was deliberate and willful in a way Eve's was not. Eve was deceived. But Adam chose to partake of the fruit Eve offered him with full knowledge that he was engaging in deliberate rebellion against God.

There is, however, an even more important reason why Adam's sin, rather than Eve's, led to the fall of all humanity. Because of Adam's unique position as head of the original family and therefore captain of the whole human race, Adam's headship had particular significance for all of humanity. God dealt with him as a kind of legal delegate for himself, his wife, and all their offspring. When Adam sinned, he sinned as our representative before God. When he fell, we fell with him. That is precisely why Scripture teaches that we are *born* sinful (see Gen. 8:21; Ps. 51:5; 58:3) and that we all share in *Adam's* guilt and condemnation (Rom. 5:18).

In other words, contrary to what many people assume, we don't fall from a state of complete innocence into sin individually, on our own. But Adam, who in effect was acting as an agent and proxy for the entire human race, plunged *all of humanity at once* into sin. In the words of Romans 5:19, "By one man's disobedience many were made sinners" (NKJV). Every one of Adam's progeny was condemned by his actions. And that is why the whole human race is said to be guilty because of what *he* did, and not because of what Eve did.

It is impossible to make sense of the doctrine of original sin if we ignore this principle of Adam's headship. Ultimately, it is impossible to make sense of Scripture at all without understanding this vital principle. In an absolutely crucial sense, even the truth of the gospel hinges on this very same idea of representative headship. Scripture says that Adam's headship over the human race is an exact parallel of Christ's headship over the redeemed race (Rom. 5:18; 1 Cor. 15:22). In the same way that Adam brought guilt on us as our representative, Christ took away that guilt for His people by becoming their head and representative. He stood as their proxy before the bar of divine justice and paid the price of their guilt before God. Jesus also did everything Adam failed to do, rendering obedience to God on behalf of His people. Therefore, "by one Man's obedience many will be made righteous" (Rom. 5:19 NKJV). In other words, Christ's righteousness counts as ours, because He took His place as the representative Head of all who trust Him. That is the gospel in a nutshell.

Don't get the idea, however, that Eve's sin was excusable because it wasn't as deliberate or as far-reaching as Adam's. Eve's sin was exceedingly sinful, and her actions demonstrated that she was a full and willing partner with Adam in his disobedience. (Incidentally, in a similar way, we all demonstrate by our own willful deeds that the doctrine of original sin is perfectly just and reasonable. No one can legitimately cast off the guilt of the human race by protesting that it is unfair for the rest of us to be tainted with guilt for Adam's behavior. Our own sins prove our complicity with him.)

Eve's sin subjected her to God's displeasure. She forfeited the paradise of Eden and inherited a life of pain and frustration instead. The divine curse against sin targeted her in a particular way.

HER HUMILIATION

The serpent was right about one thing: eating the forbidden fruit opened Eve's eyes so that she knew good and evil. Unfortunately, she knew evil by experiencing it—by becoming a willing participant in sin. And in a moment, her innocence was gone. The result was agonizing shame.

Scripture describes it in a few picturesque words: "Then the eyes of both of them were opened, and they knew that they were naked; and they sewed fig leaves together and made themselves coverings" (Gen. 3:7 NKJV).

Their famous attempt to make clothing of fig leaves perfectly illustrates the utter inadequacy of every human device ever conceived to try to cover shame. Human religion, philanthropy, education, self-betterment, self-esteem, and all other attempts at human goodness ultimately fail to provide adequate camouflage for the disgrace and shame of our fallen state. All the man-made remedies combined are no more effective for removing the dishonor of our sin than our first parents' attempts to conceal their nakedness with fig leaves. That's because masking over shame doesn't really deal with the problem of guilt before God. Worst of all, a full atonement for guilt is far outside the possibility of fallen men and women to provide for themselves.

That was the realization Adam and Eve awoke to when their eyes were opened to the knowledge of good and evil. The Lord, of course, knew all about Adam's sin before it even occurred. There was no possibility of hiding the truth from Him, and He certainly did not have to come physically to the garden to find out what the first couple were up to. But Genesis tells the story from an earthly and human perspective. What we read in Genesis 3:8–13, in essence, is what Eve heard and saw:

> *And they heard the sound of the LORD God walking in the garden in the cool of the day, and Adam and his wife hid themselves from the presence of the LORD God among the trees of the garden.*
>
> *Then the LORD God called to Adam and said to him, "Where are you?"*
>
> *So he said, "I heard Your voice in the garden, and I was afraid because I was naked; and I hid myself."*
>
> *And He said, "Who told you that you were naked? Have you eaten from the tree of which I commanded you that you should not eat?"*
>
> *Then the man said, "The woman whom You gave to be with me, she gave me of the tree, and I ate."*
>
> *And the LORD God said to the woman, "What is this you have done?"* (NKJV)

It is evident that the shame of our first parents was accompanied by a deep sense of fear, dread, and horror at the prospect of giving account to God for what they had done. That is why they tried to hide. Like the fig leaves, their hiding place was inadequate to conceal them from the all-seeing eye of God.

Adam's reply reflects his fear, as well as a note of deep sorrow. But there's no confession. Adam seems to have realized that it was pointless to try to plead innocence, but neither did he make a full confession. What he did was try to pass off the blame. He immediately pointed the finger at the one closest to him: Eve.

Also implicit in Adam's words ("The woman whom *You* gave") was an accusation against God. So quickly did sin corrupt Adam's mind that in his blame shifting, he did not shy away from making God Himself an accessory to the crime. This is so typical of sinners seeking to exonerate themselves that the New Testament epistle of James expressly instructs us, "Let no one say when he is tempted, 'I am tempted by God'; for God cannot be tempted by evil, nor does He Himself tempt anyone. But each one is tempted when he is drawn away by his own desires and enticed" (James 1:13–14 NKJV). Adam, however, was subtly trying to put at least some of the blame on God himself.

But Adam handed most of the culpability to Eve. The Lord responded, not by arguing with Adam about it, but by turning to Eve and confronting her directly. Obviously, this was not a signal that Adam was off the hook. Rather, the Lord was giving Eve an opportunity to confess her part.

But she just tried to push the blame off onto the serpent: "The woman said, 'The serpent deceived me, and I ate'" (Gen. 3:13 NKJV). That was true enough (1 Tim. 2:14), but the serpent's guilt did not justify her sin. Again, James 1:14 stands as a reminder that whenever we sin, it is because we are drawn away by *our own lust*. No matter what means Satan may use to beguile us into sin—no matter how subtle his cunning—the responsibility for the deed itself still lies with the sinner and no one else. Eve could not escape accountability for what she had done by transferring the blame.

Notice, however, that the Lord made no argument and entertained no further dialogue. There was enough to condemn Adam and Eve in their own words, despite their efforts to avoid a full confession. All their excuses were no better at concealing their guilt than the fig leaves had been.

So in Genesis 3:14–19, the Lord simply pronounces a comprehensive curse that addresses the guilty parties in turn—first the serpent, then Eve, and finally Adam:

> So the LORD God said to the serpent: "Because you have done this, you are cursed more than all cattle, and more than every beast of the field; on your belly you shall go, and you shall eat dust all the days of your life. And I will put enmity between you and the woman, and between your seed and her Seed; He shall bruise your head, and you shall bruise His heel."
>
> To the woman He said: "I will greatly multiply your sorrow and your conception; in pain you shall bring forth children; your desire shall be for your husband, and he shall rule over you."
>
> Then to Adam He said, "Because you have heeded the voice of your wife, and have eaten from the tree of which I commanded you, saying, 'You shall not eat of it': cursed is the ground for your sake; in toil you shall eat of it all the days of your life. Both thorns and thistles it shall bring forth for you, and you shall eat the herb of the field. In the sweat of your face you shall eat bread till you return to the ground, for out of it you were taken; for dust you are, and to dust you shall return." (NKJV)

To examine the entire curse exhaustively might consume many chapters. It would certainly require more space than would be reasonable for a chapter like this. What we are chiefly interested in, of course, is how this curse relates to Eve in particular. Notice that the curse has three sections. The first part is addressed to the serpent; the second part to Eve; and the third part to Adam. But all three sections had serious ramifications for Eve. In order to see this clearly, let's start with the final section, which is addressed to Adam, and work our way backward.

Bear in mind, first of all, that the curse on Adam applied not only to him personally, but also to the entire human race. It furthermore promised significant changes in the earthly environment. So the curse on Adam had immediate and automatic implications for Eve (and for all their offspring) also. The loss of paradise and the sudden change in all of nature meant that Eve's daily life would be filled with onerous consequences, just as Adam's life would be. Her toil, like his, would become a burden. The sweat, the thorns and thistles, and ultimately the reality of death would all be part of her lot in life too. So the curse on Adam was a curse on Eve as well.

It is significant, I think, that the shortest section of the curse is the part dealing with Eve directly. Eve's part is completely contained in one verse of Scripture (v. 16), and it has two elements. One direct consequence of Eve's sin would be a multiplication of the pain and sorrow associated with childbirth. The other would be a struggle that would occur in her relationship with her husband. In other words, when the curse addresses Eve in particular, it deals with the two most important relationships in which a woman might naturally seek her highest joy: her husband and her children.

The first part of verse 16 is simple and straightforward: "I will greatly multiply your sorrow and your conception; in pain you shall bring forth children." Of course, sin is what brought sorrow and misery into the world in the first place. The expression *multiply your sorrow* does not suggest that there would have been a lesser degree of anguish or distress in an uncursed Eden anyway. Presumably, even childbirth would have been as painless and as perfect as every other aspect of Paradise. But this language simply recognizes that now, in a fallen world, sadness, pain, and physical difficulties would be part and parcel of the woman's daily routine. And in *child-birth,* the pain and sorrow would be "greatly multiplied"—significantly increased over the normal woes of everyday life. The bearing of children, which originally had the potential to bring the most undiluted kind of joy and gladness, would instead be marred by severe pain and difficulty.

The second part of the verse is a little harder to interpret: "Your desire shall be for your husband, and he shall rule over you." Clear light is shed on the meaning of that expression by a comparison with Genesis 4:7, which uses exactly the same language and grammatical construction to describe the struggle we wage with sin: "Sin lies at the door. And its desire is for you, but you should rule over it" (NKJV). In other words, sin desires to gain mastery over you, but you need to prevail over it instead.

Genesis 3:16, using the very same language, describes a similar struggle that would take place between Eve and her husband. Before Adam sinned, his leadership was always perfectly wise and loving and tender. Before Eve sinned, her submission was the perfect model of meekness and modesty. But sin changed all of that. She would now chafe under his headship and desire to gain dominance over him. His tendency would be to suppress her in a harsh or domineering way. And thus we see that tensions over gender roles go all the way back to our first parents. It is one of the immediate effects of sin and the awful curse that it brought upon our race.

Paradise was utterly ruined by sin, and the severity of the curse must have shattered Eve's heart. But God's judgment against her was not entirely harsh and hopeless. There was a good deal of grace, even in the curse. To the eyes of faith, there were rays of hope that shone even through the cloud of God's displeasure.

For example, Eve might have been made subject to the serpent to whom she had foolishly acquiesced. But instead, she remained under the headship of her husband, who loved her. She might have been utterly destroyed, or made to wander alone in a world where survival would have been difficult. Instead, she was permitted to remain with Adam, who would continue to care for her and provide for her. Although their relationship would now have tensions that did not exist in Eden, she remained Adam's partner. Even though she might have justly been made an outcast and a pariah, she retained her role as a wife.

In the worst case, Eve might have even been forbidden to bear children. Instead, although the experience would now be painful and accompanied by sorrow, Eve would still be the mother of all living. In fact, her very name, given to her by Adam after the pronouncement of the curse, gave testimony to that fact. "Adam called his wife's name Eve; because she was the mother of all living" (Gen. 3:20 NKJV).

As a matter of fact, the promise that Eve would still bear children mitigated every other aspect of the curse. That one simple expectation contained a ray of hope for the whole human race. There was a hint in the curse itself that one of Eve's own offspring would ultimately overthrow evil and dispel all the darkness of sin. Eve had set a whole world of evil in motion by her disobedience; now, through her offspring, she would produce a Savior. This powerful hope had *already* been implicitly given to her, in the portion of the curse where the Lord addressed the serpent.

HER EXPECTATION

God's curse on the serpent was the most severe of all. In the most literal and obvious sense, the curse appears to be addressed to the actual reptile. But remember, *this* reptile was somehow indwelt or controlled by Satan. The true significance of the curse, therefore, actually looks beyond the snake and his species. Its primary message is a grim sentence of condemnation against Satan himself.

Still, the curse *does* have important implications for the literal serpent and his species. Don't miss the fact that the Lord implicitly declares "all cattle, and . . . every beast of the field" accursed (Gen. 3:14 NKJV). Of course, God did not hold the animal kingdom culpable for Adam's sin. (Scripture never portrays animals as morally sentient beings, and this is no exception. Even in the case of the serpent, the moral fault lay in the satanic spirit who used the reptile's form, and not in the beast itself.) But God cursed even the animals for Adam's sin. In other words, the curse on them was part of God's judgment against Adam.

Remember, the curse had negative ramifications for Adam's whole environment. Evil is infectious, and, therefore, when Adam sinned, his entire domain was tainted. The sweeping extent of the curse reflects that truth. That is why, in verse 17, the Lord cursed even the ground. Obviously, the animal kingdom would be likewise subject to the many and far-reaching effects of Adam's rebellion. Every beast of the field would henceforth live in a decaying and dying world. They, too, would be subject to disease, destruction, disaster, death, and various other hardships that all stemmed from the presence of evil. Therefore the animals were also formally included in God's curse. They were consigned to suffer the miseries of evil that Adam's sin had brought into his environment. This was all part of *Adam's* judgment, a constant reminder to him about God's displeasure over sin.

But the serpent would be cursed above all species, reduced to crawling on his belly in the dust. This seems to suggest that serpents originally had legs. We're not given a physical description of the serpent prior to the curse, but it could well have been a magnificent and sophisticated creature. From now on, however, all serpents would be demoted to the dirt, condemned to writhe on the ground, and therefore unable to avoid eating the offscouring of all kinds of filth along with their food. Whatever the glories of this creature prior to the fall, he now would take a form that signified the loathsomeness of the tempter who indwelt him.

Furthermore, the serpent would forever bear the stigma of human contempt. The very real effects of this pronouncement are clearly evident in the human species' near-universal hatred of snakes. No other creature arouses so much fear and loathing.

But again, the full meaning of this text really looks beyond the reptile and addresses the satanic spirit who controlled him. The serpent's degradation to the dust simply mirrors and illustrates Satan's own demotion from heaven. "How you are fallen from heaven, O Lucifer, son of the morning! How you are cut down to the ground" (Isa. 14:12 NKJV). The loathing of all humanity likewise applies to Satan. Although our race is fallen and spiritually aligned with Satan against God (John 8:44), the devil himself is a reproach and a disgrace among Eve's children. People, as a rule, are naturally repulsed by Satan and satanic imagery.

But that's not all this means. The important spiritual implications of the curse against the serpent are even more profound than that. And I believe Eve understood this in some measure. Genesis 3:15 is often referred to as the *Protevangelium* (meaning, literally, "the first gospel"). Here is the earliest glimmer of good news for fallen humanity, and it comes in the opening words of God's *curse!* He says to the evil spirit indwelling the snake: "I will put enmity . . . between your seed and her Seed; He shall bruise your head, and you shall bruise His heel" (NKJV).

Though framed as a malediction against the tempter, that part of the curse was a bright ray of light for Eve. Here was an explicit promise that her Seed would bruise the evil one's head. She could not possibly have grasped the full scope of the divine pledge concealed in those words, but she could hardly have failed to take heart from what she heard.

First of all, the mere mention of "her Seed" indicated that she would bear children and have the opportunity to raise a family. At the very least, she now *knew* she was not going to be instantly and abruptly destroyed because of her sin. She would not be consigned to unmitigated condemnation alongside the serpent. Instead (and Eve surely understood that this was only owing to God's great grace and mercy), she would still have the opportunity to become the mother of the human race. Moreover, God would ensure that enmity would perpetually exist between Eve's descendents and that evil creature. All of this was clearly good news from Eve's perspective.

Even better, however, was the promise that her seed would bruise the serpent's head. This was a guarantee that her race would not be hopelessly subordinated to the evil one's domination forever. In fact, whether Eve fully grasped it or not, this curse against the serpent hinted at an ultimate remedy for her sin, giving Eve reason to hope that someday one of her descendants would inflict a crushing blow to the tempter's head, utterly and finally destroying the diabolical being and all his influence—and, in effect, overturning all the wickedness Eve had helped to unleash.

Make no mistake; that is precisely what these words meant. The curse against the serpent held a promise for Eve. Her "Seed" would crush the serpent's head. Her own offspring would destroy the destroyer.

This sense of Genesis 3:15 reflects the true divine intention. And that fact is made absolutely clear by the rest of Scripture. (Indeed, it is the main plot of the story the rest of Scripture tells.) For example, there is an echo of this same language in Romans 16:20: "The God of peace will crush Satan under your feet shortly" (NKJV). Hebrews 2:14 says Christ (who, of course, *is* the eternal "God of peace") took on human form—literally became one of Eve's offspring—so "that through death He might destroy him who had the power of death, that is, the devil" (NKJV). First John 3:8 says, "For this purpose the Son of God was manifested, that He might destroy the works of the devil" (NKJV). Thus Christ, who was uniquely "born of a woman" (Gal. 4:4 NKJV)—the offspring of a virgin, and God in human form—literally fulfilled this promise that the Seed of the woman would break the serpent's head.

How much of this did Eve genuinely understand? Scripture does not say, but it seems clear that Eve clung to the hope that eventually one of her own offspring would wound her mortal enemy. To borrow words from a slightly different context, she seemed to sense that her species would, by God's grace, be "saved in childbearing" (1 Tim. 2:15 NKJV). We can be certain that her deep enmity toward the tempter never wavered as long as she lived. She must have longed for the day when one of her children would smash his head.

Evidence of that hope is seen in her great joy upon first becoming a mother. Genesis 4:1 describes the birth of Cain, Eve's eldest son. Eve said, "I have acquired a man from the LORD" (NKJV). The Hebrew expression might literally be translated, "I have acquired a man; YHWH." Some commentators have suggested that perhaps she thought Cain was

God incarnate, the promised Redeemer. Scripture gives us few reasons to think her messianic hope was quite that highly developed. Certainly, if she even assumed Cain would be the promised Seed, she was sorely disappointed. He crushed his mother's heart rather than the serpent's head, by murdering Abel, his younger brother.

Whatever Eve may have meant by that expression in Genesis 4:1, it was nonetheless a clear expression of hope and rejoicing because of God's grace, compassion, kindness, and forgiveness toward her. There's a tone of exultation in it: "I have acquired a man from the LORD."

It is also clear that her hope was personified in her own children. She saw them as tokens of God's goodness and reminders of the promise that her seed would be the instrument by which the tempter's ultimate destruction was accomplished. In fact, when Eve bore Seth—after Cain had already broken her heart by murdering Abel—Scripture says, she "named him Seth [meaning, "appointed one"], 'For God has appointed another seed for me instead of Abel, whom Cain killed'" (Gen. 4:25 NKJV). The reference to the "appointed seed" *does* suggest that her heart had laid hold of the promise concealed in the curse, and she treasured the undying hope that one day her own Seed would fulfill that promise.

Were Adam and Eve saved? I believe they were. God's grace to them is exemplified in the way He "made tunics of skin, and clothed them" (Gen. 3:21 NKJV). In order for Him to do that, some animals had to be slain. Thus the first ever blood sacrifice was made by the hand of God on their behalf. Furthermore, concealed in God's declaration that the woman's Seed would defeat the serpent was an implicit promise that their sin and all its consequences would one day be vanquished and the guilt of it would be eradicated. We know from a New Testament perspective that this promise involved the sending of God's own Son to undo what Adam's sin did.

They believed that promise, insofar as they understood it. Scripture records that Seth founded a line of godly people: "As for Seth, to him also a son was born; and he named him Enosh. Then men began to call on the name of the LORD" (Gen. 4:26 NKJV). Where would their knowledge of the Lord have come from? Obviously, it came from Adam and Eve, who had more direct and firsthand knowledge of God than anyone else since the fall. This godly line (which endures in the faith of millions even today) was to a large degree their legacy. Happily for Eve, it will eventually prove to be an infinitely more enduring legacy than her sin. After all, heaven will be filled with her redeemed offspring, and they will be eternally occupied with a celebration of the work of her Seed.

2

SARAH: HOPING AGAINST HOPE

By faith Sarah herself also received strength to conceive seed, and she bore a child when she was past the age, because she judged Him faithful who had promised.

Hebrews 11:11 NKJV

L et's be honest: there are times in the biblical account when Sarah comes off as a bit of a shrew. She was the wife of the great patriarch Abraham, so we tend to think of her with a degree of dignity and honor. But reading the biblical account of her life, it is impossible not to notice that she sometimes behaved badly. She could throw fits and tantrums. She knew how to be manipulative. And she was even known to get mean. At one time or another, she exemplified almost every trait associated with the typical caricature of a churlish woman. She could be impatient, temperamental, conniving, cantankerous, cruel, flighty, pouty, jealous, erratic, unreasonable, a whiner, a complainer, or a nag. By no means was she always the perfect model of godly grace and meekness.

In fact, there are hints that she may have been something of a pampered beauty; a classic prima donna. The name given to her at birth, *Sarai,* means "my princess." (Her name was not changed to *Sarah* until she was ninety years old, according to Genesis 17:15.) Scripture remarks repeatedly about how stunningly attractive she was. Wherever she went, she instantly received favor and privilege because of her good looks. That kind of thing can spoil the best of women.

By the way, the biblical account of Sarah's life doesn't really even begin until she was already sixty-five years old. Amazingly, even at that age, her physical beauty was so remarkable that Abraham regularly assumed other powerful men would want her for their harems. And he was right. First a pharaoh, then a king, not realizing she was Abraham's wife, had designs on obtaining her as a wife. To this day, Sarah is remembered for her legendary beauty. A famous Moslem tradition teaches that Sarah resembled Eve. (That is especially significant in light of another Moslem tradition, which says Allah gave Eve two-thirds of all beauty, and then divided what remained of beauty among all other women.) But it's not necessary to embellish Sarah's glamour with fables. From the biblical account alone, it is clear that she was an extraordinarily beautiful woman.

From the time she became Abraham's wife, Sarah desired one thing above all others, and that was to have children. But she was barren throughout her normal childbearing years. In fact, that is practically the first thing Scripture mentions about her. After recording that Abraham took her as a wife in Genesis 11:29, verse 30 says, "But Sarai was barren; she had no child" (NKJV).

She was obviously tortured by her childlessness. Every recorded episode of ill temper or strife in her household was related to her frustrations about her own barrenness. It ate at her. She spent years in the grip of frustration and depression because of it. She desperately wanted to be a mother, but she finally concluded that God Himself was restraining her from having children (Gen. 16:2). So badly did she want her husband to have an heir that she concocted a scheme that was immoral, unrighteous, and utterly foolish. She rashly persuaded Abraham to father a child by her own housemaid.

Predictably, the consequences of such a carnal ploy nearly tore her life apart and seemed to leave a lasting scar on her personality. Her bitterness seethed for thirteen years, and she finally insisted that Abraham throw the other woman out, along with the child he had fathered by her.

Sarah's faults are obvious enough. She was certainly fallen. Her faith, at times, grew weak. Her own heart sometimes led her astray. Those shortcomings were conspicuous and undeniable. If those things were all we knew about Sarah, we might be tempted to picture her as something of a battle-ax—a harsh, severe woman, relentlessly self-centered and temperamental. She wasn't always the kind of person who naturally evokes our sympathy and understanding.

Fortunately, there was much more to Sarah than that. She had important strengths as well as glaring weaknesses. Scripture actually commends her for her faith and steadfastness. The apostle Peter pointed to her as the very model of how every wife should submit to her husband's headship. Although there were those terrible flashes of petulance and even cruelty (reminders that Sarah was an embattled, fleshly creature like us), Sarah's life on the whole is actually characterized by humility, meekness, hospitality, faithfulness, deep affection for her husband, sincere love toward God, and hope that never died.

A study in contrasts and contradictions, Sarah was indeed one extraordinary woman. Although she gave birth to only one son and didn't become a mother at all until she was well past the normal age of fertility, she is the principal matriarch in Hebrew history. Although her enduring faithfulness to her husband was one of the most exemplary aspects of her character, the most notorious blunder of her life involved an act of gross *un*faithfulness. She sometimes vacillated, but she ultimately persevered against unbelievable obstacles, and the steadfastness of her faith became the central feature of her legacy. In fact, the New Testament enshrines her in the Hall of Faith: "because she judged Him faithful who had promised" (Heb. 11:11 NKJV).

The full spectacle of Sarah's amazing faith doesn't really become apparent until we contemplate the many seemingly insurmountable obstacles to that faith.

HER BACKGROUND IN UR OF THE CHALDEANS

Sarah was half-sister to her husband, Abraham. In Genesis 20:12, Abraham describes for King Abimelech his relationship with his wife: "She is truly my sister. She is the daughter of my father, but not the daughter of my mother; and she became my wife" (NKJV). Terah was father to both of them, Sarah being ten years younger than Abraham (Gen. 17:17). We're not told the names of either of their mothers.

Incidentally, that kind of half-sibling marital relationship was not deemed incestuous in Abraham's time. Abraham's brother, Nahor, married a niece; and both Isaac and Jacob married cousins. Such marriages to close relatives were not the least bit unusual or scandalous in the patriarchal era—nor in previous times extending all the way back to creation. Obviously, since Adam and Eve were the only humans God originally created, it would have been absolutely essential in the beginning for some of Adam's offspring to wed their own siblings.

Scripture made no prohibition against consanguine marriages (matrimony between close relatives) until well after Abraham's time. No doubt one of the main reasons the Lord ultimately forbid the practice was because of the accumulation of genetic mutations in the human gene pool. When you begin with two genetically perfect creatures, there is no risk of any hereditary defects. Only gradually did the dangers associated with inbreeding arise. Therefore, no legal prohibition against incest even existed until the time of Moses. Then Leviticus 18:6–18 and 20:17–21 explicitly forbade several kinds of incest, including marriage between half-siblings. But the patriarchs should not be evaluated by laws that were only handed down many generations later. It was no sin for Abraham to take Sarah as his wife.

Scripture says virtually nothing about their early years of marriage. In fact, *all* we know about that era in their lives is the bitter truth that perpetually grated on Sarah's own consciousness: "Sarai was barren; she had no child" (Gen. 11:30 NKJV). That one statement sums up everything Scripture has to say about the first sixty-five years of Sarah's life! It is no wonder if she occasionally exhibited flashes of frustration and resentment.

Notice that the biblical account of Abraham's life likewise doesn't really begin until he was seventy-five. All we are told is that he had been born and raised in Sumeria, lower Mesopotamia, near the confluence of the Tigris and Euphrates rivers. (That's close to the head of the Persian Gulf in a region that is part of present-day Iraq.) Abraham's hometown was a famous urban center known as Ur of the Chaldeans.

Ur was the heart of a sophisticated pagan culture. Sarah and Abraham would have lived there during the very height of its power and affluence. The city government was a superstitious theocracy supposedly under the Babylonian moon god. (This was the same culture that built the famous ziggurats, those massive terraced towers upon which pagan temples were set.)

Abraham, of course, was a worshiper of YHWH. His knowledge of the true God was probably passed down to him by way of his ancestors. After all, Abraham was only a ninth-generation descendent from Shem, son of Noah.

It is obvious that the world cultures of Abraham's time were highly paganized. Going back even before the tower of Babel episode, love for the truth had obviously been in sharp decline for many generations. By the time Abraham came on the scene, idolatrous worship thoroughly dominated every world culture.

But there was still a scattered remnant of true believers. It is entirely likely that dispersed here and there among the world's population were faithful families who still knew and worshiped YHWH, having maintained their faith across the generations from Noah's time. For example, judging from details given in the book of Job, including the length of Job's lifespan, Job was probably a close contemporary of Abraham's. Job and his friends (lousy counselors though they were) had a thorough familiarity with the God of their ancestors. They lived in the land of Uz. The precise location of Uz is not certain, but it was clearly in the Middle East (Jer. 25:20)—yet not in the vicinity of Ur of the Chaldeans, where Abraham's family lived. So the remnant who still worshiped YHWH were not confined to any single location or limited to any one family.

In fact, in the biblical account of Abraham's life, we are also introduced to Melchizedek (Gen. 14:18). He represented an order of itinerant priests who knew the one true God and served Him. Abraham met Melchizedek somewhere in the Dead Sea region. Clearly, a few diverse remnants of faithful YHWH worship *did* still exist in Abraham's time.

The Lord's purpose in choosing and calling Abraham was to make him the father of a great nation that would be His witness to the world. That nation, Israel, would be formally covenanted with YHWH. Through them, the truth would be kept alive and preserved in perpetuity. Scripture says "the oracles of God" were committed to them (Rom. 3:2 NKJV). In other words, from the nation that came out of Abraham, prophets would arise. Through them the Scriptures would be given to the world. God would dwell in their midst and set His sanctuary among them. By their lineage a Deliverer, the Messiah, would arise. And in Him, all the nations of the world would be blessed (Gen. 18:18).

Sarah obviously had a key role to play in this plan. Abraham could never become the patriarch of a great nation if she did not first become mother to his offspring. She was surely aware of the Lord's promises to Abraham. She certainly would have longed to see those promises fulfilled. As long as she remained childless, however, the sense that everything somehow hinged on her must have pressed on her like a great burden on her shoulders.

SARAH

HER JOURNEY TO THE LAND OF PROMISE

Apparently, while Abraham was still a young man living in Ur, the Lord spoke to him, saying, "Get out of your country, from your family and from your father's house, to a land that I will show you" (Gen. 12:1 NKJV).

Abraham obeyed, and Hebrews 11:8 expressly commends him for his obedience: "By faith Abraham obeyed when he was called to go out to the place which he would receive as an inheritance. And he went out, not knowing where he was going" (NKJV). But the journey was long and slow. It appears Abraham did not immediately separate from his family and his father's house. Instead, he took his father with him. Abraham may have been somewhat reluctant at first to sever the parental apron strings.

In fact, as Scripture recounts the first leg of the move from Ur of the Chaldeans, it appears that Abraham's father, Terah, was still acting as head of the extended family. "Terah took his son Abram and his grandson Lot, the son of Haran, and his daughter-in-law Sarai, his son Abram's wife, and they went out with them from Ur of the Chaldeans to go to the land of Canaan; and they came to Haran and dwelt there" (Gen. 11:31 NKJV). Clearly, Terah was still in charge. Scripture portrays him as the leader of the journey, with Abraham, Sarah, and Lot in tow.

But the first long leg of the journey stalled at Haran, about 650 miles northwest, roughly following the course of the Euphrates. Perhaps Terah was too old to travel anymore. We don't know how long Abraham and Sarah remained in Haran. But they did not get moving again until Terah died, and that was evidently some time. Scripture says Terah was more than two hundred years old when he died, and Abraham was seventy-five when he finally left Haran for the promised land.

That means Sarah was now sixty-five, the exact age most people today think is ideal for retirement. Sarah was by no means a *young* woman, even by the standards of the patriarchal era, when people obviously lived much longer and remained agile, healthy, and vigorous well past their sixties. The life of a nomad would be hard for anyone at sixty-five. And yet there is no sign whatsoever that she was reluctant or unwilling to go with Abraham to a land neither of them had ever seen.

In fact, what we know of Sarah suggests that far from complaining, she went eagerly, gladly, and enthusiastically with Abraham. She was utterly and completely devoted to her husband. Knowing that God wanted to make him the father of a great nation, she earnestly longed to give birth to the child who would set that whole process in motion.

Leaving Haran after burying his father, Abraham still had quite a large caravan. Scripture tells us, "Abram took Sarai his wife and Lot his brother's son, and all their possessions that they had gathered, and the people whom they had acquired in Haran, and they departed to go to the land of Canaan. So they came to the land of Canaan" (Gen. 12:5 NKJV).

That account suggests the final leg of the journey to Canaan was direct and uninterrupted. It was some 350 miles on foot (making the total journey from Ur more than a thousand miles). With a large caravan, moving a reasonable distance of eight to ten miles in a typical day, the trip from Haran to Canaan would have required only about six or seven weeks. Abraham seems not to have stopped until he reached Bethel, a fertile area with abundant springs.

Abraham's first act upon arrival there was the building of a stone altar. At that time, the Lord also appeared to Abraham. He expanded His original promises to Abraham, now adding that He would give all the surrounding land to Abraham's descendants. Although Abraham and Sarah remained nomads and vagabonds for the remainder of their days, this place and its altar remained their anchor. (This was also the very same place where Abraham's grandson Jacob would later be visited by YHWH and have that famous dream about a ladder that reached to heaven.)

But circumstances quickly forced Abraham to keep moving south.

"There was a famine in the land, and Abram went down to Egypt to dwell there, for the famine was severe in the land" (Gen. 12:10 NKJV). It was there, for the first time, that Abraham tried to pass Sarah off as his sister. He did this out of fear that if Pharaoh knew she was his wife, he would kill Abraham in order to have Sarah. Abraham's great faith wavered somewhat at this point. He succumbed to the fear of men. Had he simply trusted God, God would have protected Sarah (as He did in the end anyway).

But Scripture says that before they even entered Egypt, Abraham discussed with Sarah the dangers this place posed for a man with a beautiful wife. "When the Egyptians see you . . . they will say, 'This is his wife'; and they will kill me, but they will let you live," he told her (Gen. 12:12 NKJV). And so at Abraham's suggestion, she agreed to pose as his sister (v. 13). *Abraham's* motives were selfish and cowardly, and the scheme reflected a serious weakness in his faith. But Sarah's devotion to her husband is nonetheless commendable, and God honored her for it.

Stewards of Pharaoh saw her, pointed her out to Pharaoh, and brought her to his house. Scripture says Pharaoh showed favor to "brother" Abraham for Sarah's sake, lavishing him with livestock, apparently in anticipation of requesting her hand in marriage (v. 16). Meanwhile, by God's providence, Pharaoh did not violate her (v. 19). And to see that he did not, the Lord troubled Pharaoh's house with "great plagues" (v. 17 NKJV).

Somehow Pharaoh discovered the reason for the plagues, and he confronted Abraham with the deception, expelling the patriarch and his wife from Egypt (Gen. 12:19–20). Nonetheless, Pharaoh, preoccupied with more pressing things, did no harm to either of them, and when Abraham left Egypt, Pharaoh's favor toward Sarah had made Abraham a very wealthy man (Gen. 13:2). He and Sarah returned to Bethel, "to the place of the altar which he had made there at first. And there Abram called on the name of the LORD" (13:4 NKJV).

Henceforth, the Lord himself would be their dwelling place. Together, they "dwelt in the land of promise as in a foreign country, dwelling in tents . . . [while they] waited for the city which has foundations, whose builder and maker is God" (Heb. 11:9–10 NKJV). That is as good a summary as any of the earthly life Sarah inherited when she stepped out in faith to follow her husband: earthly inconvenience, mitigated by the promise of eternal blessing.

HER YEARNING FOR THE PROMISED BLESSING

Remember, Abraham and Sarah both came from an urban environment. They were not, as is commonly supposed, lifetime nomads or Bedouins who simply wandered all their lives because that is all they knew. Bear in mind that they did not *start* wandering until Abraham was already in his mid-seventies and Sarah was only a decade behind that. Life on the road was not something Sarah was accustomed to; it was something she had to learn to embrace.

What energized Sarah's willingness to leave all familiar surroundings, sever ties with her family, and commit to a life of rootless wandering?

Notice the nature of the vast promise God had made to Abraham: "I will make you a great nation; I will bless you and make your name great; and you shall be a blessing. I will bless those who bless you, and I will curse him who curses you; and in you all the families of the earth shall be blessed" (Gen. 12:2–3 NKJV). That is the first recorded hint of the Abrahamic Covenant, a formal pledge God made to Abraham and to his offspring forever. God's promise was unconditional and literally unlimited in the scope of its blessings. God would bless Abraham, make him a blessing, and make him a vehicle through which blessing would come to the whole world (Gal. 3:9–14). The promised blessing even had eternal implications.

In other words, redemption from sin and the means of salvation from divine judgment were part and parcel of the promise (Gal. 3:8, 16–17). Sarah understood that promise. According to Scripture, she believed it.

We know without question, from a New Testament perspective, that God's covenant with Abraham was an affirmation of the very same messianic promise God had already made to Eve in the garden when He declared that her seed would crush the head of the serpent. Just as Christ was the Seed of the woman who overthrows the serpent, He is also the Seed of Abraham by whom all the world will be blessed. Paul wrote, "Now to Abraham and his Seed were the promises made. He does not say, 'And to seeds,' as of many, but as of one, 'And to your Seed,' who is Christ" (Gal. 3:16 NKJV). This same promise is the central theme that extends all through Scripture, from Genesis 3 to its final fulfillment in the closing chapters of Revelation.

Abraham was the human channel through which the world would see the outpouring of God's redemptive plan. He understood that. Sarah understood and also embraced it. "She judged Him faithful who had promised" (Heb. 11:11 NKJV).

But despite her faith, she knew from a human perspective that her long years of childlessness already loomed large as a threat to the fulfillment of God's pledge. Sarah must have constantly pondered these things, and as time went by, the weight of her burden only increased.

Yet God kept giving her reasons to hope. In Genesis 15:7–21, YHWH restated and expanded His promise to Abraham, then formally ratified the covenant. It is significant that verse 12 says a deep sleep fell on Abraham; *then* the Lord single-handedly carried out the covenant ceremony. (Incidentally, the Hebrew word used in verse 12 is the same word describing the "deep sleep" that Adam fell into when the Lord took his rib to make Eve.) This detail about Abraham's sleep is given to stress the convenant was completely unconditional. The covenant was a unilateral promise from God to Abraham about what He, YHWH, would do. It made no demands of Abraham or Sarah whatsoever. It was a completely one-sided covenant.

If Sarah had simply realized that truth and embraced it, her whole burden would have been instantly lifted.

HER FOOLISHNESS IN THE MATTER OF HAGAR

Instead, Sarah took it upon herself to hatch a scheme that was so ill-advised and so completely fleshly that she regretted it for the rest of her days. As a matter of fact, the evil consequences of that one act had unbelievably far-reaching implications. Frankly, some of the tensions we see in the Middle East today are rooted in Sarah's foolhardy ploy to try to concoct a man-made solution to her dilemma.

To be fair, from a purely human viewpoint, we can understand Sarah's despair. Ten more fruitless years passed after Abraham and Sarah arrived in Canaan (Gen. 16:3 NKJV). Sarah was now seventy-five years old, post-menopausal, and still childless. If God planned to make her the mother of Abraham's heir, why had He not done so by now? It was natural for her to think God was deliberately withholding children from her. As a matter of fact, He was. When *His* time came for the promise to be fulfilled, no one would be able to deny that this was indeed God's doing. His plan all along was for Sarah to have her first child in her old age, after every prospect of a natural fulfillment of the prophecy was exhausted and after every earthly reason for hope was completely dead. Thus YHWH would put His power on display.

But as she considered her circumstances, Sarah concluded that a kind of surrogate parenting was the only possible solution to her predicament. If God's promise to Abraham were ever going to be fulfilled, Abraham *had* to father children by some means. Sarah thus took it upon herself to try to engineer a fulfillment of the divine promise to Abraham. She unwittingly stepped into the role of God.

Sarah had a maidservant, named Hagar, whom she had acquired during their time in Egypt. Sarah apparently reasoned that since she owned Hagar, if Abraham fathered a child by Hagar, it would in effect be Sarah's child. "So Sarai said to Abram, 'See now, the LORD has restrained me from bearing children. Please, go in to my maid; perhaps I shall obtain children by her.' And Abram heeded the voice of Sarai" (16:2 NKJV).

This was the first recorded case of polygamy in Scripture involving a righteous man. The very first bigamist on biblical record was Lamech (Gen. 4:19). He was an evil descendant of Cain. (He is not to be confused with another Lamech, described in Genesis 5:25–29, who was Noah's father and who descended from the line of Seth.)

Abraham took a concubine, at his wife's urging. "Sarai, Abram's wife, took Hagar her maid, the Egyptian, and gave her to her husband Abram to be his wife" (Gen. 16:3 NKJV). This was a sorry precedent for the patriarch of the nation to set. In generations to come, Jacob would be duped by his uncle into marrying both Leah and Rachel (29:23–31); David would take concubines (2 Sam. 5:13); and Solomon would carry polygamy to an almost unbelievable extreme, maintaining a harem of more than a thousand women (1 Kings 11:1–3).

But God's design for marriage was monogamy from the beginning. "A man shall leave his father and mother and be joined to his wife, and *the two* shall become *one flesh*" (Matt. 19:4–5 NKJV, emphasis added). Paul likewise made clear what God's ideal for marriage is: "Let each man have *his own wife,* and let each woman have *her own husband*" (1 Cor. 7:2 NKJV, emphasis added). Disobedience to that standard has always resulted in evil consequences. David's polygamous heart led to his sin with Bathsheba. Solomon's marital philandering destroyed him and divided his kingdom (1 Kings 11:4). No good has ever come from any violation of the "one-flesh" principle of monogamy. Abraham's union with Hagar is certainly no exception.

As soon as Hagar conceived, Sarah *knew* it was a grave mistake. Hagar suddenly became haughty and contentious toward Sarah: "When she [Hagar] saw that she had conceived, her mistress [Sarah] became despised in her eyes" (Gen. 16:4 NKJV).

Here, then, is the first outburst of temper we see from Sarah: "Sarai said to Abram, 'My wrong be upon you! I gave my maid into your embrace; and when she saw that she had conceived, I became despised in her eyes. The LORD judge between you and me'" (Gen. 16:5 NKJV).

It is true that Sarah was being unreasonable. This whole sordid plan was, after all, her big idea. Yes, as the spiritual head of the household, Abraham should have rejected Sarah's plan out of hand—but it's still not quite fair to pin *all* the guilt on him. On the other hand, this fit of Sarah's was deliberately provoked by Hagar. Her insolent treatment of Sarah was utterly indefensible. No doubt, Hagar knew all too well about Sarah's extreme grief over her own barrenness. Now she was deliberately putting salt in Sarah's wound. Since Hagar was the servant and Sarah the one in charge, this was the most brazen kind of deliberate impudence.

A section of the book of Proverbs deals with precisely this situation:

> *Under three things the earth quakes,*
> *And under four, it cannot bear up:*
> *Under a slave when he becomes king,*
> *And a fool when he is satisfied with food,*
> *Under an unloved woman when she gets a husband,*
> *And a maidservant when she supplants her mistress.* (30:21–23 NASB)

The truth, however, is that every party in this whole affair was guilty, and all of them ended up reaping bitter fruit from what they had sown.

Abraham recognized the legitimacy of Sarah's complaint. He might have been wise to step in as an arbitrator and seek a solution that would have been fair to both women. But given Sarah's disposition at that moment, he did what most husbands would probably do and simply let

Sarah deal with Hagar her own way. "Abram said to Sarai, 'Indeed your maid is in your hand; do to her as you please.' And when Sarai dealt harshly with her, she fled from her presence" (Gen. 16:6 NKJV).

To understand Sarah's extreme frustration, let's follow Hagar for a moment. Notice first that although Sarah dealt harshly with her maidservant, the Lord showed extreme grace to Hagar. The Angel of the Lord sought her out. In all likelihood, this was no created angel, but a visible manifestation of YHWH himself in angelic or human form. (I'm inclined to think that this Angel was actually the preincarnate Son of God. We meet the same Angel several times in the Old Testament, including Genesis 22:11–18; Exodus 3:2–5; and 1 Kings 19:5–7.) Notice that He spoke to Hagar in the first person as YHWH, not in the third person, as an angelic messenger speaking on YHWH's behalf would do.

His words to Hagar were gentle and full of mercy. He first approached her by asking where she had come from and where she was going. He addressed her directly as "Hagar, Sarai's maid," however, both to make clear that he knew exactly who she was and to remind her of her duty. Then, to make this explicit, when Hagar answered truthfully, the Angel said, "Return to your mistress, and submit yourself under her hand" (Gen. 16:9 NKJV). As a legally indentured servant, she had no right to run away, and she needed to go back and be humbly obedient.

The Angel then made an amazing, completely unsolicited promise to Hagar: "I will multiply your descendants exceedingly, so that they shall not be counted for multitude" (Gen. 16:10 NKJV). Prophetically, he described her unborn son for her, saying she would call him Ishmael and that he would be wild, yet dwell in the presence of his brethren (16:12).

She, in return, acknowledged Him by a unique name: "El-Roi," or "the God who sees," a reference to the omniscient eye that followed her and sought her out even when she tried to hide (16:13 NKJV).

Consider this, however: Sarah had never received such a promise from God. Sarah's faith resided in promises God had made to Abraham. Up to this point, Sarah had never explicitly been named in the covenant God made with Abraham. God had already confirmed His promise to Abraham on no less than three major occasions. He first told Abraham he would be the father of a great nation (12:3). He then promised to make Abraham's seed as the dust of the earth—"so that if a man could number the dust of the earth, then your descendants also could be numbered" (13:16 NKJV). When Abraham later reminded the Lord that he still lacked a legitimate heir, God promised once again that Abraham's seed would be like the stars of the sky in number (15:1–6).

On none of those occasions had God ever expressly stated that Sarah would be matriarch to the nation in question. That was her hope and expectation. But what the episode with Hagar shows is that Sarah's hope was beginning to wane. She was slowly losing heart.

HER PERSEVERANCE THROUGH YEARS OF SILENCE

When Ishmael was born to Hagar, Scripture says Abraham was eighty-six years old (Gen. 16:16). Thirteen more frustrating years passed for Sarah after that. She remained barren. By that time she was eighty-nine years old. She had lived in Canaan for twenty-four years. Her husband was about to have his hundredth birthday. If her hope was not utterly shattered, it must have hung by a very thin thread.

Here's where the greatness of Sarah's faith shines through. She had harbored hope for so long. Year after year had come and gone. She was now an old woman, and no matter how often she and Abraham tried to conceive, the promise was *still* unfulfilled. Most women would have given up long before this. A lesser woman might have despaired of ever seeing YHWH's promise fulfilled and turned to paganism instead. But we are reminded again that Sarah "judged Him faithful who had promised" (Heb. 11:11 NKJV). This is what made her so extraordinary.

Finally, when Abraham was ninety-nine, the Lord appeared to him again and once more renewed the covenant. This was an especially important restatement of the covenant. The passage is long, and there's not enough space here to cover it in detail, but the Lord once again reiterated and expanded the vital promises he had made to Abraham. Every time the promises came, they got bigger: "My covenant is with you, and you shall be a father of many nations" (Gen. 17:4 NKJV). Not just "a great nation"; not merely descendants as numerous as the stars or the dust; but "many nations." To this aged man who had managed to father only one son (and that by less than honorable means), God said, "I will make you exceedingly fruitful; and I will make nations of you, and kings shall come from you" (17:6 NKJV).

It was also at this point that God gave Abraham his name, changing it from his birth name, Abram (17:5 NKJV). *Abram* means "exalted father"; *Abraham* means "father of many nations."

The Lord also formally extended the Abrahamic Covenant across the generations, making the whole land of Canaan "an everlasting possession" for Abraham's offspring forever (17:7–8 NKJV). Finally, God gave Abraham the sign of circumcision, with instructions for how it was to be administered (17:10–14). Circumcision became the sign and the formal seal of the covenant. Everything germane to the covenant was now in place.

Significantly, at the beginning of the chapter, YHWH revealed Himself to Abraham with a new name: "Almighty God," *El Shaddai* in Hebrew (17:1 NKJV). The name deliberately highlighted God's omnipotence. After hearing these promises so many times, Abraham might have been wondering whether he would ever see the son who embodied the fulfillment of the promises. The name was a subtle reminder to Abraham that nothing was too hard for God.

Having said all that, the Lord then turned the subject to Sarah. For the first time on record, He specifically brought Sarah by name into the covenant promises: "Then God said to Abraham, 'As for Sarai your wife, you shall not call her name Sarai ["my princess"], but Sarah ["Princess"] shall be her name. And I will bless her and also give you a son by her; then I will bless her, and she shall be a mother of nations; kings of peoples shall be from her'" (17:15–16 NKJV). By removing the possessive pronoun ("my"), the Lord was taking away the limiting aspect of her name, since she was to be ancestor to many nations.

There's no indication that Sarah was present to hear this; the context suggests that she was not. We can be certain she heard *about* it from Abraham at the first opportunity. Notice his reaction: "Then Abraham fell on his face and laughed, and said in his heart, 'Shall a child be born to a man who is one hundred years old? And shall Sarah, who is ninety years old, bear a child?'" (17:17 NKJV). There was probably as much relief and gladness in the laughter as there was incredulity. Surely we can understand Abraham's amazement, perhaps even tinged with a measure of uncertainty. But don't mistake it for unbelief. In Romans 4:20–21, the apostle Paul, speaking of this very moment, says Abraham "did not waver at the promise of God through unbelief, but was strengthened in faith, giving glory to God, and [was] fully convinced that what He had promised He was also able to perform" (NKJV).

Abraham also pleaded with God not to overlook Ishmael, at this point thirteen-years-old and no doubt beloved by his father: "Abraham said to God, 'Oh, that Ishmael might live before You!'" (Gen. 17:18 NKJV).

The Lord immediately reiterated the promise regarding Sarah: "No, Sarah your wife shall bear you a son, and you shall call his name Isaac; I will establish My covenant with him for an everlasting covenant, and with his descendants after him" (v. 19 NKJV). Sarah's son, not Hagar's, would be the child in whom the covenant promises would find their fulfillment (Gal. 4:22–28).

The Lord had one thing left to say: "And as for Ishmael, I have heard you. Behold, I have blessed him, and will make him fruitful, and will multiply him exceedingly. He shall beget twelve princes, and I will make him a great nation. But My covenant I will establish with Isaac, whom Sarah shall bear to you at this set time next year" (Gen. 17:20–21 NKJV). For the first time, here was a promise, with a fixed date, assuring Sarah of her place in the covenant. With that, the interview was over, and Scripture says simply that He "went up from Abraham" (v. 22 NKJV).

Abraham must have immediately found Sarah and reported to her all that the Lord said. Whatever her reaction, she certainly understood that *Abraham* believed the promise, because he immediately was circumcised, and he had every male in his household circumcised as well, whether they had been "born in the house or bought with money from a foreigner" (vv. 23–27 NKJV).

HER JOY IN THE FULFILLMENT OF THE PROMISE

The next time the Lord appeared to Abraham, one of His express purposes was to renew the promise for Sarah's sake so that she could hear it with her own ears. Genesis 18 describes how the Lord visited Abraham with two angels. Abraham saw them far off, and (perhaps even before he realized who they were) immediately had Sarah begin preparation of a meal for them. He promised them "a little water . . . [and] a morsel of bread," but he actually had a calf slain and gave them a feast (Gen. 18:4–8 NKJV). Sarah's willingness to entertain guests so elaborately on such short notice is one of the marks of her submission to Abraham mentioned by the apostle Peter when he held Sarah up as a model for wives. Peter wrote, "In this manner, in former times, the holy women who trusted in God also adorned themselves, being submissive to their own husbands, as Sarah obeyed Abraham, calling him lord" (1 Peter 3:5–6 NKJV). This was the very instance Peter had in mind. In fact, while Sarah is always portrayed as submissive to Abraham, Genesis 18:12 is the only place in the Old Testament record where she referred to him as "my lord" (NKJV).

While they were eating, the men asked, "Where is Sarah your wife?" (Gen. 18:9 NKJV).

"Here, in the tent," Abraham replied, establishing that he knew she was within earshot. Scripture describes the details of the conversation that followed:

> And He said, "I will certainly return to you according to the time of life, and behold, Sarah your wife shall have a son." (Sarah was listening in the tent door which was behind him.)
>
> Now Abraham and Sarah were old, well advanced in age; and Sarah had passed the age of childbearing. Therefore Sarah laughed within herself, saying, "After I have grown old, shall I have pleasure, my lord being old also?"
>
> And the LORD said to Abraham, "Why did Sarah laugh, saying, 'Shall I surely bear a child, since I am old?' Is anything too hard for the LORD? At the appointed time I will return to you, according to the time of life, and Sarah shall have a son."
>
> But Sarah denied it, saying, "I did not laugh," for she was afraid. And He said, "No, but you did laugh!" (Gen. 18:10–15 NKJV)

Sarah's laughter (just like Abraham's earlier) seems to have been an exclamation of joy and amazement rather than doubt. Yet when the Lord asked, "Why did Sarah laugh?" she denied it. That denial was motivated by fear. She was afraid because she had not laughed aloud, but "within herself." As soon as she realized this stranger had such a sure and thorough knowledge of her heart, she knew instantly and definitively that it was the Lord.

The year that followed was a difficult and busy year for Abraham and Sarah. That was the year God destroyed Sodom and Gomorrah (Gen. 18:16–19:29). And during that same year, Abraham journeyed south again, this time into the land ruled by Abimelech, king of Gerar. Sarah, though now ninety, was still beautiful enough to stir the passions of a king. What had happened in Egypt twenty-five years earlier was replayed once more. Abraham again tried to pass Sarah off as his sister, and Abimelech, smitten with her beauty, began to pursue her. But God spared Sarah, by warning Abimelech in a dream that she was Abraham's wife (Gen. 20:3). Scripture underscores the fact that Abimelech was not permitted by God to touch her (20:6), lest there be any question about whose child she would soon bear.

Abimelech, having been frightened when YHWH appeared to him in the dream, was gracious to Abraham and Sarah. He lavished gifts on Abraham and said, "See, my land is before you; dwell where it pleases you" (20:15 NKJV). To Sarah he said, "Behold, I have given your brother a thousand pieces of silver; behold, it is your vindication before all who are with you, and before all men you are cleared" (20:16 NASB).

Immediately after that incident, according to Scripture, "The LORD visited Sarah as He had said, and the LORD did for Sarah as He had spoken. For Sarah conceived and bore Abraham a son in his old age, at the set time of which God had spoken to him" (21:1–2 NKJV). Sarah named him Isaac, meaning "laughter." And Sarah said, "God has made me laugh, and all who hear will laugh with me" (21:6 NKJV). Thus she confessed the laugh she had previously tried to deny.

We're given a fascinating insight into Sarah's real character by the fact that she saw genuine humor in the way God had dealt with her. "Who would have said to Abraham that Sarah would nurse children? For I have borne him a son in his old age" (v. 7 NKJV). Despite her occasional bursts of temper and struggles with discouragement, Sarah remained an essentially good-humored woman. After those long years of bitter frustration, she could still appreciate the irony and relish the comedy of becoming a mother at such an old age. Her life's ambition was now realized, and the memory of years of bitter disappointment quickly disappeared from view. God had indeed been faithful.

HER HARSHNESS IN HER TREATMENT OF ISHMAEL

Sarah plays a major role in only one more episode recounted by Scripture. Isaac was finally weaned—and from what we know of the culture, he would therefore have been a young toddler, probably two- or three-years-old. Scripture says, "Abraham made a great feast on the same day that Isaac was weaned" (21:8 NKJV). It was a time for celebration. But something happened that was the final straw for Sarah in her long struggle to accept Hagar as her husband's concubine. She saw Ishmael making fun of Isaac (v. 9). Scripture doesn't say *why* Ishmael was mocking. It was probably for some silly, childish reason. As any parent will attest, such behavior is by no means out of the ordinary for a child Ishmael's age. He was probably no older than fourteen at this point, just emerging from childhood into young manhood—old enough to be responsible for his behavior, but not old enough to be wise.

But it was too much for Sarah to endure. She immediately said, "Cast out this bondwoman and her son; for the son of this bondwoman shall not be heir with my son, namely with Isaac" (v. 10 NKJV).

For Abraham, all the joy instantly went out of the celebration. Ishmael was, after all, his firstborn son. He genuinely loved him. Remember Abraham's earlier plea to God, "Oh, that Ishmael might live before You!" (Gen. 17:18 NKJV).

Was Sarah really being overly harsh? In truth, she was not. Virtually any woman forced to share her husband with a concubine would respond to a situation like this exactly as Sarah did. She was Abraham's true wife. Hagar was an interloper. Besides, according to the promise of God Himself, Isaac was Abraham's true heir, promised by God to be the one through whom the covenant blessing would eventually see fulfillment. It confused things beyond measure for Ishmael to be in a position to claim the right of the firstborn over the one true heir appointed by God to succeed Abraham. Ishmael was a threat to God's purpose for Abraham's line as long as he remained in any position to claim that *he,* rather than Isaac, was Abraham's rightful heir.

So what may appear at first glance to be an extreme overreaction was actually another proof of Sarah's great faith in God's promise. God Himself affirmed the wisdom of her demand: "God said to Abraham, 'Do not let it be displeasing in your sight because of the lad or because of your bondwoman. Whatever Sarah has said to you, listen to her voice; for in Isaac your seed shall be called'" (21:12 NKJV).

Ishmael was by no means totally abandoned. The Lord promised to make a great nation of Ishmael too—"because he is your seed" (v. 13 NKJV). YHWH subsequently appeared to Ishmael and Hagar in their extremity and promised to meet all their needs (vv. 14–21). Furthermore, some kind of family tie was continually maintained between the lines of Ishmael and Isaac, because when Abraham died, both sons working together buried their father alongside Sarah (25:9–10).

The apostle Paul uses the expulsion of Hagar as an illustration of the conflict between law and grace. He calls it "an allegory" (Gal. 4:24 KJV), but we're not to think he is denying the historical facts of the Genesis account. Instead he is treating it as typology—or better yet, a living object lesson. Hagar, the bondwoman, represents the slavery of legalism (the bondage of trying to earn favor with God through works). Sarah, the faithful wife, represents the perfect liberty of grace. Paul was reminding the Galatian believers that "we, brethren, as Isaac was, are children of promise" (v. 28 NKJV)—saved by grace, not vainly hoping to be saved by works. "But, as he who was born according to the flesh then persecuted him who was born according to the Spirit, even so it is now" (v. 29 NKJV). Just as Ishmael taunted Isaac, so the false teachers in Galatia were persecuting true believers. Paul's conclusion? "Cast out the bondwoman and her son, for the son of the bondwoman shall not be heir with the son of the freewoman" (v. 30 NKJV). Harsh as it may have seemed, there was a very crucial, necessary, and positive spiritual principle in the expulsion of Hagar and Ishmael. This symbolized the important truth that the kind of religion that is dependent on human effort (symbolized by the carnal scheme that conceived Ishmael as an artificial fulfillment of God's promise) is utterly incompatible with divine grace (symbolized by Isaac, the true heir of God's promise). And the two are so hostile to one another that they cannot even abide in close proximity.

HER HAPPINESS IN HER WANING YEARS

After Hagar was cast out, Sarah returned to a healthy, monogamous life with her beloved husband and their child, Isaac, who was a perpetual reminder to both Sarah and Abraham of God's staunch faithfulness. As far as we know, the rest of her years were lived out in joy and peace.

Sarah doesn't even appear in the biblical account of Abraham's near sacrifice of Isaac. That whole event was uniquely meant as a test of *Abraham's* faith. Sarah seems to have been kept completely isolated from it until it was over. It occurred in the land of Moriah (Gen. 22:2). (In later generations, the city of Jerusalem surrounded the area known as Moriah, and Mount Moriah, at the heart of the city, was the precise spot where the Temple was situated, according to 2 Chronicles 3:1). Moriah was some forty-five miles from Beersheba, where Abraham was then residing (Gen. 21:33–34). In any event, Sarah's faith had already been well tested. She had long since demonstrated her absolute trust in God's promises. And the stamp of God's approval on her is contained in those New Testament passages that recognize her for her steadfast faithfulness.

In fact, in the very same way the New Testament portrays Abraham as the spiritual father of all who believe (Rom. 4:9–11; Gal. 3:7), Sarah is pictured as the spiritual matriarch and the ancient epitome of all faithful women (1 Peter 3:6). Far from isolating those memorable instances where Sarah behaved badly, it commemorates her as the very epitome of a woman adorned with "the incorruptible beauty of a gentle and quiet spirit" (1 Peter 3:4 NKJV).

That is a fitting epitaph for this truly extraordinary woman.

3

RAHAB: A HORRIBLE LIFE REDEEMED

Salmon begot Boaz by Rahab, Boaz begot Obed by Ruth, Obed begot Jesse, and Jesse begot David the king.

Matthew 1:5–6 NKJV

When Rahab first appears in the biblical account, she is one of the most unsavory characters imaginable. In fact, she is introduced as "a harlot named Rahab" (Josh. 2:1 NKJV). If you had met her before the great turning point of her life, you might have instantly written her off as completely hopeless. She was an immoral woman living in a pagan culture that was fanatically devoted to everything God hates. The culture itself was on the brink of judgment. Their long descent into the abyss of moral and spiritual corruption had been intentional, and now it was irreversible.

As far as we know, Rahab had always been a *willing* participant in her civilization's trademark debauchery. She had personally profited from the evil that permeated that whole society. Now that God had called for the complete destruction of the entire culture because of their extreme wickedness, why shouldn't Rahab also receive the just desserts of her own deliberate sin?

As far as the record of her life is concerned, there were no redeeming qualities whatsoever about Rahab's life up to this point. On the contrary, she would have been in the very *basement* of the moral hierarchy in a Gentile culture that was itself as thoroughly degenerate and as grossly pagan as any society in world history. She was a moral bottom-feeder. She made her living off that culture's insatiable appetite for unbridled debauchery, catering to the most debased appetites of the very dregs of society. It is hard to imagine a more unlikely candidate for divine honor than Rahab.

Yet in Hebrews 11:31 (though identified even there as "the harlot Rahab" [NKJV]), she is specifically singled out by name for the greatness of her faith, and she even appears in the genealogy of Christ in Matthew 1. Extraordinary? That word is an understatement in Rahab's case.

AN UNLIKELY BACKGROUND

Rahab lived in Jericho at the time of Joshua. Her house was not in some back alley of town, but perched right on the famous wall (Josh. 2:15). The wall must have been a wide affair, certainly spacious enough on top for buildings and either a walkway or a road. This was almost certainly a prime location in the high-rent business district. It is fair to assume, then, that Rahab had enjoyed phenomenal financial success in her trade.

Unfortunately, her "trade" was prostitution. She regularly sold herself to the most wicked men in that already-wicked city.

Jericho was part of the Amorite kingdom, a grotesquely violent, totally depraved, thoroughly pagan culture so hell-bent on the pursuit of everything evil that God Himself had condemned them and ordered the Israelites to wipe them from the face of the earth (Deut. 20:17). In fact, the Amorite culture had been so completely and maliciously corrupt for so long (going back at least to the time of Abraham), that their evil lifestyle was the very reason God had granted Abraham and his heirs rights to their land in the first place (Deut. 18:12; 1 Kings 21:26). The Lord had promised Abraham that his descendants would begin to possess the land as soon as the wickedness of the Amorites was complete (Gen. 15:16). That time had now come. This evil nation had reached God's maximum tolerance level.

Rahab therefore epitomized the vileness of the Amorite culture at a point when they had collectively filled the measure of human wickedness to its very brim. Her whole life had been devoted to the profane pursuit of carnal self-gratification. Her livelihood was totally dependent on consensual evil. She was enslaved to the most diabolical kinds of passion, in bondage to her own sin, and held captive by a monstrous society that was itself already under God's sentence of condemnation—indeed, marked out for *eternal* destruction. But divine grace redeemed her and liberated her from all of that, plucking her as a brand from the fire.

Here is the historical setting for Rahab's story: Moses had died (Josh. 1:1–2). The generation of Israelites who had come out of Egypt were all dead too. More than a million Israelites had originally left Egypt under Moses' leadership (Ex. 12:37). Because of that generation's collective stubbornness and persistent unbelief, when they first reached the very doorstep of the Promised Land at Kadesh-Barnea, everyone over twenty years of age was prohibited from entering. An entire generation was doomed to die in the wilderness without even seeing another glimpse of the Promised Land.

There were two significant exceptions (Num. 14:30): Joshua and Caleb. Those two men had scouted the Promised Land together for Moses. They had returned enthusiastic about the prospects of Israel's new homeland. They affirmed what God had said about the land. But when ten other spies returned with a conflicting report, discouraged, warning of the dangers that lay ahead, the people of Israel balked at entering the land. They listened to the unbelief of the pessimists rather than to the promise of YHWH. Then and there, the entire nation staged a mutiny against Moses and against God (Num. 13–14). That was the final straw. That is why Israel was made to wander for forty years. It was a divine judgment against them because of their unbelief (Num. 14:30–35). In the end, the carcasses of that whole generation (except the two faithful men) were buried in scattered graves in the wilderness, where the harsh elements eventually consumed them (vv. 32–33).

Thirty-eight years had now passed since that rebellion at Kadesh-Barnea. The book of Joshua starts with the Israelites situated again on the doorstep of Canaan—this time near Acacia Grove (Josh. 2:1; 3:1), about seven miles east of the Jordan River, almost directly across the river from Jericho. Joshua had been appointed as leader over the whole nation in Moses' place. In Joshua 1, the Lord reinforced Joshua's courage and resolve with a series of promises, and Joshua prepared the people to enter the land. The day this generation had hoped for all their lives was finally here.

Wisely, just as Moses had done years before, Joshua sent spies ahead to gather military and strategic information about what lay on the other side of the Jordan. This time, however, Joshua sent only two men, saying, "Go, view the land, especially Jericho" (2:1 NKJV).

Scripture says simply: "So they went, and came to the house of a harlot named Rahab, and lodged there" (2:1 NKJV). Thus Rahab is the very first person Scripture introduces us to in the Promised Land. By God's gracious providence, she would become one of the linchpins of Israel's military triumph. Her whole life, her career, and her future would be changed by her surprise encounter with two spies.

It is an unlikely confluence of forces for good: on the one hand, a lone pagan woman whose life up till now had been anything but heroic, and an entire nation of itinerant, lifelong refugees who had lived for the past forty years under the frown of God because of their parents' disobedience.

But the spies' collaboration with Rahab was the beginning of the downfall of Jericho. Jericho's defeat was the first dramatic conquest in one of history's greatest military campaigns ever.

AN UNEXPECTED ACT OF KINDNESS

Joshua 2:1–7 tells what happened:

> *Now Joshua the son of Nun sent out two men from Acacia Grove to spy secretly, saying, "Go, view the land, especially Jericho." So they went, and came to the house of a harlot named Rahab, and lodged there.*
>
> *And it was told the king of Jericho, saying, "Behold, men have come here tonight from the children of Israel to search out the country."*
>
> *So the king of Jericho sent to Rahab, saying, "Bring out the men who have come to you, who have entered your house, for they have come to search out all the country."*
>
> *Then the woman took the two men and hid them. So she said, "Yes, the men came to me, but I did not know where they were from.*
>
> *"And it happened as the gate was being shut, when it was dark, that the men went out. Where the men went I do not know; pursue them quickly, for you may overtake them."*
>
> *(But she had brought them up to the roof and hidden them with the stalks of flax, which she had laid in order on the roof.)*
>
> *Then the men pursued them by the road to the Jordan, to the fords. And as soon as those who pursued them had gone out, they shut the gate.* (NKJV)

Joshua deliberately kept the work of the spies secret. Apparently, even the Israelites did not know of their mission. The scouts were to report back to Joshua, not to the whole nation (vv. 23–24). Joshua wasn't asking them for feedback so that the people could discuss among themselves whether to go across the Jordan or hold back in fear. He wasn't about to make that mistake again. Israel had traveled down the dead-end road of popular opinion already, and it cost them almost forty years' time. Joshua was taking the role of a decisive commander. He would assess the spies' report personally and decide (with the Lord's help, not a vote of the populace) how his armies would proceed.

Jericho was in a strategic location, at the openings of two vital pathways through the surrounding mountains, one leading southwest toward Jerusalem, the other leading northwest toward Ai and beyond, toward Bethel. Conquering Jericho would give Israel an important foothold into all the Promised Land. No wonder Jericho was so heavily fortified. The task of the spies was to assess those fortifications and report back to Joshua.

Most likely, the spies began their covert work shortly before dusk. The Jordan River lay seven miles to the west. A two-hour brisk walk would get them to the riverbank. There were fords nearby (v. 7), where the water ran approximately chest high at its deepest point. The men could either wade or easily swim across the Jordan. They would then have another seven-mile journey by foot to Jericho. (Even if they got wet crossing the river, this afforded more than enough time to be suitably dry upon arrival.) Then they would need to enter the walled city by some means and find lodging for the remainder of the night—all without arousing suspicion.

Jericho was a large town, and visitors came and went all the time. The spies managed to get into the city before the gates were closed for the night (v. 5). Scripture doesn't say how they got in. We assume they were able to find a way without much difficulty. Perhaps they simply mingled with other travelers at rush hour.

Once inside the city, the ideal place for lodging would be an inn or a house on the wall itself. From there they could assess the city's defenses. A good way to avoid arousing suspicion or attracting undue attention would be to find some seamy district where *everyone* would understand the need for discretion.

Their search led them to Rahab, a harlot, who was prosperous enough to have a house in a prime spot on the wall. Both she and her business were probably well-known in Jericho. Here was an ideal situation for the spies. She would have opened her door to them without any questions about who they were. In her business, the strictest confidentiality was essential. She would have welcomed them and invited them inside quickly, just as she did all her clients.

The Israelite spies did not seek her out to take advantage of her for immoral purposes, of course. Perhaps that very thing is what first won them her trust. They were obviously not there to use her or abuse her, unlike virtually all the other men she ever saw. They were serious and sober, but they did not seem to have frightened her in any way. Presumably, they treated her with patient dignity and respect while they made their careful reconnaissance. No doubt they explained who they were, which meant they would have almost certainly told her something about YHWH. Mostly, they went about their business, perhaps making measurements of the wall and recording details about the battlements and the landscape.

Rahab's house was perfect for their purposes. The position afforded a close-up look at the wall, which was the city's chief defense. But the location also made possible a quick escape if necessary. City walls are designed to keep out intruders, of course. But a person *on* the wall with a long enough rope can easily get out. By God's sovereign providence, everything they needed was in place. Also, by God's sovereign design, Rahab's heart was ready to believe in YHWH.

Somehow, it appears, the presence of the spies was known almost as soon as they entered Rahab's house. Of course, everyone in Jericho certainly already knew that the entire Israelite nation was camped across the river, within walking distance. All of Jericho had heard about Israel's miraculous escape from Pharaoh across the Red Sea and the drowning of the entire Egyptian army (v. 10). The story of Israel's subsequent wanderings in the wilderness was also well-known throughout the region. Rahab herself tells the spies that all the inhabitants of the land were

fainthearted because of what they had heard about Israel and God's dealings with them. In Rahab's words, "As soon as we heard these things, our
hearts melted; neither did there remain any more courage in anyone
because of you" (v. 11 NKJV).

Still, aside from Rahab herself, the people of Jericho do not seem to
have been *sufficiently* fearful of YHWH's power or Israel's military might.
Perhaps the tales about forty years of aimless wandering had a tendency
to counterbalance the Canaanites' fear over Israel's military might. Whatever the reason for their complacency, residents of Jericho were obviously
too smug in the security of their walled fortress.

They were nonetheless on guard for intruders, and officials had probably given strict orders to report anything suspicious to the king. The
"king" functioned like a city mayor, but he had military control. Therefore,
he was the one to be notified if intruders were spotted.

Perhaps someone from whom the spies had asked directions turned
them in. Or maybe sentries near Rahab's house spotted them and recognized them as Israelites from their clothing. In any case, their presence
was quickly reported to Jericho's king. The information he received
included exact details about where the spies had gone, so the king sent
messengers to check out Rahab's house.

Here's where Rahab utterly surprises us. Remember, she made her living by selling herself for evil purposes. There was probably a handsome
reward in it for her if she had turned in the spies. But she didn't. She hid
them. She misdirected the officials and saved the lives of the two spies,
even though this put her at considerable risk. Obviously, the king's representatives *knew* the spies had been in her home. When they were unable
to find any evidence that the men had really left the city, they would probably be back to question Rahab again. She had put her own life in jeopardy by protecting these strangers. Her sudden expression of faith,
therefore, is not only unexpected; it seems to run counter to every instinct
that normally would motivate a woman like Rahab.

Rahab's actions in protecting the spies involved the telling of a lie. Was that justified? By commending her for her faith, is Scripture also condoning her methods? Good men have argued over that question, all the way back to the earliest rabbinical history. Let's face it. It is not an *easy* question. Scripture says, "Lying lips are an abomination to the LORD, but those who deal truthfully are His delight" (Prov. 12:22 NKJV). God Himself *cannot* lie (Titus 1:2; Num. 23:19; 1 Sam. 15:29), and therefore He cannot condone or sanction a lie. Some have tried to argue that because of the circumstances, this was not, technically, a "lie," but a military feint, a legitimate stratagem designed to trick or outwit the enemy in warfare. Others argue that even lying is acceptable if the motive is a greater good. Such a situational approach to ethics is fraught with very serious problems.

I see no need to try to justify Rahab's lie. Was it *necessary* for a greater good? Certainly not. Shadrach, Meshach, and Abednego might have escaped punishment by lying too. And they might have argued convincingly that it was for a "greater good." But there is no greater good than the truth, and the cause of truth can never be served by lying. Shadrach and friends told the truth—in fact they seized the opportunity to glorify God's name—and God was *still* able to save them from the furnace. He certainly could have saved Rahab and the spies without a lie.

Still, that isn't the point of Rahab's story. There's no need for clever rationalization to try to justify her lie. Scripture never commends *the lie*. Rahab isn't applauded for her *ethics*. Rahab is a positive example of *faith*.

At this moment, her faith was newborn, weak, and in need of nurture and growth. Her knowledge of YHWH was meager. (She makes it clear in Joshua 2:9–11 that she knew *something* about Him, having developed a keen interest in YHWH from the stories about Israel's escape from Egypt. But it's likely she had never met any true YHWH-worshipers before this night.) She most likely had no understanding of the value He put on truthfulness. Meanwhile, she was a product of a corrupt culture where ethics were virtually nonexistent. Lying was a way of life in her society—

and especially in her profession. The way she responded is just what we might expect from a brand-new believer under those circumstances.

The point is that Rahab's faith, undeveloped as it was, immediately bore the fruit of action. She "received the spies with peace" (Heb. 11:31 NKJV)—meaning that she not only hid them, but also implicitly embraced their cause. She thereby entrusted her whole future to their God. And the proof of her faith was not the lie she told, but the fact that "she received the messengers and sent them out another way" (James 2:25 NKJV)—when she might have handed them over for money instead. The *lie* is not what made her actions commendable. It was the fact that she turned down an easy reward, put herself in jeopardy, and thus staked everything on the God of Israel.

Nothing but faith could have made such a dramatic, instantaneous change in the character of such a woman. She had obviously developed a great curiosity about YHWH from the tales of His dealings with Israel. Now that she had met flesh-and-blood people who knew Him and worshiped Him, she was ready to throw her lot in with them.

AN AMAZING EXPRESSION OF FAITH

Rahab's quick thinking saved the spies. The narrative suggests that she quickly hid the men *after* the king's messengers knocked on her door and inquired about the spies. She heard the request, "*then* . . . took the two men and hid them," before giving an answer (Josh. 2:3–4 NKJV). The speed and ingenuity of her scheme to hide them suggests that she was experienced in this kind of thing. Apparently the stalks of flax, "which she had laid in order on the roof" (v. 6 NKJV), were there for precisely that purpose, in case a jealous wife came looking for a client. Rahab had a long rope handy too (v. 15 NKJV). No doubt she had arranged similar escapes, but for different reasons, in the past.

The hiding place certainly served a high and holy purpose this time.

Presumably, the king's messengers searched Rahab's house quickly and failed to find the spies before heading off in pursuit of the phony trail—which took them all the way to the fords of the Jordan.

After it was clear that the king's messengers were gone for the night, Rahab went back up to the roof to speak with the spies. She gave them an explicit testimony of the faith that motivated her. Here is the biblical account:

> *Now before they lay down, she came up to them on the roof, and said to the men: "I know that the LORD has given you the land, that the terror of you has fallen on us, and that all the inhabitants of the land are fainthearted because of you. For we have heard how the LORD dried up the water of the Red Sea for you when you came out of Egypt, and what you did to the two kings of the Amorites who were on the other side of the Jordan, Sihon and Og, whom you utterly destroyed. And as soon as we heard these things, our hearts melted; neither did there remain any more courage in anyone because of you,* for the LORD your God, He is God in heaven above and on earth beneath. *Now therefore, I beg you, swear to me by the LORD, since I have shown you kindness, that you also will show kindness to my father's house, and give me a true token, and spare my father, my mother, my brothers, my sisters, and all that they have, and deliver our lives from death."*
>
> *So the men answered her, "Our lives for yours, if none of you tell this business of ours. And it shall be, when the LORD has given us the land, that we will deal kindly and truly with you."*
>
> *Then she let them down by a rope through the window.* (Josh. 2:8–14 NKJV, emphasis added)

Notice that Rahab's faith was accompanied by *fear.* There is nothing wrong with that. Indeed, "The fear of the LORD is the beginning of wisdom" (Ps. 111:10 NKJV). In Rahab's case, fear is partly what motivated her faith. She had heard powerful evidence of the Lord's supremacy over Egypt. She understood that it was the Lord's might (not sheer military skill) that had triumphed over Sihon and Og, two fearsome Amorite kings (Josh. 2:10 NKJV). She probably understood something of YHWH's sovereign authority over Israel from the tales of their forty years in the wilderness. Hers was a healthy kind of fear. It had convinced her that YHWH was indeed the one true God. The psalmist wrote, "Men shall speak of the might of Your awesome acts, and I will declare Your greatness" (Ps. 145:6 NKJV). That is precisely the kind of testimony that had brought Rahab to faith.

The spies swore an oath to deal kindly with her when they conquered her city. But they gave her one condition. She was to hang a scarlet cord from the window where she let them down (Josh. 2:17–18). This would mark her house in the sight of all Israel, and anyone inside the house would be spared when the city was overthrown. The Hebrew word for "cord" in verse 18 is different from the word for "rope" in verse 15. This cord would have been a brightly colored band of woven threads, used for decorative purposes. The color would make it easily visible from beneath the wall. Both its appearance and its function were reminiscent of the crimson sign of the blood sprinkled on the doorposts at the first Passover. Many commentators believe the scarlet color is also a deliberate typological symbol for the blood of the true Paschal Lamb. Perhaps it is. It certainly stands as a fitting symbol of Christ's blood, which turns away the wrath of God.

From Rahab's perspective, however, the significance of the scarlet cord was nothing arcane or mystical. It was a simple, expedient emblem suited to mark her window discreetly so that her house would be easily distinguishable from all the rest of the houses in Jericho.

After making their solemn agreement to safeguard Rahab's household and sealing their pledge with an oath (vv. 17–20), the spies descended under cover of darkness via the rope into the valley outside Jericho's walls. Rahab had advised them to hide in the mountains for three days until the king gave up the search (v. 16), and they did so. Scripture says,

"The pursuers sought them all along the way, but did not find them" (v. 22 NKJV).

When the men finally returned to Joshua, their report contrasted sharply with the report the ten unfaithful spies had brought to Moses nearly forty years before. It was exactly what Joshua hoped to hear: "Truly the LORD has delivered all the land into our hands, for indeed all the inhabitants of the country are fainthearted because of us" (v. 24 NKJV).

AN ENDURING LEGACY

Israel's miraculous victory over Jericho is a familiar account to most people. It is a classic illustration of how spiritual triumph is always obtained: "'Not by might nor by power, but by My Spirit,' says the LORD of hosts" (Zech. 4:6 NKJV). God does not work exclusively by miracles. In fact, the times are relatively rare when He sets aside normal means in order to accomplish his purposes. Few of Israel's military battles were ever won solely by the miraculous intervention of God. The armies of Israel had to fight. But by the same token, *none* of their battles was ever won without the Lord's power.

In this case, God purposefully intervened in a way that made clear to everyone in Canaan that He was fighting for Israel. He demolished the massive walls of Jericho without any military means whatsoever. This was not a chance earthquake. To prove it, God had the Israelites march around the city with the ark of the covenant once each day for six consecutive days (Josh. 6). On the seventh day, they marched around the city seven times, blew a ram's horn, and shouted. Instantly, the wall of the city fell down flat (Josh. 6:20).

All except one part of the wall, that is. Rahab and her house were spared. "Joshua had said to the two men who had spied out the country, 'Go into the harlot's house, and from there bring out the woman and all that she has, as you swore to her.' And the young men who had been spies went in and brought out Rahab, her father, her mother, her brothers, and all that she had. So they brought out all her relatives and left them outside the camp of Israel" (vv. 22–23 NKJV). The writer of Joshua (probably Joshua himself) added, "So she dwells in Israel to this day" (v. 25 NKJV).

Rahab is a beautiful example of the transforming power of faith. Although she had few spiritual advantages and little knowledge of the truth, her heart was drawn to YHWH. She risked her life, turned her back on a way of life that did not honor God, and walked away from everything but her closest family members (whom she brought into the community of God's people along with her). From that day on, she lived a completely different kind of life, as a true hero of faith. She has a place of honor in Hebrews 11 alongside some notable names in that "great cloud of witnesses" who testify to the saving power of faith.

After the account of Jericho's destruction in Joshua 6, Rahab is never again mentioned by name in the Old Testament. Of course, when Joshua noted that Rahab was still living in Israel, this was probably many years after the fall of Jericho. Apparently, she lived out her life in quiet dignity and grace amid the people of God. She was wholly changed from the kind of woman she once had been. She was, and is still, a living symbol of the transforming effect of saving faith. That is the primary message of her life.

In fact, when we *do* meet Rahab again on the pages of Scripture, it is in the New Testament. Her name is mentioned there three times. Two of those honor her for her remarkable faith (Heb. 11:31; James 2:25). She is held up as an example of faith for both men and women. James, in particular, cites her case to show that faith produces action. Indeed, Rahab's faith did not lie dormant long. Remember, it was only after she hid the spies that she verbalized to them her belief that YHWH was the one true God. Her faith was seen in the fruit of her works before she even had an opportunity to verbalize it on her tongue. James says genuine faith is always active and fruitful like that. "Faith without works is dead" (James 2:26 NKJV). Rahab's faith was anything but dead.

The most amazing occurrence of Rahab's name, though, in the New Testament is the very first time it appears there, on the very first page, in the very first paragraph of the first gospel. Matthew began his account of Christ's life with a lengthy genealogy tracing the entire lineage of Jesus from the time of Abraham. Matthew's goal, of course, was to prove by Jesus' pedigree that He qualified to be the promised Seed of Abraham, and that He is also rightful heir to the Davidic throne. There, in the list of Jesus' ancestors, we unexpectedly find Rahab's name: "Salmon begot Boaz by Rahab, Boaz begot Obed by Ruth, Obed begot Jesse" (Matt. 1:5 NKJV).

It is highly unusual for women to be named in Hebrew genealogies at all. (Notice that the record of Adam's offspring in Genesis 5 omits any reference to his daughters.) Yet Matthew mentions five women, and all of them are notable: Tamar (1:3), Rahab (v. 5), Ruth (v. 5), Bathsheba (v. 6), and Mary (v. 16). At least three of them were Gentiles. Three of them were disgraced because of their own sin. In fact, all of them, for various reasons, knew what it was to be an outcast—to have some infamy or stigma attached to their reputations:

- Tamar was a Canaanite woman whose husband had died, leaving her childless. She posed as a prostitute and seduced her own father-in-law, Judah, in order to bear a child. Interestingly enough, a scarlet thread also plays a role in Tamar's tragic life story (Gen. 38:13–30).

- Rahab we already know about, including the shame of her sordid background.

- Ruth (whom we will soon meet) was from the Moabite nation, a people generally despised in Israel (Ruth 1:3).

- Bathsheba (whom Matthew doesn't name but refers to simply as "the wife of Uriah") committed adultery with King David (2 Sam. 11).

- Mary, of course, bore the disgrace of an out-of-wedlock pregnancy.

Collectively, they illustrate how God is able to work all things together for good. From a human perspective, the whole genealogy is checkered with outcasts and examples of failure. The women, in particular, underscore how scandal colored so much of the messianic line. It was filled with foreigners, outcasts, and those who were pariahs for various reasons. Still, they nevertheless all found a place in the plan of God to bring His Son into the world.

The scandal motif in Christ's lineage was no accident. In His incarnation, Christ willingly "made Himself of no reputation, taking the form of a bondservant" (Phil. 2:7 NKJV). He *became* an outcast and a public disgrace, being made a curse on our behalf (Gal. 3:13). He remains even now "a stone of stumbling and a rock of offense" (1 Peter 2:8 NKJV). The gospel message, too, is a public scandal—mere foolishness and shame as far as those who perish are concerned. But to those who are saved, it is the power of God (1 Cor. 1:18).

Then again, "Those who are well have no need of a physician, but those who are sick. [Christ] did not come to call the righteous, but sinners, to repentance" (Mark 2:17 NKJV). Rahab was the very embodiment of that truth. This is why the New Testament repeatedly brings her up as a real-life example of the fruit of saving faith. She is a living reminder that even the worst of sinners can be redeemed by divine grace through faith. "For by grace you have been saved through faith, and that *not of yourselves; it is the* gift of God, not of works, lest anyone should boast. For we are *His* workmanship" (Eph. 2:8–10 NKJV, emphasis added).

Rahab was redeemed not because of any meritorious works she did. She did not earn God's favor by any good deeds. Remember, even what she *did* do right—harboring the spies—was morally tainted because of the way she handled it. She lied. But she is not given to us as an example of the power of human works. She is not a lesson in how to better ourselves through self-improvement. She is a reminder that God by *His* grace can redeem even the most horrible life.

Some of the scholastic rabbis just prior to Jesus' time became embarrassed by the fact that a woman with Rahab's background was spared in the destruction of Jericho and brought into Israel as a proselyte. They proposed a different understanding of the Hebrew word for *harlot* in Joshua 2:1 (also 6:17, 25). The Hebrew term is similar to a word meaning "to feed," they claimed. Perhaps Rahab was really just an innkeeper or a hostess, they countered.

The problem is, the actual Hebrew word really can mean only one thing: "harlot." That was the uncontested understanding of this text for centuries. In fact, there is no ambiguity whatsoever in the Septuagint (an ancient Greek translation of the Old Testament dating to the second century BC) or in the Greek texts of Hebrews 11:31 and James 2:25. The Greek word used to describe Rahab is *porne,* meaning "harlot." (Notice that the term comes from the same root as the English term *pornography* and has similar negative moral overtones.)

The idea of sanitizing Rahab's background was revived by some churchmen with overly delicate sensibilities in the Victorian era. C. H. Spurgeon, the best-known Baptist preacher in late nineteenth-century London, replied, "This woman was no mere hostess, but a real harlot . . . I am persuaded that nothing but a spirit of distaste for free grace would ever have led any commentator to deny her sin."

He was exactly right, of course. Remove the stigma of sin, and you remove the need for grace. Rahab is extraordinary precisely because she received extraordinary grace. There's no need to reinvent her past to try to make her seem less of a sinner. The disturbing fact about what she once *was* simply magnifies the glory of divine grace, which is what made her the extraordinary woman she *became.* That, after all, is the whole lesson of her life.

4

RUTH: LOYALTY AND LOVE

Your people shall be my people, and your God, my God.

Ruth 1:16 NKJV

The Old Testament book of Ruth is a flawless love story in a compact format. It's not an epic tale, but a short story. (The entire account is given in only eighty-five verses.) Still, it runs the full range of human emotions, from the most gut-wrenching kind of grief to the very height of glad-hearted triumph.

Ruth's life was the true, historical experience of one genuinely extraordinary woman. It was also a perfect depiction of the story of redemption, told with living, breathing symbols. Ruth herself furnished a fitting picture of every sinner. She was a widow and a foreigner who went to live in a strange land. Tragic circumstances reduced her to abject poverty. She was not only an outcast and an exile, but also bereft of any resources—reduced to a state of utter destitution from which she could never hope to redeem herself by *any* means. In her extremity, she sought the grace of her mother-in-law's closest kinsman. The story of how her whole life was changed is one of the most deeply touching narratives in the whole of Scripture.

287

RUIN

Ruth's story began near the end of the era of the Judges in the Old Testament. It was about a century before the time of David, in an age that was often characterized by anarchy, confusion, and unfaithfulness to the law of God. There was also a severe famine in Israel in those days.

We are introduced to the family of Elimelech in Ruth 1:1–2. Elimelech had a wife, Naomi, and two sons, named Mahlon and Chilion. Their hometown was Bethlehem, famous as the burial place of Rachel, Jacob's wife (Gen. 35:19). Bethlehem in future generations would gain more lasting fame as the hometown of David, and then, of course, as the birthplace of Christ. The story of Elimelech's family became a key link in the chain tying the messianic line to Bethlehem.

The famine in Israel forced Elimelech and family to seek refuge in Moab, just as a similar famine had once driven Abraham into Egypt. These must have been desperate times, because Moab itself was a mostly desolate region, a high tableland bounded on the west by the Dead Sea and on the east by arid desert wasteland. Its boundaries on the north and south were two deep river gorges (the Arnon and the Zered, respectively), and these were virtually dry most of the year. Moab was fertile but dry, and therefore the land was largely destitute of trees, good mostly for grazing flocks and herds.

The Moabites were descendants of Lot's eldest daughter through her incestuous relationship with her own father. The child born of that illicit union was named Moab. He was, of course, a second cousin of Jacob. (Remember that Lot was Abraham's nephew.) But even though their ancestries had that close relationship, the Moabites and the Israelites generally despised one another.

During the time of Israel's wilderness wanderings, Moabite women deliberately seduced Israelite men, then enticed them to participate in sacrifices to idolatrous gods (Num. 25). Moab was the same nation whose king, Balak, engaged the hireling prophet, Balaam, to prophesy against Israel. So throughout the Old Testament, relations between Israel and Moab ranged from uneasy tension to outright hostility.

The Moabites worshiped a god whom they called Chemosh. (He was their chief deity, but Numbers 25:2 suggests that they worshiped many others also.) Scripture calls Chemosh "the abomination of Moab" (1 Kings 11:7; 2 Kings 23:13 NKJV). Worship of this idol was grotesque, at times even involving human sacrifices (2 Kings 3:26–27). As the events of Numbers 25 suggest, Moabite worship was also filled with erotic imagery and lewd conduct. Moabite paganism typified everything abominable about idolatry. The Moabite culture practically epitomized everything faithful Israelites were supposed to shun.

We are therefore meant to be somewhat shocked and appalled by the fact that Elimelech and family sought refuge in Moab. Elimelech was a landowner in Bethlehem, and prominent enough to be called "our brother" by the city elders there (Ruth 4:2–3 NKJV). His name means, "My God is king." That, together with Naomi's faith and character, suggests that he and his family were devout Jews, not careless worldlings. The fact that Elimelech would take his family to Moab is a measure of the famine's frightening severity. The land of Israel was evidently both spiritually and physically parched, and times were desperate.

Tragedy quickly mounted for this family. First, Elimelech died in Moab, leaving Naomi a widow with the responsibility of two sons. Fortunately for her, Mahlon and Chilion were approaching adulthood, and they soon married. Unfortunately, the wives they took were Moabites (Ruth 1:3–4). No devout Israelite would have regarded such a marriage as auspicious. Israelite men were expressly forbidden to marry Canaanite women, lest the men be turned away to other gods (Deut. 7:1–3). Common sense suggests that for similar reasons, marriage to a Moabite wasn't deemed appropriate, either. Nevertheless, Naomi and her sons must have felt trapped by their desperate circumstances, so Naomi seems to have graciously accepted these daughters-in-law. One was named Orpah (meaning "stubborn") and the other, Ruth ("friendship"). Ruth married Mahlon (Ruth 4:10), who was apparently the elder of the two sons. Orpah, then, would have been the wife of Chilion. Ruth 1:4 says Naomi and her sons dwelt in Moab ten years. (That is probably the total time they spent in Moab rather than the amount of time that passed after the young men married, because neither of the young couples seem to have had children. That would have been very unusual after ten years of marriage, even in a time of famine.)

Meanwhile, circumstances did not appear to be improving for Naomi. In fact, matters took a turn for the worse. Both Mahlon and Chilion died, leaving the three women to fend for themselves. In that culture, this was a nearly impossible situation. Three widows, with no children and no responsible relatives, in a time of famine, could not hope to survive for long, even if they pooled their meager resources. We're not told what caused any of the husbands to die, but the fact that all three perished is a measure of how hard life was in the adversity of those days. Mahlon and Chilion seem to have died in quick succession, suggesting they perhaps fell victim to a disease, very likely related to the famine.

Naomi, Ruth, and Orpah had been brought to the brink of ruin. So when word reached Naomi that the drought was broken in Israel, she quickly made up her mind to return. She was now childless, widowed, impoverished, and aging (Ruth 1:12), destitute of all land and possessions, and without any relatives close enough to count on them to care for her. Still, she longed for her homeland and her own people, and she decided to go back to Bethlehem.

Both daughters-in-law began the difficult journey with Naomi, but as Naomi considered their circumstances (especially the hardships these two young women might face if they staked their futures to hers), she decided to release them back to their own families. It seemed to Naomi as if the hand of the Lord was against her (v. 13). She no doubt struggled with bitter regret over having come to Moab in the first place. Now she would be leaving her husband and both of her sons buried in that God-forsaken place. She seems to have been overcome with remorse and perhaps a feeling that she had somehow incurred the Lord's displeasure by going to Moab. Why should her daughters-in-law suffer because God's hand of discipline was against her? So she tried to persuade the young women to turn back.

The biblical description of the scene—especially the bitter anguish shared by all three women—is heart-rending:

> Then she arose with her daughters-in-law that she might return from the country of Moab, for she had heard in the country of Moab that the LORD had visited His people by giving them bread. Therefore she went out from the place where she was, and her two daughters-in-law with her; and they went on the way to return to the land of Judah. And Naomi said to her two daughters-in-law, "Go, return each to her mother's house. The LORD deal kindly with you, as you have dealt with the dead and with me. The LORD grant that you may find rest, each in the house of her husband." Then she kissed them, and they lifted up their voices and wept.
>
> And they said to her, "Surely we will return with you to your people."
>
> But Naomi said, "Turn back, my daughters; why will you go with me? Are there still sons in my womb, that they may be your husbands? Turn back, my daughters, go; for I am too old to have a husband. If I should say I have hope, if I should have a husband tonight and should also bear sons, would you wait for them till they were grown? Would you restrain yourselves from having husbands? No, my daughters; for it grieves me very much for your sakes that the hand of the LORD has gone out against me!"
>
> Then they lifted up their voices and wept again; and Orpah kissed her mother-in-law, but Ruth clung to her. (Ruth 1:6–14 NKJV)

RESOLVE

Ruth was determined to stay with Naomi, regardless of the personal cost. The still-young Moabite girl probably felt that she quite literally had nothing left to lose anyway. In keeping with the meaning of her name, Ruth seems to have developed a close bond of friendship and attachment to her mother-in-law.

Naomi still tried to dissuade Ruth from going any farther with her. "She said, 'Look, your sister-in-law has gone back to her people and to her gods; return after your sister-in-law'" (Ruth 1:15 NKJV). Naomi no doubt felt it was not in Ruth's best interests to be shackled to an aged widow. On the other hand, she certainly could not have truly believed that it would be a good thing for Ruth to go back to her people *"and to her gods."* In all likelihood, Naomi was testing Ruth, hoping to coax from her an explicit verbal profession of faith in YHWH. It would be wrong to take Ruth to Israel and place a widow without financial support in that society if she had no genuine commitment to Israel's God.

Ruth's reply is a beautiful piece of poetry in Hebrew style:

> *Entreat me not to leave you,*
> *Or to turn back from following after you;*
> *For wherever you go, I will go;*
> *And wherever you lodge, I will lodge;*
> *Your people shall be my people,*
> *And your God, my God.*
> *Where you die, I will die,*
> *And there will I be buried.*
> *The LORD do so to me, and more also,*
> *If anything but death parts you and me.* (Ruth 1:16–17 NKJV)

Thus Ruth expressed her firm resolve to stay with Naomi. Her affection for her mother-in-law was sincere. She still desired to remain part of that family. Above all, her devotion to the God of Israel was real. This was an amazingly mature and meaningful testimony of personal faith, especially in light of the fact that it came from the lips of a young woman raised in a pagan culture. The witness of Naomi and her family must have made a powerful impression on Ruth.

When Naomi saw the firm resolve of Ruth, Scripture says, "she stopped speaking to her" (v. 18 NKJV)—meaning, of course, that she gave up trying to dissuade Ruth from coming with her to Bethlehem. Their souls and their destinies were bound together by their friendship and their common faith.

After ten years or more in Moab, Naomi returned to people who remembered her and knew her name. Naomi's return caused no small stir. Scripture says, "All the city was excited because of them; and the women said, 'Is this Naomi?'" (v. 19 NKJV). *Naomi* means "pleasant," and in an earlier time it must have been a perfect description of Naomi. The fact that so many women remembered her and were so glad to see her suggests that she had once been a gregarious soul, beloved by all who knew her. But now her life was so colored with sadness that she told the other women, "Do not call me Naomi; call me Mara [meaning 'bitter'], for the Almighty has dealt very bitterly with me. I went out full, and the LORD has brought me home again empty. Why do you call me Naomi, since the LORD has testified against me, and the Almighty has afflicted me?" (vv. 20–21 NKJV).

This was not a complaint as much as a heartfelt lament. She knew, as Job did, that it is the Lord who gives and takes away. She understood the principle of God's sovereignty. In calling herself "Mara," she was not suggesting that she had become a bitter person; but (as her words reveal) that Providence had handed her a bitter cup to drink. She saw the hand of God in her sufferings, but far from complaining, I think she was simply acknowledging her faith in the sovereignty of God, even in the midst of a life of bitter grief. Everything Scripture tells us about Naomi indicates that she remained steadfast in the faith throughout her trials. She was not unlike Job—she was a woman of great faith who withstood almost unimaginable testing without ever once wavering in her love for YHWH and her commitment to His will. So hers is actually an impressive expression of faith, without an ounce of resentment in it.

Elimelech had a wealthy relative named Boaz, who had prospered despite the years of famine. He was a landowner of vast holdings and considerable influence. Scripture says he was "a relative of Naomi's husband" (Ruth 2:1 NKJV), but does not spell out the relationship. He might have been Elimelech's brother, but that seems unlikely, since he wasn't, technically, Naomi's next of kin (Ruth 3:12). He was more likely a cousin or a nephew of Elimelech.

Boaz was also a direct descendant of Rahab. Matthew 1:5 says, "Salmon begot Boaz by Rahab" (NKJV), and that agrees with Ruth 4:21, but the number of years spanning the time between the fall of Jericho and the start of the Davidic dynasty suggest that there must be more generations between Salmon and David than either Matthew 1 or Ruth 4 explicitly name. Hebrew genealogy often used a kind of shorthand, skipping generations between well-known ancestors. Matthew seems to do this deliberately to achieve a kind of numerical symmetry in the genealogical listing (Matt. 1:17)—probably as an aid to memorization. So rather than being the immediate son of Rahab, Boaz may very well have been a great-grandson. He was nonetheless in Rahab's direct line. He undoubtedly knew her story well and gloried in his heritage. His connection with Rahab would certainly have inclined his heart to be sympathetic to the plight of a foreign woman like Ruth who had embraced YHWH with a faith reminiscent of Rahab's.

REDEMPTION

In agreeing to return to Bethlehem with Naomi, Ruth was agreeing to help support the aging woman. The biblical data suggest that Ruth was still quite young and physically strong. So she went to work in the fields, gleaning what the harvesters left behind in order to provide enough grain to eke out an existence.

Biblical law established this as a means by which even the most destitute in Israel could always earn a living. Leviticus 19:9–10; 23:22, and Deuteronomy 24:19–21 all required that when a field was harvested, whatever fell from the sheaves should be deliberately left behind. When fruit was picked from trees and vines, some of it was to be left unplucked. The remains of the harvest were then free to be gleaned by anyone willing to do the work.

Ruth's options were limited to that, and that alone. She had no relatives other than her mother-in-law. Naomi's own next of kin weren't even close enough to be legally obliged to support her. With no visible means of support, Ruth saw the necessity of working the barley fields, so she sought and obtained Naomi's permission (Ruth 2:2).

As it happened, she gleaned in one of Boaz's fields, and he saw her. The language of the text suggests that this was purely by happenstance—"she happened to come to the part of the field belonging to Boaz" (v. 3 NKJV)—but we know from the clear teaching of Scripture that God Himself providentially orchestrated these events (Prov. 16:33). Nothing happens by "chance," but God is always behind the scenes, working all things together for the good of His people (Rom. 8:28). There is no such thing as "luck" or "fate" for believers.

Boaz visited his fields that very day, to see the progress of the harvest. When he noticed Ruth, he took an immediate interest. She was obviously young, able, and diligent. Boaz sought out the foreman of his crew and inquired about Ruth.

The chief servant replied, "It is the young Moabite woman who came back with Naomi from the country of Moab. And she said, 'Please let me glean and gather after the reapers among the sheaves.' So she came and has continued from morning until now, though she rested a little in the house" (Ruth 2:6–7 NKJV).

Boaz immediately realized, of course, that this woman was his relative by marriage, so he began to show her special favor. He encouraged her to glean only in his fields and to stay close by his harvesters. He gave her permission to drink from the water he supplied his servants, and he instructed his young men not to touch her.

Ruth, moved by his gentle kindness and generosity, knew very well that such extreme liberality was highly unusual, especially toward an impoverished woman from a foreign land. "She fell on her face, bowed down to the ground, and said to him, 'Why have I found favor in your eyes, that you should take notice of me, since I am a foreigner?'" (v. 10 NKJV).

Boaz explained that he had heard of her extraordinary faithfulness to Naomi and the great sacrifices she had made to come to a foreign land. Then he gave her an unusual blessing that reveals what a godly man he was: "The LORD repay your work, and a full reward be given you by the LORD God of Israel, under whose wings you have come for refuge" (v. 12 NKJV).

Her reply was equally gracious, and beautiful for its humility: "Let me find favor in your sight, my lord; for you have comforted me, and have spoken kindly to your maidservant, though I am not like one of your maidservants" (v. 13 NKJV).

In that first meeting, Boaz immediately seemed smitten with Ruth. He invited her to eat with his workers at mealtime and personally saw that she had enough to be satisfied (vv. 14–16). He instructed his workers to permit her to glean among his sheaves, and he even encouraged them to let grain fall purposely from the bundles for her sake. Thus he lightened the load of her labor and increased the reward of it.

Ruth nonetheless continued to work hard all day. "She gleaned in the field until evening, and beat out what she had gleaned, and it was about an ephah of barley" (v. 17 NKJV). That was a full half bushel, approximately enough to sustain Ruth and Naomi for five days or more. This was about four times as much as a gleaner could hope to gather on a typical good day. Ruth took the grain, as well as some leftover food from lunch, and gave it to Naomi.

Naomi was clearly surprised and pleased at Ruth's amazing prosperity.

She seemed to have instinctively understood that Ruth could not possibly have done so well without someone's help. So she asked where Ruth had gleaned and pronounced a special blessing on "the one who took notice of you" (v. 19 NKJV).

When Ruth told her the man who had been her benefactor was named Boaz, Naomi instantly saw the hand of God in the blessing. "Naomi said to her daughter-in-law, 'Blessed be he of the LORD, who has not forsaken His kindness to the living and the dead!' And Naomi said to her, 'This man is a relation of ours, one of our close relatives'" (v. 20 NKJV).

The Hebrew word translated "one of our close relatives" is *goel*. It is a technical term that means much more than "kinsman." The *goel* was a relative who came to the rescue. The word *goel* includes the idea of redemption, or deliverance. In fact, in order to express the idea more perfectly in English, Old Testament scholars sometimes speak of the *goel* as a "kinsman-redeemer." In Scripture, the word is sometimes translated as "redeemer" (Job 19:25 NKJV) and sometimes as "avenger" (Num. 35:12 NKJV).

A *goel* was usually a prominent male in one's extended family. He was the official guardian of the family's honor. If the occasion arose, he would be the one to avenge the blood of a murdered relative (Josh. 20:2–9). He could buy back family lands sold in times of hardship (Lev. 25:23–28). He could pay the redemption-price for family members sold into slavery (Lev. 25:47–49). Or (if he were a single man or widower and thus eligible to marry) he could revive the family lineage when someone died without an heir by marrying the widow and fathering offspring who would inherit the name and the property of the one who had died. This was known as the law of levirate marriage, and Deuteronomy 25:5–10 presented it as a *duty* in cases where one brother (obviously unmarried and presumably younger) was living in the household of a married brother who died. If the surviving brother refused to fulfill the duty of the *goel* by marrying his brother's widow, he was treated with contempt by all of society.

The Old Testament places a great deal of emphasis on the role of the *goel.* There was a significant redemptive aspect to this person's function. Every kinsman-redeemer was, in effect, a living illustration of the position and work of Christ with respect to His people: He is our true Kinsman-Redeemer, who becomes our human Brother, buys us back from our bondage to evil, redeems our lives from death, and ultimately returns to us everything we lost because of our sin.

Boaz would become Ruth's *goel.* He would redeem her life from poverty and widowhood. He would be her deliverer—and Naomi grasped the potential of this glad turn of events the very moment she learned it was Boaz who had taken an interest in Ruth. He was not only a kinsman; he had the means to be a redeemer too. Naomi strongly encouraged Ruth to follow Boaz's instructions and stay exclusively in his fields. Ruth did this until the end of the harvest season (Ruth 2:21–23).

Naomi saw it as her duty as mother-in-law to seek long-term security for this faithful Moabite girl who had so graciously proven her loyalty, generosity, diligence, and strength of character throughout the hot and difficult harvest season. In a culture where arranged marriages were the norm, this meant doing what she could to orchestrate a marriage between Ruth and Boaz.

Because she was a woman, protocol forbade Naomi from approaching Boaz to arrange a marriage for Ruth. In fact, there was no suggestion that Naomi had spoken to Boaz at all about anything since her return from Moab. Yet from the very beginning, Naomi clearly had an intuition about Boaz's interest in Ruth. Having watched and waited through the long harvest season, Naomi apparently decided Boaz needed some subtle help to get the ball rolling. The way things finally played out suggests that Naomi's instincts were right on target.

If Boaz had ever been married, Scripture does not mention it. According to Jewish tradition, he was a lifelong bachelor. He may have had some physical imperfection or personality quirk that stood in the way of a suitable marriage arrangement. At the very least, he desperately needed prodding. Although he obviously took a keen interest in Ruth from the moment he first saw her, it does not seem to have entered his mind to pursue the *goel's* role on her behalf. By his own testimony (Ruth 3:10), he was surprised that Ruth didn't deem him unsuitable for marriage.

Naomi had sized up the situation correctly though, and she instructed Ruth on what to do. Naomi's scheme was bold and utterly unconventional. Of course, Ruth, as a foreigner, could always plead ignorance of Jewish custom, but if Naomi's plan had been known in advance by people in the community, the propriety police certainly would have been up in arms. Of course, the scheme did not involve any *real* unrighteousness or indecency. Naomi certainly would not have asked Ruth to compromise her virtue or relinquish godly modesty.

Still, what Naomi advised Ruth to do was shockingly forward. (Even to enlightened twenty-first-century minds, it seems surprisingly plucky.) Naomi's plan, in essence, was for Ruth to propose marriage to Boaz! She told Ruth, "Wash yourself and anoint yourself, put on your best garment and go down to the threshing floor; but do not make yourself known to the man until he has finished eating and drinking. Then it shall be, when he lies down, that you shall notice the place where he lies; and you shall go in, uncover his feet, and lie down; and he will tell you what you should do" (Ruth 3:3–4 NKJV). By the custom of the time, this would indicate Ruth's willingness to marry Boaz.

It was the end of the harvest. The threshing floor was a site, most likely out of doors, where grain was winnowed. This involved tossing grain into the air in a breeze so that the light husks of chaff would be blown away. Boaz would work late, sleep outdoors at the threshing floor all night, then arise early and go back to threshing. Thus he both extended his work hours and guarded his grain through the night. He worked well into the night, had a short meal, and laid down next to the grain pile to sleep. Scripture says "his heart was cheerful" (Ruth 3:7 NKJV).

The harvest had been abundant. After years of famine, Boaz was exhilarated at his prosperity.

In accordance with Naomi's instructions, Ruth "came softly, uncovered his feet, and lay down" (v. 7 NKJV). Boaz was so fatigued that he did not notice her until he awakened at midnight and was startled to find a woman lying at his feet.

He said, "Who are you?"

She answered, "I am Ruth, your maidservant. Take your maidservant under your wing, for you are a *[goel]*" (v. 9 NKJV). Ruth was borrowing language ("under your wing") from the blessing Boaz had given her (2:12). This was, in effect, a marriage proposal.

This came as an overwhelming and unexpected blessing to Boaz. According to Ruth 3:10–13:

> *Then he said, "Blessed are you of the LORD, my daughter! For you have shown more kindness at the end than at the beginning, in that you did not go after young men, whether poor or rich. And now, my daughter, do not fear. I will do for you all that you request, for all the people of my town know that you are a virtuous woman. Now it is true that I am a close relative; however, there is relative closer than I. Stay this night, and in the morning it shall be that if he will perform the duty of a close relative for you—good; let him do it. But if he does not want to perform the duty for you, then I will perform the duty for you, as the LORD lives! Lie down until morning."* (NKJV)

Scripture doesn't identify the man who was Naomi's actual next of kin. (He would almost certainly have been either an older brother or cousin of Boaz.) Boaz knew immediately who it was, and he knew that custom required him to defer to this other relative. He explained the situation to Ruth, swore to her his own willingness to be her *goel* if it were possible, and urged her to remain at his feet through the night.

Nothing immoral occurred, of course, and Scripture is clear about that. But Boaz, being protective of Ruth's virtue, awoke her and sent her home just before dawn. He gave her a generous portion of grain as a gift for Naomi, saying, "Do not go empty-handed to your mother-in-law" (v. 17 NKJV).

Naomi, of course, was anxiously awaiting word of what had happened. Ruth told her the whole story, and Naomi, whose feminine intuition was impeccable, said, "Sit still, my daughter, until you know how the matter will turn out; for the man will not rest until he has concluded the matter this day" (v. 18 NKJV).

She was exactly right. Boaz went immediately to the city gate and found Naomi's true next of kin. The two of them sat down in the presence of ten city elders and negotiated for the right to be Ruth's *goel*.

That role involved, first of all, the buy-back of Elimelech's property. In Israel, land portions were part of each family's lasting legacy from generation to generation. Plots of family land could not be permanently sold (Lev. 25:23). Real estate that was "sold" to pay debts remained in the possession of the buyer only until the year of Jubilee, at which time it reverted to the original owner's family. This arrangement helped keep Israel's wealth evenly distributed, and it meant that land-sale deals were actually more like long-term leases. Land sold for debt relief could also be redeemed at any time by the seller or his *goel*. As long as Elimelech had no heirs, the property he and Naomi had sold to pay their debts would automatically become the permanent possession of anyone who acted as Naomi's *goel* by redeeming her property. This made the prospect extremely appealing.

Boaz said, "If you will redeem it, redeem it; but if you will not redeem it, then tell me, that I may know; for there is no one but you to redeem it, and I am next after you."

"I will redeem it," the other relative replied (Ruth 4:4 NKJV).

But then Boaz explained that there was a catch. While Elimelech had no surviving heir, the man who would have been his rightful heir (Mahlon) had left a widow. Therefore, Boaz explained, "On the day you buy the field from the hand of Naomi, you must also buy it from Ruth the Moabitess, the wife of the dead, to perpetuate the name of the dead through his inheritance" (v. 5 NKJV).

This changed things a bit. Because if Ruth *did* remarry someone under the principle of levirate marriage, and she produced any heir in Mahlon's name, rights to Elimelech's land would automatically pass to Ruth's off-spring. The only way to eliminate that risk would be to marry Ruth. The unnamed close relative was either unable or unwilling to marry Ruth. And he didn't want to take an expensive risk that might jeopardize his own children's inheritance. So he told Boaz, "I cannot redeem it for myself, lest I ruin my own inheritance. You redeem my right of redemption for yourself, for I cannot redeem it" (v. 6 NKJV).

A formal contract was then publicly sealed in the customary fashion: the relative removed his sandal and gave it to Boaz (v. 8), in effect granting Boaz the right to stand in his stead as *goel* for Ruth and Naomi.

And Boaz said to the elders and all the people, "You are witnesses this day that I have bought all that was Elimelech's, and all that was Chilion's and Mahlon's, from the hand of Naomi. Moreover, Ruth the Moabitess, the widow of Mahlon, I have acquired as my wife, to perpetuate the name of the dead through his inheritance, that the name of the dead may not be cut off from among his brethren and from his position at the gate. You are witnesses this day" (vv. 9–10 NKJV).

Everyone loves a good love story, and the people of Bethlehem were no exception. As word got out about the unusual transaction taking place in the city gate, the inhabitants of the city began to congregate. They pronounced a blessing on Boaz and his bride-to-be. "We are witnesses," they told Boaz. "The LORD make the woman who is coming to your house like Rachel and Leah, the two who built the house of Israel; and may you prosper in Ephrathah and be famous in Bethlehem. May your house be like the house of Perez, whom Tamar bore to Judah, because of the offspring which the LORD will give you from this young woman" (vv. 11:1–12 NKJV).

The blessing proved to be prophetic. Boaz and Ruth were married, and the Lord soon blessed them with a son. At the birth of this child, the women of Bethlehem gave a blessing to Naomi as well: "Blessed be the LORD, who has not left you this day without a close relative; and may his name be famous in Israel! And may he be to you a restorer of life and a nourisher of your old age; for your daughter-in-law, who loves you, who is better to you than seven sons, has borne him" (vv. 14–15 NKJV).

All of that came true as well. As verse 17 explains, "The neighbor women gave him a name, saying, 'There is a son born to Naomi.' And they called his name Obed. He is the father of Jesse, the father of David" (NKJV). In other words, Ruth was David's great-grandmother.

That is how Ruth, a seemingly ill-fated Moabite woman whose loyalty and faith had led her away from her own people and carried her as a stranger into the land of Israel, became a mother in the royal line that would eventually produce that nation's first great king. Her best-known offspring would be Abraham's Seed and Eve's hoped-for Deliverer.

Ruth is a fitting symbol of every believer, and even of the church itself—redeemed, brought into a position of great favor, endowed with riches and privilege, exalted to be the Redeemer's own bride, and loved by Him with the profoundest affection. That is why the extraordinary story of her redemption ought to make every true believer's heart resonate with profound gladness and thanksgiving for the One who, likewise, has redeemed us from our sin.

5

HANNAH: A PORTRAIT OF FEMININE GRACE

Hannah prayed and said: "My heart rejoices in the LORD; My horn is exalted in the LORD. I smile at my enemies, Because I rejoice in Your salvation."

1 Samuel 2:1 NKJV

annah's name means "grace." It's a fitting designation for a woman whose life was crowned with grace and who became a living emblem of the grace of motherhood. A study of her life reveals the classic profile of a godly mother.

Yet Hannah almost despaired of ever *becoming* a mother. Her experience strongly echoes Sarah's. Like Sarah, she was childless and distraught over it. Both women's marriages were plagued with stress because of their husbands' bigamy. Both of them ultimately received the blessing they sought from God, and in both cases, the answers to their prayers turned out to be exceedingly and abundantly more significant than they had ever dared to ask or think. Hannah's son, Samuel, was the last of the judges. He was also a priest—the one who formally inaugurated the true royal line of Israel by anointing David as king. Samuel became a towering figure in Israel's history. Thus Hannah's life often mirrored that of the original matriarch, Sarah. Most of all, she mirrored Sarah's amazing faith and perseverance.

In a similar way, Hannah also foreshadowed Mary, the mother of Jesus. Hannah's prayer of dedication in 1 Samuel 2:1–10 was the model for Mary's Magnificat in Luke 1:46–55. Both Hannah and Mary formally dedicated their firstborn sons to the Lord (1 Sam. 1:24–28; Luke 2:22–24). Surrender to God's will cost each of them dearly in terms of emotional suffering. (In Hannah's case, this meant the painful sorrow of separation from her own child. Samuel left home to begin his full-time training in the tabernacle when he was still a young toddler, at a time when most children still enjoy the comfort of their mothers' arms.)

A CHERISHED HOPE

Hannah was unique among the women we have studied so far because she was not in the genealogical line of the Messiah. But Hannah's famous dedicatory prayer, when she offered her son to God, is actually a prophetic paean to Israel's Messiah. Clearly, she cherished the very same messianic hope that framed the worldview of every one of the extraordinary women we are studying.

As a matter of fact, since Hannah is the last of the Old Testament women we'll be dealing with, it is worth mentioning how prominent the messianic expectation is in the Old Testament—not only in the lives of these few women, but throughout the law, the psalms, and the prophets (Luke 24:44). The theme runs like a brilliant scarlet thread woven into the tapestry of the Old Testament. Here and there, it comes boldly to the surface in explicit prophecies and promises, but it is usually concealed just underneath, where it remains a constant undertone—always discernible but seldom conspicuous, and never really very far from the center of the picture. It is the true foundation for every *other* theme in the Old Testament.

I especially love how the messianic hope comes right to the forefront whenever we consider the principal women of the Old Testament. The truth is, every truly righteous man and woman in the Old Testament shared the same fervent longing for the Messiah to come. He was the focus and the theme of all their future hopes.

In other words, Christ has *always* been the one true object of all saving faith—even in Old Testament times. Long before He was explicitly revealed in human flesh, the Redeemer was promised. Although the Old Testament saints' understanding of Him was dim and shadowy, the promised Redeemer truly was the focus of all their hopes for salvation. Job, whose story is one of the most ancient expressions of faith recorded in Scripture, gave this testimony at the lowest point of his worst troubles: "I know that my Redeemer lives, and He shall stand at last on the earth; and after my skin is destroyed, this I know, that in my flesh I shall see God, whom I shall see for myself, and my eyes shall behold, and not another. How my heart yearns within me!" (Job 19:25–27 NKJV). Job's faith even included the expectation of his own bodily resurrection!

The faith of true believers has *always* had that Christ-centered perspective. No wonder the messianic expectation was so prominent in the hearts and minds of these extraordinary women. It was the very essence of the faith by which they laid hold of God's promises. It was therefore the key to everything that made them truly extraordinary!

A GODLY HERITAGE

Hannah was an obscure woman living in a remote part of Israel with her husband, Elkanah. Hannah and Elkanah made their home in the territory occupied by the tribe of Ephraim. First Samuel 1:1 lists Elkanah's great-great-grandfather, Zuph, as an "Ephraimite," but this clearly designates only the territory the family lived in, and not their line of descent. We know this because 1 Chronicles 6:22–27 gives a detailed genealogy for Elkanah, showing that he actually descended from Levi by way of Kohath.

The Kohathites were one of the three major lines in the tribe of Levi.

This was an important clan. Moses and Aaron were Kohathites, according to 1 Chronicles 6:2–3. The sons of Kohath were assigned responsibility for the most sacred furnishings of the tabernacle, including the ark of the covenant (Num. 3:30–31). When Israel moved camp from one place to another in the wilderness, it was the Kohathites' duty to disassemble the Holy of Holies and transport the ark and all the sacred utensils according to a strict procedure (4:4–16).

Once Israel occupied the Promised Land permanently and the tabernacle was finally situated at Shiloh, the Kohathites seem to have devoted themselves to other priestly functions—especially leading music, prayer, and praise in the tabernacle (1 Chron. 6:31–33). Thus one of Elkanah's close ancestors was known as "Heman the singer," according to verse 33.

The Levites were the only tribe in Israel allotted no independent territory of their own because they were the priestly tribe, and the Lord Himself was their inheritance (Num. 18:20). So when the land of Israel was divided and distributed according to the twelve other tribes, the Levites were scattered throughout the whole nation. They were given modest plots of pastureland and fields to cultivate in selected cities throughout Israel. Elkanah's ancestors, probably as far back as the earliest generation after the conquest of Canaan, had lived among the tribe of Ephraim. That's why Zuph (Elkanah's ancestor) is called an "Ephraimite," even though this was clearly a family of Kohathites, from the tribe of Levi.

Men from the tribe of Levi took turns every year (for a few weeks at a time) serving in the tabernacle. In those days, the tabernacle was situated at Shiloh. Since the Levites had this duty to minister in the tabernacle, taking them away from their land and homes for an extended time each year, their income was supplemented with tithes collected from all Israel (Num. 18:24–32).

Hannah faithfully traveled with Elkanah to the tabernacle every year to worship and offer a sacrifice. Scripture portrays them as a devout family, yet living in a dismal period of Israel's history. The Bible reminds us that at the time Elkanah made regular trips to Shiloh to worship and offer his sacrifice, "the two sons of Eli, Hophni and Phinehas, the priests of the LORD, were there" (1 Sam. 1:3 NKJV).

Hophni and Phinehas were two of the *worst* priests we ever meet on the pages of Scripture. They were greedy men who illegally—and sometimes forcibly—took the best portions of people's offerings for themselves (1 Sam. 2:13–16). Worse yet, they used their position as priests to seduce young women (v. 22). They had, in effect, turned the tabernacle into a bawdy house, and they had formed a kind of priestly mafia, bullying worshipers and flagrantly showing contempt for God's law. The obvious result was that the people of Israel grew to abhor bringing their offerings to the Lord (v. 17). All the people of Israel were aware of what Hophni and Phinehas were doing, but their father Eli made only a half-hearted attempt to rebuke them, even though he was the high priest (v. 24).

Of course, the visible manifestation of God's glory that once resided over the ark of the covenant was long gone. The ark itself had come to mean little to the Israelites. Hophni and Phinehas treated it like a talisman. The low point came when they took it into battle against the Philistines, presuming it would guarantee Israel a victory. Instead, the Philistines soundly defeated Israel's army and captured the ark. The ark was never again returned to the tabernacle at Shiloh. (After its recovery from the Philistines, the ark remained in virtual neglect for about a hundred years in a private house in Kiriath-Jearim, until David retrieved it and brought it to Jerusalem in preparation for the temple Solomon would build there.)

The loss of the ark (1 Sam. 4:10–11) occurred just a few short years after Hannah is introduced to us in Scripture (1:2). It was the climactic and defining moment of that backslidden era. Incidentally, in that same battle in which the ark was captured, Hophni and Phinehas were killed. Eli fell over from shock as soon as he heard the news. He died too—from injuries sustained in that fall. Phinehas's wife delivered a child shortly after that, and she named him Ichabod, meaning "the glory has departed" (4:12–22 NKJV). It was an apt description of that whole era of Israel's history. This was indeed a time of great spiritual darkness.

In those dry and gloomy days, Hannah stood out as a ray of light. Not only was she the quintessential godly mother and wife, but in a spiritually cold generation she exemplified patience, prayerfulness, faith, meekness, submission, spiritual devotion, and motherly love.

A HOLY AMBITION

In spite of her gracious character, Hannah's home life was often troubled and sorrowful. Her husband was a bigamist. In the words of Scripture, "He had two wives: the name of one was Hannah, and the name of the other Peninnah. Peninnah had children, but Hannah had no children" (1 Sam. 1:2 NKJV). Obviously, this situation caused severe tension in the family. Peninnah—called Hannah's "rival" (v. 6 NKJV)—deliberately provoked her, goading her about the fact that the Lord had withheld children from her.

Elkanah preferred Hannah, whom he loved deeply, but that only magnified the bitter rivalry between the women. Such strife was an inevitable side effect of Elkanah's bigamy. Of course, one of the obvious reasons God designed marriage as a monogamous relationship in the first place was to avoid this kind of strife within families.

Hannah was in constant anguish because of her own infertility. She was further tormented by Peninnah's carping taunts. The burden and stress made life almost unbearable. Hannah wept bitterly, and she literally could not even eat at times (1:7). She longed to be a mother. This was her one ambition in life.

I am convinced it was no selfish aspiration. The way Hannah immediately dedicated her first son to the Lord and gave him over to serve in the tabernacle at such a young age demonstrates the purity of her motives.

She understood that motherhood is the highest calling God can bestow on any woman.

That is not to suggest, of course, that motherhood is the *only* proper role for women. Scripture recognizes that it is God's will for some women to remain single (1 Cor. 7:8–9). In the wisdom of His providence, He has also ordained that some married women will remain perpetually childless (see Psalm 127:3). A woman is by no means *required* to be a wife or a mother before she can be useful in the Lord's service. Miriam (Moses' sister) and Deborah (who served as a judge and deliverer in Israel) are biblical examples of women whom God used mightily apart from marriage or motherhood. (Deborah was married, but she gained renown in a role that had nothing to do with being a wife or mother.)

Still, Scripture frequently portrays marriage as "the grace of life" (1 Pet. 3:7 NKJV) and motherhood as the *highest* calling any woman could ever be summoned to. It is, after all, the one vocation that God uniquely designed women to fulfill, and no man can ever intrude into the mother's role. Perhaps you have already noticed how the glory and dignity of motherhood stood out in one way or another as a major theme in the life of every woman we have dealt with so far. That is true of *most* of the key women in Scripture. Scripture honors them for their faithfulness in their own homes. Or, as in the case of Rahab and Ruth, we remember them because by faith they were liberated from the bondage of the world and raised to the more exalted role of wife and mother. Only rarely in Scripture were women singled out and praised for exploits or careers outside the domestic realm. Honor and eminence for women in the Bible was nearly always closely associated with home and family. Hannah understood that, and she earnestly desired to enter into the noble role of a mother.

Of course, the Bible's exaltation of motherhood is often scorned by our more "enlightened" age. In fact, in this generation, motherhood is frequently derided and belittled even in the name of "women's rights." But it has been God's plan from the beginning that women should train and nurture godly children and thus leave a powerful imprint on society through the home (1 Tim. 5:10; Titus 2:3–5). Hannah is a classic illustration of how that works. She is a reminder that mothers are the makers of men and the architects of the next generation. Her earnest prayer for a child was the beginning of a series of events that helped turn back the spiritual darkness and backsliding in Israel. She set in motion a chain of events that would ultimately usher in a profound spiritual awakening at the dawn of the Davidic dynasty.

We first encounter Hannah when Israel was in desperate need of a great leader and a great man. Hannah became the woman whom God used to help shape that man. Samuel proved to be the one man who could fill the leadership void. His character bore the clear stamp of his mother's influence, even though he left home at such an early age.

I believe Hannah's influence as a godly wife and mother is traceable to the three great loves of her life.

LOVE FOR HER HUSBAND

From the beginning of Scripture's account of her family, it is evident that Hannah had a deep love for Elkanah, as he did for her. When they made a peace offering to the Lord (a sacrifice in which the offerer roasted the sacrificial animal and partook of a feast unto the Lord), Elkanah gave portions to Peninnah and all her children, but he gave a double portion to Hannah because of his great love for her (1 Sam. 1:4–5). This was a public honor that he regularly and deliberately bestowed on her in the presence of others at a feast.

Obviously, Hannah's marriage was not a perfect one, chiefly because of the jealousy and rivalry her husband's polygamous marriage caused. Hannah seemed to be the first wife, since she is named first (v. 2). Apparently Elkanah later married Peninnah because of Hannah's barrenness. Remember, it was deemed vitally important in that culture to have children who could maintain the family inheritance and the family name. This was the same reason Abraham entered into a polygamous relationship with Hagar. It is undoubtedly the main reason we see so much polygamy in the Old Testament.

But Hannah's marriage, though marred by tensions, was solid. Elkanah obviously loved Hannah with a sincere affection, and he knew her love for him was reciprocal. In fact, he tried to comfort her by tenderly reminding her of his love for her: "Hannah, why do you weep? Why do you not eat? And why is your heart grieved? Am I not better to you than ten sons?" (v. 8 NKJV). This plea *did* help, at least for the moment, because Hannah immediately arose and ate, then went to the tabernacle (v. 9).

Hannah's love for her husband is the first key to understanding her profound influence as a mother. Contrary to popular opinion, the most important characteristic of a godly mother is not her relationship with her *children*. It is her love for her *husband*. The love between husband and wife is the real key to a thriving family. A healthy home environment cannot be built exclusively on the parents' love for their children. The properly situated family has *marriage* at the center; families shouldn't revolve around the children.

Furthermore, all parents need to heed this lesson: what you communicate to your children through your marital relationship will stay with them for the rest of their lives. By watching how mother and father treat one another, they will learn the most fundamental lessons of life—love, self-sacrifice, integrity, virtue, sin, sympathy, compassion, understanding, and forgiveness. Whatever you teach them about those things, right or wrong, is planted deep within their hearts.

That emphasis on the centrality of marriage was very evident between Elkanah and Hannah. With all their domestic issues, they nonetheless had a healthy marriage and an abiding love for one another. Their inability to have children together was like an open wound. But it was an experience that drew out of Elkanah tender expressions of love for his wife. And even in a home environment with a second wife and multiple children—a chaos created by the folly of Elkanah's bigamy and made even more dysfunctional by Peninnah's ill temperament—Hannah and Elkanah clearly loved one another deeply.

They worshiped God together, and they did so regularly. Verse 3 says, "This man went up from his city *yearly* to worship and sacrifice to the LORD of hosts in Shiloh" (NKJV). But that doesn't mean Hannah and Elkanah visited the tabernacle *only* once a year. All Israelite men were required to attend three annual feasts (Deut. 16:1–17). Most likely, Elkanah took his family with him on those journeys. They probably traveled to Shiloh together on other occasions too. (The journey from the family home in Ramathaim Zophim to Shiloh was a distance of about twenty-five miles along the edge of the Jordan Valley. The trip could easily be made in two days or less.) Worship seemed to have been a central aspect of Hannah and Elkanah's lives together. This was what kept their love for one another strong in the face of so much adversity.

It also explains the second reason why Hannah was such an influential mother. As much as she loved Elkanah, there was an even greater love that motivated her.

LOVE FOR HEAVEN

Hannah obviously had a deep and abiding love for God. Her spiritual passion was seen in the fervency of her prayer life. She was a devout woman whose affections were set on heavenly things, not on earthly things. Her desire for a child was no mere craving for self-gratification. It wasn't about her. It wasn't about getting what she wanted. It was about self-sacrifice—giving herself to that little life in order to give him back to the Lord. Centuries earlier, Jacob's wife Rachel prayed, "Give me children, or else I die!" (Gen. 30:1 NKJV). Hannah's prayer was more modest than that. She did not pray for "children," but for one son. She begged God for one son who would be fit to serve in the tabernacle. If God would give her that son, she would give him back to God. Hannah's actions proved that she wanted a child not for her own pleasure, but because she wanted to dedicate him to the Lord.

Naturally, then, the Lord was the One to whom she turned to plead her case. It was significant, I think, that despite the bitter agony Hannah suffered because of her childlessness, she never became a complainer or a nag. There's no suggestion that she ever grumbled against God or badgered her husband about her childlessness. Why should she whine to Elkanah? Children are an inheritance from the Lord (Ps. 127:3; Gen. 33:5). Hannah seems to have understood that, so she took her case straight to the Lord. Despite her disappointment and heartache, she remained faithful to YHWH. In fact, frustration seems to have turned her more and more *to* the Lord, not *away* from him. And she persisted in prayer.

That's a beautiful characteristic, and it was Hannah's distinctive virtue: constant, steadfast faith. First Samuel 1:12 speaks of her prayer as continual: "She *continued* praying before the LORD" (NKJV, emphasis added). She stayed before the Lord, even with a broken heart, pouring out tearful prayers. Her trials thus had the benefit of making her a woman of prayer. She truly exemplified what it meant to "pray without ceasing" (1 Thess. 5:17; Luke 18:1–8).

The value of persistent and passionate prayer is one of the central lessons from Hannah's life. Notice how the passion of her praying is described in 1 Samuel 1:10–11: "And she was in bitterness of soul, and prayed to the LORD and wept in anguish. *Then she made a vow* and said, 'O LORD of hosts, if You will indeed look on the affliction of Your maidservant and remember me, and not forget Your maidservant, but will give Your maidservant a male child, then I will give him to the LORD all the days of his life, and no razor shall come upon his head'" (NKJV, emphasis added).

There were two parts to Hannah's vow. One was the promise to give the child to the Lord. Subsequent events indicated that by this pledge she intended to devote him to full-time service in the tabernacle. The last part of Hannah's promise entailed a vow never to cut his hair. This was one of three provisions of the ancient Nazirite vow (Num. 6:1–9). While it was not clear whether Hannah's promise also entailed all the other provisions of the Nazirite vow, if it had, her son would have also been required to abstain from wine (or any product of grapes) and not come in contact with anything that would cause ceremonial defilement. These restrictions were signs of consecration to God.

Both parts of Hannah's vow consecrated her son for life to duties that normally would have been only temporary. Levites, as we have seen, took turns serving in the tabernacle. No one had the responsibility for life. Nazirite vows were usually only temporary too. Of course, God had expressly commanded Samson's mother to make him a Nazirite for life (Judg. 13:2–7). (Since Samson's mother had been barren before Samson was conceived, Hannah's knowledge of that history may be what prompted her to make this vow.) John the Baptist also seemed to have been under a similar lifelong vow (Luke 7:33). But normally such vows lasted a few weeks or years at the most.

Hannah obviously wanted her son to be a godly man, serving and glorifying the Lord all his life. These were not promises she made lightly, and when God finally answered her prayer, she did not recoil from the difficult duty her vow had placed on her as Samuel's mother.

The intensity of Hannah's prayer made her conspicuous in the tabernacle, especially in that backslidden era. She was so totally consumed by the passion of her prayer and so distraught with weeping (1 Sam. 1:10) that she caught the attention of the old priest, Eli. He had probably never witnessed more passionate, heartfelt praying, though he didn't even know it was that:

> *And it happened, as she continued praying before the LORD, that Eli*
> *watched her mouth. Now Hannah spoke in her heart; only her lips moved,*

but her voice was not heard. Therefore Eli thought she was drunk. So Eli said to her, "How long will you be drunk? Put your wine away from you!"

And Hannah answered and said, "No, my lord, I am a woman of sorrowful spirit. I have drunk neither wine nor intoxicating drink, but have poured out my soul before the LORD. Do not consider your maidservant a wicked woman, for out of the abundance of my complaint and grief I have spoken until now."

Then Eli answered and said, "Go in peace, and the God of Israel grant your petition which you have asked of Him." (1 Sam. 1:12–17 NKJV)

Eli's insensitive response was typical of him. It showed how utterly he lacked any sense of discernment or even basic courtesy. This is a large part of the explanation for why he was so incompetent in his roles as high priest to the nation and father to his own sons. His accusation against Hannah was the same accusation the unbelieving mob made against the disciples on the day of Pentecost (Acts 2:13). Eli evidently did not recognize that she was praying.

A couple of factors may have contributed to his confusion. In the first place, it was customary in Israel to pray aloud, not silently. Hannah seems to have understood that God sees right into the human heart. He knows our thoughts even before they become words; and He knows our words before they are formed on our lips (Ps. 139:1–4). Furthermore, we are taught in the New Testament that the Holy Spirit intercedes for us with groanings that can't even be uttered (Rom. 8:26). So there was no need for Hannah to pray aloud. She wasn't doing it for ceremony. She knew that the Lord knew her heart. By contrast, private prayer seemed to have been so foreign to Eli that he could not even recognize prayer when he saw it, unless it conformed to ceremonial customs.

A second thing that may have obscured Eli's discernment was the fact that his own sons were known to consort with loose women right there in the tabernacle (1 Sam. 2:22). Eli certainly did not approve of his sons' behavior, but he failed to take strong enough measures to keep it from happening. Apparently he was more accustomed to seeing immoral women at the tabernacle than godly ones, so he may have assumed that Hannah was one of those women.

His rebuke was nonetheless foolish and uncalled for. Drunkenness usually makes people noisy and boisterous. Hannah was silent and keeping completely to herself. There was no reason whatsoever for Eli to scold her like that.

Hannah answered with characteristic grace and humility. Of course, she was horrified by his accusation and denied it with a clear tone of chagrin. She explained that she was merely pouring out her heart in sorrow. She didn't tell Eli the reason for her sorrow. There was no need for that. She understood that only God could answer her prayer; that was why her prayers had been silent in the first place.

For his part, Eli quickly changed his tone. He must have been somewhat embarrassed and chastened to learn how badly he had misjudged this poor woman. Because of that, he blessed her and called on the Lord to grant her petition.

Hannah's final response to Eli revealed another of her positive spiritual traits. "And she said, 'Let your maidservant find favor in your sight.' So the woman went her way and ate, and her face was no longer sad" (1:18 NKJV). Hannah cast her whole burden upon the Lord and left her sense of frustration there at the altar. She did what she had come to the tabernacle to do. She had brought her case before the Lord. Now she was content to leave the matter in His hands.

That demonstrates how genuine and patient her faith truly was. Scripture says, "Cast your burden on the LORD, and He shall sustain you" (Ps. 55:22 NKJV). Some people will pray, "O God, here's my problem," and then leave His presence in complete doubt and frustration, still shouldering the same burden they originally brought before the Lord, not really trusting Him to sustain them. Hannah truly laid her troubles in the lap of the Lord, totally confident that He would answer her in accord for what was best for her. There's a real humility in that kind of faith, as the apostle Peter noted: "Humble yourselves under the mighty hand of God, that He may exalt you in due time, casting all your care upon Him, for He cares for you" (1 Peter 5:6–7 NKJV).

When God finally *did* answer Hannah's prayer by giving her the son she had asked for, her thankful soul responded with a pure, unbroken stream of praise. Her words, recorded for us in 1 Samuel 2:1–10, are a masterpiece. In the chapter that follows, we'll examine Mary's Magnificat, which is a close parallel to this passage both in its style and its substance:

> *And Hannah prayed and said:*
>
> *"My heart rejoices in the LORD;*
> *My horn is exalted in the LORD.*
> *I smile at my enemies,*
> *Because I rejoice in Your salvation.*
>
> *"No one is holy like the LORD,*
> *For there is none besides You,*
> *Nor is there any rock like our God.*
>
> *"Talk no more so very proudly;*
> *Let no arrogance come from your mouth,*
> *For the LORD is the God of knowledge;*
> *And by Him actions are weighed.*
>
> *"The bows of the mighty men are broken,*
> *And those who stumbled are girded with strength.*
> *Those who were full have hired themselves out for bread,*
> *And the hungry have ceased to hunger.*
> *Even the barren has borne seven,*
> *And she who has many children has become feeble.*

"The LORD kills and makes alive;
He brings down to the grave and brings up.
The LORD makes poor and makes rich;
He brings low and lifts up.
He raises the poor from the dust
And lifts the beggar from the ash heap,
To set them among princes
And make them inherit the throne of glory.

"For the pillars of the earth are the Lord's,
And He has set the world upon them.
He will guard the feet of His saints,
But the wicked shall be silent in darkness.

"For by strength no man shall prevail.
The adversaries of the LORD shall be broken in pieces;
From heaven He will thunder against them.
The LORD will judge the ends of the earth.

"He will give strength to His king,
And exalt the horn of His anointed." (NKJV)

There's enough solid content in that brief thanksgiving anthem that we could spend many pages analyzing it. If it were given to me as a text to preach on, I would undoubtedly have to preach a series of several sermons just to unpack its prophetic and doctrinal significance completely. Obviously, we don't have enough space for that kind of thorough study of Hannah's hymn of praise. But even the briefest overview reveals how thoroughly familiar Hannah was with the deep things of God.

She acknowledged, for example, God's holiness, His goodness, His sovereignty, His power, and His wisdom. She worshiped Him as Savior, as

Creator, and as sovereign judge. She acknowledged the fallenness and depravity of human nature, as well as the folly of unbelief and rebellion. In short, her few stanzas were a masterpiece of theological understanding.

But this was not mere academic theology. Hannah spoke about God from her own intimate knowledge of Him. Her words of praise were filled with love and wonder. That love for God, and a love for all things heavenly, was one of the keys to Hannah's lasting influence as a mother.

LOVE FOR HER HOME

A third major characteristic of Hannah was her devotion to home and family. We see evidence of this from the beginning, in her love for Elkanah and his love for her. We see it in the way she rose above the petty strife and feuding Peninnah deliberately tried to sow within her own household with no other intention than to exasperate Hannah. We see it again in Hannah's intense longing to be a mother. We see it best in how committed she was to her child in his infancy.

When Hannah and Elkanah returned home after her encounter with Eli in the tabernacle, Scripture says, "Elkanah knew Hannah his wife, and the LORD remembered her. So it came to pass in the process of time that Hannah conceived and bore a son" (1:19–20 NKJV). She named him Samuel, but the meaning of *Samuel* is not entirely clear. It could literally be translated "name of God." Some commentators suggest it could mean "asked from God," and others say "heard by God." In Hebrew, the name is very similar to Ishmael, which means, "God shall hear." Whatever the actual significance of the name, the essence of what it meant to Hannah is clear. Samuel was a living answer to prayer and a reminder that God had heard what she asked and granted her heart's desire.

Hannah devoted herself solely to Samuel's care for the next few years. When the time came to make the first trip to Shiloh after the baby's birth, Hannah told her husband she planned to stay at home with Samuel until he was weaned. "Then," she said, "I will take him, that he may appear before the LORD and remain there forever" (v. 22 NKJV).

She knew her time with Samuel would be short. Mothers in that culture nursed their children for about three years. She would care for him during his most formative years, while he learned to walk and talk. As soon as he was weaned, though, she was determined to fulfill her vow.

In the meantime, she would be a fixture in his life. She became the very model of a stay-at-home mom. No mother was ever more devoted to home and child. She had important work to do—nurturing him, caring for him, and helping him learn the most basic truths of life and wisdom. She taught him his first lessons about YHWH. She made her home an environment where he could learn and grow in safety. And she carefully directed the course of his learning and helped shape his interests.

Hannah seemed to understand how vital those early years are, when 90 percent of personality is formed. "Train up a child in the way he should go, and when he is old he will not depart from it" (Prov. 22:6 NKJV). She prepared Samuel in those formative years for a lifetime of service to God—the high calling to which she had consecrated him before he was ever born. History tells us that she did her job well. Samuel, obviously a precocious child, grew in wisdom and understanding. Those early years set a course for his life from which he never deviated. The only blot on his record came in his old age, when he made his sons judges and they perverted justice (1 Sam. 8:1–3). Samuel's own failure as a father was the one aspect of his life that obviously owed more to the influence of Eli, the old priest, than to the example of Hannah.

Hannah's devotion to home and motherhood was exemplary in every way. Her devotion to her son in those early years makes her ultimate willingness to hand Samuel over to a life of service in the tabernacle seem all the more remarkable. It must have been intensely painful for her to send him off at such a tender age. In effect, the tabernacle became his boarding school and Eli his tutor. But it is apparent that Hannah's influence on

Samuel remained far more of a guiding force in his life than the spiritually feeble example of Eli.

No doubt Hannah kept as close to Samuel as the arrangement would allow. She and Elkanah naturally would have increased their visits to Shiloh in light of Hannah's intense love for Samuel. It seems safe to surmise that they probably extended the duration of each visit too. Scripture says she "used to make him a little robe, and bring it to him year by year when she came up with her husband to offer the yearly sacrifice" (1 Sam. 2:19 NKJV). Again, "yearly" in this case doesn't mean "just once a year." It speaks of the regularity and faithfulness of their visits. Hannah thus continued to exercise a strong maternal influence on Samuel throughout all his formative years.

Scripture says God blessed Hannah with five more children—three sons and two daughters (v. 21). Her home and family life became rich and full. She was blessed by God to be allowed to achieve every ambition she had ever longed to fulfill. Her love for heaven, husband, and home are still the true priorities for every godly wife and mother. Her extraordinary life stands as a wonderful example to women today who want their homes to be places where God is honored, even in the midst of a dark and sinful culture. Hannah showed us what the Lord can do through one woman totally and unreservedly devoted to Him.

May her tribe increase.

6

MARY: BLESSED AMONG WOMEN

The virgin's name was Mary. And having come in, the angel said to her, "Rejoice, highly favored one, the Lord is with you; blessed are you among women!"

Luke 1:27–28 NKJV

Of all the extraordinary women in Scripture, one stands out above all others as the most blessed, most highly favored by God, and most universally admired by women. Indeed, no woman is more truly remarkable than Mary. She was the one sovereignly chosen by God—from among all the women who have ever been born—to be the singular instrument through which He would at last bring the Messiah into the world.

Mary herself testified that all generations would regard her as profoundly blessed by God (Luke 1:48). This was not because she believed herself to be any kind of saintly superhuman, but because she was given such remarkable grace and privilege.

While acknowledging that Mary was the most extraordinary of women, it is appropriate to inject a word of caution against the common tendency to elevate her *too much*. She was, after all, a woman—not a demigoddess or a quasi-deiform creature who somehow transcended the rest of her race. The point of her "blessedness" is certainly not that we should think of her as someone to whom we can appeal for blessing; but rather that she herself was supremely blessed by God. She is never portrayed in Scripture as a source or dispenser of grace, but is herself the recipient of God's blessing. Her Son, not Mary herself, is the fountain of grace (Ps. 72:17). *He* is the long-awaited Seed of Abraham of whom the covenant promise spoke: "In your seed all the nations of the earth shall be blessed" (Gen. 22:18 NKJV).

Various extrabiblical religious traditions and many superstitious minds have beatified Mary beyond what is reasonable, making her an object of religious veneration, imputing to her various titles and attributes that belong to God alone. A long tradition of overzealous souls throughout history have wrongly exalted her to godlike status. Unfortunately, even in our era, Mary, not Christ, is the central focus of worship and religious affection for millions. They think of her as more approachable and more sympathetic than Christ. They revere her as the perfect Madonna, supposedly untouched by original sin, a perpetual virgin, and even co-redemptrix with Christ Himself. Catholic dogma teaches that she was taken bodily to heaven, where she was crowned "Queen of Heaven." Her role today, according to Catholic legend, is mediatory and intercessory. Therefore, multitudes direct their prayers to her instead of to God alone—as if Mary were omnipresent and omniscient.

As a matter of fact, many people superstitiously imagine that Mary regularly appears in various apparitions here and there, and some even claim that she delivers prophecies to the world through such means. This extreme gullibility about apparitions of Mary sometimes rises to almost comical proportions. In November 2004, a stale grilled-cheese sandwich sold for $28,000 in an eBay auction because the sandwich purportedly had an image of Mary supernaturally etched in the burn marks of the toast. A few months later, thousands of worshipers in Chicago built a makeshift shrine to Mary in the walkway of a freeway underpass because someone claimed to see an image of her in salt stains on the concrete wall of the abutment.

No less than Pope John Paul II declared his total devotion to Mary. He dedicated his whole pontificate to her and had an M for Mary embroidered in all his papal garments. He prayed to her, credited her with saving his life, and even left the care of the Roman Catholic Church to her in his will. Rome has long fostered the cult of Marian devotion, and superstition about Mary is more popular today than it has ever been. So much homage is paid to Mary in Catholic churches around the world that the centrality and supremacy of Christ is often utterly obscured by the adoration of His mother.

All such veneration of Mary is entirely without biblical warrant. In fact, it is completely *contrary* to what Scripture expressly teaches (Rev. 19:10). But the tendency to make Mary an object of worship is nothing new. Even during Jesus' earthly ministry, for example, there were those who showed undue reverence to Mary because of her role as His mother. On one occasion, Scripture says, a woman in the crowd raised her voice and said to Jesus, "Blessed is the womb that bore You, and the breasts at which You nursed."

His reply was a rebuke: "On the contrary, blessed are those who hear the word of God, and observe it" (Luke 11:27–28 NASB).

Mary herself was a humble soul who maintained a consistently low profile in the gospel accounts of Jesus' life. Scripture expressly debunks some of the main legends about her. The idea that she remained a perpetual virgin, for example, is impossible to reconcile with the fact that Jesus had half-brothers who are named in Scripture alongside both Joseph and Mary as their parents: "Is this not the carpenter's son? Is not His mother called Mary? And His brothers James, Joses, Simon, and Judas?" (Matt. 13:55 NKJV). Matthew 1:25 furthermore says that Joseph abstained from sexual relations with Mary only "till she had brought forth her firstborn Son" (NKJV). On any natural reading of the plain sense of Scripture, it is impossible to support the idea of Mary's perpetual virginity.

Mary's immaculate conception and her supposed sinlessness are likewise without any scriptural foundation whatsoever. The opening stanza of Mary's Magnificat speaks of God as her "Savior," thus giving implicit testimony from Mary's own lips that she needed redemption. In such a biblical context, that could refer only to salvation from sin. Mary was in effect confessing her own sinfulness.

In fact, far from portraying Mary with a halo and a seraphic stare on her face, Scripture reveals her as an average young girl of common means from a peasants' town in a poor region of Israel, betrothed to a working-class fiancé who earned his living as a carpenter. If you had met Mary before her firstborn Son was miraculously conceived, you might not have noticed her at all. She could hardly have been more plain and unassuming. From everything we know of her background and social standing, not much about her life or her experience so far would be deemed very extraordinary.

MARY'S HERITAGE

Mary did have some illustrious ancestors, though. Luke gave us her genealogy in detail (Luke 3:23–38). Matthew, likewise, listed Joseph's (Matt. 1:1–16). Both Joseph and Mary descended from David. Therefore, prior to David, they shared the same genealogy. Mary's branch of David's family tree can be traced through David's son named Nathan, while Joseph's branch is the royal line, through Solomon. In light of this, Christ inherited David's throne through his stepfather. It was his birthright as a firstborn son. Jesus' blood relationship to David, however, came through Mary who descended from an otherwise inconsequential branch of David's family.

Remember that Matthew included several women in the genealogy of Christ. Since all those women came between Abraham and David, all of them were ancestors of both Joseph and Mary—including Rahab and Ruth. Of course, Sarah (though unnamed in the New Testament genealogies) was the wife of Abraham and the mother of Isaac. And Eve was the mother of all living. Therefore, with the single exception of Hannah, every one of the extraordinary women we have examined so far was an ancestor of Mary. She seems to have inherited the best traits of all of them. (As we're going to see, she also reflected the best aspects of Hannah's character.) Most significant of all, her faith was an extraordinary example of the kind of faith Jesus blessed. She was sincere, earnestly worshipful, childlike in her trust of the Lord, and utterly dependent on Him.

Then she found herself unexpectedly thrust into the very role each one of her illustrious ancestors had longed to fulfill. She would become the mother of the promised Redeemer.

THE ANNOUNCEMENT THAT CHANGED HER LIFE

When we first meet Mary in Luke's gospel, it is on the occasion when an archangel appeared to her suddenly and without fanfare to disclose to her God's wonderful plan. Scripture says, simply, "The angel Gabriel was sent by God to a city of Galilee named Nazareth, to a virgin betrothed to a man whose name was Joseph, of the house of David. The virgin's name was Mary" (Luke 1:26–27 NKJV).

Mary is the equivalent of the Hebrew "Miriam." The name may be derived from the Hebrew word for "bitter." (As we saw in the story of Ruth, her mother-in-law Naomi referred to herself as "Mara," a reference to the bitterness of her trials.) Mary's young life may well have been filled with bitter hardships. Her hometown was a forlorn community in a poor district of Galilee. Nazareth, you may recall, famously bore the brunt of at least one future disciple's disdain. When Philip told Nathanael that he had found the Messiah and the Anointed One was a Galilean from Nazareth, Nathanael sneered, "Can anything good come out of Nazareth?" (John 1:45–46 NKJV). Mary had lived there all her life, in a community where, frankly, good things probably were pretty scarce.

Other details about Mary's background can be gleaned here and there in Scripture. She had a sister, according to John 19:25. There's not enough data in the text to identify accurately who the sister was, but Mary's sister was herself obviously a close enough disciple of Jesus to be present with the other faithful women at the crucifixion. Mary was also a close relative of Elizabeth, mother of John the Baptist (Luke 1:36). The nature of that relationship isn't specifically described. They might have been cousins, or Elizabeth might have been Mary's aunt. Luke's account describes Elizabeth as already "in her old age." Mary, on the other hand, seems to have been quite young.

In fact, at the time of the Annunciation, Mary was probably still a teenager. It was customary for girls in that culture to be betrothed while they were still as young as thirteen years of age. Marriages were ordinarily arranged by the bridegroom or his parents through the girl's father. Mary was betrothed to Joseph, about whom we know next to nothing—except that he was a carpenter (Mark 6:3) and a righteous man (Matt. 1:19).

Scripture is very clear in teaching that Mary was still a virgin when Jesus was miraculously conceived in her womb. Luke 1:27 twice calls her a virgin, using a Greek term that allows for no subtle nuance of meaning. The clear claim of Scripture, and Mary's own testimony, is that she had never been physically intimate with any man. Her betrothal to Joseph was a legal engagement known as *kiddushin,* which in that culture typically lasted a full year. *Kiddushin* was legally as binding as marriage itself. The couple were deemed husband and wife, and only a legal divorce could dissolve the marriage contract (Matt. 1:19). But during this time, the couple lived separately from one another and had no physical relations whatsoever. One of the main points of *kiddushin* was to demonstrate the fidelity of both partners.

When the angel appeared to Mary, she was already formally bound to Joseph by *kiddushin.* Luke 1:28–35 describes Mary's encounter with the angel:

> *And having come in, the angel said to her, "Rejoice, highly favored one, the Lord is with you; blessed are you among women!"*

But when she saw him, she was troubled at his saying, and considered what manner of greeting this was.

Then the angel said to her, "Do not be afraid, Mary, for you have found favor with God. And behold, you will conceive in your womb and bring forth a Son, and shall call His name JESUS. He will be great, and will be called the Son of the Highest; and the Lord God will give Him the throne of His father David. And He will reign over the house of Jacob forever, and of His kingdom there will be no end."

Then Mary said to the angel, "How can this be, since I do not know a man?"

And the angel answered and said to her, "The Holy Spirit will come upon you, and the power of the Highest will overshadow you; therefore, also, that Holy One who is to be born will be called the Son of God." (NKJV)

We have seen throughout this book how numerous godly women in Mary's ancestry, going all the way back to Eve, had fostered the hope of being the one through whom the Redeemer would come. But the privilege came at a high cost to Mary personally, because it carried the stigma of an unwed pregnancy. Although she had remained totally and completely chaste, the world was bound to think otherwise. Even Joseph assumed the worst. We can only imagine how his heart sank when he learned that Mary was pregnant, and he knew he was not the father. His inclination was to divorce her quietly. He was a righteous man and loved her, so Scripture says he was not willing to make a public example of her, but he was so shaken by the news of her pregnancy that at first he saw no option but divorce. Then an angel appeared to him in a dream and reassured him: "Joseph, son of David, do not be afraid to take to you Mary your wife, for that which is conceived in her is of the Holy Spirit. And she will bring forth a Son, and you shall call His name JESUS, for He will save His people from their sins" (Matt. 1:20–21 NKJV).

Common sense suggests that Mary must have anticipated all these difficulties the moment the angel told her she would conceive a child. Her joy and amazement at learning that she would be the mother of the Redeemer might therefore have been tempered significantly at the horror of the scandal that awaited her. Still, knowing the cost and weighing it against the immense privilege of becoming the mother of the Christ, Mary surrendered herself unconditionally, saying simply, "Behold the maidservant of the Lord! Let it be to me according to your word" (Luke 1:38 NKJV).

There's no evidence that Mary ever brooded over the effects her pregnancy would have on her reputation. She instantly, humbly, and joyfully submitted to God's will without further doubt or question. She could hardly have had a more godly response to the announcement of Jesus' birth. It demonstrated that she was a young woman of mature faith and one who was a worshiper of the true God. Her great joy over the Lord's plan for her would soon be very evident.

MARY'S RESPONSE OF WORSHIP

Mary, filled with joy and bubbling over with praise, hurried to the hill country to visit her beloved relative, Elizabeth. There's no suggestion that Mary was fleeing the shame of her premature pregnancy. It seems she simply wanted a kindred spirit to share her heart with. The angel had explicitly informed Mary about Elizabeth's pregnancy. So it was natural for her to seek out a close relative who was both a strong believer and also expecting her first son by a miraculous birth, announced by an angel (Luke 1:13–19). While Elizabeth was much older, maybe even in her eighties, and had always been unable to conceive, and Mary was at the beginning of life—both had been supernaturally blessed by God to conceive. It was a perfect situation for the two women to spend time rejoicing together in the Lord's goodness to both of them.

Elizabeth's immediate response to the sound of Mary's voice gave Mary independent confirmation of all that the angel had told her. Scripture says,

> It happened, when Elizabeth heard the greeting of Mary, that the babe leaped in her womb; and Elizabeth was filled with the Holy Spirit. Then she spoke out with a loud voice and said, "Blessed are you among women, and blessed is the fruit of your womb! But why is this granted to me, that the mother of my Lord should come to me? For indeed, as soon as the voice of your greeting sounded in my ears, the babe leaped in my womb for joy. Blessed is she who believed, for there will be a fulfillment of those things which were told her from the Lord." (Luke 1:41–45 NKJV)

Elizabeth's message was prophetic, of course, and Mary instantly understood that. Mary had learned from an angel about Elizabeth's pregnancy. Nothing indicates that Mary had sent word of her own circumstances ahead to Elizabeth. Indeed, Mary's sudden arrival had all the hallmarks of a surprise to her relative. Elizabeth's knowledge of Mary's pregnancy, therefore, seems to have come to her by revelation, in the prophecy she uttered when the Holy Spirit suddenly filled her.

Mary replied with prophetic words of her own. Her saying is known as the Magnificat (Latin for the first word of Mary's outpouring of praise). It is really a hymn about the incarnation. Without question, it is a song of unspeakable joy and the most magnificent psalm of worship in the New Testament. It is the equal of any Old Testament psalm, and as we have noted before, it bears a strong resemblance to Hannah's famous hymn of praise for the birth of Samuel. It is filled with messianic hope, scriptural language, and references to the Abrahamic covenant:

> My soul magnifies the Lord,
> And my spirit has rejoiced in God my Savior.

For He has regarded the lowly state of His maidservant;
For behold, henceforth all generations will call me blessed.
For He who is mighty has done great things for me,
And holy is His name.
And His mercy is on those who fear Him
From generation to generation.
He has shown strength with His arm;
He has scattered the proud in the imagination of their hearts.
He has put down the mighty from their thrones,
And exalted the lowly.
He has filled the hungry with good things,
And the rich He has sent away empty.
He has helped His servant Israel,
In remembrance of His mercy,
As He spoke to our fathers,
To Abraham and to his seed forever. (Luke 1:46–55 NKJV)

It is clear that Mary's young heart and mind were already thoroughly saturated with the Word of God. She included not only echoes of two of Hannah's prayers (1 Sam. 1:11; 2:1–10), but also several other allusions to the law, the psalms, and the prophets:

Luke 1 (NKJV)	Old Testament (NKJV)
• "My soul magnifies the Lord" (46).	• "My heart rejoices in the Lord" (1 Sam. 2:1). • "My soul shall make its boast in the Lord" (Ps. 34:2). • "My soul shall be joyful in the Lord" (Ps. 35:9). • "I will greatly rejoice in the Lord, my soul shall be joyful in my God" (Isa. 61:10).

Luke 1 (NKJV)	Old Testament (NKJV)
• "And my spirit has rejoiced in God my Savior" (47).	• "God is my salvation" (Isa. 12:2). • "There is no other God besides Me, a just God and a Savior" (Isa. 45:21).
• "For He has regarded the lowly state of His maidservant" (48).	• "If You will indeed look on the affliction of Your maidservant and remember me, and not forget Your maidservant" (1 Sam. 1:11). • "He shall regard the prayer of the destitute, and shall not despise their prayer" (Ps. 102:17). • "Who remembered us in our lowly state, for His mercy endures forever" (Ps. 136:23).
• "For behold, henceforth all generations will call me blessed" (48).	• "Then Leah said, 'I am happy, for the daughters will call me blessed'" (Gen. 30:13). • "And all nations will call you blessed" (Mal. 3:12).
• "For He who is mighty has done great things for me" (49).	• "Your righteousness, O God, is very high, You who have done great things" (Ps. 71:19). • "The Lord has done great things for us, and we are glad" (Ps. 126:3).
• "And holy is His name" (49).	• "No one is holy like the Lord" (1 Sam. 2:2). • "Holy and awesome is His name" (Ps. 111:9). • "The High and Lofty One Who inhabits eternity, whose name is Holy" (Isa. 57:15).
• "And His mercy is on them who fear Him from generation to generation" (50).	• "So great is His mercy toward those who fear Him" (Ps. 103:11). • "The mercy of the Lord is from everlasting to everlasting on those who fear Him, and His righteousness to children's children" (Ps. 103:17).

Luke 1 (NKJV)	Old Testament (NKJV)
	• "My righteousness will be forever, and My salvation from generation to generation" (Isa. 51:8).
• "He has shown strength with His arm" (51).	• "You have a mighty arm; strong is Your hand, and high is Your right hand" (Ps. 89:13). • "He has done marvelous things; His right hand and His holy arm have gained Him the victory" (Ps. 98:1). • "The Lord has made bare His holy arm in the eyes of all the nations" (Isa. 52:10).
• "He has scattered the proud in the imagination of their hearts" (51).	• "You have scattered Your enemies with Your mighty arm" (Ps. 89:10). • "The imagination of man's heart is evil from his youth" (Gen. 8:21).
• "He has put down the mighty from their thrones, and exalted the lowly" (52).	• "The Lord kills and makes alive; He brings down to the grave and brings up. The Lord makes poor and makes rich; He brings low and lifts up. He raises the poor from the dust and lifts the beggar from the ash heap, to set them among princes and make them inherit the throne of glory" (1 Sam. 2:6–8). • "He breaks in pieces mighty men without inquiry, and sets others in their place" (Job 34:24).
• "He has filled the hungry with good things; and the rich He has sent away empty" (53).	• "He satisfies the longing soul, and fills the hungry soul with goodness" (Ps. 107:9).

Luke 1 (NKJV)	Old Testament (NKJV)
• "He has helped His servant Israel, in remembrance of His mercy, as He spoke to our fathers, to Abraham and to his seed forever" (54–55).	• "He has remembered His mercy and His fulness to the house of Israel" (Ps. 98:3). • "O Israel, you will not be forgotten by Me!" (Isa. 44:21). • "You will give truth to Jacob and mercy to Abraham, which You have sworn to our fathers from days of old" (Mic. 7:20). • "O seed of Abraham . . . He remembers His covenant forever, the word which He commanded, for a thousand generations, the covenant which He made with Abraham" (Ps. 105:6–9).

Those who channel their religious energies into the veneration of Mary would do well to learn from the example of Mary herself. God is the *only* One she magnified. Notice how she praised the glory and majesty of God while repeatedly acknowledging her own lowliness. She took no credit for anything good in herself. But she praised the Lord for His attributes, naming some of the chief ones specifically, including His power, His mercy, and His holiness. She freely confessed God as the one who had done great things for her, and not vice versa. The song is all about *God's* greatness, *His* glory, the strength of *His* arm, and *His* faithfulness across the generations.

Mary's worship was clearly from the heart. She was plainly consumed by the wonder of His grace to her. She seemed amazed that an absolutely holy God would do such great things for one as undeserving as she. This was not the prayer of one who claimed to be conceived immaculately, without the corruption of original sin. It was, on the contrary, the glad rejoicing of one who knew God intimately as her *Savior.* She could celebrate the fact that God's mercy is on those who fear Him, because she herself feared God and had received His mercy. And she knew firsthand how God exalts the lowly and fills the hungry with good things, because she herself was a humble sinner who had hungered and thirsted after righteousness, and was filled.

It was customary in Jewish prayers to recite God's past faithfulness to His people (Ex. 15; Judg. 5; Pss. 68; 78; 104; 105; 114; 135; 136; 145; and Hab. 3). Mary followed that convention here in abbreviated fashion. She recalled how God had helped Israel, in fulfillment of all His promises. Now her own child would be the living fulfillment of God's saving promise. No wonder Mary's heart overflowed with such praise.

HER RELATIONSHIP TO HER SON

Throughout Christ's earthly ministry, Mary appeared in only three scenes. On two of those occasions, Jesus Himself explicitly repudiated the notion that her earthly authority over Him as His mother entitled her to manage any aspect of His saving work. He did this without showing her the least bit of disrespect, of course, but He nonetheless clearly and completely disclaimed the idea that Mary was in any sense a mediator of His grace.

The first of these occasions was during the wedding at Cana, when Jesus performed His first miracle. The apostle John recorded what happened: "When they ran out of wine, the mother of Jesus said to Him, 'They have no wine'" (John 2:3 NKJV). The host at the wedding was undoubtedly a close family friend whom Mary cared a great deal for. (Notice how verse 1 says "the mother of Jesus was *there*"; but verse 2 says, "Jesus and His disciples were *invited*." Mary was evidently helping to coordinate the reception for her friend. Hence, she was one of the first to see that the wine supply was not going to be enough.) Mary also knew full well that Christ had the means to solve this embarrassing social dilemma, and she was subtly asking Him to do something about it. Whether she anticipated the kind of miracle He performed is not clear. She might have simply been prodding Him to make a suitable announcement and help cover the embarrassment for the hosts. Or, as it seems likely, she fully understood that He was the Prophet whom Moses foretold, and she was expecting Him, like Moses had so often done, to work a miracle that would supply what was lacking. She made no overt request, but her meaning was obviously plain to her Son.

For His part, Jesus had every intention of miraculously replenishing the wine, because that is what He subsequently did. He was never prone to vacillate, hesitate, or change His mind (Heb. 13:8). The fact that He ultimately performed the miracle is proof that He *planned* to do it.

Yet Scripture suggests His reply to Mary was somewhat terse. He was just as direct with Mary as she had been subtle with Him: "Jesus said to her, 'Woman, what does your concern have to do with Me? My hour has not yet come'" (John 2:4 NKJV). He was not being rude, and nothing suggests that Mary was in any way grieved or offended by His reply. "Woman" was a typical formal address in that culture. Again, it was curt without being impertinent. But there's no escaping the mild rebuke in His words and in His tone. The question, "What does your concern have to do with Me?" is a challenge seen several times in Scripture (Judg. 11:12; 2 Sam. 16:10; Ezra 4:2–3; Matt. 8:29). It conveyed a clear tone of displeasure and strong admonishment. Still, there's no suggestion that Mary took this as an affront. *His* intent was not to wound, but to correct and instruct.

Mary may have recalled a similar incident years before. As a young boy just entering young adulthood, Jesus was separated from His parents at the temple. After a frantic search, they found Him, and Mary mildly scolded Him for allowing them to be worried. He replied, with what appears to be genuine amazement, "Why did you seek Me? Did you not know that I must be about My Father's business?" (Luke 2:49 NKJV). He was, in effect, disclaiming any notion that His earthly father's parental interests could ever override the higher authority of His heavenly Father.

Here, at the Cana wedding, His message to Mary was similar. In spiritual matters, her earthly role as His mother did not give her any right to attempt to manage His mission as it pertained to fulfilling the Father's will on the Father's timetable. As a man, He was her Son. But as God, He was her Lord. It was not her business to command Him in spiritual matters. The way He spoke to her simply reminded her of that fact without showing her any real disrespect.

Then He turned the water to wine.

After that, Mary always remained in the background. She never sought or accepted the kind of preeminence so many seem determined to try to thrust on her. She never again attempted to intercede with Him for miracles, special favors, or other blessings on behalf of her friends, her relatives, or anyone else. It is only sheer folly that causes so many to imagine she has now usurped that role from her position in heaven.

Mary appeared again during Jesus' earthly ministry when the throngs who clamored for miracles from Christ had become larger than ever. Mark records that the demands of Jesus' ministry were such that He didn't even have time to eat (Mark 3:20). Jesus' own close family members began to be concerned for His safety, and they concluded (wrongly, of course) that He was beside Himself (v. 21). Scripture says they went to Him intending to physically pull Him away from the crowds and the heavy demands that they were making on Him.

Meanwhile, some scribes came from Jerusalem and accused Jesus of casting out demons in the power of Beelzebub (v. 22). Mark painted a vivid picture of chaos, opposition, and vast multitudes of needy people all pressing in on Jesus. It was into this context that His immediate family members came, seeking to get Him away from the multitudes for His own safety and sanity's sake. Mark 3:31–35 tells what happened:

Then His brothers and His mother came, and standing outside they sent to Him, calling Him. And a multitude was sitting around Him; and they said to Him, "Look, Your mother and Your brothers are outside seeking You."

But He answered them, saying, "Who is My mother, or My brothers?" And He looked around in a circle at those who sat about Him, and said, "Here are My mother and My brothers! For whoever does the will of God is My brother and My sister and mother." (NKJV)

Jesus sent the same message again. As far as His spiritual work was concerned, His earthly relatives had no more claim on Him than anyone else. He certainly did not set Mary on any exalted plane above His other disciples. He knew better than she did the limits of His human strength. He would not, even at her urging, leave what He was doing. He would not be interrupted or allow Himself to be sidetracked, even by her sincere maternal concern. As always, He must be about His *Father's* business, and she did not need to be consulted for that.

Once again, however, we see Mary learning to submit to Him as her Lord, rather than trying to control Him as His mother. She became one of His faithful disciples. She seems to have come to grips with the reality that He had work to do, and she could not direct it. She ultimately followed Him all the way to the cross, and on that dark afternoon when He died, she was standing nearby with a group of women, watching in grief and horror. The crucifixion was the third and final time Mary appeared alongside Jesus during the years of His public ministry.

THE SWORD THAT PIERCED HER SOUL

Mary had probably always had an inkling that this day would come. She had surely heard Jesus speak (as He did often) of His own death. As a matter of fact, the cloud of this inevitable reality had probably hung over Mary's mind since Jesus' infancy. It was no doubt one of the things she kept and pondered in her heart (Luke 2:19, 51). Luke's gospel recounts how the first hint of impending tragedy crept into Mary's consciousness.

When Jesus was yet a newborn infant, His earthly parents took Him to the temple to dedicate Him to the Lord in accordance with the instructions of Exodus 13:2, 13: "Consecrate to Me all the firstborn, whatever opens the womb among the children of Israel . . . All the firstborn of man among your sons you shall redeem" (NKJV). Joseph and Mary came with a sacrifice of two turtledoves (Luke 2:24), which was what the law prescribed for people too poor to afford a lamb (Lev. 12:8). On that day, the little family from Nazareth encountered two elderly saints, Simeon and Anna. (Anna will be the subject of the following chapter.)

Simeon was an old man whom Scripture describes as "just and devout, waiting for the Consolation of Israel" (Luke 2:25 NKJV). The Spirit of God had revealed to Simeon that he would have the privilege of seeing the Messiah before he died. On the day Joseph and Mary dedicated Jesus at the temple, the Holy Spirit led Simeon there also (v. 27 NKJV).

As soon as Simeon saw Jesus, he knew this child was the Lord's Anointed One. Scripture says he took the infant Jesus up in his arms and uttered a prophecy. Then, turning to Mary, he told her, "Behold, this Child is destined for the fall and rising of many in Israel, and for a sign which will be spoken against (yes, *a sword will pierce through your own soul also),* that the thoughts of many hearts may be revealed" (vv. 34–35 NKJV, emphasis added).

It is almost certain that in the process of writing his gospel, Luke sought details about Jesus' birth and life from Mary. Luke 1:1–4 indicates that he had access to the testimony of many eyewitness reports. Since he included several details that only Mary could have known, we can be fairly sure that Mary herself was one of Luke's primary sources. Luke's inclusion of several facts from Jesus' early life (2:19, 48, 51) suggests that this was the case. Mary's own eyewitness testimony must also have been Luke's source for the account of Simeon's prophecy, for who but she could have known and recalled that incident? Apparently, the old man's cryptic prophecy had never left her mind.

Years later, as Mary stood watching a soldier thrust a sword into Jesus' side, she must have truly felt as if a sword had pierced her own soul also. At that very moment, she might well have recalled Simeon's prophecy, and suddenly its true meaning came home to her with full force.

While Mary quietly watched her Son die, others were screaming wicked taunts and insults at Him. Her sense of the injustice being done to Him must have been profound. After all, no one understood Jesus' absolute, sinless perfection better than Mary did. She had nurtured Him as an infant and brought Him up through childhood. No one could have loved Him more than she did. All those facts merely compounded the acute grief any mother would feel at such a horrible sight. The pain of Mary's anguish is almost unimaginable. Yet she stood, stoically, silently, when lesser women would have fled in horror, shrieked and thrashed around in panic, or simply collapsed in a heap from the overwhelming distress. Mary was clearly a woman of dignified grace and courage.

Mary seemed to understand that her steadfast presence at Jesus' side was the only kind of support she could give Him at this dreaded moment. But even that was merely a public show of support. Mary's personal suffering did not represent any kind of participation in His atoning work. Her grief added no merit to His suffering for others' guilt. *He* was bearing the sins of the world. She could not assist with that. Nor did He need her aid as any kind of "co-redemptrix" or "co-mediatrix." "There is one God and one Mediator between God and men, the Man Christ Jesus" (1 Tim. 2:5 NKJV). Mary herself did not try to intrude into that office; it is a shame so many people insist on trying to put her there.

As a matter of fact, in the waning hours of Jesus' life, it was *Jesus* who came to *her* aid. Already in the final throes of death, He spotted Mary standing nearby with a small group of women and John, the beloved disciple. For the final time, Jesus acknowledged His human relationship with

Mary. In his own gospel account, John describes what happened: "When Jesus therefore saw His mother, and the disciple whom He loved standing by, He said to His mother, 'Woman, behold your son!' Then He said to the disciple, 'Behold your mother!' And from that hour that disciple took her to his own home" (John 19:26–27 NKJV).

So one of Jesus' last earthly acts before yielding up His life to God was to make sure that for the rest of her life, Mary would be cared for.

That act epitomizes Mary's relationship with her firstborn Son. She was His earthly mother; but He was her eternal Lord. She understood and embraced that relationship. She bowed to His authority in heavenly matters just as in His childhood and youth He had always been subject to her parental authority in earthly matters (Luke 2:51). As a mother, she had once provided all His needs, but in the ultimate and eternal sense, He was *her* Savior and provider.

Mary was like no other mother. Godly mothers are typically absorbed in the task of training their children for heaven. Mary's Son was the Lord and Creator of heaven. Over time, she came to perceive the full import of that truth, until it filled her heart. She became a disciple and a worshiper. Her maternal relationship with Him faded into the background. That moment on the cross—Jesus placing His mother into the earthly care of John—formally marked the end of that earthly aspect of Mary's relationship with Jesus.

After Jesus' death, Mary appears only once more in the Bible. In Luke's chronicle of the early church, she is listed among the disciples who were praying together in Jerusalem at Pentecost (Acts 1:14). Her name is never mentioned in the epistles. It is clear that the early church never thought of making her an object of religious veneration the way so many have done in the subsequent annals of various Christian traditions.

Mary herself never claimed to be, or pretended to be, anything more than a humble handmaiden of the Lord. She was extraordinary because God used her in an extraordinary way. She clearly thought of herself as perfectly *ordinary*. She is portrayed in Scripture only as an instrument whom God used in the fulfillment of His plan. She herself never made any pretense of being an administrator of the divine agenda, and she never gave anyone any encouragement to regard her as a mediatrix in the dispensing of divine grace. The lowly perspective reflected in Mary's Magnificat is the same simple spirit of humility that colored all her life and character.

It is truly regrettable that religious superstition has, in effect, turned Mary into an idol. She is certainly a worthy woman to emulate, but Mary herself would undoubtedly be appalled to think anyone would pray to her, venerate images of her, or burn candles in homage to her. Her life and her testimony point us consistently to her Son. *He* was the object of her worship. *He* was the one she recognized as Lord. *He* was the one she trusted for everything. Mary's own example, seen in the pure light of Scripture, teaches us to do the same.

7

ANNA: THE FAITHFUL WITNESS

She gave thanks to the Lord, and spoke of Him to all those who looked for redemption in Jerusalem.

Luke 2:38 NKJV

I t is truly remarkable that when Jesus was born, so few people in Israel recognized their Messiah. It was not as if no one was watching for Him. Messianic expectation in the early first century was running at an all-time high.

Daniel's famous prophecy about "Messiah the Prince" (Dan. 9:24–27 NKJV) had practically set the date. Daniel wrote, "Seventy weeks are determined . . . Know therefore and understand, that from the going forth of the command to restore and build Jerusalem until Messiah the Prince, there shall be seven weeks and sixty-two weeks." If Daniel's "weeks" (literally, "sevens" in the Hebrew) are understood as seven-year periods, Daniel is describing a period of 483 years total: "seven weeks" (forty-nine years) plus "sixty-two weeks" (434 years). "The command to restore and build Jerusalem" seems to be a reference to the decree of Artaxerxes (Neh. 2:1–8), which was issued in 444 or 445 BC. If the years are reckoned by a lunar calendar of 360 days, Daniel's timetable would put the appearance of

"Messiah the Prince" around AD 30, which was the year of His triumphal entry.

Scripture records that when John the Baptist began his ministry, "The people were in expectation, and all reasoned in their hearts about John, whether he was the Christ or not" (Luke 3:15 NKJV). As a matter of fact, several of the disciples first encountered Christ for the very reason that they were watching expectantly for Him to appear, and they came to John the Baptist, who pointed the way to Christ (John 1:27–37).

The fact is, virtually all faithful believers in Israel were already expectantly awaiting the Messiah and looking diligently for Him at the exact time Jesus was born. The irony is that so very few recognized Him, because He met none of their expectations. They were looking for a mighty political and military leader who would become a conquering king; He was born into a peasant family. They probably anticipated that He would arrive with great fanfare and pageantry; He was born in a stable, almost in secret.

The only people in Israel who *did* recognize Christ at His birth were humble, unremarkable people. The Magi of Matthew 2:1–12, of course, were foreigners and Gentiles, and they were very rich, powerful, and influential men in their own culture. But the only *Israelites* who understood that Jesus was the Messiah at His birth were Mary and Joseph, the shepherds, Simeon, and Anna. All of them were basically nobodies. All of them recognized Him because they were told who He was by angels, or by some other form of special revelation. Luke recounts all their stories in succession, as if he is calling multiple witnesses, one at a time, to establish the matter.

The final witness he calls is Anna. Everything Scripture has to say about her is contained in just three verses: Luke 2: 36–38. She is never mentioned anywhere else in the Bible. But these three verses are enough to establish her reputation as a genuinely extraordinary woman:

Now there was one, Anna, a prophetess, the daughter of Phanuel, of the tribe of Asher. She was of a great age, and had lived with a husband seven years from her virginity; and this woman was a widow of about eighty-four years, who did not depart from the temple, but served God with fastings and prayers night and day. And coming in that instant she gave thanks to the Lord, and spoke of Him to all those who looked for redemption in Jerusalem. (NKJV)

The scene is the same one we left near the end of our previous chapter. Simeon had just picked up the infant Jesus and pronounced a prophetic blessing on Him. "In that instant," Luke says, Anna happened by and immediately understood what was going on and who Christ was. Perhaps she overheard Simeon's blessing. She probably already knew Simeon personally. Anna herself was clearly a fixture in the temple, and Simeon was described as "just and devout" (v. 25 NKJV). Both were very old. It seems unlikely that their paths had never crossed. Probably knowing Simeon's reputation as a righteous man whose one expectation in life was to see "the Consolation of Israel" with his own eyes before dying, Anna stopped and took notice when she heard the joyous blessing he pronounced on Jesus.

Like every other extraordinary woman we have seen so far, Anna's hopes and dreams were full of messianic expectation. She knew the Old Testament promises, and she understood that salvation from sin and the future blessing of Israel depended on the coming of the Messiah. Her longing to see Him was suddenly and surprisingly fulfilled one day as she went about her normal routine in the temple.

Anna appears only in a very brief vignette of Luke's gospel, but her inclusion there elevates the importance of her life and testimony. She was blessed by God to be one of a handful of key witnesses who knew and understood the significance of Jesus' birth. And she made no attempt to keep it a secret. Thus she became one of the first and most enduring witnesses to Christ. No doubt wherever Luke's gospel is proclaimed, her testimony is still bringing others to the Savior. Thus she deserves a prominent place in any list of extraordinary women.

Actually, quite a lot about Anna's extraordinary life can be gleaned from the three brief verses of Scripture that are devoted to her story. Luke's narrative is loaded with key phrases that give us a surprisingly rich understanding of Anna's life and character.

"SHE WAS A PROPHETESS"

Luke introduced her this way: "There was one, Anna, a prophetess" (Luke 2:36 NKJV). Her name in Hebrew is identical to "Hannah." Remember, from the story of Samuel's mother Hannah, the name means "grace"—an appropriate name for a godly, dignified woman. Anna's character does bear some striking similarities to her Old Testament namesake. Both women were singled out for their practice of prayer and fasting. Both were perfectly at home in the temple. Both prophesied. In Hannah's case, you'll recall, her celebratory prayer (1 Sam. 2:1–10) was also a prophetic psalm about the Messiah. Anna is said to be a prophetess whose heart was prepared for the coming of the Messiah.

What did Luke mean by *prophetess*? He was not suggesting that Anna predicted the future. She was not a fortune-teller. He didn't necessarily even suggest that she received special revelation from God. The word *prophetess* simply designated a woman who spoke the Word of God. Any preacher who faithfully proclaims the Word of God would be a "prophet" in the general biblical sense. And a prophetess would be a woman uniquely devoted to declaring the Word of God.

Anna may have been a teacher of the Old Testament to other women. Or she may have simply had a private ministry there in the temple offering words of encouragement and instruction from the Hebrew Scriptures to other women who came to worship. Nothing suggests that she was a source of revelation, or that any special revelation ever came to her directly. Even her realization that Jesus was the Messiah seemed to have come from the revelation given to Simeon and subsequently overheard by her. She is nonetheless called a prophetess because it was her habit to declare the truth of God's Word to others. This gift for proclaiming God's truth ultimately played a major role in the ministry she is still best remembered for.

In all the Old Testament, only five women are ever referred to as "prophetess." The first was Miriam, Moses' sister, identified as a prophetess in Exodus 15:20, where she led the women of Israel in a psalm of praise to God about the drowning of Pharaoh and his army. The simple one-stanza psalm Miriam sang was the substance of her only recorded prophecy (v. 21). The fact that God had once spoken through her, unfortunately, later became an occasion for pride and rebellion (Num. 12:1–2), and the Lord disciplined her for that sin by temporarily smiting her with leprosy (vv. 9–15).

In Judges 4:4, we are introduced to the second woman in the Old Testament designated as a prophetess: "Deborah, a prophetess, the wife of Lapidoth" (Judg. 4:4 NKJV). She was the only female among the varied assortment of judges who led the Jewish people before the monarchy was established in Israel. In fact, she was the only woman in all of Scripture who ever held that kind of leadership position and was blessed for it. The Lord seemed to raise her up as a rebuke to the men of her generation who were paralyzed by fear. She saw herself not as a usurper of men, but as a woman who functioned in a maternal capacity, while men like Barak were being raised up to step into their proper roles of leadership (5:12). That's why she referred to herself as "a mother in Israel" (v. 7 NKJV). She gave instructions to Barak from the Lord (Judg. 4:6), so it seems she received revelation from God, at least on that one occasion.

In 2 Kings 22:14, Scripture mentions Huldah as a prophetess. In verses 15–20, she had a word from the Lord for Hilkiah the priest and others. Nothing about her, or her background, is known. In fact, she is mentioned only here and in a parallel passage in 2 Chronicles 34:22–28.

The only two other women called prophetesses in the Old Testament were an otherwise unknown woman named Noadiah (Neh. 6:14), who was classified among the *false* prophets; and Isaiah's wife (Isa. 8:3), who was called a prophetess only because she was married to Isaiah, not because she herself prophesied (unless her decision to name her son "Maher-Shalal-Hash-Baz" could be counted as a prophecy).

Rarely did God speak to his people through women, and never did any woman have an ongoing prophetic ministry similar to that of Elijah, Isaiah, or any of the other key Old Testament prophets. In other words, there is nothing anywhere in Scripture to indicate that any women ever held a prophetic *office*. The idea that "prophetess" was a technical term for an official position or an ongoing ministry of direct revelation is simply nowhere to be found in Scripture.

Luke's identification of Anna as a "prophetess," therefore, did not necessarily mean that she personally received divine revelation. When Luke called her a "prophetess," we are not to imagine that this was an *office* she filled. Most likely, it meant that she had a reputation as a gifted teacher of other women and a faithful encourager of her fellow worshipers in the temple. When she spoke, it was about the Word of God. She had evidently spent a lifetime hiding God's Word in her heart. Naturally, that was the substance of what she usually had to say. So when Luke called her a "prophetess," he gave insight into her character and a clue about what occupied her mind and her conversation.

"OF THE TRIBE OF ASHER"

Anna is further identified as "the daughter of Phanuel, of the tribe of Asher" (Luke 2:36 NKJV). Her heritage is given because it was rather unusual. Asher was the eighth son of Jacob. He was the offspring of Zilpah, Leah's maid and Jacob's concubine (Gen. 30:12–13). The tribe that descended from Asher belonged to the apostate northern kingdom of Israel.

If you remember Old Testament history, you know that the kingdom split after Solomon's time. The ten tribes in the north formed an independent nation, with their own king (who was not the rightful heir to David's throne, but a usurper). From then on, in the Old Testament, the name "Israel" applied to the apostate northern kingdom. The southern kingdom took the name "Judah." (That was because Judah was by far the larger of the two remaining tribes in the south—the other one being Benjamin.)

The southern kingdom remained loyal to the Davidic throne. Of course, the city of Jerusalem lay in the heart of the southern kingdom close to the border between Judah and Benjamin. The temple there was still the only place where the true priesthood could offer sacrifices. A few faithful Israelites from each of the ten tribes migrated south so that they weren't cut off from the temple, but in doing so, they gave up their family lands and their inheritance.

Judah and Israel remained independent from one another for generations. At times they were uneasy allies. Most of the time, however, their kings were bitter rivals. Apostasy and idolatry plagued both nations continually. Prophets were sent by God to warn the northern as well as the southern tribes about their spiritual decline, but the prophets were mostly spurned on both sides of the border. Evil kings sat on both thrones. Judah had a few good and godly kings in the mix, but every one of the kings of Israel was evil.

Naturally, apostate Israel built new places of worship and established an alternative priesthood. That quickly led to the total corruption of the Jewish religion in the northern kingdom. Ever more sinister forms of paganism saturated the culture. Finally, in 722 BC, the Assyrians conquered the ten northern tribes and took most of the people into captivity. Only a handful ever returned.

Anna's descent from the tribe of Asher suggests that her heritage owed much to God's grace. Her ancestors had either migrated south before the Assyrian conquest of Israel, or they were among the small and scattered group of exiles who returned from captivity. Either way, she was part of the believing remnant from the northern kingdom, and she was therefore a living emblem of God's faithfulness to His people.

"THIS WOMAN WAS A WIDOW"

By the time of Jesus' birth, Anna was already advanced in years. She had not enjoyed a particularly easy life. Her whole world was shattered by tragedy when she was still quite young, apparently before she had even borne children. Her husband died seven years after their marriage, and she had remained single ever since.

The Greek text is ambiguous as to her exact age. ("This woman was a widow of about eighty-four years.") It might mean literally that she had been a widow for eighty-four years. Assuming she married very young (remember, thirteen was a typical age for engagement in that society), then lived with her husband seven years before he died, that would make her at least 104—very old indeed, but entirely possible.

More likely, what the text is saying is that she was now an eighty-four-year-old widow. She was married for seven years when her husband died, and having never remarried, she had now lived as a widow for more than six decades.

Widowhood in that society was extremely difficult. It virtually guaranteed a life of extreme poverty. That's why, in the early church, the apostle Paul urged young widows to remarry (1 Tim. 5:14) so that the church was not overly burdened with their support.

Anna probably either lived on charity or supported herself out of the remnants of her family's inheritance. Either way, she must have led a very frugal, chaste, and sober life. Luke adds that she "served God with fastings and prayers night and day" (Luke 2:37 NKJV)—which rounds out the picture of this elderly, dignified, quiet, devoted woman's life and ministry.

"WHO DID NOT DEPART FROM THE TEMPLE"

Luke gave another significant detail about Anna: "[She] did not depart from the temple" (Luke 2:37 NKJV). That's an emphatic statement, which suggests that Luke meant it in a literal sense. Evidently, Anna lived right there on the temple grounds. There were some apartments in the outer courts (Neh. 13:7–9). These were modest chambers, probably used as temporary dwelling places for priests who lived on the temple grounds while doing their two weeks' annual service.

Perhaps because of her long faithfulness, her obvious spiritual gifts, her steadfast devotion to the Lord, and her constant commitment to her ministry of prayer and fasting, temple officials had given her a small chamber. She was now too old to be employed as a caretaker, but perhaps she had once served in that capacity, and her living quarters had been given to her for life. In any case, it was ultimately the Lord who had graciously provided her a place in His house and sovereignly orchestrated whatever arrangement she might have had with the temple custodians.

It is obvious that Anna was a most extraordinary woman in the eyes of everyone who knew her. She lived the simplest kind of life. She could *always* be found at the temple. She was singularly and completely devoted to the service and worship of God—mostly through her prayers and fasting.

The manner of her praying, accompanied by fasting, speaks of her own self-denial and sincerity. Fasting by itself is not a particularly useful exercise. Abstaining from food *per se* has no mystical effect on anything spiritual. But fasting *with prayer* reveals a heart so consumed with praying, and so eager to receive the blessing being sought, that the person simply has no interest in eating. That is when fasting has real value.

Anna apparently had been doing this as a pattern for sixty-four years or longer. Here was a passionate woman! What do you think Anna had been praying about? She surely prayed about many things, but there is little doubt that one of the main subjects of her prayers was an earnest plea for the very same thing Simeon was so eager for: "the Consolation of Israel" (Luke 2:25 NKJV). Her hope, like Eve's, was for the Seed who would crush the serpent's head. Her longing, like Sarah's, was for the Seed of Abraham, who would bless all the nations of the world. She was praying that God would soon send the promised deliverer, the Messiah.

Anna's amazing faith stemmed from the fact that she believed all the promises that filled the Old Testament. She took the Word of God seriously. She knew in her heart that the Messiah was coming, and without any doubt whatsoever her first and foremost prayer was that it would happen soon.

I'm convinced that Anna had a remarkable knowledge of spiritual truth. Remember, she belonged to the believing remnant, not the apostate majority. She had no part in the error and hypocrisy that Jesus would later rebuke among the scribes and Pharisees. She was not a participant in the money-changing system at the temple that stirred His wrath. She knew the Pharisees were corrupt legalists. She understood that the Sadducees were spiritually bankrupt liberals. She truly loved her God. She understood His heart and mind. She genuinely believed His Word. She was a wonderfully remarkable woman indeed—perhaps one of the *most* devout people we meet anywhere on the pages of Scripture. No one else comes to mind who fasted and prayed faithfully for more than sixty years!

God was about to give her an answer to her prayers in the most dramatic fashion. Verse 38 says that just when Simeon pronounced his prophetic blessing on the infant Christ and His earthly parents, "in that instant" (NKJV), she came along. Now, Herod's temple was a massive building, and the temple complex was huge, surrounded by a courtyard with thousands of people milling around at almost any given time.

Joseph and Mary did not know Simeon, but by God's providence and through the sovereign direction of His Spirit, He had brought them together (v. 27). At that very instant, just while Simeon was blessing the child with inspired words of prophecy, the Spirit of God providentially led this elderly woman to a place where she was within earshot. Luke's description is typically understated: "Coming in that instant she gave thanks to the Lord" (v. 38 NKJV).

Suddenly everything she had been praying and fasting for was right there in front of her face, wrapped in a little bundle in Simeon's arms. By faith, she knew instantly that Simeon's prophecy was true and that God had answered her prayers. She immediately began giving thanks to God, and all those many, many years of petition turned to praise.

We can only imagine how Anna felt after long decades of focused prayer and fasting, yearning for God to reveal His glory again, praying and fasting for the salvation of Israel, and beseeching God to send the Messiah. Finally, the answer to her prayers had come in flesh and blood.

"SHE . . . SPOKE OF HIM TO ALL"

Suddenly Anna's prophetic giftedness came boldly to the forefront: "[She] spoke of Him to all those who looked for redemption in Jerusalem" (Luke 2:38 NKJV). The verb tense signifies continuous action. It literally means that she continually spoke of Him to all who were looking for the Redeemer. This became her one message for the rest of her life.

Notice that Anna knew who the believing remnant were. She could identify the *true* worshipers—the ones who, like her, were expectantly awaiting the Messiah. She sought such people out, and at every opportunity from then on, she spoke to them about *Him*.

That is how this dear woman who had spent so many years mostly talking to God became best known for talking to people about Christ. The Messiah had finally come, and Anna was one of the very first to know who He was. She could not keep that news to herself. She thus became one of the very first and most enduring witnesses of Christ.

What became of Anna after this is not recorded. She was undoubtedly in heaven by the time Christ began his public ministry some thirty years later. The day of His dedication was probably her one and only glimpse of Him. But it was enough for her. She literally could not stop talking about Him.

And that is the most endearing part of this wonderful woman's extraordinary legacy.

8

The Samaritan Woman: Finding the Water of Life

Come, see a Man who told me all things that I ever did. Could this be the Christ?

John 4:29 NKJV

In John 4 we meet an unnamed Samaritan woman with a rather sordid background. Jesus met her when she came to draw water at a well, and the encounter transformed her whole life. The apostle John devoted forty-two verses to telling the tale of this woman's amazing encounter with the Lord. Such a significant section of Scripture would not be given to this one episode unless the lessons it contained were supremely important.

At first glance, much about the scene seems ordinary and unimportant. Here is an anonymous woman who performed the most mundane of everyday tasks: she came to draw her daily ration of water for her household. She came alone, at an hour when she probably expected to find no one else at the well. (That was probably an indication of her status as an outcast.) Jesus, traveling through the region on His way to Jerusalem, was resting near the well. His disciples were purchasing food in the nearby village. Jesus, having no utensil or rope with which to draw water, asked the woman to fetch Him a drink. It was not the stuff of great drama, and this was certainly not a scene that would lead us to expect one of the most profound theological lessons in all the Bible was just ahead.

A REMARKABLE SETTING

Look closer, however, and it turns out that many details in this picture are enormously significant.

In the first place, this was Jacob's well, located on a plot of land well known to students of the Old Testament. It was a field that Jacob purchased so that he could pitch his tent in the land of Canaan (Gen. 33:18–19). He built an altar on the site, "and called it El Elohe Israel," meaning "the God of Israel" (v. 20 NKJV). This very field was the first inhabitable piece of real estate recorded in Scripture that any Israelite ever owned in the Promised Land. Abraham had previously purchased the field of Ephron, which contained a cave that became his and Sarah's burial place (Gen. 23:17–18; 25:9–10). But *this* property actually became Jacob's home base.

John 4:5 reminds us that this was the same parcel of ground Jacob deeded to his favorite son, Joseph (Gen. 48:21–22). It later became the very place where Joseph's bones were finally put to rest (Josh. 24:32). Remember that when Moses left Egypt, he took Joseph's coffin (Gen. 50:24–26; Ex. 13:19). The Israelites carried Joseph's remains around with them for forty years in the wilderness. One of their first acts after conquering the Promised Land was the final interment of those bones. This was all done at Joseph's own behest (Heb. 11:22). To the Israelites, the tale of Joseph's bones was a significant reminder of God's faithfulness (Acts 7:15–16).

The well that was on the property was not mentioned in the Old Testament, but its location was well established in Jesus' day by centuries of Jewish tradition, and the site remains a major landmark even today. The well is very deep (John 4:11), accessible only by a very long rope through a hole dug though a slab of soft limestone. The reservoir below is spring-fed, so its water is always fresh, pure, and cold. It is the *only* well, and the finest water, in a vicinity where brackish springs abound. The existence of such a well on Jacob's property was deemed by the Israelites as a token of God's grace and goodness to their patriarch. Hence, the location had a very long and meaningful history in Jewish tradition.

In Jesus' era, though, that plot of ground lay in Samaritan territory, and this is another surprising and significant detail about the setting in John 4. For Jesus to be in Samaria at all was unusual (and perhaps even somewhat scandalous). The Samaritans were considered unclean by the Israelites. Jesus was traveling from Jerusalem to Galilee (v. 3). A look at any map reveals that the most direct route goes straight through Samaria. But in Jesus' time, any self-respecting Jew would always travel a different way. The preferred route went east of the Jordan River, then north through Decapolis before crossing the Jordan again into Galilee. This alternate route went many miles out of the way, but it bypassed Samaria, and that was the whole point.

Samaritans were a mixed-race people descended from pagans who had intermarried with the few remaining Israelites after the Assyrians con-quered the northern kingdom (722 BC). As early as Nehemiah's time (the mid-fifth century BC), the Samaritans posed a serious threat to the purity of Israel. Secular history records that Nehemiah's main nemesis, Sanballat, was an early governor of Samaria (Neh. 4:1–2). The Jewish high priest's grandson married Sanballat's daughter, incurring Nehemiah's wrath. "I drove him from me," Nehemiah wrote (13:28 NKJV). Such a marriage "defiled the priesthood and the covenant of the priesthood and the Levites" (v. 29 NKJV).

By the first century, the Samaritans had a distinct culture built around a syncretistic religion, blending aspects of Judaism and rank paganism. Their place of worship was on Mount Gerizim. Sanballat had built a temple there to rival the temple in Jerusalem. The Samaritan temple was served by a false priesthood, of course. Remember that the Israelites in the northern kingdom had already corrupted Judaism several centuries before this by establishing a false priesthood. That defiled flavor of Judaism was precisely what gave birth to Samaritanism. So the Samaritan religion was twice removed from the truth. But they did hold to selected elements of Jewish doctrine. Samaritans regarded the Pentateuch (the first five books of the Old Testament) as Scripture. They rejected the psalms and the prophets, however.

During the Maccabean period, less than a century and a half before the time of Christ, Jewish armies under John Hyrcanus destroyed the Samaritan temple. Gerizim nevertheless remained sacred to the Samaritans and the center of worship for their religion. (A group of Samaritans still worships there even today.)

The Jews' contempt for the Samaritans was so intense by the first century that most Jews simply refused to travel through Samaria, despite the importance of that land to their heritage.

Jesus deliberately broke with convention. John 4:4 says, "He *needed* to go through Samaria" (NKJV, emphasis added). He had a purpose to fulfill, and it required Him to travel through Samaria, stop at this historic well, talk to this troubled woman, and make an unprecedented disclosure of His true mission and identity.

Seen in that light, virtually *everything* about the setting of John 4 becomes remarkable. It is unusual to find Jesus alone. It is amazing to realize that God incarnate could grow physically weary (v. 6) or become thirsty (v. 7). It is startling that Jesus would intentionally seek out and initiate a conversation with a wretched Samaritan woman like this one. It was astonishing even to *her* that any Jewish man would speak to her (v. 9). It was equally shocking for the disciples to find Him speaking to her (v. 27). It would have been considered outrageous for Him to drink from an unclean vessel that belonged to an unclean woman. It seems odd for a woman like this to enter so quickly into an extended theological dialogue. It is marvelous to see how rich Jesus' teaching could be, even in a context like this. (The heart and soul of everything Scripture teaches about authentic worship is condensed in just a few words Jesus spoke to this woman in verses 21–24.) It is astounding that her own sin was such a large issue in her own heart and mind (v. 29), even though Jesus had only referred to it obliquely (v. 18) and even though she initially seemed to try to dodge the point (vv. 19–20).

But what is staggeringly unexpected about this whole fantastic account is that Jesus chose *this* time and *this* place and *this* woman to be part of the setting where He would (for the first time ever) formally and explicitly unveil His true identity as the Messiah.

And that singular fact automatically gives this woman a prominent place in the "extraordinary" category.

A CURIOUS CONVERSATION

Jesus' conversation with the woman started out simply and naturally enough—he asked her for a drink. The well was deep, and He had no way to draw water from it, so He said: "Give Me a drink" (v. 7 NKJV). He probably said it casually and in a friendly enough way, but He expressed it in the form of a command, not a question.

She obviously didn't think the request, or the way He phrased it, was rude. She certainly didn't act offended. Instead, she immediately expressed surprise that He would even speak to her, much less drink from her vessel: "How is it that You, being a Jew, ask a drink from me, a Samaritan woman?" (v. 9 NKJV). Gender taboos, racial divisions, and the class system would normally keep a man of Jesus' status from conversing with a woman such as she, much less drinking from a water container that belonged to her.

Bypassing her actual question, Jesus said, "If you knew the gift of God, and who it is who says to you, 'Give Me a drink,' you would have asked Him, and He would have given you living water" (v. 10 NKJV). He was already hinting at the real message He intended to give her.

She immediately understood that He was making an amazing claim. She replied, "Sir, You have nothing to draw with, and the well is deep. Where then do You get that living water? Are You greater than our father Jacob, who gave us the well, and drank from it himself, as well as his sons and his livestock?" (vv. 11–12 NKJV).

As a matter of fact, He *was* greater than Jacob, and that is precisely the point He wanted to demonstrate for her. But once more, instead of answering her question directly, He continued speaking of the living water. Indeed, He assured her, the water He offered was infinitely better than the water from Jacob's well: "Whoever drinks of this water will thirst again, but whoever drinks of the water that I shall give him will never thirst. But the water that I shall give him will become in him a fountain of water springing up into everlasting life" (vv. 13–14 NKJV).

Now she was supremely curious, and she asked Him to give her the living water (v. 15). I think by now she probably understood that He was speaking of spiritual water. Parables and metaphors were standard teaching tools in that culture. Jesus was obviously some kind of rabbi or spiritual leader. It is unlikely that she was still thinking in literal terms. But her reply simply echoed the same metaphorical language He had used with her: "Sir, give me this water, that I may not thirst, nor come here to draw" (v. 15 NKJV).

Jesus' next words unexpectedly drew her up short: "Go, call your husband, and come here" (v. 16 NKJV).

Now she was in a quandary. The truth about her life was so horrible that she could not admit it to Him. He seemed to be assuming she was a typical woman with a respectable home and an honorable husband. She was nothing like that. But instead of exposing all her disgrace to this rabbi, she told him only a small fraction of the truth: "I have no husband" (v. 17 NKJV).

To her utter chagrin, He knew the full truth already: "Jesus said to her, 'You have well said, 'I have no husband,' for you have had five husbands, and the one whom you now have is not your husband; in that you spoke truly'" (vv. 17–18 NKJV). Notice that He did not rebuke her as a liar; on the contrary, He *commended* her for speaking truthfully. She wasn't denying her sin. But she obviously wasn't proud of it, either. So in order to retain whatever shred of dignity she could, she had simply sidestepped the implications of His question without actually lying to cover anything up.

No matter. He knew all about her sin right down to the infinitesimal details. When she later recounted her meeting with Jesus, this was the fact that left the strongest impression on her mind: He told her everything she ever did (vv. 29, 39). Moments before, she had questioned whether He was greater than Jacob. Now she knew.

I love the low-key, almost droll simplicity with which she acknowledged her own guilt: "Sir, I perceive that You are a prophet" (v. 19 NKJV). He had unmasked her completely. Whoever He was, He obviously knew all about her. And yet, far from spurning her or castigating her, He had offered her the water of life!

At this point, a thousand thoughts and questions must have filled her mind. She certainly must have wondered exactly who this was and how He knew so much about her. It is obvious that He was quite prepared to tell her who He was. He Himself had raised that issue almost immediately (v. 10). But instead of pursuing that question, she turned the conversation in a bizarre direction. She brought up what was to her mind the biggest point of religious contention between the Jews and the Samaritans: "Our fathers worshiped on this mountain, and you Jews say that in Jerusalem is the place where one ought to worship" (v. 20 NKJV). She actually didn't frame it as a question, but I don't think she meant it as a challenge. I think she was genuinely hoping that this rabbi, who seemed to know *everything*, could straighten out what seemed to her to be the fundamental debate of the ages: Who was right? The Jews or the Samaritans? Gerizim or Jerusalem?

Jesus did not brush her sincere question aside. He didn't reproach her for changing the subject. He gave her a brief but very potent answer in John 4:21–24:

Woman, believe Me, the hour is coming when you will neither on this mountain, nor in Jerusalem, worship the Father. You worship what you do not know; we know what we worship, for salvation is of the Jews. But the hour is coming, and now is, when the true worshipers will worship the Father in spirit and truth; for the Father is seeking such to worship Him. God is Spirit, and those who worship Him must worship in spirit and truth. (NKJV)

With that reply, He accomplished several things. First, he let her know that *where* you worship isn't the issue. True worshipers are defined by whom and how they worship.

Second, He made it clear that the religious tradition she had grown up in was totally and utterly false: "You worship what you do not know; we know what we worship, for salvation is of the Jews" (v. 22 NKJV). He did not airbrush the reality or trouble Himself with trying to be delicate. He answered the real question she was asking.

Third, He subtly steered her back to the main subject by telling her that a new age was dawning when neither Gerizim nor Jerusalem would have a monopoly on the priesthood. The era of the New Covenant was just on the horizon. There was a subtle expression of messianic expectation in His words, and she got it.

She replied with these amazing words: "'I know that Messiah is coming' (who is called Christ). 'When He comes, He will tell us all things'" (v. 25 NKJV).

Is it not significant that this Samaritan woman, born and raised in a culture of corrupt religion, had the same messianic hope shared by every other godly woman in Scripture?

Now, consider the implications of her statement. She *knew* the Messiah was coming. That was a definitive expression of confidence. It was embryonic faith waiting to be born. And how did she think the true Messiah would identify Himself? "When He comes, He will tell us all things" (v. 25 NKJV). Jesus had already demonstrated His full knowledge of all her secrets. As she later testified to the men of her city, "[He] told me all things that I ever did" (v. 29 NKJV).

She was strongly hinting that she suspected Jesus Himself might be the Messiah. When the apostle Peter later confessed his faith that Jesus *was* the Christ, the Son of the living God, Jesus told him, "Blessed are you, Simon Bar-Jonah, for flesh and blood has not revealed this to you, but My Father who is in heaven" (Matt. 16:17 NKJV). The same thing was true of this woman. The Holy Spirit was working in her heart. God the Father was drawing her irresistibly to Christ, revealing truth to her that eye had never seen and ear had never heard.

Now Jesus was ready to pull back the curtain and reveal His true identity in an unprecedented way.

AN ASTONISHING REVELATION

No sooner had she broached the subject of the Messiah, than Jesus said, "I who speak to you am He" (John 4:26 NKJV). This is the single most direct and explicit messianic claim Jesus ever made. Never before in any of the biblical record had He said this so forthrightly to anyone. Never again is it recorded that He declared Himself this plainly, until the night of His betrayal.

Of course, when Peter made his great confession, Jesus affirmed that Peter had it right (Matt. 16:17–19). But He immediately "commanded His disciples that they should tell no one that He was Jesus the Christ" (v. 20 NKJV). When Jewish crowds demanded, "If You are the Christ, tell us plainly" (John 10:24 NKJV), He never denied the truth, but He avoided explicitly stating the words they were clamoring to hear. Instead, He appealed to His works as evidence of who He was: "I told you, and you do not believe. The works that I do in My Father's name, they bear witness of Me" (v. 25 NKJV).

It was not until His trial before Caiaphas, in the early-morning hours just before His crucifixion, that Jesus once again revealed His identity as plainly as He did for this Samaritan woman.

The high priest asked Him, "Are You the Christ, the Son of the Blessed?" (Mark 14:61 NKJV).

Jesus said, "I am. And you will see the Son of Man sitting at the right hand of the Power, and coming with the clouds of heaven" (v. 62 NKJV).

That was the very declaration that ultimately cost Him His life. Mark wrote, "The high priest tore his clothes and said, 'What further need do we have of witnesses? You have heard the blasphemy! What do you think?' And they all condemned Him to be deserving of death" (vv. 63–64 NKJV).

In light of all that, it is absolutely astonishing that the very *first* time Jesus chose to reveal Himself as Messiah, it was to a Samaritan woman with such a shady past. But His self-revelation is a testimony to her faith. The fact that He declared Himself so plainly is proof positive that the tiny germ of hope that had her looking for the Messiah in the first place was either about to develop into authentic, full-fledged faith—or else it already had sprouted. Jesus would not have committed Himself to an unbeliever (John 2:24).

Scripture says it was precisely "at this point" that the disciples returned from their errand, "and they marveled that He talked with a woman" (John 4:27 NKJV). The Greek expression is emphatic, suggesting they returned just in time to hear Him declare Himself Messiah. They were shocked speechless at the scene. John, himself an eyewitness, wrote, "No one said, 'What do You seek?' or, 'Why are You talking with her?'" (v. 27 NKJV).

AN AMAZING TRANSFORMATION

Soon after the disciples arrived, the woman left the well, leaving behind her water pot. It wasn't absent-mindedness that caused her to leave it; she fully intended to come back. Her plan was to bring the leading men of the city and introduce them to Christ. She was privy to amazing knowledge that must not be kept secret.

Her response was typical of new believers, one of the evidences of authentic faith. The person who has just had the burden of sin and guilt lifted always wants to share the good news with others. The woman's excitement would have been palpable. And notice that the first thing she told the men of her town was that Jesus had told her everything she ever did. No longer was she evading the facts of her sin. She was basking in the glow of forgiveness, and there is simply no shame in that.

Her enthusiasm and determination were apparently hard to resist, because the men of the city went back with her to the well where they all met Jesus.

The immediate impact of this woman's testimony on the city of Sychar was profound. John wrote, "Many of the Samaritans of that city believed in Him *because of the word of the woman* who testified, 'He told me all that I ever did'" (v. 39 NKJV, emphasis added).

What a contrast this makes with the reception Jesus got from the scribes and Pharisees in Jerusalem! Luke wrote, "The Pharisees and scribes *complained,* saying, 'This Man receives sinners and eats with them'" (Luke 15:2 NKJV, emphasis added). The religious leaders were disgusted with Him because He was willing to converse with rogues and scoundrels such as this woman. They mocked Him openly, saying, "Look, a glutton and a winebibber, a friend of tax collectors and sinners!" (Matt. 11:19 NKJV). They were offended, for example, when Jesus went to the house of Zacchaeus. "They all complained, saying, 'He has gone to be a guest with a man who is a sinner'" (Luke 19:7 NKJV).

But Samaritans lacked the phony scruples of religious hypocrisy. The leading men of that Samaritan village were in many ways the polar opposites of the religious leaders in Jerusalem. The Jewish leaders, of course, were convinced that when the Messiah came, He would vindicate them. He would banish the Romans and set up His kingdom over the whole world, with Israel at the hub. He would triumph over all Israel's enemies, including the Samaritans, and rule and reign through the very political and religious structures they represented. Their messianic expectations were high for that very reason, and their contempt for Christ was acute for the *same* reason. He fit none of their preconceived notions of what the Messiah ought to be. He rebuked the religious leaders while fellowshiping openly with publicans and sinners. The Jewish leaders hated Him for it.

The Samaritans had the opposite perspective. They knew the Messiah was promised. Although the books of Moses were the only part of the Old Testament they believed, the messianic promises were there. As Jesus told the Pharisees, "If you believed Moses, you would believe Me; for he wrote about Me" (John 5:46 NKJV). In Deuteronomy 18:18, for example, God promised a great Prophet—a national spokesman on the order of Moses, or greater: "I will raise up for them a Prophet like you from among their brethren, and will put My words in His mouth" (NKJV). The Pentateuch also included all the familiar promises about the Seed of the woman who would crush the serpent, and the Seed of Abraham, in whom all the nations would be blessed. That is why the Samaritan woman knew the Messiah was coming.

But Samaritan society had been degraded and debased by years of false religion and immorality. Samaritans had a definite sense that they were sinners. They lacked the self-righteous swagger that colored the religion of the Pharisees and Sadducees. When they pondered the coming Messiah, they probably anticipated His advent with a degree of fear.

So when this woman announced so boldly that she had found the Messiah and that He knew everything about her sin but received her anyway, the men of Sychar welcomed Jesus with great enthusiasm. "They urged Him to stay with them; and He stayed there two days. And many more believed because of His own word. Then they said to the woman, 'Now we believe, not because of what you said, for we ourselves have heard Him and we know that this is indeed the Christ, the Savior of the world'" (John 4:40–42 NKJV). This was an amazing revival, and it must have utterly transformed that little town.

Jesus had indeed found a true worshiper. Scripture doesn't tell us what ultimately became of the Samaritan woman. Her *heart* was clearly changed by her encounter with Christ. It is an absolute certainty that her *life* changed as well, because "If anyone is in Christ, [she] is a new creation; old things have passed away; behold, all things have become new" (2 Cor. 5:17 NKJV).

Within three years after the Samaritan woman's meeting with Christ at Jacob's well, the church was founded. Its influence quickly spread from Jerusalem into all Judea and Samaria, and from there to the uttermost parts of the earth (Acts 1:8). That meant the Samaritan woman and the men of her city would soon be able to find fellowship and teaching in a context where there was neither Hebrew nor Samaritan, Jew nor Greek, slave nor free, male nor female; but where all were one in Christ Jesus (Gal. 3:28). I think it is a certainty that the Samaritan village of Sychar became a center of gospel activity and witness. Having gone out of His way to reveal Himself to that village, having given them the water of life that quenched their spiritual thirst, we can be certain He did not simply abandon them. This woman, who had begun her new life by bringing many others to Christ, no doubt continued her evangelistic ministry. She even continues it today through the record of Scripture. Multitudes have come to Christ through the influence of John 4 and "because of the word of the woman who testified, 'He told me all that I ever did'" (v. 39 NKJV). Only heaven will reveal the vast and far-reaching fruits of this extraordinary woman's encounter with the Messiah.

9

MARTHA AND MARY: WORKING AND WORSHIPING

Mary . . . sat at Jesus' feet and heard His word. But Martha was distracted with much serving.

Luke 10:39–40 NKJV

I n this chapter, we meet *two* extraordinary women—Martha and Mary. We'll consider them together because that is how Scripture consistently presents them. They lived with their brother, Lazarus, in the small village of Bethany. That was within easy walking distance of Jerusalem, about two miles southeast of the Temple's eastern gate (John 11:18)—just over the Mount of Olives from Jerusalem's city center. Both Luke and John recorded that Jesus enjoyed hospitality in the home of this family. He went there on at least three crucial occasions in the gospels. Bethany was apparently a regular stop for Him in His travels, and this family's home seems to have become a welcome hub for Jesus during His visits to Judea.

Martha and Mary make a fascinating pair—very different in many ways, but alike in one vital respect: both of them loved Christ. By now, you're surely beginning to notice that this is the consistent hallmark of every woman whom the Bible treats as exemplary. They all point to Christ.

Everything praiseworthy about them was in one way or another centered on *Him*. He was the focus of earnest expectation for every one of the outstanding women in the Old Testament, and He was greatly beloved by all the principal women in the New Testament. Martha and Mary of Bethany are classic examples. They became cherished personal friends of Jesus during His earthly ministry. Moreover, He had a profound love for their family. The apostle John, who was a keen observer of whom and what Jesus loved, made it a point to record that "Jesus loved Martha and her sister and Lazarus" (John 11:5 NKJV).

We're not told how this particular household became so intimate with Jesus. Since no family ties are ever mentioned between Jesus' relatives and the Bethany clan, it seems likely that Martha and Mary were simply two of the many people who heard Jesus teach early in His ministry, extended Him hospitality, and built a relationship with Him that way. In whatever way this relationship began, it obviously developed into a warm and deeply personal fellowship. It is clear from Luke's description that Jesus made Himself at home in their house.

The fact that Jesus actively cultivated such friendships sheds light on the kind of man He was. It also helps explain how He managed to have an itinerant ministry in Judea without ever becoming a homeless indigent, even though He maintained no permanent dwelling of His own (Matt. 8:20). Apparently, people like Martha and Mary regularly welcomed Him into their homes and families, and He was clearly at home among His many friends.

Certainly hospitality was a special hallmark of *this* family. Martha in particular is portrayed everywhere as a meticulous hostess. Even her name is the feminine form of the Aramaic word for "Lord." It was a perfect name for her because she was clearly the one who presided over her house. Luke 10:38 speaks of the family home as *Martha's* house. That, together with the fact that her name was usually listed first whenever she was named with her siblings, implies strongly that she was the elder sister. Lazarus appears to be the youngest of the three, because he was named last in John's list of family members (John 11:5), and Lazarus rarely comes to the foreground of any narrative—including John's description of how Lazarus was raised from the dead.

Some believe Martha's position as owner of the house and dominant one in the household indicates that she must have been a widow. That's possible, of course, but all we know from Scripture is that these three siblings lived together, and there is no mention that any of them had ever been married. Nor is any hint given about how old they were. But since Mary was literally at Jesus' feet each time she appeared, it would be hard to imagine them as very old. Furthermore, the starkly contrasting temperaments of Martha and Mary seem unmellowed by much age. I'm inclined to think they were all three still very young and inexperienced. Indeed, in their interaction with Christ, He always treated them much the same way an elder brother would, and many of the principles He taught them were profoundly practical lessons for young people coming of age. A few of those lessons rise to particular prominence in the episode we will soon examine.

THREE SNAPSHOTS OF MARTHA AND MARY TOGETHER

Scripture gives three significant accounts of Jesus' interaction with this family. First, Luke 10:38–42 describes a minor conflict between Martha and Mary over how best to show their devotion to Christ. That is where we initially meet Martha and Mary in the New Testament. The way Luke described their clashing temperaments was perfectly consistent with everything we see in two later incidents recorded by John. (We'll return to focus mostly on the end of Luke 10 in this chapter because that's where the contrasting personalities of these two are seen most clearly.)

A second close-up glimpse at the lives of these two women comes in

John 11. Virtually the entire chapter is devoted to a description of how their brother Lazarus died and was brought back to life by Christ. Jesus' personal dealings with Martha and Mary in this scene highlighted their individual characteristics. Although we don't have space enough to consider the event thoroughly, we'll later return briefly just to take note of how the death and subsequent raising of Lazarus affected both Martha and Mary profoundly, but differently, according to their contrasting personalities. John gave very detailed and poignant descriptions of how deeply the sisters were distressed over their loss, how Jesus ministered to them in their grief, how He mourned with them in a profound and personal way, and how He gloriously raised Lazarus from the dead at the very climax of the funeral. More than any other act of Jesus, that one dramatic and very public miracle was what finally sealed the Jewish leaders' determination to put Him to death because they knew that if He could raise the dead, people would follow Him, and the leaders would lose their power base (John 11:45–57). They obstinately refused to consider that His power to give life was proof that He was exactly who He claimed to be: God the Son.

Martha and Mary seemed to understand that Jesus had put Himself in jeopardy in order to give them back the life of their brother. In fact, the full depth of Mary's gratitude and understanding was revealed in a third and final account where both of these women appeared together one more time. John 12 (with parallel accounts in Matthew 26:6–13 and Mark 14:3–9) records how Mary anointed the feet of Jesus with costly ointment and wiped His feet with her hair. Although both Matthew and Mark described the event, neither of them mentioned Mary's name in this context. It was nonetheless clear that they were describing the same incident we read about in John 12. Both Matthew 26:12 and John 12:7 indicated that Mary, in some sense, understood that she was anointing Jesus for burial. She must have strongly suspected that her brother's resurrection would drive Jesus' enemies to a white-hot hatred, and they would be determined to put Him to death (John 11:53–54). Jesus Himself had gone to the relative safety of Ephraim right after the raising of Lazarus, but Passover brought Him back to Jerusalem (vv. 55–56). Mary (and probably Martha as well) seemed to grasp more clearly than anyone how imminent the threat to Jesus was. That surely intensified their sense of debt and gratitude toward Him, as reflected in Mary's act of worship.

MARY, THE TRUE WORSHIPER

According to Matthew and Mark, Mary's anointing of Jesus' feet took place at the home of "Simon the leper." Of course, a person with an active case of leprosy would not have been able to *attend* a gathering like this, much less *host* it in his own home. Lepers were considered ceremonially unclean, therefore banished from populated areas (Lev. 13:45–46), so Simon's nickname must signify that he was a *former* leper. Since Scripture says Jesus healed all who came to Him (Luke 6:19), Simon was probably someone whom Jesus had healed from leprosy. (Just such an incident is described in Luke 5:12–15).

Simon also must have been a well-to-do man. With all the disciples present, this was a sizable dinner party. He may also have been an unmarried man, because Martha seems to have been acting as hostess at this gathering. Some have suggested that she might have made her living as a professional caterer. More likely, Simon was a close friend of the family, and she volunteered to serve. Lazarus was present too (John 12:2). It appears that the gathering was a close group of Jesus' friends and disciples. Perhaps it was a formal celebration of Lazarus's return from the dead. If so, this group of friends had come together mainly to express their gratitude to Jesus for what He had done.

Mary knew exactly how best to show gratitude. Her action of anointing Jesus was strikingly similar to another account from earlier in Jesus' ministry (Luke 7:36–50). At a different gathering, in the home of a different man, a Pharisee (who was coincidentally also named Simon), a woman "who was a sinner" (v. 37 NKJV)—apparently a repentant prostitute (v. 39)—had once anointed Jesus' feet and wiped them with her hair, exactly like Mary in the John 12 account. In all likelihood, the earlier incident was well known to Martha and Mary. They knew the lesson Jesus taught on that occasion: "Her sins, which are many, are forgiven, for she loved much" (v. 47 NKJV). Mary's reenactment would therefore have been a deliberate echo of the earlier incident, signifying how much she also loved Jesus and how supremely grateful to Him she was.

Both Matthew and Mark indicate that Jesus' willingness to accept such a lavish expression of worship is what finally sealed Judas's decision to betray Christ. According to John, Judas resented what he pretended to perceive as a "waste," but his resentment was really nothing more than greed. He was actually pilfering money from the disciples' treasury (John 12:4–6).

So the lives of these two women inadvertently intersected *twice* with the sinister plot to kill Jesus. The raising of their brother first ignited the plot among the Jewish leaders that finally ended with Jesus' death. Mary's munificent expression of gratitude to Jesus then finally pushed Judas over the edge.

MARTHA, THE DEVOTED SERVANT

Reluctantly setting that aside, our main focus in this chapter is that famous incident described at the end of Luke 10 when Jesus gave Martha a mild rebuke and a strong lesson about where her real priorities ought to lie. The passage is short but rich. Luke writes:

Now it happened as they went that He entered a certain village; and a certain woman named Martha welcomed Him into her house. And she had a sister called Mary, who also sat at Jesus' feet and heard His word. But Martha was distracted with much serving, and she approached Him and said, "Lord, do You not care that my sister has left me to serve alone? Therefore tell her to help me."

And Jesus answered and said to her, "Martha, Martha, you are worried and troubled about many things. But one thing is needed, and Mary has chosen that good part, which will not be taken away from her." (10:38–42 NKJV)

Martha seemed to be the elder of the two sisters. Luke's description of her behavior is one of the things that supports the idea that these three siblings were still young adults. Martha's complaint sounds callow and girlish. Jesus' reply, though containing a mild rebuke, has an almost grandfatherly tone to it.

Jesus had apparently come at Martha's invitation. She was the one who welcomed Him in, signifying that she was the actual master of ceremonies in this house. On this occasion, at least, she wasn't merely filling in as a surrogate hostess for a friend; she was plainly the one in charge of the household.

In Luke 7:36–50, when Jesus visited the home of Simon the Pharisee (where the *first* anointing of His feet took place), He was clearly under the scrutiny of His critics. The hospitality was notoriously poor on that occasion; Simon did not offer Jesus water to wash His feet or even give Him a proper greeting (Luke 7:44–46)—two *major* social snubs in that culture. The washing of a guest's feet was the first-century Middle Eastern equivalent of offering to take a guest's coat (John 13:1–7). Not to do it was tantamount to implying that you wished the guest would leave quickly. And to omit the formal greeting was tantamount to declaring him an enemy (2 John 10–11).

Martha, to her great credit, was at the opposite end of the hospitality spectrum from Simon the Pharisee. She fussed over her hostessing duties. She wanted everything to be just right. She was a conscientious and considerate hostess, and these were admirable traits. Much in her behavior was commendable.

I love the way Jesus came across in this scene. He was the perfect houseguest. He instantly made Himself at home. He enjoyed the fellowship and conversation, and as always, *His* contribution to the discussion was instructive and enlightening. No doubt His disciples were asking Him questions, and He was giving answers that were thought-provoking, authoritative, and utterly edifying. Mary's instinct was to sit at His feet and listen. Martha, ever the fastidious one, went right to work with her preparations.

THE CONFLICT BETWEEN THEM

Soon, however, Martha grew irritable with Mary. It's easy to imagine how her exasperation might have elevated. At first, she probably tried to hint in a "subtle" way that she needed help, by making extra noise—maybe moving some pots and pans around with a little more vigor than the situation really required, and then by letting some utensils or cookware clatter together loudly in a washbasin. Martha might have cleared her throat or exhaled a few times loudly enough to be heard in the next room. Anything to remind Mary that her sister was expecting a little help. When all of that failed, she probably tried to peek around the corner or walk briskly through to the dining room, hoping to catch Mary's eye. In the end, however, she just gave up all pretense of subtlety or civility and aired her grievance against Mary right in front of Jesus. In fact, she complained *to* Him and asked Him to intervene and set Mary straight.

Jesus' reply must have utterly startled Martha. It didn't seem to have occurred to her that she might be the one in the wrong, but the little scene earned her the gentlest of admonitions from Jesus. Luke's account ends there, so we're probably safe to conclude that the message penetrated straight to Martha's heart and had exactly the sanctifying effect Christ's words always have on those who love Him.

Indeed, in the later incident recorded in John 12, where Mary anointed

Jesus' feet, Martha once again is seen in the role of server. But this time *Judas* was the one who complained (John 12:4–5). He apparently tried his best to drum up a general outcry against Mary's extravagance and managed to stir some expressions of indignation from some of the other disciples (Matt. 26:8). But Martha wisely seems to have held her peace this time. She no longer seemed resentful of Mary's devotion to Christ. Martha herself loved Christ no less than Mary did, I believe. He clearly loved them both with deepest affection (John 11:5).

Some important lessons emerge from Jesus' reprimand of Martha. We would all do well to heed these admonitions.

A LESSON ABOUT THE PREFERENCE OF OTHERS OVER SELF

Jesus' gentle admonition to Martha is first of all a reminder that we should honor others over ourselves. Scripture elsewhere says, "Be kindly affectionate to one another with brotherly love, in honor giving preference to one another" (Rom. 12:10 NKJV). "Be submissive to one another, and be clothed with humility, for 'God resists the proud, but gives grace to the humble'" (1 Peter 5:5 NKJV). "Let nothing be done through selfish ambition or conceit, but in lowliness of mind let each esteem others better than himself. Let each of you look out not only for his own interests, but also for the interests of others" (Phil. 2:3–4 NKJV).

Humility had been a constant theme in Jesus' teaching, and a difficult lesson for most of His disciples to learn. Even on the night of Jesus' betrayal, each of the disciples had ignored basic hospitality rather than take a servant's role and wash the others' feet (John 13:1–7).

In the Luke 10 account, Martha's external behavior at first appeared to be true servanthood. She was the one who put on the apron and went to work in the task of serving others. But her treatment of Mary soon revealed a serious defect in her servant's heart. She allowed herself to become censorious and sharp-tongued. Such words in front of other guests were certain to humiliate Mary. Martha either gave no thought to the hurtful effect of her words on her sister, or she simply didn't care.

Furthermore, Martha was wrong in her judgment of Mary. She assumed Mary was being lazy. "Who are you to judge another's servant? To his own master he stands or falls" (Rom. 14:4 NKJV). Did Martha imagine that she, rather than Christ, was Mary's true master?

In reality, Mary was the one whose heart was in the right place. Her motives and desires were more commendable than Martha's. Jesus knew it, even though no mere mortal could ever make that judgment by observing the external behavior of the two women. But Jesus knew it because He knew the hearts of both women.

Martha's behavior shows how subtly and sinfully human pride can corrupt even the best of our actions. What Martha was doing was by no means a bad thing. She was waiting on Christ and her other guests. In a very practical and functional sense, she was acting as servant to all, just as Christ had so often commanded. She no doubt began with the best of motives and the noblest of intentions.

But the moment she stopped listening to Christ and made something other than Him the focus of her heart and attention, her perspective became very self-centered. At that point, even her service to Christ became tainted with self-absorption and spoiled by a very uncharitable failure to assume the best of her sister. Martha was showing an attitude of sinful pride that made her susceptible to several other kinds of evil as well: anger, resentment, jealousy, distrust, a critical spirit, judgmentalism, and unkindness. All of that flared up in Martha in a matter of minutes.

Worst of all, Martha's words impugned the Lord Himself: "Lord, do You not care . . . ?" (Luke 10:40 NKJV). Did she really imagine that *He* did not care? She certainly knew better. Jesus' love for all three members of this family was obvious to all (John 11:5).

But Martha's thoughts and feelings had become too self-focused.

Because of that, she also fell into an all-too-common religious trap described by Paul in his letter to the Corinthians: "They, measuring themselves by themselves, and comparing themselves among themselves, are not wise" (2 Cor. 10:12 NKJV). She turned her attention from Christ and began watching Mary with a critical eye. Naturally, it began to ruin the whole evening for Martha.

Mary, by contrast, was so consumed with thoughts of Christ that she became completely oblivious to everything else. She sat at His feet and listened to Him intently, absorbing His every word and nuance. She was by no means being lazy. She simply understood the *true* importance of this occasion. The Son of God Himself was a guest in her home. Listening to Him and worshiping Him were at that moment the very best use of Mary's energies and the one right place for her to focus her attention.

One thing that stood out about Mary of Bethany was her keen ability to observe and understand the heart of Christ. Mary's temperament seemed naturally more contemplative than Martha's. In Luke 10, she wanted to listen intently to Jesus, while Martha bustled around making preparations to serve the meal. In John 11, when Jesus arrived after Lazarus had already died, Martha ran out of the house to meet Him, but Mary remained in the house, immersed in grief (John 11:20). She was absorbed, as usual, in deep thoughts. People like Mary are not given to sudden impulse or shallow activity. Yet while Jesus had to *coax* a confession of faith from Martha (vv. 23–27)—and even that was pretty shaky (v. 39)—Mary simply fell at His feet in worship (v. 32).

Mary seemed to be able to discern Jesus' true meaning even better than any of the twelve disciples. Her gesture of anointing Him in preparation for His burial at the beginning of that final week in Jerusalem shows a remarkably mature understanding. That was the fruit of her willingness to sit still, listen, and ponder. It was the very thing that always made Mary such a sharp contrast to Martha, whose first inclination was usually to act—or react. (Martha had a lot in common with Peter in that regard.)

If Martha had truly preferred Mary over herself, she might have seen in Mary a depth of understanding and love for Christ that surpassed even her own. She could have learned much from her more quiet, thoughtful sister. *But not right now.* Martha had a table to set, a meal to get out of the oven, and "many things" she was "worried and troubled about" (Luke 10:41 NKJV). Before she knew it, her resentment against Mary had built up, and she could no longer restrain herself. Her public criticism of Mary was an ugly expression of pride.

A LESSON ABOUT THE PRIORITY OF WORSHIP OVER SERVICE

It's interesting to read this narrative and try to imagine how the average woman might respond if placed in a situation like Martha's. My strong suspicion is that *many* women would be inclined to sympathize with Martha, not Mary. After all, it would normally be considered rude to let your sister do all the hard work in the kitchen while you sit chatting with guests.

So in a real sense, Martha's feelings were natural and somewhat understandable. That may be one reason Jesus' rebuke was so mild. In normal circumstances, any older sister would think it obligatory for the younger sister to help in serving a meal to guests. In other words, what Martha expected Mary to do was, in itself, perfectly fine and good.

Nevertheless, what Mary was doing was better still. She had "chosen that good part" (Luke10:42 NKJV). She had discovered the one thing needful: true worship and devotion of one's heart and full attention to Christ. That was a higher priority even than service, and the good part she had chosen would not be taken away from her, even for the sake of something as gracious and beneficial as helping Martha prepare Jesus a meal. Mary's humble, obedient heart was a far greater gift to Christ than Martha's well-set table.

This establishes worship as the highest of all priorities for every Christian. Nothing, including even service rendered to Christ, is more important than listening to Him and honoring Him with our hearts. Remember what Jesus told the Samaritan woman at the well: God is seeking true worshipers (John 4:23). Christ had found one in Mary. He would not affirm Martha's reprimand of her, because it was Mary, not Martha, who properly understood that worship is a higher duty to Christ than service rendered on His behalf.

It is a danger, even for people who love Christ, that we not become so concerned with *doing things for Him* that we begin to neglect *hearing Him* and *remembering what He has done for us.* We must never allow our service for Christ to crowd out our worship of Him. The moment our works become more important to us than our worship, we have turned the true spiritual priorities on their heads.

In fact, that tendency is the very thing that is so poisonous about all forms of pietism and theological liberalism. Whenever you elevate good deeds over sound doctrine and true worship, you ruin the works too. Doing good works for the works' sake has a tendency to exalt self and depreciate the work of Christ. Good deeds, human charity, and acts of kindness are crucial expressions of real faith, but they must flow from a true reliance on *God's* redemption and *His* righteousness. After all, our own good works can never be a means of earning God's favor; that's why in Scripture the focus of faith is always on what God has done for us, and never on what we do for Him (Rom. 10:2–4). Observe any form of religion where good works are ranked as more important than authentic faith or sound doctrine, and you'll discover a system that denigrates Christ while unduly magnifying self.

Not that Martha was guilty of gross self-righteousness. We shouldn't be any more harsh in our assessment of her than Christ was. She loved the Lord. Her faith was real, but by neglecting the needful thing and busying herself with mere activity, she became spiritually unbalanced. Her behavior reminds us that a damaging spirit of self-righteousness can slip in and contaminate even the hearts of those who have sincerely embraced Christ as their true righteousness. Martha's harshness toward Mary exposed precisely that kind of imbalance in her own heart.

Jesus' gentle words of correction to Martha (as well as His commendation of Mary) set the priorities once more in their proper order. Worship (which is epitomized here by listening intently to Jesus' teachings) is the one thing most needed. Service to Christ must always be subordinate to that.

A LESSON ABOUT THE PRIMACY OF FAITH OVER WORKS

A third vital spiritual principle goes hand in hand with the priority of worship over service and is so closely related to it that the two actually overlap. This third principle is the truth (taught from the beginning to the end of Scripture) that what we *believe* is ultimately more crucial than what we *do.*

Martha's "much serving" was a distraction (Luke 10:40 NKJV) from the "one thing" (v. 42 NKJV) that was really needed—listening to and learning from Jesus. Religious works often have a sinister tendency to eclipse faith itself. Proper good works always flow from faith and are the fruit of it. What we do is vital, because that is the evidence that our faith is living and real (James 2:14–26). But faith must come first and is the only viable foundation for true and lasting good works. All of that is wrapped up in the truth that works are not the instrument of justification; faith is (Rom. 4:4-5).

Martha seems to have forgotten these things momentarily. She was acting as if Christ needed her work for Him more than she needed His work on her behalf. Rather than humbly fixing her faith on the vital importance of Christ's work for sinners, she was thinking too much in terms of what she could do for Him.

Again, this seems to be the natural drift of the human heart. We wrongly imagine that what we do for Christ is more important than what He has done for us. Every major spiritual decline in the history of Christianity has come when the church has lost sight of the primacy of faith and begun to stress works instead. Virtually every serious doctrinal deviation throughout church history has had this same tendency at its core—beginning with the error of the Judaizers, who insisted that an Old Covenant ritual (circumcision) was essential for justification. They denied that faith alone could be instrumental in justification, and that undermined the very foundation of the gospel.

Human instinct seems to tell us that what we *do* is more important than what we *believe*. But that is a false instinct, the product of our fallen self-righteousness. It is a totally wrong way of thinking—*sinfully* wrong. We must never think more highly of our works for Christ than we do of His works on our behalf.

Of course, such a thought would never consciously enter Martha's mind. She loved Christ. She genuinely trusted Him, although her faith had moments of weakness. Still, on this occasion, she allowed her anxiety about what she must do for Christ to overwhelm her gratitude over what He would do for her.

I'm very grateful that Christ's rebuke of Martha was a gentle one. I must confess that it is very easy for me to identify with her. I love the privilege of serving the Lord, and He has blessed me with more than enough to stay busy. It is tempting at times to become swept up in the activity of ministry and forget that faith and worship must always have priority over work. In these hectic times, we all need to cultivate more of Mary's worshipful, listening spirit and less of Martha's scrambling commotion.

Martha and Mary also remind us that God uses all kinds of people. He has gifted us differently for a reason, and we're not to despise one another or look at others with contempt, just because we have differing temperaments or contrasting personalities.

Martha was a noble and godly woman with a servant's heart and a rare capacity for work. Mary was nobler still, with an unusual predisposition for worship and wisdom. Both were remarkable in their own ways. If we weigh their gifts and their instincts *together*, they give us a wonderful example to follow. May we diligently cultivate the best instincts of both of these extraordinary women.

10

MARY MAGDALENE: DELIVERED FROM DARKNESS

Now when He rose early on the first day of the week, He appeared first to Mary Magdalene, out of whom He had cast seven demons.

Mark 16:9 NKJV

Mary Magdalene is one of the best-known and least-understood names in Scripture. Scripture deliberately draws a curtain of silence over much of her life and personal background, but she still emerges as one of the prominent women of the New Testament. She is mentioned by name in all four gospels, mostly in connection with the events of Jesus' crucifixion. She has the eternal distinction of being the first person to whom Christ revealed Himself after the resurrection.

Church traditions dating back to the early fathers have identified Mary Magdalene with the anonymous woman (identified only as "a sinner") in Luke 7:37–38, who anointed Jesus' feet and wiped them with her hair. But there is absolutely no reason to make that connection. Indeed, if we take the text of Scripture at face value, we have every reason to think otherwise. Since Luke first introduced Mary Magdalene by name in a completely different context (8:1–3) only three verses after he ended his narrative about the anointing of Jesus' feet, it seems highly unlikely that Mary Magdalene could be the same woman whom Luke described but did not name in the preceding account. Luke was too careful a historian to neglect a vital detail like that.

Some early commentators speculated that Mary Magdalene was the woman described in John 8:1–12, caught in the very act of adultery and saved from stoning by Christ, who forgave her and redeemed her. There is no basis for that association, either.

Mary Magdalene has also been the subject of a lot of extrabiblical mythology since medieval times. During the early Middle Ages, some of the gnostic heresies virtually co-opted the character of Mary Magdalene and attached her name to a plethora of fanciful legends. Apocryphal books were written about her, including one purporting to be Mary Magdalene's account of the life of Christ, *The Gospel of Mary.* Another, the gnostic *Gospel of Philip,* portrayed her as an adversary to Peter.

In recent years, some of those legends have been resurrected, and many of the long-discredited apocryphal stories about Mary Magdalene have been republished. She has become something of an icon for women in the "spiritual" fringe of the feminist movement who like the idea of Mary Magdalene as a kind of mythical goddess figure. Many of the ancient gnostic tales about her are well suited for that perspective. On a different front, one bestselling novel, *The Da Vinci Code* by Dan Brown, adapted several long-forgotten gnostic legends about Mary Magdalene and wove them into an elaborate conspiracy theory that included the blasphemous suggestion that Jesus and Mary Magdalene were secretly married and even had children. (According to that view, she, not the apostle John, was the beloved disciple mentioned in John 20:2 and 21:20.) Stacks of books ranging from utterly frivolous speculations to quasi-scholarly works have further revived selected gnostic fabrications about Mary Magdalene. A few highly sensationalized television documentaries have further reinforced the popularity of the revived myths.

So while Mary Magdalene is currently being talked about more than ever, much of the discussion is mere hype and hyperbole borrowed from ancient cults. What Scripture actually says about her is extraordinary enough without any false embellishment. Let's not allow this truly remarkable woman to get lost in the fog of ancient heretics' mystical and devilish fantasies.

DARKNESS

Mary Magdalene *did* have a dark past. Nothing indicates that her conduct was ever lewd or sordid in any way that would justify the common association of her name with sins of immorality. But Mary was indeed a woman whom Christ had liberated from demonic bondage. Luke introduced her as "Mary called Magdalene, out of whom had come seven demons" (Luke 8:2 NKJV). Mark 16:9 also mentioned the seven demons. It's the only detail we have been given about Mary Magdalene's past, except for a clue that we derive from her surname.

Actually, "Magdalene" is not a surname in the modern sense. She wasn't from a family that went by that name; she was from the village of Magdala. She was called "Magdalene" in order to distinguish her from the other women named *Mary* in the New Testament, including Mary of Bethany and Mary, the mother of Jesus.

The tiny fishing village of Magdala (mentioned only once by name in Scripture, in Matthew 15:39) was located on the northwest shore of the Sea of Galilee, some two or three miles north of the Roman city of Tiberias, and about five and a half miles south and west from Capernaum. (Capernaum, on the north shore of the lake, was Peter's hometown and a sort of home base for Jesus' Galilean ministry. Mary's hometown was within easy walking distance, or accessible by a short boat trip across the corner of the lake.) Jesus' ministry involved a number of exorcisms in that region. It seems to have been a hotbed of demonic activity.

The symptoms of demonic possession in the New Testament were varied. Demoniacs were sometimes insane, as in the case of the two demon-possessed men who lived in a graveyard and behaved so fiercely that no one dared approach them (Matt. 8:28–34; Mark 5:1–5). At least one of them, Mark tells us, was given to the nightmarish habit of deliberately mutilating himself with stones (Mark 5:5). More frequently, demonic possession was manifest in physical infirmities, such as blindness (Matt. 12:22), deafness (Mark 9:25), an inability to speak (Matt. 9:32–33), fits and seizures (Mark 1:26; Luke 9:38–40), and general infirmity (Luke 13:11–13).

Don't imagine (as many do) that the biblical descriptions of demon possession are merely crude accommodations to human superstition, as if the maladies characterized as demonic possession in the Bible were actually manifestations of epilepsy, dementia, or other purely psychological and physiological afflictions. Scripture *does* make a clear distinction between demon possession and diseases, including epilepsy and paralysis (Matt. 4:24). Demon possession involves bondage to an evil spirit—a real, personal, fallen spirit-creature—that indwells the afflicted individual. In several cases, Scripture describes how evil spirits spoke through the lips of those whom they tormented (Mark 1:23–24; Luke 4:33–35). Jesus sometimes forced the demonic personality to reveal itself in that way, perhaps to give clear proof of His power over evil spirits (Mark 5:8–14).

In every case, however, demon possession is portrayed as an affliction, not a sin, per se. Lawlessness, superstition, and idolatry undoubtedly have a major role in opening a person's heart to demonic possession, but none of the demonized individuals in the New Testament is explicitly associated with immoral behavior. They are always portrayed as tormented people, not willful malefactors. They suffered wretched indignities at the hands of evil spirits. They were all miserable, sorrowful, lonely, heartsick, forlorn, and pitiable creatures. Most of them were regarded as outcasts and pariahs by polite society. Scripture invariably presents them to us as victims with utterly ruined lives.

Such was Mary Magdalene, we can be certain. Satan tormented her with seven demons. There was nothing any mere man or woman could do for her. She was a veritable prisoner of demonic afflictions. These undoubtedly included depression, anxiety, unhappiness, loneliness, self-loathing, shame, fear, and a host of other similar miseries. In all probability, she suffered even *worse* torments, too, such as blindness, deafness, insanity, or any of the other disorders commonly associated with victims of demonic possession described in the New Testament. Whatever her condition, she would have been in perpetual agony—at least seven kinds of agony. Demoniacs in Scripture were always friendless, except in rare cases when devoted family members cared for them. They were perpetually restless because of their inability to escape the constant torments of their demonic captors. They were continually joyless because all of life had become darkness and misery for them. And they were hopeless because there was no earthly remedy for their spiritual afflictions.

That is all that can be said with certainty about the past of Mary Magdalene. Scripture deliberately and mercifully omits the macabre details of her dreadful demon-possession. But we are given enough information to know that at the very best, she must have been a gloomy, morose, tortured soul. And it is quite likely (especially with *so many* demons afflicting her) that her case was even worse. She might well have been so demented as to be regarded by most people as an unrecoverable lunatic.

DELIVERANCE

Christ had delivered her from all that. Luke and Mark seem to mention her former demonization only for the purpose of celebrating Christ's goodness and grace toward her. Without dredging up any squalid details from her past, they record the fact of her bondage to demons in a way that magnifies the gracious power of Christ.

One intriguing fact stands out about all the demonic deliverances that are recorded in Scripture: demon-possessed people never came to Christ to be delivered. Usually they were brought to Him (Matt. 8:16; 9:32; 12:22; Mark 9:20). Sometimes He called them to Himself (Luke 13:12), or He went to them (Matt. 8:28–29). On occasions when demons were already present upon His arrival, they would sometimes speak out with surprise and dismay (Mark 1:23–24; Luke 8:28).

Evil spirits never voluntarily entered the presence of Christ. Nor did they ever knowingly allow one whom they possessed to come close to Him. They often cried against Him (Luke 4:34). They sometimes caused violent convulsions in a last-gasp effort to keep the wretched souls they possessed away from Him (Mark 9:20), but Christ sovereignly drew and delivered multitudes who were possessed by demons (Mark 1:34, 39). Their emancipation from demonic bondage was always instantaneous and complete.

Mary Magdalene was one of them. How and when she was delivered is never spelled out for us, but Christ set her free, and she was free indeed. Having been set free from demons and from sin, she became a slave of righteousness (Rom. 6:18). Her life was not merely reformed; it was utterly transformed.

At one point in His ministry, Jesus gave a rather poignant illustration of the inadequacy of the religion of self-reform:

When an unclean spirit goes out of a man, he goes through dry places, seeking rest; and finding none, he says, "I will return to my house from which I came." And when he comes, he finds it swept and put in order. Then he goes and takes with him seven other spirits more wicked than himself, and they enter and dwell there; and the last state of that man is worse than the first. (Luke 11:24–26 NKJV)

It's intriguing that Mary Magdalene herself was possessed by seven demons. Perhaps she had tried to reform her own life and learned the hard way how utterly futile it is to try to free oneself from Satan's grip. Good works and religion don't atone for sin (Isa. 64:6), and no sinner has it within his power to change his own heart (Jer. 13:23). We can make cosmetic changes (sweeping the house and putting it in order), but that doesn't remove us from the dominion of darkness into the kingdom of light. Only God can do that (1 Peter 2:9). Only the same "God who commanded light to shine out of darkness" has the power to shine "in our hearts to give the light of the knowledge of the glory of God in the face of Jesus Christ" (2 Cor. 4:6 NKJV). That is precisely what the Lord did for Mary Magdalene.

Mary owed everything to Christ. She knew it too. Her subsequent love for Him reflected the profound depth of her gratitude.

DISCIPLESHIP

Mary Magdalene joined the close circle of disciples who traveled with Jesus on His long journeys. Her deliverance from demons may have occurred relatively late in Christ's Galilean ministry. Luke is the only one of the gospel writers who names her in any connection prior to the crucifixion. Notice the context in which she is named:

> Now it came to pass, afterward, that He went through every city and village, preaching and bringing the glad tidings of the kingdom of God. And the twelve were with Him, and certain women who had been healed of evil spirits and infirmities; Mary called Magdalene, out of whom had come seven demons, and Joanna the wife of Chuza, Herod's steward, and Susanna, and many others who provided for Him from their substance. (Luke 8:1–3 NKJV)

There was certainly nothing inappropriate about Jesus' practice of allowing women disciples to be His followers. We can be certain that whatever traveling arrangements were made for the group, Jesus' name and honor (as well as the reputations of *all* the men and women in the group) were carefully guarded from anything that might hint at any reproach. After all, Jesus' enemies were looking desperately for reasons to accuse Him. If there had been any way whatsoever for them to drum up doubts about the propriety of Jesus' relationships with women, that issue would have been raised. But even though His enemies regularly lied about Him and even accused Him of being a glutton and a winebibber (Matt. 11:19), no accusations against Him were ever made on the basis of how He treated the women in His band of disciples. These were godly women who devoted their whole lives to spiritual things. They evidently had no family responsibilities that required them to stay home. If they had been in breach of any such duties, you can be certain that Jesus would not have permitted them to accompany Him. There is never the slightest hint of unseemliness or indiscretion in the way any of them related to Him.

It is true that most rabbis in that culture did not normally allow women to be their disciples. But Christ encouraged men and women alike to take His yoke and learn from Him. This is yet another evidence of how women are honored in Scripture.

Luke said Mary Magdalene and the other women were among many who "provided for Him from their substance" (Luke 8:3 NKJV). Perhaps Mary had inherited financial resources that she used for the support of Jesus and His disciples. The fact that she was able to travel with Jesus in the inner circle of His disciples may be a clue that she was unmarried and otherwise free from any obligation to parents or close family. She might well have been a widow. There is no evidence that she was a very young woman. The fact that her name appears at the head of the list of this band of women seems to indicate that she had a special place of respect among them.

Mary Magdalene remained Jesus' faithful disciple even when others forsook Him. In fact, she first appeared in Luke's gospel at a time when opposition to Jesus had grown to the point that He began to teach in parables (Matt. 11:10–11). When others became offended with His sayings, she stayed by His side. When others walked no longer with Him, she remained faithful. She followed Him all the way from Galilee to Jerusalem for that final Passover celebration. She ended up loyally following Him to the cross, and even beyond.

DISASTER

Matthew, Mark, and John all record that Mary Magdalene was present at the crucifixion. Combining all three accounts, it is clear that she stood with Mary, the mother of Jesus, Salome (mother of the apostles James and John), and another, lesser-known Mary (mother of James the Less and Joses).

There's an interesting progression in the gospel accounts. John, describing the state of affairs near the beginning of the crucifixion, said the women "stood by the cross" (John 19:25 NKJV). They were close enough to hear Him speak to John and Mary when He committed His mother to the beloved disciple's care (vv. 26–27).

But Matthew and Mark, describing the end of the ordeal, said the women were "looking on from afar" (Matt. 27:55; Mark 15:40 NKJV). As the crucifixion wore on, crowds of taunting miscreants moved in, elbowing the women back. The women probably drew back instinctively, too, as the scene became steadily more and more gruesome. It was as if they could not bear to watch—but they could not bear to leave.

They remained until the bitter end. There was nothing for them to do but watch and pray and grieve. It must have seemed the greatest possible disaster, to have the One whom they loved and trusted above all torn from their midst so violently. There they stood, in a crowd of bloodthirsty fanatics who were screaming for the death of their beloved Lord. With the screaming-mad furor of hatred at the very pinnacle of intensity, they could easily have become victims of the mob. But they never shrank away completely. They never left the scene until the bitter end. And even then, they stayed close to Jesus' body. Such was the magnetism of their loyalty and love for Christ.

In fact, it was only thanks to Mary Magdalene that the disciples even learned where Jesus' body was laid after His death. Mark records that Joseph of Arimathea asked Pilate for the body of Christ in order to give it a proper burial. Joseph had access to Pilate because he was a prominent member of the Sanhedrin, the ruling council of Jewish leaders (Mark 15:43). They were the same group who had conspired to bring Jesus to trial, condemned Him, and voted to put Him to death that very morning. Joseph, however, was a secret disciple of Jesus (John 19:38), and "he had not consented to their decision and deed" (Luke 23:51 NKJV). All four gospels record Joseph's action of retrieving Jesus' body. Mark added that Mary Magdalene and Mary the mother of Joses secretly followed Joseph to the tomb and "observed where He was laid" (Mark 15:47 NKJV).

The apostle John described how Joseph of Arimathea, together with Nicodemus (who was "a ruler of the Jews," according to John 3:1 NKJV, and therefore probably also a member of the Sanhedrin and a secret disciple), "took the body of Jesus, and bound it in strips of linen with the spices, as the custom of the Jews is to bury" (John 19:40 NKJV). John says Nicodemus had purchased about a hundred pounds of "myrrh and aloes" (v. 39 NKJV). These were scented spices and resins used by the Jews in lieu of embalming. The two men speedily anointed Jesus' body and bound Him tightly in linen strips (v. 40). They would have needed to hurry to finish the task before the Sabbath started (v. 42).

Mary Magdalene's love for Christ was as strong as anyone's. She took note of where and how He had been laid in the tomb. After all He had done for her, it must have broken her heart to see His lifeless, mangled body so poorly prepared and laid in a cold tomb. She was determined to wash and anoint His body properly. So Luke 23:55–56 says she and the other Mary began the preparation of their own burial spices before the Sabbath began. Mark 16:1 adds that they purchased still more spices as soon as the Sabbath was officially over (sundown on Saturday). First thing in the morning, they planned to give Him a burial worthy of Someone so profoundly loved.

DAYBREAK

Mary Magdalene had remained longer than any other disciple at the cross. Then she was also the first to reach His tomb at daybreak on the first day of the week. Her devotion was never more plain than in her response to His death, and that devotion was about to be rewarded in an unimaginably triumphant way.

There was evidently no thought of resurrection in Mary Magdalene's mind. She had seen up close the devastating effects of the bitter blows Jesus had received on the way to the cross. She had witnessed firsthand as His life ebbed from Him. She had watched as His lifeless body was unceremoniously wrapped in linen and hastily prepared ointment and left alone in the tomb. The one thought that filled her heart was a desire to do properly what she had seen done so hurriedly and haphazardly by Nicodemus and Joseph. (She might have recognized them as members of the hostile Sanhedrin. Otherwise, she probably did not know them at all.) She thought she was coming to the tomb for one final expression of love to her Master— to whom she knew she owed everything.

The apostle John, himself an eyewitness to some of the the dramatic events of that morning, gives the best description:

Now on the first day of the week Mary Magdalene went to the tomb early, while it was still dark, and saw that the stone had been taken away from the tomb. Then she ran and came to Simon Peter, and to the other disciple, whom Jesus loved, and said to them, "They have taken away the Lord out of the tomb, and we do not know where they have laid Him."

Peter therefore went out, and the other disciple, and were going to the tomb. So they both ran together, and the other disciple outran Peter and came to the tomb first. And he, stooping down and looking in, saw the linen cloths lying there; yet he did not go in. Then Simon Peter came, following him, and went into the tomb; and he saw the linen cloths lying there, and the handkerchief that had been around His head, not lying with the linen cloths, but folded together in a place by itself. Then the other disciple, who came to the tomb first, went in also; and he saw and believed. For as yet they did not know the Scripture, that He must rise again from the dead. Then the disciples went away again to their own homes.

But Mary stood outside by the tomb weeping, and as she wept she stooped down and looked into the tomb. And she saw two angels in white sitting, one at the head and the other at the feet, where the body of Jesus had lain. Then they said to her, "Woman, why are you weeping?"

She said to them, "Because they have taken away my Lord, and I do not know where they have laid Him." (John 20:1–13 NKJV)

Matthew 28:2 records that the rolling away of the stone was accompanied by "a great earthquake" (NKJV). We also know from Matthew and Mark that at least two other women ("the other Mary" and Salome) had come to help. They had discussed the difficulty of rolling the great stone (a massive wheel-shaped slab that rested in a trough) away from the mouth of the tomb, but by the time they arrived, the stone was already rolled away.

Mark 16:5 and Luke 24:3 both say the women went inside the sepulchre and found it empty. Mary's first inclination was to assume that someone had stolen Jesus' body. She immediately ran out of the tomb and back up the same trail she had come from, apparently planning to go for help. Before running far, though, she encountered Peter and John, on their way to the burial site. She breathlessly told them about the empty tomb, and they both took off running to see for themselves. John makes a point of recording that he outran Peter, but he stopped at the mouth of the tomb to peer inside, and Peter ran past him into the sepulchre itself. There Peter found the empty grave clothes and a headpiece folded and set aside. John joined him inside the tomb. Seeing the grave clothes still intact but empty was enough, John says, for him to believe. He and Peter left the scene immediately (Luke 24:12). It was probably at that point that the other women went into the tomb again to see for themselves (Mark 16:4).

Meanwhile, Mary Magdalene, overwrought with the new grief of thinking someone had stolen the body, remained outside the tomb alone. She stooped to peer in, and it was then that two angels appeared inside the tomb (John 20:12). Matthew, Mark, and Luke tell the story in abbreviated fashion, deliberately truncating some details. Each account gives different aspects of the story, but they are easy to harmonize. Of course, all the women saw the angels. Only one of the angels spoke. To the women inside the tomb, he said, "He is not here; for He is risen" (Matt. 28:6; see Mark 16:6; Luke 24:6 NKJV). Then the angel instructed them, "Go quickly and tell His disciples that He is risen from the dead" (Matt. 28:7 NKJV). At that point, all but Mary seem to have left. According to Matthew, "they went out quickly from the tomb with fear and great joy" (v. 8 NKJV).

Mary seemed to have remained outside the tomb, still disconsolate over the missing body. Evidently she had taken no notice of the empty grave clothes. It seems clear that she had neither heard the angel's triumphant news, nor did she understand how elated Peter and John were when they left the tomb. The angel came and spoke directly to her: "Woman, why are you weeping?" (John 20:13 NKJV).

Through her broken-hearted sobs, Mary replied, "Because they have taken away my Lord, and I do not know where they have laid Him" (John 20:13 NKJV).

It was just then that she turned and saw Jesus. At first, through her tear-filled eyes, she did not recognize Him at all. (She was not the only one who did not instantly perceive who He was after His resurrection. Later that day, according to Luke 24:13–35, two of His disciples traveled some distance with Him on the road to Emmaus before their eyes were opened to realize who He was.) His countenance was different—glorified. If He looked the way John described Him in Revelation 1:14, "His head and hair were white like wool, as white as snow, and His eyes like a flame of fire" (NKJV).

Jesus spoke: "Woman, why are you weeping? Whom are you seeking?" (John 20:15 NKJV).

Mary, thinking He was the gardener, pleaded with Him to show her where they had taken the body of Christ.

All He had to say was her name, and she instantly recognized Him. "He calls his own sheep by name . . . [and] they know his voice" (John 10:3–4 NKJV).

"Rabboni!" Mary's grief instantly turned to inexpressible joy (John 20:16 NKJV), and she must have tried to clasp Him as if she would never let Him go.

His words, "Do not cling to Me" (v. 17), testified in a unique way to the extraordinary character of Mary Magdalene. Most of us are too much like the apostle Thomas—hesitant, pessimistic. Jesus urged Thomas to touch Him, in order to verify Jesus' identity (v. 27). It is remarkable and sad—but true—that most of Jesus' disciples, especially in this postmodern age, constantly need to be coaxed nearer to Him. Mary, by contrast, did not want to let go.

Jesus thus conferred on her a unique and unparalleled honor allowing her to be the first to see and hear Him after His resurrection. Others had already heard and believed the glad news from the mouth of an angel.

Mary got to hear it first from Jesus Himself. The biblical epitaph on her life was recorded in Mark 16:9: "When He rose early on the first day of the week, He appeared first to Mary Magdalene" (NKJV).

That was her extraordinary legacy. No one can ever share that honor or take it from her. But we can, and should, seek to imitate her deep love for Christ.

11
LYDIA: A HOSPITABLE HEART OPENED

Now a certain woman named Lydia heard us. She was a seller of purple from the city of Thyatira, who worshiped God. The Lord opened her heart to heed the things spoken by Paul.

Acts 16:14 NKJV

L ydia is best remembered as the original convert for the gospel in Europe. She was the first person on record ever to respond to the message of Christ during the apostle Paul's original missionary journey into Europe. Her conversion marked the earliest foothold of the church on a continent that ultimately became the hub of the gospel's witness worldwide. (Europe has only relinquished that distinction to North America in the past hundred years or so.)

Ironically, however, Lydia herself was not European. Her name was also the name of a large Asian province, which was probably the region of her birth. The capital city of Lydia was Sardis. That territory's last and best-known ruler was Croesus, who ruled in the sixth century BC and whose very name is synonymous with wealth. (He was defeated by Cyrus, ruler of Medo-Persia in Ezra's time. Cyrus used the captured wealth of Croesus to help him conquer most of the known world.) In Roman times, the once-great land of Lydia was merely one of the provinces of Asia Minor. But by the end of the apostolic age, the province of Lydia was also a thriving center of Christianity. Sardis (still the region's capital city in the apostle John's time) was home to one of the seven churches in the book of Revelation (3:1–6).

Lydia's actual hometown was the city of Thyatira. Thyatira, in the province of Lydia, was home to one of the seven churches of Revelation (2:18–29). Significantly, Thyatira was located in the very region of Asia Minor where Luke tells us Paul, Silas, and Timothy "were forbidden by the Holy Spirit to preach the word" (Acts 16:6 NKJV).

Shortly after all doors were closed to Paul for any further church-planting in Asia Minor, God sovereignly led the missionary party into Europe by means of a dream in which a Macedonian man "stood and pleaded with [Paul], saying, 'Come over to Macedonia and help us'" (v. 9 NKJV). Macedonia in those days was the name of a Roman province that covered much of the upper peninsula of Greece, extending from the Adriatic to the Aegean. The area where Paul ministered lies in modern-day Greece. (Modern Macedonia is a considerably smaller region, distinct from Greece.) "Immediately," Luke says, "we sought to go to Macedonia, concluding that the Lord had called us to preach the gospel to them" (v. 10 NKJV).

The ironies are many. Instead of reaching Lydia in the region she regarded as home, the gospel pursued her to Europe, where she was engaged in business. Although Paul saw a Macedonian man in his vision, an Asian woman became the first convert on record in Europe.

Lydia was a remarkable woman who appeared suddenly and unexpectedly in the biblical narrative, reminding us that while God's sovereign purposes usually remain hidden from our eyes, He is always at work in secret and surprising ways to call out a people for His name.

HOW THE GOSPEL CAME TO LYDIA

Lydia's story is brief but compelling. It is told in just a few verses near the start of Luke's narrative about the apostle Paul's second missionary journey. This was an extended missionary trip whose description spans Acts 15:36–18:22. Paul's main companions on that long journey were Silas and Timothy. Luke apparently joined them just before they crossed the narrow strait from Troas (in Asia Minor) into Macedonia (entering Europe). Luke's enlistment in the missionary team was signaled by an abrupt change to first-person pronouns, starting in Acts 16:10 (NKJV) ("immediately we sought to go to Macedonia"). From that point on, Luke wrote as an eyewitness. It was at that very point Lydia's story came into play.

The sovereign hand of God's providential guidance was evident to Paul's entire group. Luke didn't explain all the circumstances, but by some means they had been forbidden by the Spirit of God to journey into the heart of Asia Minor. Every other door of ministry in Asia was also closed to them (16:6–8). That's when Paul received a revelation calling him across to the European continent. God had made it perfectly clear to all that there was just one way ahead—Macedonia. They wasted no time crossing to the Greek mainland.

Luke gives a detailed account of the route they took to Macedonia: "Sailing from Troas, we ran a straight course to Samothrace [an island in the Aegean, where they harbored overnight], and the next day came to Neapolis, and from there to Philippi, which is the foremost city of that part of Macedonia, a colony. And we were staying in that city for some days" (16:11–12 NKJV). The short two- or three-day journey was mostly by sea. The route from Troas to Neapolis covered about 140 nautical miles. Neapolis was the port city adjacent to Philippi, which lay some ten miles farther inland.

Philippi took its name from Philip II of Macedon, father of Alexander the Great. It was the eastern terminus of a famous Roman road known as the Egnatian Way. Thessalonica, where Paul would later found a famous church, lay another 150 miles west, at the other end of the Egnatian Way.

In Paul's day, Philippi was a thriving, busy community at the crossroads of two trade routes (one by land via the highway from Thessalonica; the other by sea, via the port at nearby Neapolis). Luke describes Philippi as "a colony" (Acts 16:12 NKJV), which means it was a colony of Rome, with a Roman government and a large population of Roman citizens. History records that Philippi had become a Roman colony in 31 BC. That meant the city had its own local government accountable directly to Rome, completely independent of the provincial Macedonian government. Its citizens were also exempt from Macedonian taxes. So this was a prosperous and flourishing city, bustling with trade and commerce from all over the world. It was a strategic place for introducing the gospel to Europe.

Paul and company spent "some days" in Philippi, apparently waiting for the Sabbath. Paul's normal evangelistic strategy was to take the gospel first to the local synagogue, because if he went to the Gentiles first, the Jews would never listen to anything he had to say. Philippi, however, was a thoroughly Gentile town with no synagogue.

There were a few Jews in Philippi, but very few—not even enough to support a synagogue. In order to start a synagogue in any community, Jewish custom required a quorum (known as a minyan) of at least ten Jewish men (any adult males beyond the age of Bar Mitzvah would qualify). The number was supposedly derived from the biblical account of the destruction of Sodom and Gomorrah, in which God told Abraham He would spare those cities for the sake of ten righteous men (Gen. 18:32–33). But the minyan rule was a classic example of rabbinical invention. Biblical law made no such restriction.

According to the tradition, in communities without synagogues, Jewish women could pray together in groups if they liked, but men had to form a legitimate minyan before they could partake in any kind of formal, public, communal worship—including prayer, the reading of the Torah, or the giving of public blessings.

Since Philippi's Jewish community was apparently not large enough to form a legitimate minyan, Paul and his group learned the place where Jewish women gathered to pray on the Sabbath, and they went there instead. Luke writes, "On the Sabbath day we went out of the city to the riverside, where prayer was customarily made; and we sat down and spoke to the women who met there" (Acts 16:13 NKJV). The river was a small stream known as the Gangitis, just west of the town. Apparently, the small group of women who gathered there constituted the only public gathering of Jews anywhere in Philippi on a typical Sabbath day. In keeping with his principle of bringing the gospel "[to] the Jew first" (Rom. 1:16 NKJV), Paul went to the riverside to preach.

Ironically, the one woman who responded most eagerly was not Jewish at all. Lydia was a worshiper of YHWH, at least externally. But she was a Gentile, an active seeker of the true God who had not even yet become a formal Jewish proselyte. Luke described his first meeting with Lydia this way: "A certain woman named Lydia heard us. She was a seller of purple from the city of Thyatira, who worshiped God" (Acts 16:14 NKJV).

She was, in effect, a businesswoman. She sold purple dye and fancy purple cloth, manufactured by a famous guild in her hometown of Thyatira. (Archaeologists have uncovered several Roman inscriptions dating from the first century and referring to the guild of dyers in Thyatira.) The rare and expensive dye (actually more crimson than purple) was made from a spiny-shelled mollusk known as the murex. The process had been invented in ancient Tyre, and the dye was (and is still) known as Tyrian dye. Manufacturers in Thyatira had perfected a better method of obtaining the dye from the mollusks. They also had developed a less expensive dye of similar color from the root of the madder plant. This was a popular alternative to the more costly color, especially among working-class people. But the more expensive Tyrian dye was the basis for royal purple, and that substance was one of the most precious of all commodities in the ancient world. So Lydia must have been a woman of some means. The mention of a household in Acts 16:15 would indicate that she maintained a home in Philippi, most likely, with household servants. All of this confirms that she was a wealthy woman.

HOW THE GOSPEL CAPTURED LYDIA'S HEART

The manner of Lydia's conversion is a fine illustration of how God always redeems lost souls. From our human perspective, we may think we are seeking Him, that trusting Christ is merely a "decision" that lies within the power of our own will to choose, or that we are sovereign over our own hearts and affections. In reality, wherever you see a soul like Lydia's truly seeking God, you can be certain God is drawing her. Whenever someone trusts Christ, it is God who opens the heart to believe. If God Himself did not draw us to Christ, we would never come at all. Jesus was quite clear about this: "No one can come to Me unless the Father who sent Me draws him" (John 6:44 NKJV). "No one can come to Me unless it has been granted to him by My Father" (v. 65 NKJV).

The fallen human heart is in absolute bondage to sin. Every sinner is just as helpless as Mary Magdalene was under the possession of those seven demons. Romans 8:7–8 says, "The carnal mind is enmity against God; for it is not subject to the law of God, nor indeed can be. So then, those who are in the flesh cannot please God" (NKJV). We are powerless to change our own hearts or turn from evil in order to do good: "Can the Ethiopian change his skin or the leopard its spots? Then may you also do good who are accustomed to do evil?" (Jer. 13:23 NKJV). The love of evil is part of our fallen nature, and it is the very thing that makes it impossible for us to choose good over evil. Our wills are bent in accordance with what we love. We are in bondage to our own corruption. Scripture portrays the condition of every fallen sinner as a state of hopeless enslavement to sin.

Actually, it's even worse than that. It is a kind of death—an utter spiritual barrenness that leaves us totally at the mercy of the sinful lusts of our own flesh (Eph. 2:1–3). We are helpless to change our own hearts for the better.

Acts 16:14 describes Lydia as a woman "who worshiped God" (NKJV). Intellectually, at least, she already knew that YHWH was the one true God. She apparently met regularly with the Jewish women who gathered to pray on the Sabbath, but she had not yet become a convert to Judaism.

Luke recorded that Lydia "heard us" (Acts 16:14 NKJV). He used a Greek word that meant she was listening intently. She did not merely absorb the sound, but she was carefully attentive to the meaning of the words. She was not like Paul's companions on the road to Damascus, who heard the noise of a voice (Acts 9:7) but didn't understand the meaning of it (22:9). She listened with rapt attention and understanding as Paul and his companions explained the gospel message.

Her heart was truly open. She was a genuine seeker of God. But notice Luke's whole point: it was not that Lydia opened her own heart and ears to the truth. Yes, she was seeking, but even that was because God was drawing her. She was listening, but it was God who gave her ears to hear. She had an open heart, but it was God who opened her heart. Luke expressly affirms the sovereignty of God in Lydia's salvation: "The Lord opened her heart to heed the things spoken by Paul" (16:14 NKJV).

A lot of people struggle to come to grips with this truth. It is a difficult idea, but I am very glad for the truth of it. If it were not for God's sovereign work drawing and opening the hearts of sinners to believe, no one would ever be saved. This is the very thing Paul has in mind in Ephesians 2, after stressing the utter spiritual deadness of sinners, when he says salvation—all of it—is a gift of God (Eph. 2:8–9).

Did you realize that even faith is God's gift to the believer? We don't reach down into our own hearts and summon faith from within by sheer willpower. God is the one who opens our hearts to believe. Repentance is something He graciously bestows (Acts 11:18; 2 Tim. 2:25).

I think all Christians have some intuitive understanding of this truth.

That is why we pray for the salvation of our loved ones. (If salvation were solely dependent on own free-will choice, what would be the point of praying to God about it?) We also know in our hearts that we cannot boast of being wiser or more learned than our neighbors who still do not believe. We know in our hearts that our salvation is wholly and completely the work of God's grace, and not in any sense our own doing. All believers, like Lydia, must confess that it was God who first opened our hearts to believe.

The language is significant. A lot of people imagine that the doctrine of God's sovereignty has Him somehow forcing people against their wills to believe. Theologians sometimes use the expression "irresistible grace" when they describe the way God brings sinners into the kingdom. Don't imagine for a moment that there is any kind of violent force or coercion involved when God draws people to Christ. Grace doesn't push sinners against their wills toward Christ; it draws them willingly to Him—by first opening their hearts. It enables them to see their sin for what it is and empowers them to despise what they formerly loved. It also equips them to see Christ for who He truly is. Someone whose heart has been opened like that will inevitably find Christ Himself irresistible. That is precisely the meaning of the expression "irresistible grace." That is how God draws sinners to Himself. Luke's description of Lydia's conversion captures it beautifully. The Lord simply opened her heart to believe— and she did.

God's sovereign hand is seen clearly in every aspect of Luke's account. The Lord clearly orchestrated the circumstances that brought Paul to Macedonia. It was a similar providence that brought Lydia there and drew her to the riverside on a Sabbath morning with a seeking heart. It was the Spirit of God who sovereignly opened her heart, gave her spiritual ears to hear, and gave her spiritual eyes to see the irresistible appeal of Christ.

For her part, she responded instantly. God's sovereignty does not leave the sinner out of the process. Lydia heard and heeded. She willingly embraced the truth of the gospel and became a believer that very morning. She became a participant in the fulfillment of the promise made long before to Eve. The seed of the woman crushed the serpent's head for her.

HOW THE GOSPEL TRANSFORMED LYDIA'S LIFE

Lydia's faith immediately was evident in her actions. Almost incidentally, Luke said, "And when she and her household were baptized . . ." (Acts 16:15 NKJV). Remember, the meeting took place next to a river. Apparently, Lydia, like the Ethiopian eunuch, needed little encouragement to take that first step of obedience to Christ. She was baptized then and there.

Notice also that Scripture mentioned her "household." This could describe her actual family, but nothing in the context indicated she was married. It would have been highly unusual in that culture for a married woman with family responsibilities to be involved in an import-export business requiring her to travel from continent to continent. Besides, she was clearly the head of her household. It was, after all, "her" household, and verse 40 (NKJV) speaks of "the house of Lydia," signifying that she was the owner of the building.

Lydia may have been a widow. Her household most likely included servants. She may also have had grown children who lived and traveled with her. But whoever was included in the household, they all came to faith and were baptized right along with Lydia. She was already leading others to Christ. And God was graciously opening their hearts too.

Lydia was also quick to show hospitality to the missionaries. According to Luke, she "begged" them to be her guests: "If you have judged me to be faithful to the Lord, come to my house and stay" (Acts 16:15 NKJV). Luke added (with characteristic understatement), "So she persuaded us" (v. 15 NKJV).

Lydia's hospitality to these strangers who had come in the name of the Lord was commendable. Again, her eagerness to host them reminds us that she was a woman of means. We know for sure that the group included Paul, Silas, Timothy, and Luke. In all likelihood there were others. This may have been a large team. It would be no easy task, even today, to host so many strangers. Since they had no plans for where to go next (they were there, after all, to plant a church), she was offering to keep them indefinitely.

Moreover, the real cost to Lydia was potentially much higher than the monetary value of room and board for a group of missionaries. Remember that Philippi was where Paul and Silas were beaten badly, thrown in jail, and clamped in stocks. They were ultimately freed by a miraculous earthquake, and the jailer and all his household became Christians in the process. But if preaching the gospel was deemed a jailable offense, Lydia was exposing herself to possible trouble—a loss of business, bad will in the community, and even a prison sentence for herself—by housing these strangers and thus giving them a base from which to evangelize.

Her wonderful act of hospitality nevertheless opened the way for the church to penetrate Europe. Paul and the missionaries apparently stayed with Lydia for a long time. Verse 18 describes a demon-possessed woman who harassed them "for *many* days" (NKJV, emphasis added), until Paul, "greatly annoyed, turned and said to the spirit, 'I command you in the name of Jesus Christ to come out of her.' And he came out that very hour."

The possessed woman was a slave whose owners had profited greatly from her fortune-telling abilities (v. 16). After the demon left her, she could no longer do whatever trick gave her credibility as a seer. The girl's owners therefore drummed up the public opposition that soon landed Paul and Silas in jail.

After the conversion of the jailer, when Paul and Silas were finally freed, Luke said, "They went out of the prison and entered the house of Lydia; and when they had seen the brethren, they encouraged them and departed" (Acts 16:40 NKJV).

That indicates that they had been in Philippi long enough to found a fledgling church. Apparently, a number of people had responded to the gospel. Naturally, their first meeting place was Lydia's home. By opening her home to the apostle Paul, Lydia had the honor of hosting in her own living room the earliest meetings of the first church ever established in Europe! She gained that honor for herself by showing such warm hospitality to this team of missionaries whom she barely knew. She epitomized the kind of hospitality Scripture demands of all Christians.

Lydia's hospitality was as remarkable as her faith. Because of her generosity to Paul and his missionary team, the gospel obtained a solid foothold in Philippi. A few short years later, Paul penned the epistle that bears the name of that church. It is obvious from the tone of his epistle that opposition to the gospel was still strong in Philippi. But the gospel was more powerful yet, and from Philippi the testimony of Christ sounded out into all of Europe. It continues to spread to the uttermost parts of the earth, even today.

Lydia's reward in heaven will surely be great. She was a truly extraordinary woman. Like all the women in our study, everything that made her exceptional was a result of God's work in her heart. Scripture is explicit about that, especially in Lydia's case—but it is true of every woman we have studied.

EPILOGUE

The twelve women whose lives we have studied are a representative sampling of all the women whom Scripture commends. All twelve of these women—together with every other godly woman from the pages of the Bible—share several characteristics in common.

First, and most prominently, their faith and their hopes were absolutely and resolutely Christ-centered. That is the single, central, dominant truth that emerges from a study of all the godly women in Scripture, and I trust it has come through clearly as you have worked your way through this book. If these twelve women teach us anything, it is to center our lives, our faith, and our perspective of the future on Christ and Christ alone. After all, in a nutshell, that is the same response the gospel demands of us. It is not only the central theme proclaimed by the *women* of the Bible; it is the very heart of the entire biblical message.

Notice, furthermore, that the main lessons of these twelve lives are all about spiritual character and feminine virtue. The women whose lives we have been studying aren't memorable solely because of their physical beauty, their natural abilities, their personal accomplishments, or some position they attained. They aren't distinguished for any of the typical reasons celebrity is conferred on certain women these days. Most of them did not marry into any kind of fame or influence. (Did you notice that not one of our twelve extraordinary women is noteworthy exclusively because of whom she was married to? These women did not derive their identities or their reputations solely from their husbands.) Most of them did not gain any kind of celebrity at all in the eyes of the world. Among the twelve we have studied, not one of them distinguished herself through a great career, some worldly accomplishment, or anything that would even stand out in the eyes of a cultural observer. All of them were basically modest, in every sense of the word—as "is proper for women professing godliness" (1 Tim. 2:10 NKJV). Frankly, some of these women would not be deemed important at all if they were not expressly singled out in Scripture as women of faith.

So we are brought back once again to the issue of their faith. Bear this in mind: faith was the root and the quintessence of everything that made these women extraordinary. But in no case did their excellence stop with *bare* faith. The fruit of their faith was virtue. The accounts of each of them illustrate, in some significant way, a particular moral quality or spiritual trait that is worthy of emulation. With Eve, it was her perseverance in faith and expectation, even after her world had been totally shattered by her own sin. In Sarah's case, it was her steadfast hope that persevered against unbelievable obstacles. The lesson of Rahab's life is seen in the example of her remarkable conversion, because she reminds us of how dramatically God's grace can rebuild a sin-ravaged life. Ruth was a living example of devotion, love, trust, and humility. Hannah exemplified the dedication of motherhood and the importance of making one's home a place where God is honored above all. Mary, the mother of Christ, was a model of humble submission. Anna was an apt illustration of how to be a faithful witness to the grace and glory of God. The Samaritan woman personified an eager response to the gospel message. Martha and Mary embodied the twin virtues of worship and service, prompted by deep devotion to Christ. Mary Magdalene was a living example of how Christ's deliverance and forgiveness prompts great love (Luke 7:47). And Lydia is best remembered for a heart that was wide open to Christ.

Not one of those women was perfect, of course. Their flaws and failures are evident, too, and those are also recorded for our admonition (1 Cor. 10:8–11). The sins of the saints in Scripture are always recounted with simple candor and never in a way that excuses or glorifies the wrongdoing. While standing as a rebuke to our sin, such stories also comfort us with the reminder that throughout history, God has used imperfect vessels, "that the excellence of the power may be of God and not of us" (2 Cor. 4:7 NKJV). After all, Christ came to seek and to save the lost—not the righteous, but sinners (Luke 19:10; Mark 2:17). These women all depict the truth of that promise, and that certainly ought to be a rich encouragement when we consider our own fallenness.

To sum up, everything that made these women extraordinary was ultimately owing to the work of the glorious Savior whom they loved and served. *God* was the truly extraordinary one, and He was simply conforming these women to their Savior's likeness (Rom. 8:29).

Extraordinary as they seem, what God was doing in their lives is really no different from what He does in the life of every true believer: "But we all, with unveiled face, beholding as in a mirror the glory of the Lord, are being transformed into the same image from glory to glory, just as by the Spirit of the Lord" (2 Cor. 3:18 NKJV).

May the extraordinary results of that process be the everyday experience of your life.

NOTES

1. Tertullian, *On the Apparel of Women,* book II, chapter 11.
2. Ibid, chapter 12.
3. Ibid, chapter 13.
4. Chrysostom, *Letter to a Young Widow,* 2.

ABOUT THE AUTHOR

JOHN MACARTHUR, one of today's foremost Bible teachers, is the author of numerous best-selling books that have touched millions of lives. He is pastor-teacher of Grace Community Church in Sun Valley, California, and president of The Master's College and Seminary. He is also president of Grace to You, the ministry that produces the internationally syndicated radio program Grace to You and a host of print, audio, and Internet resources—all featuring John's popular, verse-by-verse teaching. He also authored the notes in *The MacArthur Study Bible*, which has been awarded the Gold Medallion and has sold more than 500,000 copies. John and his wife, Patricia, have four children (all married), who have given them fourteen grandchildren.

For more details about John MacArthur and all his
Bible-teaching resources,
contact Grace to You at:

800-55-GRACE
or
www.gty.org